On the Margins of Modernism

CONTRAVERSIONS
Critical Studies in Jewish Literature, Culture, and Society

Daniel Boyarin and Chana Kronfeld, General Editors

On the Margins of Modernism

Decentering Literary Dynamics

Chana Kronfeld

UNIVERSITY OF CALIFORNIA PRESS

Berkeley / Los Angeles / London

Anthem written by Leonard Cohen. Copyright 1993 Leonard
Cohen Strange Music, Inc. Used by permission. All rights
reserved.

Chapter 5 and parts of Chapters 4 and 7 are adaptations of
articles previously published as "Allusion: An Israeli
Perspective," *Prooftexts* 5, no. 2:137–63, and "Fogel and
Modernism: A Liminal Moment in Hebrew Literary History,"
Prooftexts 13, no. 1:45–63.

University of California Press
Berkeley and Los Angeles, California

University of California Press, Ltd.
London, England

© 1996 by
The Regents of the University of California

Library of Congress Cataloging-in-Publication Data

Kronfeld, Chana.
    On the margins of modernism : decentering literary
dynamics / Chana Kronfeld.
        p.   cm — (Contraversions ; 2)
    Includes bibliographical references and index.
    ISBN 0-520-08346-6 (alk. paper). — ISBN 0-520-08347-4 (pbk. :
alk. paper)
    1. Literary theory.   2. Hebrew poetry, Modern—History and
criticism.   3. Yiddish poetry—History and criticism.
4. Marginality, in literature.   I. Title.   II. Series.
PJ5024.K76   1996   96-3452
892'.41091—dc20   CIP

Printed in the United States of America

9 8 7 6 5 4 3 2 1

The paper used in this publication meets the minimum requirements
of American National Standard for Information Sciences—Perma-
nence of Paper for Printed Library Materials, ANSI Z39.48-1984.

For Amichai and Maya, my loves

Ring the bells that still can ring.
Forget your perfect offering.
There is a crack in everything.
That's how the light gets in.

—from *Anthem*, by Leonard Cohen
© 1993 Leonard Cohen Stranger Music (BMI)

Contents

Acknowledgments

The conceptual framework for this book evolved during the months I spent as the Bernard Osher Fellow at the Townsend Center for the Humanities at the University of California at Berkeley. I am grateful to Paul Alpers, Tina Gillis, Pat Branch, and all the participants of the Townsend Fellows Seminar for the stimulating and inspiring context they provided.

My thoughts about marginal prototypes and the selective modeling of literary history continued to take shape over a period of several years and I was fortunate to be able to present them in an ongoing research seminar on Hebrew and comparative literature at Berkeley. Only in these graduate seminars did I begin to learn, with and from my students, how to apply my general ideas about literary trends to a range of textual and critical issues, from the reading of a poem to the critique of literary historiography. During this period I was lucky enough to work with some of the most brilliant students around, many of whom have since become colleagues. In effect, they were colleagues all along. What made the difference for me, however, was this group's collaborative spirit and their active resistance to the "capitalism of ideas" that is the norm in academic culture. In joint projects as well as in widely divergent individual endeavors, their boundless intellectual generosity—with me and with each other—has contributed to a sense of community that I truly cherish.

The conventional money market metaphors that dominate the discourse of acknowledgments—an economy in which the author/ owner of a book checks off a list of "debts owed" and "credit due"—

get in the way of expressing what this working/learning together has meant for me, and what each and every one of "my" (ex)students has contributed to "my" book. It is therefore with a troubling awareness of the inadequacies of this discourse that I wish to thank all participants of the graduate seminar group; and to enumerate, in alphabetical order, my more specific gratitudes to those of the group who have had direct input into the book.

Michael (Miki) Gluzman, intellectual soulmate, opened new critical perspectives for me in his own work on the exclusion of women and non-Zionist poets from the Hebrew modernist canon. He often knew what I was trying to say before I did and provided both vital criticism and empathic feedback that nurtures and informs every page of this book. I have greatly benefitted from his rare abilities in critical reading, his rigorous standards of scholarship, and what I can only describe as the most amazing intellectual openmindedness I have ever encountered. I am grateful to Ruthi Rost Kadish for sharing with me her research on the poet Esther Raab in Israel. My thanks to Barbara Mann for her cogent comments on the poetry and for her crucial contribution to the research and the bibliography. Ilana Pardes's work on women's countertraditions in the Bible and in modern Hebrew poetry, in particular her inspired readings of the Song of Songs and of Yocheved Bat-Miriam, helped challenge and expand my own approach. Her notes on the early versions of the manuscript and especially her critical comments on Chapter 4 were extremely helpful. Naomi Seidman not only provided crucial criticism on the Introduction and Chapter 7 but also taught me a lot in her own work on Fogel and on the gender politics of Hebrew/Yiddish relations. Her astonishing mind and endless creativity have enriched my own thinking on most of the topics this book touches on. Nanette Stahl's study of liminal moments in biblical law and narrative was highly instructive for my model of marginal prototypes. I have learned a lot from Jennifer Sylvor's nuanced analysis of the Russian-Hebrew-Yiddish modernist connection. I am grateful to Ruth Tsoffar for several important theoretical references, especially for Chapter 2. Eric Zakim was indispensable to all the crucial stages of research and writing. His astute critical observations and his probing eye for textual detail saved me from many an error. His insights on interartistic modernisms and on the poetry of David Fogel were extremely illuminating. I am also deeply grateful to him for providing artful translations of Hebrew poems into English and for his skillful stylistic editing. All in all, I can attest to the validity of that old Hebrew precept, "I've learned from all who've taught me, but from my students most of all."

My thinking on literature and the basic tools I use in reading poetic and critical texts have benefitted more than I can ever express from the extraordinary mentors I have had over the years. Benjamin Harshav (formerly Hrushovski) has taught me the value of theoretical rigor in the face of so much soft thinking, and has developed many of the tools I find useful in the elucidation of the wondrous stylistic and sonorous web of the poetic text. In his breathtaking studies of the Yiddish and Hebrew cultural revolutions, Harshav continues to model for me the need to extend theory to the historical and cultural dimensions of literary production and reception. The great interdisciplinary breakthroughs of his written work and the hybridity of his academic and artistic identities have had a liberating effect on my own thinking, even when we have not agreed. And I've only recently come to realize how empowering his actual poetic practice has been for me. Through the unsettling Hebrew poetry written by the persona Gabi Daniel, he has allowed me to be proud of being the daughter of the survivors to whom David Ben-Gurion referred as "human dust." And as the last great Yiddish modernist, H. Benyomin, he has shown me that such dusts [*shtoybn*; the name of his first volume of poetry, composed in the Vilna Ghetto] are where poetic gold is to be found.

I have been privileged to know Robert (Uri) Alter first as a teacher and now, for the past ten years, as a close colleague. His phenomenal erudition, his clarity of thought, and the virtuosity of his critical prose have been admired ideals I can only marvel at. My understanding of many of the historical, stylistic, and intertextual aspects of Hebrew literature is greatly obligated to him. Alter's epoch-making reconstruction of biblical poetics is paralleled in importance, from my perspective, by a less widely known revision of modern Hebrew literary history. I'm referring to his stylistic analysis of anti-*nusach* (roughly, antiformulaic) prose fiction as a distinct literary phase with close links to European modernism. This analysis has had a great influence on my own project of recovering liminal modernisms in Hebrew and Yiddish poetry. His insightful comments on earlier versions of the manuscript were particularly crucial in propelling the project along. His constant encouragement and unfailing support even in the face of real political differences has meant more than I can ever express.

Ziva Ben-Porat's theory of literary allusion, and her model of intertextuality in general, provided me with a theoretical framework that informs all sections of this book and is the topic of discussion in Chapter 5. Of no less importance to me, however, have been Ben-Porat's great intellectual generosity with students and colleagues and the model she supplied early on of noncompetitive, collaborative research. I am proud to claim her as a (much too young) intellectual mother.

It is my good fortune to have dear friends who are also shrewd critics and extremely careful readers. These colleagues/friends have given me the benefits of their expertise and erudition in commenting on various parts of this book and I am deeply grateful to them. Rutie Adler, a dear and close friend of twenty years, continues to be an invaluable source of linguistic savvy and keen stylistic insight. Her comments were particularly helpful in the articulation of Chapters 1 and 4. Her own work on deixis in Hebrew contributed to my understanding of textual cohesion in many of the poems discussed in this book. Her wonderfully sarcastic optimism—her license plate reads "*eeye tov*" [things will turn out O.K.]—has been a constant source of encouragement.

Ruth Berman's astute and insightful suggestions helped tremendously with the stylistic function of tense and aspect in Chapter 4. And so did her hug and words of friendship in a particularly difficult time. David Biale provided very helpful comments on the Introduction and Conclusion and much needed encouragement and support. Daniel Boyarin gave not only important feedback on the Introduction but the push that helped get the project off the ground. His brilliance and the fervor of his creativity helped me a great deal. I wish to thank Audri Durchslag Litt, a dear friend of over twenty years, who first introduced me to the great—and still largely ignored—modernist poetry of Else Lasker-Schüler, which Audri translated into English together with Jeanette Litman-Demeestère.

As this book goes to press I am grieving over the premature death of Amos Funkenstein, great mind, gentle friend, formidable colleague. I wish I had a chance to thank Amos for the conversations on the poetry of Yehuda Amichai that were very helpful with the revisions of Chapters 5 and 6.

If Bluma Goldstein had given me only the feel of family that her friendship has provided me with, *dayeynu:* that would have been enough. Her affection, her generosity, and the sheer joy of her company have a lot to do with making Berkeley a real home. But she has also influenced my work in a number of important ways. Bluma read earlier versions of the manuscript with extreme care, some chapters more than once, and made many exceptionally helpful comments that formed the blueprints for my revisions. I am particularly grateful for her rigorous critique of the Introduction and for extensive help with the articulation of early versions of Chapter 8. Her studies of Kafka in the dual contexts of German modernism and Jewish literature were highly instrumental in forming my own views.

George Lakoff and the Berkeley linguistics and cognitive science circle at large have had a profound influence on my work. Lakoff should not be held responsible, however, for my hybrid versions of prototype semantics and metaphor theory. I am grateful to him for his friendship and support, and for the wonderful discussions of Yehuda Amichai's poetry that inform Chapters 4–6.

My beloved friend Gail Holst Warhaft's work on women's lament in Greek literature provided an admirable model for an alternative literary history. Her strength, her pain, and her poetry were in my heart throughout this writing process. Diane Wolf's award-winning study of factory daughters in Indonesia provided an important counterexample to the elitism of universalizing postmodernist theory. Her friendship has been very important to me.

I was lucky to have had the opportunity to work with an exceptionally dedicated, talented, and ever so patient group of editors at the University of California Press in Berkeley. I am deeply grateful to Doris Kretschmer and Scott Norton for their expert guidance, unending kindness, and handholding support throughout the different stages of the book-birthing process. To Nola Burger my thanks for her beautiful design job, and my gratitude to Pam Fischer and especially to Kim Zetter for the truly heroic trilingual copyediting.

Eliyah Arnon deserves special thanks for providing invaluable help with the final stages of manuscript preparation, copyright, bibliography, and proofreading. His singlemindedness, dedication, and resourcefulness were quite unlike anything I had seen before.

Parts of some chapters were presented, in earlier versions, at a variety of forums, including the Yale Symposium on the Revival of Hebrew Language, Literature and Culture; annual conferences of the Association for Jewish Studies and the National Association of Professors of Hebrew; and during a lecture series at the University of Chicago, Emory University, and the University of California at Berkeley. I am grateful to the audiences for their comments. I also wish to thank the anonymous readers who reviewed the manuscript for the Press for their many useful suggestions. A special gratitude goes to Richard Fein and David Neal Miller, the editors of what was to be *The Yiddish Poem Itself*, for their detailed comments on earlier versions of Chapter 8. Though that project never materialized, it encouraged me to do the kind of close reading of Yiddish poetry this book concludes with. I wish to thank Alan Mintz and David Roskies, editors of *Prooftexts*, for their comments on earlier versions of Chapter 5, which appeared in their journal as Kronfeld 1985, and parts of Chapters 4 and 7, which appeared as Kronfeld 1993.

Amichai Kronfeld's rigorous criticism, and equally rigorous love, pushed each and every chapter of this book to be the toughest piece of thinking, the clearest piece of writing, the most subtle job of reading I was capable of at the time. Although I'd often feel eclipsed by the incisiveness of his mind, it was his gentleness, sensitivity, and ultimately his friendship that made it possible for me to see this project through. And it didn't hurt that he could be such a nuanced reader of poetry as well. Our daughter Maya Kronfeld was at all times eager to help—and indeed was very helpful—not only with proofreading but also with translating poems from Hebrew into English. Her uncanny sense of language and rhythm, and above all her unabashed passion for literature and art, have sustained me throughout the writing process. To the two of them, loves of my life, this book is dedicated.

Grateful acknowledgment is made to the following publishers and individuals for permission to reprint poems and translations: Schocken Ltd. for "Jacob and the Angel" ("Ya'akov ve-ha-mal'akh"), "On the Day My Daughter Was Born No One Died" ("Ba-yom she-bo nolda biti lo met af ish"), "To the Full Extent of Mercy" ("Bekhol chumrat ha-rachamim"), and "The Verb Pattern Sonnet" ("Sonet ha-binyanim"), by Yehuda Amichai; Ha-Kibbutz Ha-Meuchad Ltd. for "At the End of Day" ("Bi-netot ha-yom"), "On Autumn Nights" ("Be-leylot ha-stav"), and "Slowly the Horses Climb" ("Le'at olim susay"), by David Fogel; Isaac Halpern for "My Screamingness" ("Mayn Shrayedikayt"), "A Night" ("A Nakht"), and "Sunset on Trees" ("Zunfargang oyf Beymer"), by Moyshe Leyb Halpern; Levia Hofshteyn for "I Saw Her by the River" ("Kh'hob Derzen Zi Baym Taykh") and "The Ice Floe Is Moving" ("Di Kri'ye Geyt"), by Dovid Hofshteyn; Sifriat Poalim Ltd. for "You Are Hereby" ("Harey Yat"), by Avraham Shlonsky; and Peter Everwine for his translation of "As Sand" ("Kemo chol"), by Nathan Zach.

Minor Modernisms

Beyond Deleuze and Guattari

(First Century Jerusalem. A crowd of followers congregates outside the hovel where Brian, an anachronistic, parodic double for Christ, lives with his mother. The chanting mob arouses Brian from his first night with his lover, Judith, who is the sole female member of the Peoples' Front of Judea, an ineffectual splinter group fighting against the Roman occupation. Reluctantly, Brian opens the window and tries to get the noisy crowd to disperse.)

Crowd: A blessing! A blessing!
    (*more pandemonium*)
Brian: No, please. Please. Please listen.
    (*they quieten*)
    I've got one or two things to say.
Crowd: Tell us. Tell us both of them!!
Brian: Look . . . You've got it all wrong.
    You don't need to follow me.
    You don't need to follow anybody.
    You've got to think for yourselves.
    You're all individuals.
Crowd: Yes, we're all individuals.
Brian: You're all different.
Crowd: Yes, we *are* all different.
Dennis: I'm not.
Crowd: Sssshhh!

         —Monty Python, *The Life of Brian*

The 1979 movie *The Life of Brian* offers itself, in Monty Python's irreverent parodic logic, as parable and prelude for this study on the margins of modernism.[1] Difference iterated and echoed in unison ("Yes, we *are* all different") is difference erased, a gesture that can be met only with resistance, with a refusal to be different in the manner prescribed by the consensus ("I'm not"). From its collective vantage point outside Brian's door, the crowd embraces otherness as a force that consolidates a majority. In the process, they turn Brian, that antiheroic mock-Christ, into a figure of absolute yet vacuous authority. But it is Dennis, the little bearded man in the left-hand corner of the frame on whom I wish to turn the spotlight in this study, the one who mumbles "I'm not" and is silenced by the crowd, never to be heard from again.

What does it mean to be that writer, that reader on the margins of international modernism, in the corner of the picture yet part of it, when the crowd at the center clusters around a homogenized, privileged construction of difference? What does it mean for the visibility or audibility of that writer, that reader, when the center, in the process of championing difference, denies both that writer's modernism and his or her minor status?[2] Finally, what does it mean for the field if the very theoretical models that aim to uncover "the damage inflicted on minority cultures" structurally, institutionally participate in replicating it (JanMohamed and Lloyd, 1990:9)?

Modernism is famous for its affinity for the marginal, the exile, the "other." Yet the representative examples of this marginality typically are those writers who have become the most canonical high modernists. Their "narrative of unsettlement, homelessness, solitude and impoverished independence" (Williams, 1989:34) may indeed have been cast in minor, discordant tones, but those tones were composed in the major key of the most commonly read European languages: English, French, German. While they sometimes acknowledge the multicultural, international nature of the movement, handbooks as well as theoretical debates on modernism and minor writing consistently focus on -isms and writers that are well within this major linguistic and geopolitical key. Consequently, even hugely influential trends within European modernism itself are sometimes made to sound like a casual codetta: Scandinavian modernism, by many accounts the overture to all later trends; or the two very different variations on futurism, the Italian and the Russian; or the still resonant din of Rumanian dada (described by most critics as French).[3] These modernisms usually get the cursory nod, while the focus of discussion remains on the canonically privileged modalities of difference in Kafka and Pound, Proust and Joyce.

Very few of the discussions of international modernism available in English or French or German include Russian acmeism or Russian imaginism, although important poets who see themselves as affiliated with these trends can be found not only in Russia but also all the way over in the Palestine of the 1920s and 1930s. We love to read the acmeists Anna Akhmatova and Osip Mandelstam, even the imaginist Sergey Yesenin, in translation, but this doesn't make our view of international modernism more inclusive.[4] This is perhaps only natural, since historical and theoretical discourse on literature is always tacitly based on what I call a "selective modeling" of literary production, a modeling that both constitutes and serves its own cultural prototypes. But the selective processes, their tendentiousness and utility, should be opened up for analysis and not simply accepted as inevitable, built-in blinders.

Raymond Williams exposes the link between consolidating a Euro-American modernist canon from what was once a marginal literary trend and erasing unprivileged formations of marginality. His words resonate with special poignancy because they may have been among his last. These are his notes for the first chapter of an unfinished book, brilliantly edited and introduced by Tony Pinkney in the posthumous volume *The Politics of Modernism:*

> After Modernism is canonized, however, by the post-war settlement and its accompanying, complicit academic endorsements, there is then the presumption that since Modernism is *here* in this specific phase or period, there is nothing beyond it. The [once] marginal or rejected artists become classics of organized teaching and of travelling exhibitions in the great galleries of the metropolitan cities. 'Modernism' is confined to this highly selective field and denied to everything else in an act of pure ideology, whose first, unconscious irony is that, absurdly, it stops history dead.
> . . . [W]e must search out and counterpose an alternative tradition taken from the neglected works left in the wide margins of the century. (Williams, 1989:34–35)

Searching out and counterposing such alternative traditions on the margins of modernism is, indeed, my primary project in this book. Many minor modernisms remain "in the wide margins of this century," excluded from standard accounts of this international movement simply because they lie outside the official borders of the unarticulated yet powerful cartographic paradigm: international modernism = Europe + United States. Let me offer just one example. Malcolm Bradbury and James McFarlane's excellent critical anthology *Modernism 1890–1930* ([1976] 1981) is much more sensitive than most traditional treatments of modernism to the movement's diversity and heterogeneity. It nevertheless adheres implicitly to the cartographic formula, never straying beyond the boundaries of Europe and the United States. Not coincidentally, this same anthology also systematically marginalizes the crucial role women writers and editors played in the dynamics of international modernism, minimizing even the contribution of those women who were active within the Euro-American frame.[5]

How to search out and counterpose an alternative tradition and alternative theory of marginal modernisms without universalizing them out of existence? How to account, within a theoretically rigorous model, both for the women and minorities traditionally marginalized within the Euro-American canon and for the diverse groups and individual female and male writers outside the cartographic and linguistic mainstream? Writers the world over have self-consciously participated in—not simply been influenced by—the great international experiment with the -isms of modernism. But, ironically, Arabic, Hebrew, Senegalese, Japanese, and Yiddish literatures (among many others) have been excluded from recent theories of minor writing by the theoretical premises of the very same recovery project that should have made their voices audible.

Nevertheless, current theories of the minor have had an important effect in a number of ways. They have refocused attention on the decentering, deterritorializing, indeed the revolutionary and innovative force of minor writing. At the same time they have also underscored the potential appropriation of the minor by the major canonical system; and they have pointed out ways in which a minor literature can replicate exclusionary practices in its attempt to model itself after the hegemonic literary canon. Recent discussions have also helped reinscribe the association between minor and modernist, charging the old alliance between the two concepts with a new political urgency. All these perspectives have proven exceedingly helpful to me in exploring the history and theory of marginal modernisms.

Yet coming as I do from the perspective of two literatures, Hebrew and Yiddish, whose (different) modernisms and modes of minor writing do not fit into the postcolonial models now in vogue, I am troubled by what I see as the exclusionary effect of current definitions of the minor. All too often the selective modeling of minor literature—as of "international modernism"—on a Euro-American geopolitics and linguistics effectively leaves all that is not English, French, or German (or "deterritorialized" versions thereof) outside our purview. This exclusion is not merely a result of some bad choice of examples but is logically entailed by the explicitly articulated principles of the most detailed theories of minor writing available to date.[6] Only if we construct the major through the minor, not—as current wisdom has it—the minor through the major, can we begin to discern the regionalism, contextual diversity, and interdependence of even the most highly canonical forms of modernism. Theories of modernism that are modeled on belated, decentered, or linguistically minor practices may provide some insight into the processes that have become automatized or rendered imperceptible in the canonical center. Through the multiple, broken prisms of the minor, the mystified notion of a unified canonical modernism is exploded, subjecting the very language of center and periphery itself to a critique that exposes its own historicity.[7]

Perhaps the best-known representatives of the current direction in theorizing about minor literature are Gilles Deleuze and Félix Guattari, whose intent is undoubtedly progressive but whose effect may be quite restrictive. Their famous essay, "What Is a Minor Literature?" (Chapter 3 of Deleuze and Guattari, [1975] 1986)[8], elaborated on somewhat critically by David Lloyd (1987 and 1990)[9] and somewhat less critically by others (compare Renza, 1984), explicitly restricts minor, deterritorialized writing to "oppositional" writing in a major language[10]: "[a] minor literature doesn't come from a minor language; it is rather that which a minority constructs within a major language" (Deleuze and Guattari, 1986:16). But, according to the same authors, minor literature (linguistically thus restricted) becomes the most, in fact the only, privileged category in the new theory and politics of culture: "there is nothing that is major or revolutionary except the minor" (1986:26). Furthermore, "the minor no longer designates specific literatures but the revolutionary conditions for every literature within the heart of what is called great (or established) literature" (1986:18).[11]

Deleuze and Guattari's highly influential essay and its offshoots in English and American postcolonial cultural criticism present a challenge I want to address in some detail. I believe their position has highly restrictive theoretical and methodological consequences for a discussion of both modernist and minor writing. In a nutshell, I think Deleuze and Guattari's restriction of the minor to the language of the major culture precludes any alternative modeling of an international literary trend such as modernism on its "non-major" linguistic practices. Furthermore, their account privileges and universalizes the "minor within the major" as that which "no longer designates specific literatures but the revolutionary conditions of every literature" (Deleuze and Guattari, 1986:18). In the process of setting up the "truly minor" as this essentialist achievement term, the historically, culturally, and linguistically diverse formations of minor writing become— yet again—invisible. Anticipating the exclusionary potential of their critical project, Dana Polan, the gifted translator of Deleuze and Guattari's *Kafka*, includes the following rather strongly worded cautionary note in the introduction to the 1986 American edition: "Dangerously, despite all the efforts of Deleuze and Guattari to deconstruct hierarchies, American literary criticism may treat them . . . as aesthetes of a high-culture avant-garde closed in on its own fetishes of interiority. . . . One hopes that a translation of *Kafka* will be something that readers will question, as well as use" (xxvi).

More significantly for our purposes, Polan forewarns the readers that a "picking up of Deleuze and Guattari, then, would have to examine not only what they enable but also what they disenable, what they close off" (xxvi). It is precisely the consequences of this disenabling potential that I wish to argue against, with an eye to reinscribing those marginal modernisms that Deleuze and Guattari's model would write off as not "truly minor" and, by implication, as not fully capable of being agents of social and aesthetic change. Through this critique I wish to prepare the ground for what I believe to be a less exclusionary theoretical and historical model of marginal modernisms, elaborated and applied to the production and reception of Hebrew and Yiddish poetic modernisms. Of greatest interest to me, therefore, is the slippage between the concepts of the minor and the modernist, a slippage that is implicit in Deleuze and Guattari's account and becomes self-critically explicit in Lloyd's extended version.

Underlying both Deleuze and Guattari's three characteristics of minor literature and Lloyd's extended conditions for minor writing is the same fundamental principle: a minor literature is not written in a minor language. I will have more to say about this linguistic imperative later on. But, to begin, here are the conditions for the minor (within the language of the major), according to Deleuze and Guattari: "The three characteristics of minor literature are the deterritorialization of language, the connection of the individual to a political immediacy, and the collective assemblage of enunciation" (1986:18).

Lloyd provides a more nuanced and historicized interpretation of what he himself describes as Deleuze and Guattari's "impressionistic" and "mostly synchronic" account (1987:5). Yet his analysis reproduces the basic structure and methodological grid of their argument. As Gluzman astutely points out, both theories try to squeeze the highly diffuse and open-ended category of minor literature into a "checklist" of "necessary and sufficient conditions for membership in the category of minor writing."[12]

Lloyd's conditions for minor writing (as distinct from minority writing) expand and interpret each of Deleuze and Guattari's. Their first and second characteristics of the minor are further divided by Lloyd into two conditions each, and the third is interpreted as having three interrelated parts. Here are Lloyd's conditions for the minor: (1) "[e]xclusion from the canon and, by extension, from the 'canonical form' of the state"; (2) sustained "oppositional relationship to the canon and the state"; (3) "[c]ommon perpetuating of non-identity"; and (4) refusal "to represent the attainment of autonomous subjectivity" (1987:21–22). Conditions (1) and (2) may be read as politicized, historicized extensions of Deleuze and Guattari's first characteristic, the deterritorialization of language. Conditions (3) and (4) may be seen as a more socially nuanced articulation of their second characteristic, the connection of the individual to political immediacy. Lloyd proposes further a triad of concrete stylistic strategies for minor writing that correlate roughly with Deleuze and Guattari's highly suggestive but unclear third characteristic, the "collective assemblage [agencement] of enunciation [énonciation]" (1986:18). These for Lloyd are three distinct but interrelated modes of intertextuality: parody, translation, and citation.

These criteria, and their attendant rhetorical devices, while much more coherent than Deleuze and Guattari's, preserve some of the original theory's methodological and historical difficulties. As Lloyd himself acknowledges, they fit not only minor writing but also— modernism!

> A minor literature so defined overlaps in many respects with what has become known as modernism, and in most respects with post-modernism. . . . If minor literature belongs to the general field of

modernism, it does so only as the negative critical aspect of modernism. In other words, wherever the writer continues to conceive the work as playing in some sense a prefigurative and reconciling role, that work remains, whatever its stylistic features, assimilated to a canonical aesthetic. Hence modernists such as Eliot, Pound, and Yeats clearly belong within a major paradigm by right of the claims to transcending division and difference that constantly inform their works.

This ascription evidently initially has to ignore the difficulties these writers have in maintaining such claims in their historical moment, and to overlook the "minor" stylistic features to which they constantly have recourse. But these stylistic features . . . are symptomatic of a crisis of canonicity that is definitive of modernism itself. (1987: 23–24)

The attempts at separating the notion of the minor and the modernist seem to create more difficulties than they resolve. Minor literatures are modernist only in that they take a critical or oppositional stance within the canon. But in order to take such a stance they have to be minor (by Lloyd's conditions 1 and 2). Since the same negative characteristics (or negations of "major" ones) define both critical modernism and minor writing, perhaps one way out of the impasse is to do away with the stylistic features or treat them as necessary but not sufficient conditions: if a writer possesses the stylistic features of a minor writer (parody, translation, citation) but turns out to serve some reconciling function in the canon (whichever way that is to be assessed), then that writer will not count as minor, despite those intertextual strategies. But in what sense are these stylistic features related to minor status and not simply typical of (major or minor) modernism? And if, as Lloyd acknowledges finally, "the crisis of canonicity . . . is definitive of modernism itself," how then can it be used to define only the oppositional (the minor) formations of modernism?

What I find far more troubling, however, than this logical slippage is the implicit dehistoricization of both the minor and the modernist that accompanies it. Clearly, minor writing existed before modernism, even according to Deleuze and Guattari's linguistic principles, and will continue to exist after it; but to conflate the minor and the modernist without providing any historical criteria of contextualization is to blur the temporality and cultural specificity of both. Similarly, to identify as major those modernists whose works have come only later to be assimilated to a canonical aesthetic, is to disregard the resistant, even revolutionary role they may have played in the literary and political system of their time. And cannot the aesthetic-historical processes that constitute literary canonization turn the role of a once minor poet into a "major" (canon preserving) one? As Raymond Williams pointedly observed in the passage I quoted above, "The marginal or rejected (modernist) artists become classics of organized teaching" (1989:34); or is Lloyd suggesting that some positions or stylistic strategies are "essentially," "eternally" critical? The reification of critical categories is no less a danger for progressive approaches than for conservative ones.

Let us consider for a brief moment an intriguingly analogous example taken from the opposite end of the literary-critical spectrum. Hugh Kenner is one of the modernist canon's most astute readers and an active participant in its formation and preservation. In his well-known article "The Making of the Modernist Canon" Kenner (1984) identifies "the supranational movement called International Modernism" exclusively, unabashedly with Irish and American "decentralized" English writing. To be a modernist is indeed to be an expatriate, a decentered writer, but it has to be in the one and only language of modernism: English. And not, God forbid, the English of African or African American or even Australian and Canadian modernisms. The deterritorialization that Kenner privileges is exclusively Amero-Irish, even if he gives this non-English English the name "International Modernism": "Though the language of International Modernism, like that of air control towers, proved to be English, none of its canonical works came either out of England or out of any mind formed there. International Modernism was the work of Irishmen and Americans. Its masterpieces include *Ulysses, The Waste Land,* the first thirty *Cantos*" (1984:367).

Kenner goes to some lengths to make his case by arguing first, that French, German, Russian, and Italian models were important only in nonverbal modernisms and in (technological) modernity, and second, that none of the important English proponents of International Modernism was in fact English. For that purpose he has to brutally de-canonize Virginia Woolf: "She is not part of International Modernism; she is an English novelist of manners, writing village gossip;" (1984: 371). He also needs to perform some acrobatics to deterritorialize those (male) "International Modernists" he does not wish to decanonize: "By contrast [with the expatriate American talent Pound, Eliot, H.D.] the native talent is apt to seem unimportant, or else proves not to be native: even Wyndham Lewis, who went to an English public school (Rugby), had been born near a dock at Amherst, Nova Scotia, on his American father's yacht" (1984:369).

This blatantly biased selective modeling of "International" Modernism would be quite amusing if it weren't so symptomatic. Although Deleuze and Guattari end up with a much more convincing illustration of modernist deterritorialization, their monolingual construction of the minor-within-the-major has a similarly exclusionary effect. This is the underlying premise of their famous reading of Franz Kafka as the prototypical example of minor writing. Let me stress that it is not the interpretive accuracy of their reading of Kafka that I am concerned with here, nor do I intend this as a critical reading of Kafka's own views about German, Yiddish, and Hebrew. What I focus on, instead, are the consequences of Deleuze and Guattari's use of Kafka as the paradigmatic example for their theory of minor writing. Their account of Kafka as a model for the minor runs into difficulties in three ways: the very choice of Kafka, the manner in which his minor status is constructed, and the modes of oppositional minority literature that such a construction excludes.

First, choosing one of the major writers of the international modernist canon as the example of minor literature immediately calls into question the usefulness of the category of minor writing itself. Nevertheless, one might argue, Kafka's major status within the canon was not part of the conditions under which his writing was shaped; furthermore, as Bluma Goldstein has observed, while Kafka is certainly highly canonical in the context of international modernism and as a contributor to that old category "world literature," his position in the German literary system is much more ambivalent.[13] Clearly, however, this choice pulls the category of the minor away from the senses of "marginalized," "suppressed," "excluded"—namely, away from a focus on the minor as a feature of the history and politics of a work's reception.

Second, in the process of constructing Kafka's minor position as a Jew writing in the hegemonic German within a Czech environment, Deleuze and Guattari in effect erase all the non-German dimensions of his literary affiliation—a remarkable feat since in the foreground of their narrative are pronouncements about multiculturalism, polylingualism, and in particular the "situation of the German language in Czechoslovakia, as a fluid language intermixed with Czech and Yiddish," which is what "will allow Kafka the possibility of invention" (1986:20). But upon closer examination it becomes clear that Deleuze and Guattari uncritically adopt the view (which Kafka himself may have held) that Yiddish is in principle just an oral, popular resource that a writer like Kafka can use only to deflate German; not a full-fledged language but a means to achieve that underlying goal of all minor writing, the deterritorialization of the major language, while rejecting Hebrew and Czech altogether:

> Kafka does not opt for a reterritorialization through the Czech language. Nor toward a hypercultural use of German with all sorts of oneiric or symbolic or mythic flights (even Hebrew-ifying ones), as was the case with the Prague school. Nor toward an oral, popular Yiddish. Instead, using the path that Yiddish opens up to him, he takes it in such a way as to convert it into a unique and solitary form of writing. . . . He will tear out of Prague German all the qualities of underdevelopment that it has tried to hide. (1986:25–26)

In order to reduce Kafka's project to that one "truly minor" goal of deterritorializing German, Deleuze and Guattari need to radically ignore Kafka's profound (yet resistant and therefore minor on their own account!) engagement with the intertextual echo chambers of Yiddish and Hebrew literary culture. Even if Kafka, like many of the Hebrew and Yiddish modernists of his time, did choose to resist the ornate allusive pastiche of biblical and liturgical phrases, to reject the "oneiric," symbolic mode of premodernist engagement with Jewish literary sources, this should not be mistaken for a total rejection of Hebrew as a literary-cultural affiliation. On the contrary, this move might be precisely what draws Kafka so much closer to the minimalist project in the Hebrew and Yiddish modernisms that emerge in the Vienna and Berlin (but also in the Moscow, Warsaw, Kiev, Tel Aviv, and New York) of Kafka's time.[14] Other critics have observed Kafka's resistant, abstracted thematization of the reading strategies and the interpretive models developed within Hebrew and Yiddish literatures (parable, midrash, Hasidic tale, textual commentary) in place of the customary citational style of premodernist Jewish textual traditions.[15] What remains to be studied, however, are the ways in which Kafka's meta-textual practices may in fact point to partial affiliation (simultaneous with his other central European ones) with the liminal modernisms of the Hebrew anti-*nusach* (antiformulaic) modernists (Uri Nissan Gnessin, Avraham Ben-Yitzhak, David Fogel, and Yosef Chaim Brenner).[16] What also needs to be explored is Kafka's possible alignment—not in terms of influence but as historicized intertextual affiliation—with the general project of Yiddish minimalist expressionism whose resistance to the citational model was articulated in the aesthetic principles of *nakete linyes* (naked lines) and *nakete lider* (naked poems). (See Eric, [1922] 1973.)

Deleuze and Guattari's reduction of Kafka's literary cross-cultural project to an essentially monolingual tension between "good" and "poor" (i.e., Jewish) German is therefore, at best, an instance of what I describe in this book as the single-lens construction of literary affiliation. My argument is that many of the exclusionary practices of literary theory and historiography can be traced back to an optical difficulty with stereoscopic and kaleidoscopic vision: the difficulty to see writers like Kafka, for example, as simultaneously maintaining multiple literary affiliations, and to view these multiple affiliations as partial, potentially contradictory, and ambivalent. But that is precisely the kind of critical vision I believe we need.

Deleuze and Guattari's narrative, slipping in and out of a suggestive but highly misleading *erlebte Rede* with the text of Kafka's diaries, letters, and lecture on Yiddish (1948–49; 1954) denies not only the links between his work and the textual practices of Hebrew and Yiddish literature but the very possibility of producing such oppositional literatures in the non-major languages. This third problem is to my mind the most critical one, for it is here that Deleuze and Guattari's model, and others based on its fundamental premises, come closest to Kenner's exclusion of the whole world except Ireland and the United States from international modernism: Kafka's modernism could only have been German and it could only have been oppositional (in the privileged sense) in German. Hebrew, on this account, cannot be the language of a minor literature during Kafka's period because it is associated with Zionism, mysticism, and a reterritorialization of language in the service of a nation building process—all ways in which a minority literature replicates the formations of a hegemonic, major culture. Yiddish fares even worse since it is considered to be not a language but a "graft"; it is denied minor status and access to independent literariness because it is nothing but impoverished German and therefore useful only for the purpose of a modernist dismantling of German from within (1986:25).

Interestingly, the denial of minor status to these (and, by their first principle, all other!) literatures in "indigenous" minority languages is correlated with the erasure of Hebrew and Yiddish modernisms. Deleuze and Guattari deny, or are simply ignorant of, the unparalleled creative explosion of Hebrew and Yiddish modernism, in fact of several different modernisms, across the shifting centers of Jewish literature but also, significantly, in the cities where German was the dominant language of culture. Vibrant and oppositional, the project of these modernists needs to be understood both in its internal gesture of resisting and disrupting the whole structure of Jewish cultural/ textual tradition, and, externally, in its self-conscious, ambivalent affiliations with the European modernist trends whose margins these writers inhabited and whose borders they wished to stretch.

Both Hebrew and Yiddish modernisms remained, to a large extent, deterritorialized expressive systems and not only during the first quarter of this century, before the center of Hebrew literature moved to Palestine. Yiddish, which never had a territory, reveals all the linguistic marks of a deterritorialized language, marks which Deleuze and Guattari, following Vidal Sephiha, call "tensors" (1986:22). As the proverbial landless language (its writers joke bitterly about imaginary trips to "yiddishland"), Yiddish became an ideal vehicle for international radical experimentation with modernism. Its breathtaking project was halted only with the decimation of the Yiddish writers and readers in the Nazi genocide and the Stalinist purges. From about 1910 on, and especially during the years between the two world wars, Yiddish poets, writers, and dramaturgs created some of the most innovative modernist writing in Europe—impressionist, futurist, expressionist—in groups that clustered around literary magazines like *Albatros, Khalyastre* (the gang), *Ringen* (rings), *Milgroym* (pomegranate). In the movement's perpetually shifting centers, Berlin and Warsaw, Kiev and Moscow, the Yiddish modernists participated in a critique of major European culture launched from the deterritorialized linguistic, cultural, and often political margins. In the period immediately after World War I, at least nineteen Yiddish-language journals and periodicals were published in Berlin alone (Alt, 1987). It is perhaps not accidental that Deleuze and Guattari's model reveals the greatest anxiety (conveyed by them ventriloquistically through Kafka's own anxiety, 1986:25) about Yiddish, for Yiddish modernism is the ultimate counter example to their exclusive association of deterritorialization with minor/modernist writing in a major language.

In the chapters that follow I address the many ways in which the trends and subversions of Hebrew modernism call into question the simple opposition of minor and major literature, and expose the fuzziness of the distinction between a deterritorialized and a reterritorialized language. My goal is to show that theories of minor writing will continue to replicate the exclusionary practices of the major if they dismiss those forms of oppositionality which resist, quite literally, the idiom of the hegemonic culture: the ultimate refusal to obey the linguistic imperative to write in the language of the major modernisms of European culture.[17] Let me offer a single glimpse, by way of closure and preview, of one particularly intriguing form of resistance to the crowd's iteration/erasure of difference ("I'm not.") with which I began this introduction.

In Vienna, as early as 1908, the first modernist Hebrew poet, Avraham Ben-Yitzhak (Sonne) (1883–1950), developed the initial forms of a radically new liminal modernism that, as I argue in this book, was later to become the foundation for an alternative direction in Hebrew letters, a direction shaped to a large extent by an unprecedented number of women poets and by the non-Zionist male poet David Fogel. Marked, as Miron has observed, by a minimalist aesthetic of "thinness" (1991b:89–90) and obsessed with meta-artistic questions of perception and expression, Ben-Yitzhak's poetic project, like Fogel's later one, was lodged uneasily, critically, in the space between impressionism and expressionism, testing the limits of both.[18] By the time he moved to Vienna from his native Galicia, Ben-Yitzhak already possessed remarkable erudition in European letters. In Vienna he met Fogel, the Hebrew poet who would develop and refine the Viennese-Hebrew versions of marginal modernism that I describe in this book as an anti-*nusach* (antiformulaic) poetics.

During these years Ben-Yitzhak also met and befriended some of the central literary and artistic figures of the period who sought out his company because of his profound engagement in the literary questions of the time: James Joyce, Arnold Schoenberg, Georg Brandes, Robert Musil, Hugo von Hofmannsthal, Arthur Schnitzler, and others. Herman Broch maintained a lifelong literary correspondence with him and even offered him a chair of philosophy and Hebrew literature at an American university (Hever, 1992:107; see also Silberschlag, 1985:39–40, and Ha-Ephrati, 1976: 162–66, 172–75).

In his memoirs of the 1930s, Elias Canetti, Ben-Yitzhak's devoted friend, describes him as an admired figure and role model: "The greatest Viennese writers were attracted to him as if spellbound. . . . In many ways he was a model. Once I had known him no one else could become a model for me."[19] By the time Canetti met him, Ben-Yitzhak had already stopped writing (Hebrew) and had become instead a sort of oral vehicle for (one is tempted to say almost an embodiment of) a modernist poetics. The language of Canetti's extraordinary memoirs underscores this unique role throughout, but let me quote here some particularly suggestive examples. Canetti characterizes his daily need to listen to "Dr. Sonne" speak as "an addiction, such as I had not experienced for any other intellectual." Listening to him one "forgot that the speaker was a human being . . . [one] never regarded him as a character; he was the opposite of a character" (1986:133–135). At this point Canetti develops a detailed analogy between Ben-Yitzhak's "oral poetics" and a written—though unfinished—text that serves as Canetti's most prototypical example of the decentered formations of Viennese modernism to which he has apprenticed himself:

> But though I would not presume to reproduce his [Ben-Yitzhak/ Sonne's] statements, there is a literary creation to which I believe he can be likened. In those years I read Musil. I could not get enough of *The Man without Qualities*, the first two volumes of which, some thousand pages, had been published. It seemed to me that there was nothing comparable in all of literature. And yet, wherever I chanced to open these books, the text seemed surprisingly familiar. This was a language I knew, a rhythm of thought that I had met with, and yet I knew for sure that there were no similar books in existence. It was some time before I saw the connection. Dr. Sonne *spoke* as Musil *wrote.* . . . Day after day I was privileged to hear chapters from a second *Man without Qualities* that no one else ever heard of. For what he said to others—and he did speak to others, though not every day—was a *different* chapter. (1986:136; emphases in the original)

What the Hebrew critics have always referred to as Ben-Yitzhak's "silent period," from 1930 to his death in Israel twenty years later, is here recorded not as a turning away from a hopelessly marginal (Hebrew) modernism, but as a resort to an oral (German) modernism, an art that is all process: "It was always new, it had just come into being" (Canetti, 1986:135). The fact that in Vienna, in the early and mid 1930s, Ben-Yitzhak "foresaw the worst and said so" (1986:145) underlines how untenable the option to write in German had become for him by that time. In fact we now know that Ben-Yitzhak actively tried out "the German option" earlier on. In an extraordinary piece of archival work which resulted in a two-volume annotated edition and monograph on Ben-Yitzhak's poetry and poetics, Hanan Hever discovered that six of the Hebrew poems in the *opus posthumous* also had German versions and that two were apparently written in German first and in Hebrew only later (Hever, 1992:85).

Yet Hebrew was to remain the language in which Ben-Yitzhak conducted his only written modernist experiment on Viennese soil. For a poet of Ben-Yitzhak's interests, sensibilities, and background the choice of Hebrew as the language of modernist minimalism was as far from self-evident as can be imagined. Not only was Hebrew not his native tongue, but it was not the first language of his readers either, in many cases not even the second. Hebrew had been the tongue of sacred intertextual study for the better part of its history, although it always maintained a minor, secular (and, intertextually, more pared down) strand. By the time Ben-Yitzhak started writing, Hebrew had already come a long way in the short span of time since its revival as a language of modern poetry in the 1890s in the work of Chaim Nachman Bialik and Shaul Tchernichovski. But it was still, in the first decade of the twentieth century, a largely textual language, severely lacking not only in the registers of colloquial speech and slang but also in popular and subcanonical literature. The heritage of *melitsah*, the intertextual pastiche of fixed expressions borrowed from biblical, Talmudic and liturgical citations was still very much there, now more as a stylistic memory, tempting with its rich metaphoricity and with the resonance of its intertextual echo chamber. As Bialik, the major Hebrew premodernist had forewarned, the status of Hebrew wasn't going to change until the language "got a life" and became a vehicle for unmarked, normal discourse.[20]

The Hebrew that Ben-Yitzhak so stubbornly stuck to even though he had another, more mainstream medium open to him, must have seemed a very unlikely instrument for minimalist, pared down expression. Yet that was precisely the challenge that Ben-Yitzhak and others after him undertook, a challenge that—in that particular respect—is not unlike Kafka's attempt, in Deleuze and Guattari's construction, to deterritorialize German from within. Ben-Yitzhak's project, which Deleuze and Guattari's model would not recognize as minor, is the ultimate act of modernist oppositionality: to write from a position of dialogic tension with German impressionism and expressionism and with the forerunners and paragons of international modernism as a whole; to critique the modernist project and try to explore it further but to do so in a language these major modernists could not understand. By grafting a radically modern idiom onto an ironically biblical, strongly antirabbinic Hebrew, Ben-Yitzhak revived but thoroughly secularized the silences and gaps that mark biblical literature as a new model for modernism, in the process forcing He-

brew to do what it had never done before. But the price was enor-
mous. Ben-Yitzhak published only twelve poems in his lifetime and
went into total (written) silence after 1930. Yet he continues to be,
perhaps because of his enabling, liminal position between cultural
and linguistic categories, a revered, almost mythologized figure in the
small world of Hebrew letters.[21] I believe that in making the choice to
write in Hebrew, Ben-Yitzhak knew that he would be denied entry
into the modernist canon, a canon that would nevertheless continue to
describe itself as a truly minor, truly international modernism. He
refused to constitute his minor modernist project as productive, in
Lloyd's sense of the term.[22] And yet, in abdicating a high modernist
canonicity, in resisting reterritorialization, identity, and income, Ben-
Yitzhak both asserted and denied the possibility of his project ever
leaving a mark. The opening lines of the last poem published during
his lifetime can be read as an ambiguous midrash on the success/
failure of his—and Hebrew's—minor modernism:

אַשְׁרֵי הַזּוֹרְעִים וְלֹא יִקְצֹרוּ
כִּי יַרְחִיקוּ נְדוֹד.

Happy are the sowers that will not reap
For they will wander a long way off.[23]

PART ONE

Modeling Modernism

CHAPTER 1

Modernism
through the Margins

From Definitions to Prototypes

The term "modernism," though highly equivocal, commonly refers to a cluster of international movements and trends in literature and the arts. Beyond this rudimentary labeling, however, there is little agreement about the term's meaning and scope. In some cultural centers one talks of modernism as early as the 1880s; in others, as late as the 1950s. Although there seems to be some consensus that modernism's "high points"—itself a charged and problematic description—were reached during the first thirty years of this century, critical opinions are as divergent about the meaning of modernism now as they were fifty years ago, despite the massive literature devoted to the subject in recent years.

Three logically distinct sets of difficulties seem to have led to this impasse, each at a different level of discourse: the sense of the *term* itself, the nature of the *category* modernism constitutes, and the general *conceptual map* of literary groupings of which it is part. Distinguishing among these three levels of discussion is only a preliminary methodological gesture but—it seems to me—quite a necessary one given the conceptual fog in which the debate over modernism is often conducted.

(a) *The term.* "Modernism" remains a complex and contradictory literary label which, in the very process of naming, provokes some fundamental questions: Is modernism by any other name ("modernity," "avant-garde") still the same? How does the meaning of the label change when it is applied across media (literature, art, architecture, music); across genres within the same medium; and, still more problematically, across cultures, geopolitical centers, languages, even generations? Since my focus is on modernist poetry, the most relevant questions for my purposes deal with literature proper: Do the modernist labels "Russian futurism," "German expressionism," or "Anglo-American imagism," actually refer to the same literary phenomenon? And within the same subtrend or current, is there any sense in which the modernist label means the same thing when applied to mainstream, dominant European literary systems, as when it is used to describe Hebrew or Yiddish (or Arabic, Latin American, Carribean, African, Japanese) poetry? Clearly, there are reasons to expect an expressionist Hebrew poem written in Palestine in 1947 to be radically different in its expressionism from an expressionist poem written in Germany in the mid-twenties.[1] But are differences within a period or trend all we are left with, as deconstructive literary criticism would have us believe, with no possibility of internal semantic cohesion of any kind?[2]

My response to these problems will focus on the ways in which the various senses and uses of "modernism" define a dynamic semantic hierarchy. In Part 1 of this book I describe the shifting pragmatic contexts of the term's use, its historicity and tendentiousness, as well as my own bias (for I am yet another reader trying to effect yet another change in modernism's signification to fit my own cultural—literary, social, linguistic, political—conceptual scheme). In the process, I reject both the extreme skepticism of focusing exclusively on difference, which may deny modernism any signification at all, and the extreme positivism of reducing the term's complexity and heterogeneity to the lowest common denominator. Specifically, I propose that the semantic structure of "modernism"—as that of other terms designating literary groupings—be described as a "fuzzy set" of meaning horizons determined functionally and contextually, and clustered in dynamic hierarchies of degrees of salience.[3] The salience of one modernist position (or set of positions) over another is determined pragmatically by the particular aesthetic, social, and political contexts in which it is used.

(b) *The category.* The critical literature (as well as the manifestoes and other meta-poetic pronouncements of the modernists themselves) exhibit a persistent confusion about the categorization and classification of the concept *modernism:* Is it a period, a trend, a style? Is it a literary, an artistic, a cultural, or a political phenomenon? Is modernism, ontologically speaking, a process or an essence? Do certain conditions need to exist in order for a work or a poet to be considered modernist, or does modernism (or any of its subtrends, such as expressionism, imagism, futurism) include simply all those poets who are affiliated with one of its international branches? And how is affiliation determined?

Many of the methods of categorizing and classifying modernism run into serious difficulties. My job in Part 1 of this study will be to illustrate these difficulties and identify the extreme positivism or extreme nominalism behind them as procedures for analyzing literary categories and classes. Subsequently, I provide the rudiments of an alternative conceptual framework for the analysis of the literary category *modernism,* a framework which does not need to suppress either modernism's special kind of cohesiveness or its fluidity, opaqueness, and open-endedness. I show that although categories such as modernism evade classical criterial definitions, they are marked nevertheless by strong and salient features about which readers, critics, and artists all have strong intuitions—and opinions.

(c) *The conceptual map.* Scholars writing about modernism—as well as readers and writers of modernist texts—do not, as a rule, have access to any viable theoretical model for literary movements or trends as such. What, if anything, does modernism as a literary movement or trend have in common—in its conceptual structure— with periodic literary groupings such as epoch, period, or generation? What, if anything, does it have in common with typological literary groupings, like genre, mode, style? Is the very distinction between periodization and typology a viable one? By describing modernism as a transitional concept between classical notions of period and genre, I try to establish the motivation for a more pluralist model of literary groupings, a model which treats trends and movements as symptomatic of these categories' heterogeneity rather than as murky notions that resist all analysis.

Where, as far as these three questions are concerned, have the last fifty or so years of theorizing about modernism left us? To the extent that critics have attempted a conceptual analysis of modernism (and most of them have not),[4] they have usually been content with the questions raised in (a) above, acknowledging the complexity and vagueness of the label and little else. Very few have gone beyond this level to an exploration of (b), the special kind of category that constitutes the concept *modernism,* and even fewer have examined (c), the implications of modernism's semantic and classificatory complexity for a general theory of literary movements or trends. Accounts of modernism have never been informed by a sustained comparative theory of literary groupings (genre, period, school, generation, trend, movement) for the simple reason that no such theory is as yet available.

It would be a shame, I think, to resort to extreme skepticism or nominalism in order to address these questions if only because critics usually want to preserve the intuitions on which literary consumers and producers have been acting for so long—namely, that what they were engaged in was somehow, however vaguely, part of a real international, cross-cultural movement (or period or trend). Indeed, such a universalist feeling permeated much of the modernist experiment itself, even if at times only in hindsight. At the same time, it would be a shame for the critical account of the complex and contradictory label *modernism* to remain classicist and positivist if only because many modernist trends themselves embraced contradiction, antinomy, and antithesis in their implicit and explicit poetics, in a direct challenge to traditional, set-theoretical notions of meaning and categorization. That modernism's contradictory tenets were enhanced, even determined, by the drastically different historical and geopolitical conditions of each modernist wave and center goes without saying.

The salience of modernism's own valorization of the universal and the incongruous, the common and the contradictory, gives pause to persistent critical treatments of difference and similarity as an all-or-nothing proposition. Moreover, given alternative theories of meaning and categorization, such as frame and prototype semantics,[5] it no longer follows that if "modernism" is interpreted as having a set of different senses, then the label ceases to signify altogether; and, similarly for the other extreme, the term "modernism" can have meaning without being reduced to a fixed checklist of common and distinctive features. Thus, both modernism itself and contemporary theories of meaning and cognition suggest that critics may want to question their own methodological dichotomies and develop flexible procedures for determining the semantic structure of heterogeneous categories such as modernism.

Given the three levels of discussion sketched out above and their attendant conceptual confusions, it should be clearer now why discussions of modernism have so often gotten stuck in one of two methodological extremes. When they have followed the tradition of classical genre theory, accounts of modernism have tended to provide inventories of modernist traits, styles, and themes, and to ignore the difficulties which modern genre theory has had to confront; Jürgen Fohrmann (1988: 277) asks "how . . . *changes* [can] . . . be explained when the model is constructed as essentially classificatory" and he expresses skepticism about working "in terms of *identity* in *temporal contexts*" (italics in the original). Indeed, the classical notion of genre, according to Michał Głowiński (1969: 14) is "anchored so deeply in the literary consciousness" as a model for literary classification that "it has been accepted without reservations, as if it were a gift of nature."[6] When, however, critics have followed the period model, they have tended to reduce modernism to periodical divisions which, as René Wellek and Austin Warren ([1949] 1963: 262) realized a long time ago "devoutly respect the date lines" but are "unjustified by any reason save the practical need for some limit." This most common approach has traditionally denied modernism even the unsatisfactory treatment that it received under the typological model of genre. It would often result in the assimilation of the discussion of modernism into period studies of "twentieth-century literature" or the "interbellum generation," rarely providing an account of the many ways in which modernism as a literary trend does not fully correlate with the total literary production and consumption of the period.

Both the positivism of the classical model of genre and the extreme nominalism of the dateline approach have proven quite useless for the analysis of modernism. Among studies that do not abandon the categorization project altogether, though abdicating the classical model, the most exciting advances have occurred in a variety of apparently unrelated systems-theory approaches to literature. From formalism, through text and story grammar, to French and German socioliterary and evolutionary-system models, researchers have developed differentiated, dynamic methodologies for dealing with the central issues of literary history. However, little of this research has focused directly on the literary trend, which is still subsumed for the most part under either periodization or a more historically sophisticated version of typological genre studies. Within the genre or the period model, the emphasis seems to be, almost exclusively, on transitions or borderlines between periods or genres rather than on the internal structure of the category itself.[7] This emphasis also holds beyond the systems approach, as is evidenced by the global, trendy, and voluminous dispute over modernism versus postmodernism. This dispute, which, by the way, the present study carefully sidesteps, may well prove to be one of the last vestiges of bipolar thinking in modern critical theory, lagging behind the radical disruptions of conceptual dichotomies with which both the modernists and the postmodernists are so strongly associated.

As literary trends go, modernism is probably one of the most heterogeneous and fuzzy categories around. No list of common traits or goals can apply to all or most versions of modernism even if we restrict ourselves to poetry alone. Furthermore, as I suggested above, contradictory features can be found, and in many instances were even self-consciously embraced, within the same modernist subtrend, poet, or individual work. In fact, the tendency of these -isms toward schism has been described by Bradbury and McFarlane ([1976] 1981: 202) as perhaps the movement's only unifying trait. Yet, this negative formula does not really provide a way out of the impasse either because modernism is not the only trend to embrace oppositions, contradictions, and schism, even though it may do so in a way that is perceived as more radical. In other words, while schism may turn out to be a necessary condition for membership in the category modernism, it cannot claim to be a sufficient one: two of the trends that typically flank modernism—romanticism and postmodernism—have also been construed as embracing oppositionality in various ways.

Despite the overwhelming evidence that modernism defies reduction to simple common denominators, one study after another, after asserting the complexity and heterogeneity of the various manifestations of modernism, proceeds to attempt the impossibly positivist task of providing a definition of modernism; and this usually means, explicitly or tacitly, an attempt at what logicians call an *intensional definition*—namely, a list of necessary and sufficient conditions for all modernist trends. (See, for example, Gorsky, [1974] 1981:78–79; and Leonard, 1957:289–90.) It is no accident that this definitional drive is usually shared by critics who still uphold the classical genre paradigm of literary classification—what Tzvetan Todorov (in, for example, 1981:63) describes as the "organic model." While it would be nice for a theory of modernism to have the explanatory power that an intensional definition can facilitate (by showing clearly what makes all the branches of modernism part of one distinctive movement or trend), such an approach would force us to restrict severely the extension of what we could term modernist. Many important works, authors, and even entire groups that identified themselves as modernist and that are commonly perceived to be subsumed under this admittedly tattered and oversized umbrella would have to be kept out. There simply is no set of distinctive features that can apply to all the subgroupings of modernism (from futurism to surrealism) and separate them from all nonmodernist groupings (classicism, baroque, romanticism, and so forth).

Let me offer here one brief example to illustrate this point. For quite some time it has been a commonplace belief among scholars, from Harry Levin's seminal paper "What Was Modernism?" (in Levin, 1966:271–295) to Paul de Man's famous article "Literary History and Literary Modernity" (1971:142–65), that modernism was fundamentally antihistorical. This proposition is certainly true for Italian futurists, whose call to burn down museums and libraries and destroy the Latin past is well known. However, antihistoricism is certainly not typical of other branches of international modernism, such as Anglo-American imagism and vorticism, with their emphasis on classical allusion and historicist (though unchronological!) theories about tradition and the individual talent. Similar exclusions result from critical attempts to formulate the *differentia specifica* of modernism on the basis of any number of thematic or stylistic features, from an aestheticist focus on the "poetic function" to the "crisis of the subject" and the "explosion of form."[8] What critics present as a set of distinctive features is actually always only a selective modeling of modernism, determined by the critic's special purposes and perspectives.

If a list of necessary and sufficient conditions for all modernist trends proves to be too positivistic a methodological requirement, the second common approach—which attempts to define the scope of modernism simply by enumerating and describing the various -isms that are conventionally associated with it—strikes me as too relativistic. Beginning with symbolism and impressionism as early or proto-modernism, these descriptions move through futurism, expressionism, and imagism as representatives of high modernism, leading up to surrealism and dada as late or neo-modernism. This practice, common in various periodization-oriented handbooks on modernism and typical of the dateline approach in general, is implicitly based on the logical concept of an *extensional definition*. It does end up including everything one would want to include but preserves little explanatory power since it cannot tell us what makes all these -isms part of one heterogeneous yet oddly distinctive international movement.

The alternative which I outline in this study aims to set up a less positivistic—and, I hope, more rigorous—rudimentary framework for the discussion of modernism. While I believe this framework may be appropriate—with certain modifications—for the study of literary trends in general, it is particularly well suited to the special needs of the modernist poetic trends examined in this book: the two or three waves of Hebrew modernism in Europe and then in Israel;[9] and the two waves of Yiddish modernism in the United States and their counterparts in Eastern Europe. I explore the conceptual structure of the category *modernism*, its limits and internal organization, and I treat these marginal poetries as emblematic and symptomatic of modernist poetry rather than as historical anecdotes. In the process, I also examine and call into question the poetics and politics of canon formation in general.

The informal model which I am proposing here has three components, based on theories developed within several disciplines. These three components are extensions and fusions of Ludwig Wittgenstein's concept of family resemblance; Eleanor Rosch's, Charles Fillmore's, and George Lakoff's work on prototype and frame semantics and theory of categorization; and Itamar Even-Zohar's and Benjamin Harshav's [Hrushovski's] work on literary dynamics.[10]

Lakoff has pointed out in his important book, *Women, Fire, and Dangerous Things,* that Wittgenstein's theory of family resemblance was "the first major crack in the classical theory" of categorization (1987:16). To the classical conception of a category as having clear boundaries and being defined by a common checklist of properties, Wittgenstein offers a more pliable alternative. Although family resemblance is the illustration that became synonymous with his approach as a whole, Wittgenstein uses other illustrations, each of which sheds a slightly different light on the ways in which a category such as modernism may be constructed. Here I summarize briefly only three of his major examples. First is the example of family resemblance proper. Members of one family share a variety of similar features: eyes, gait, hair color, temperament. But—and this is the crucial point—there need be no one set of features shared by all family members. The second example concerns the concept of game. There is no set of features which all games share. Some are forms of group play, without any winning or losing, others involve luck, still others—skill; some have rigid rules, others are free form; and so on. While some share some properties, no one feature is common to all (Lakoff, 1987: 16). The final illustration, which Wittgenstein develops the least, may nevertheless be the most applicable to diachronic literary categories such as modernism. It has come to be known as the rope analogy, even though Wittgenstein (1972, Part 1, Section 67) actually talks about a thread: "In spinning a thread we twist fibre on fibre. And the strength of the fibre does not reside in the fact that some one fibre runs through its whole length, but in the overlapping of many fibres."[11]

Within this framework, modernism can remain one clear category even though no two subtrends within it may share the same features. Although I do suspect that few other literary and linguistic categories answer to lists of necessary and sufficient conditions, I am not claiming here that all such categories are constructed on the model of family resemblance. It does not trivially follow that if modernism is a "fuzzy" category in Zadeh's sense (1965), it is therefore necessarily structured on the principle of family resemblance. As Lawrence Barsalou (1983) has pointed out, ad hoc categories, constructed solely to achieve a certain goal, do not even show family resemblance among their members.[12]

While the model of family resemblance (in its three different formulations) aptly describes modernism as a category "with blurred edges" (Wittgenstein, 1972, Part 1, Section 71), in itself it cannot adequately account for the way the center of the category is conceived. In other words, we need to understand not only why we are sometimes uncertain whether a work is modernist, antimodernist, or postmodernist (the "blurred edges") but also why particular works, poets, or positions have come to be conceived as better examples of modernism than others. In their treatment of these questions recent contributions to prototype theory of categorization and cognitive semantics may prove useful. Briefly, a *prototype*, in the technical sense developed by Rosch and others, is a member of a category (for example, birds) which is considered a "best example" of that category (sparrow, swallow, or robin, but not turkey, penguin, or chicken).[13] Note that even though this example uses objects as category members, the prototype model is neutral with respect to the ontological status of its constituents. It is therefore possible for me to argue, in Chapter 2, against any essentialist view of modernism and, at the same time, to advocate the prototype model as a functional construct which allows people to zero in on relevant segments of a heterogeneous category.

The question whether a member of a category is more or less prototypical of that category marks a centrality gradience for the various members. In the example above, sparrow has a higher centrality gradience within the category *bird* than penguin does, although both are members of the class. When, as Wittgenstein has already pointed out, the category itself has unclear boundaries (unlike birds but like red or tall things), we can distinguish not just a centrality gradience within the category but also a membership gradience marking degrees of membership in that category (Lakoff, 1987:12–13). In other words, something either is or is not a bird (no membership gradience), but something can be kind of red and kind of not, tallish rather than tall. It seems to me that modernism presents so many difficulties for the literary theorist partly because in its different constructions it involves both centrality and membership gradience. Thus, a poet or a work may be more or less modernist, or both modernist and anti- or postmodernist (in different aspects of his or her poetics), as is the case with most of the Hebrew and Yiddish poets I discuss. Modernism, furthermore, is a category with diachronically and culturally fuzzy boundaries, where "best examples" or prototypes of each subtrend are often quite atypical. And yet they tend to (misleadingly and at times subversively) stand for the whole.

A literary prototype, in my view, need not have more features in common with more members of a category than a nonprototype. Diverse and complex factors, such as experiential grounding, cultural convention, the specific social and historical context, and the discourse conditions of a given text may combine to affect judgments of literary prototypicality. In certain contexts, this variability may even be true of prototypes in general.[14] For example, in most cases the reason robin can serve as an excellent example of a bird probably has something to do with the tendency to focus—in the absence of particular contextual constraints—on flying as the most salient property of birds. But this salience is itself context-dependent. When the discourse purposes change, and the goal is to teach someone how to cook a bird (as, say, in a cookbook), turkey suddenly becomes a much better prototype than robin, and flying ability ceases to be the most salient feature.

For the purposes of literary theory, a dynamic, context-sensitive conception of the hierarchy of prototypical members within a category becomes particularly crucial. While this flexibility is important for all literary categories, it becomes absolutely vital for those literary systems that are diachronically or synchronically on the margins. The need for some such alternative model is even more poignant for the recovery of marginalized or submerged currents—whether within dominant or decentered literary systems—such as the poetry of

women and minorities. This double marginality is certainly charac-
teristic of Hebrew and Yiddish modernisms. It is, to a certain extent,
also typical of American—as opposed to British—modernist poetry.
In order to account for the importance of these decentered positions
in molding the dynamic, heterogeneous make-up of modernism, I
propose to combine the perspectives of family resemblance and pro-
totype theory with modern systems theory. I am interested in the
possibilities opened up by a critical, historicist revision of Israeli neo-
formalist models of literary dynamics, which, following the Russian
formalist model, describe the movement between center and periph-
ery, marginal properties and dominant ones, as necessary for literary
change.

It is no accident that these neoformalist models were developed in
part as a response to (and within the same intellectual and poetic
climate as) the Israeli neomodernism of the Statehood Generation
poets of the 1950s and 1960s. Nor is it accidental that the theoretical
and ideological roots of these models lead back to Russian formalist
poetics, which in turn was intimately affiliated with and was respond-
ing to the needs of its contemporary early modernists, the Russian
futurist poets. That poetics and poetry go hand in hand, forming part
of the same system, is as true of the modernist era as it was of earlier
ones. My own theoretical collage, perhaps itself a throwback to the
modernisms that formed my taste in art and literature, is thus in a
sense also a product of the poetic system. This perspective, however,
delimits the bias and tendentiousness of my own project: to revise the
map of both "international" and Hebrew and Yiddish modernisms to
include those voices which I particularly want to hear. Here then in a
nutshell is the "empirical" motivation "from the field" for adding
such a third system-dynamic component to the analysis of the cate-
gory *modernism.*

My investigations of Hebrew and Yiddish modernist poetry have
consistently presented a fascinating paradox: that although many
modernists defined very clearly their poetic principles (typically for-
mulated in rather strong terms by group manifestoes or individual
aesthetic credos), the best examples—or prototypes—that came to
represent these trends (individual poets or even individual works) are
often quite atypical of or only marginally consistent with the princi-
ples of the group. Focusing on these modernist prototypes tends to
foreground one or two highly salient poetic features which fulfill or
match some particular (artistic, linguistic, ideological, or social) need.

In each case, there are specific reasons, which need to be reconstructed and analyzed, why a particular feature came to be perceived as exemplary within the particular conditions for the creation and reception of a particular brand of modernism at a particular historical and cultural juncture. This contextually motivated salience raising[15] creates, among other things, a series of "deviant prototypes," artistic paragons and exemplary texts that do not centrally belong to any trend but have nevertheless come to represent it.[16]

I use this model of marginal prototypes to analyze some puzzling aspects of the dynamics of modernism in Hebrew and Yiddish poetry. What I describe as the first wave of Hebrew modernism, the antiformulaic poetry (anti-*nusach*) (the first innovative volumes of which were published between 1910 and 1923), went almost unnoticed by the contemporary reading public. The one poet who eventually came to be most prototypically associated with that wave, David Fogel, was canonized and enshrined as a model for emulation some forty years later, primarily by Nathan Zach. In manifestoes that establish the principles of the third modernist wave (*dor ha-mdina*, or Statehood Poets), Zach uses Fogel's example to attack rather mercilessly the poetry of the second modernist wave (the *moderna* poets of the pre-Statehood Generation). Thus, as in the Russian formalist model, a literary son rebels against the father by embracing the poetics of an (adopted) uncle.

Fogel's case is particularly instructive because his demarginalization succeeded against all odds. His brand of modernism was a truly unique mixture of impressionism and expressionism, the transition often taking place in the course of one brief poem; moreover, one of his major poetic principles was the blending or blurring of stylistic distinctions (such as mixtures of biblical aspectual grammar with a modern tense system). His poetry consistently and quite self-consciously adopts a low membership gradience in the category it is used to define; it inhabits those "blurred edges" between adjacent categories (impressionism and expressionism, for example); and, to top it all off, it is exceptionally low-key and self-effacing in its rhetorical stance, at a moment in Hebrew literary history when the opposite traits are the common practice.[17] Nevertheless, Fogel's poetry became most instrumental two generations after its original publication, as a retrospective prototype used to discredit the extroverted maximalism and high centrality gradience of the second modernist wave, which immediately followed Fogel's (and, one may add, of the

similarly maximalist premodernist national romanticism of Chaim
Nachman Bialik's generation, which immediately preceded it).

In order to understand the belatedness of Fogel's salience we need
to look at the forces within the Hebrew literary system which caused
the entire modernist wave of antiformulaic, minimalist poetry to re-
main submerged and largely unrecognized to this day. That many of
the practitioners of this modernist style were women (Rachel, Esther
Raab, the early Yocheved Bat-Miriam, and the early Leah Goldberg)
was no doubt an important factor in maintaining this modernist
trend's prolonged invisibility. Thus, even when Zach adopted Fogel
as a model for the poetry of his late-modernist Statehood Generation,
it was only as an individual paragon (Lakoff, 1987:87–88 ff) and not as
a prototype of a collective current.

A different kind of salience raising of prototypes from the periph-
ery comes up in my discussions of Yiddish modernist poetry in the
United States and the Soviet Union. One of the most outstanding
representatives of the impressionist/aestheticist group *di yunge* ["The
Young Ones"], the first Yiddish modernist trend in North America,
was the poet Moyshe Leyb Halpern. Though centrally featured in the
group, he was in fact all along writing intensely idiosyncratic expres-
sionist verse that prefigured—in its implicit poetics—many of the
major subversions of *di yunge*'s principles, which the next wave of
modernists, the introspectivists of the *in zich* group, later on adopted
and used in their direct attacks against their predecessors. This seems
to be one of the general tendencies in the dynamics of modernist
trends and perhaps of literary trend change in general: the implicit
poetics of a deviant or marginal prototype of one wave becomes the
explicit poetics (manifestoes, articles) of the dominant, activist proto-
types of the next wave. Unlike Fogel, Halpern was never clearly ac-
knowledged by the introspectivists as a proleptic paragon, perhaps
because he already was highly salient within *di yunge,* the group of
which he came to be such an atypical and reluctant prototype.

Finally, the great contemporary Hebrew poet Yehuda Amichai has
become, for a variety of reasons, a prototype of what I describe as the
third wave of Hebrew modernism, *dor ha-mdina,* or the Statehood
Generation. Yet Amichai's use of allusion and metaphor, his populist
views of poetry and ordinary language, and his "archaeological"
view of personal and collective history provide both paradigmatic
examples and devastating critiques of major modernist tenets.
Thus, Amichai's example illustrates an important fact about literary

categories: that the same poet, work, or trend may have both a high and a low membership gradience in the same category. Furthermore, Amichai's self-acknowledged ties to the work of two great modernist foremothers, the German Else Lasker-Schüler and the Hebrew Leah Goldberg, deepens the motivation for a revision of the modernist Hebrew canon, a revision that would unveil the major role that women and antiformulaic poets played in Hebrew literary dynamics, albeit almost tacitly and from the sidelines.

The various theoretical contexts from which my model for modernism is drawn cannot be applied without some major modifications because of the difference in the object (or rather subject) of study and in the questions one asks in each framework. First, the notion of best example, which underlies prototype semantics and categorization theory, needs to be revised if it is to apply to literary groupings such as modernism. Marginal prototypes need to be acknowledged as necessary for the very life of the linguistic-literary system, and categorization has to be viewed as a process that changes with time, place, and context. All this rather complicates the tasks of both literary theory and prototype semantics, but I believe complexity should not deter rigorous investigation.

Second, the formalist model of literary dynamics, with its two emphases—the center-periphery shift and the uncle-nephew line of heritage[18]—while still a productive conceptual paradigm, needs to be revised to allow for a less mechanistic—and nonsexist—approach to the literary system. Instead, we may want to talk about hierarchies of context-dependent specific types and degrees of centrality or marginality, and about aunts and nieces and a variety of other family members.

Third, as the example of modernism suggests, we need to make our semantic and historical models more messy and nuanced and less mechanistic and predictable. Our contemporary postmodernist, post-structuralist spirit of (anti)literary (anti)theory notwithstanding, it is possible to strive for a relatively clear and more or less precise conceptual analysis of the literary groupings readers, writers, and—yes—especially critics employ so confusingly and yet so intuitively. The fuzziness and opaqueness of the literary category under discussion need not generate a fuzzy or opaque study of that category.

CHAPTER 2

Theory / History

Between Period and Genre;
Or, What to Do with a Literary Trend?

In the early 1970s, Claudio Guillén (1971:465–66) faulted scholarship in the field of literary history for not having developed a vocabulary for dealing with the literary movement, school, current, or generation. Apart from Renato Poggioli's important distinction between the static groupings of the past (schools) and the dynamic groupings prevalent since romanticism (movements, currents),[1] Guillén sadly concluded, very little is available: "The truth is that our vocabulary supplies us with a wealth of advice on the level of critical classification, interpretation, and analysis, but not on that of literary history" (1971:466–67). Over twenty years later, Guillén, while applauding the growing frequency of studies of periodization as "one of the basic themes of comparativism" (1993:291), still deplores the fact that "the basic vocabulary available [for literary history] is much more limited than that available in the field of criticism; . . . criticism can still rely on the legacy of poetics and rhetoric, which antedates the historical preoccupation of modern times. Even today one need only page through any specialized dictionary to become aware of the paucity of vocabulary for literary history" (1993:290). I do not believe, however, that the main problem is necessarily "the absence of an appropriate terminology," (1971:465) or "the paucity of vocabulary" (1993:290). Rather, I see the terminological confusion as symptomatic of a conceptual uncertainty about the distinctions among trends, movements, periods, and styles. Typically, this uncertainty is not articulated or developed in any systematic way but instead remains implicit in various discussions of modernism and of other specific trends/periods/styles.

Periodization vs. Typology

In the absence of a tradition of theorizing about the literary trend as a distinct type of literary grouping, critics have tended to subsume the concept of trend under one of the more established categories forming the two poles of a critical continuum that traditionally has dealt with literary classifications: (1) the general problem of periodization, considered central to literary history; and (2) the problem of literary typology, modeled on conventional classifications of genres, modes, and styles, and considered central to literary theory.

The period model often coincides with an *extensional* definition of a literary trend (see chap. 1): modernism (or romanticism, symbolism, postmodernism, and so forth) is said to be the collection of works that were written during the modernist (romantic, symbolist, postmodernist) period (the chronological view); or by poets who characterized themselves or were characterized by others as modernists (romantics, symbolists) (the nominalist view). In its extreme formulations, which are, in fact, still quite the norm, the period model lumps together indiscriminately the heterogeneous literary production of an entire era, delimiting it by the beginning or end of a century, the reign of a monarch, the duration of a war. Datelines marking extraliterary events like "twentieth-century literature," "the Elizabethan age," or (in Israeli literature) "the 1948 generation" still appear in course and textbook titles as well as in scholarly works as telltale markers of literary categories.[2] Even critics of the period model find it difficult to avoid the allure of chronological quantification. Ulrich Weisstein, after criticizing what he describes as "annalistic" periodization, himself fails to go beyond it when he suggests that one concept is distinguished from another along the periodological map by the sheer length of the designated time period: from the longer epoch and age to the shorter generation and movement (1973a:68–71).

The genre model, however, is frequently associated with what I described in Chapter 1 as an *intensional*, or criterial, definition: all modernist (and, similarly, all romanticist, symbolist) works are said to share a set of common and distinctive features which constitute necessary and sufficient conditions for membership in the class, modernism (romanticism), or for application of the attribute, modernist (romanticist). This model is also commonly associated with the antihistoricist reduction of periodization to typology: the recovery of modernist, romanticist, mannerist, or baroque features in the literature of periods dissociated from these trends.[3] Strict typological approaches may, for example, talk about a modernist style in medieval or in seventeenth-century poetry, or about the baroque as "ecstatic expressionism."[4] Most treatments of literary trends, whether they explicitly identify themselves as concerned with periodization or with typology, in practice present some mixture of the two approaches, a tendency I find quite symptomatic. While this means that logically and methodologically the discussions may tend to be inconsistent and even confused, it also suggests that the need for a more pluralistic account may be indicated by the literary corpus itself. My own perspective will focus on the principles implicit in the prevalent practice of this critical "mixed mode."

The schematic conceptual map presented in Figure 1 is not, then, a representation of a model of literary groupings I would advocate. Rather, it is a heuristic device for describing the general principles embedded in common critical treatments of the subject. Instead of a strict dichotomy of period and genre, as would perhaps have been expected in pre-twentieth-century critical literature, most accounts now seem to presuppose a more graded distinction, presented here as a continuum of degrees between "pure" periodization on the left and "pure" typology on the right, with the literary movement or trend marking off a set of transitional concepts which vacillate between the two poles. Different periodological and typological approaches are distinguished from one another by the segment of the continuum on which they concentrate, the particular concept they privilege, or the pole toward which they gravitate. My own approach is no exception. By diagrammatically presenting the distinction as a continuum of degrees, my account pushes the traditionally central notions of period and genre literally to the margins, while foregrounding the much neglected literary movement or trend in the visual and normative center of the map.

Although different theories describe the transitions between concepts along this continuum differently, there appears to be some consensus about the fundamental divisions. Roughly, the first third of the

PERIODIZATION   TYPOLOGY

PERIOD → AGE → GENERATION → MOVEMENT — TREND → SCHOOL → STYLE → MODE → GENRE
(epoch, era, century)   (circle, current, salon, etc.)

dynamic →   ← static
diachronic →   ← synchronic
heterogeneous →   ← homogeneous
extra-literary →   ← intra-literary

Fig. 1. Literary groupings as a continuum.

continuum, from period to generation, is still under the dominance of the period model, with size (number of years or people involved in each grouping) considered the major distinctive factor. The literary movement and its cognate concepts, the literary current, circle, or cenacle,[5] are on this account still subsumed under a partonomy of periodization.[6] The last third of the continuum, from literary school through style and mode to the literary genre proper, is most commonly treated as a typological variant of a literary taxonomy, with mode usually considered a limit case of genre, and style a limit case of the literary school. In this account, the literary trend[7] and its smaller or more static cognates, the literary salon or school, are no longer seen primarily as period units defined by their social, political, or historical circumstances but rather as distinct, intraliterary poetic types. Finally, the first half of the continuum is more frequently associated with later literature from romanticism onward, whereas the second half is more commonly thought of in connection with preromantic and classical poetics. Thus, for example, Poggioli points out that "whereas we did and do call the old-fashioned regroupings 'schools,' we call the modern ones 'movements' " (1968:17).[8]

Clearly, this rough conceptual map represents only a series of critical reductions, acceptable neither as periodization nor as typology, and certainly not adequate as a model of literary trends (movements, currents). One of the main thrusts of the research in historical poetics in recent years has been to emphasize that intraliterary criteria should apply to periodization as well as to typology and, concomitantly, that literary styles cannot claim to be free of extraliterary periodological determinants. The same goes for the other attributes so one-sidedly associated with each pole: dynamic vs. static, diachronic vs. synchronic, heterogeneous vs. homogeneous. Critiques of "pure" periodization often point to the differences of "style" within a period, while critiques of the classical genre model emphasize the historicity and variability of all literary typologies. Increasingly, literary trends and movements are invoked as evidence of the typological facets of periodization and the periodological facets of literary types.

The continuum can therefore serve only as a methodological stepping stone for a critique of reductionist approaches to literary groupings. It remains to be seen whether this schematic representation can also serve as a heuristic device for correlating views of period, trend, and style with a more general critical philosophy. Thus, one might want to ask whether socially and historically inclined critics would more often tend to assimilate the question of literary trends leftward, toward the dynamic/diachronic/heterogeneous/extraliterary period model, while formalist, structuralist, New Critical and other "intrinsic" critics would be more likely to assimilate it rightward, in the political as well as the diagrammatic sense, toward the static/synchronic/homogeneous/intraliterary genre model. My own major concern will be to observe whether more systemic and pluralistic critical approaches that combine the periodological and the typological perspectives would indeed also tend to focus on the central section of the continuum. If so, could these approaches form the foundation for a theory of the literary trend as a model for literary groupings at large rather than as a borderline case that defies precise description?[9]

This, then, is where my own approach is located: in exposing the failings of the traditional emphases on period and genre, I hope to develop within an emergent methodological pluralism the beginnings of a focused discussion of the literary trend. I have therefore been on the lookout for those systemic or pluralist approaches whose point of departure is either a critique of the "pure" (chronological or nominalist) period model or a rejection of the "pure" (static, ahistorical) genre model. In the field of genre theory, I have found quite a proliferation of such systemic and pluralistic approaches which challenge and indeed present alternatives to the classical conceptions of genres as static checklists of necessary and sufficient conditions. The research is at a much more preliminary state in the area of literary historiography in general, and theories of periodization in particular, yet primarily within this framework the discussion of the literary trend takes shape.

The Trouble with the Period Model

The major critiques of the period model in this century were themselves not unrelated to the rise, since the advent of romanticism, of literary trends and movements as dominant forms of literary grouping. At the same time, the critiques of periodization also formed a response to the shrinking periodic time span, "the increasingly smaller zones of demarcation with constantly shifting and highly flexible limits" of literary periods in the so-called modern age

(Weisstein, 1973a:71).[10] The views I present below played an impor-
tant role in setting in motion a process of radically rethinking the
traditional conceptions of period and periodization, a process in
which literary historians are still very much engrossed today.

Pioneering work in this area was done by René Wellek, who laid
down—in a series of critiques of chronological and nominalist "period
terms" (Wellek, 1941, 1970, [1963] 1973; Wellek and Warren, [1949]
1963)—the foundations for the shift of theoretical emphasis from pe-
riod to trend. Without Wellek's work it is difficult to conceive of
subsequent explorations, preliminary though they still are, into the
concepts of trend, current, and movement in the work of Poggioli
(1968), Guillén (1971 and 1993), and Douwe Fokkema (Fokkema, 1984;
Fokkema and Ibsch, 1987). Yet, despite the relative pluralism of their
positions, these critics still operate very much within the conceptual
map whose reductionism they so aptly criticize. Thus, for example,
Wellek and Warren, in their classic *Theory of Literature* ([1949] 1963:262),
while warning against the "dateline approach" to literary periodiza-
tion, still assimilate movements and trends to periodization, whereas
they devote a special chapter to genre theory. In practice, however, a
different focus seems to be emerging, for Wellek's concrete discussions
typically deal with terms designating not just a chronological period
but also a "style," such as "baroque," "romanticism," and "symbol-
ism."[11]

More than other critics, Wellek consistently focuses on the forma-
tion, spread, and distribution of what he calls "period terms." He is
therefore able to confront the nominalist versions of the period model
head on, challenging the automatic identification between label and
propositional content. His discussion of symbolism starts out with
this general methodological admonition: "[T]he history of the word
need not be identical with the history of the concept as we might
today formulate it. We must ask, on the one hand, what the contem-
poraries meant by it, who called himself [by it], or who wanted to be
included in a movement called [by that name], and on the other hand,
what modern scholarship might decide about who is to be included
and what characteristics of the period seem decisive" (1970:90).

The distinction between the history of the term and the history of
the concept is, indeed, crucial for literary trends in particular. As
Frank Kermode (1988:119) has observed with respect to specific labels
such as "metaphysical poetry," "baroque," or "rococo," "*Isms* . . .
and period descriptions have the same ambivalent quality, quite often

starting life as sneer words and then being converted by other users into eulogism." Perhaps the most important component of Kermode's argument is his admonition, with Jean Rousset, that "isms [are only] a kind of grid constructed by us. . . . One must avoid confusing the grid and the artists, the interpretive schema and the works undergoing interpretation" (1988:122–23). Kermode argues convincingly that the use of a period term involves not only chronological and typological classification but often also ideological and evaluative choices. Furthermore, he asserts that period concepts themselves, not just their labels, "inevitably involve valuation" (1988:121) because they are used in shaping and reshaping the canon with "the clear purpose of making a usable past, a past which is not simply past but also new" (1988:116). But when he describes the workings of this mutual implication of periodization, valuation, and canon formation, Kermode's account becomes increasingly troubling. He claims that "the characteristics [of a period] thought to confer value (or its opposite) can be sought anywhere" (1988:121). And because periods and movements are value-laden constructs imposed by "a consensus of a relatively small number of people" (1988:125), the power and legitimacy of these "authoritative choices" mustn't be challenged lest we lose "our" precious contact with the past, rewritten and reevaluated as it may be: ". . . in the end the question is not whether [the grids we impose on the past] are unfairly selective, but whether we want to break the only strong link we have with the past . . ." (1988:126).

Wellek's critique of nominalism, unlike Kermode's, betrays the belief that it is not necessary to limit the meaning of modernism, for example, to the conventional extension of that label because it is still possible to decide "what characteristics of the period seem decisive" (1970:90). Wellek holds on to this last vestige of intensionalism, considering some form of definition still implicitly viable. Kermode's work, by contrast, seems to take the critique of period labels to such an extreme that in its profound relativism it begins to meld into the nominalism which it originally criticized. As a result, the concepts, and not only the terms, designating literary trends emerge as arbitrary a posteriori constructs, inventions aimed at making history manageable. Only the isolated works themselves are endowed with factuality, and historical poetics is reduced to a heuristic device for maintaining—through constant reinterpretation—canonical monuments and making them usable for a new audience. By focusing exclusively on the retrospective usefulness of trend labels in maintaining a canonically "usable past," Kermode's argument diminishes the multiplicity of social and subjective contexts within which that past—when still present—was created. It downgrades both the literary group as a sociopoetic force and those marginal or censored currents on the periphery of a dominant trend that form and inform the very processes of change in literary systems.

In the final analysis, Kermode's critique of nominalism turns full circle to reveal a cynical acceptance, if not a defense, of the period-ological status quo, ruled though it may be by arbitrary label and institutional convention:

> There must be institutional control of interpretation, . . . and self-perpetuating institutions resist not only those they think of as incompetent for reasons of ignorance, but also the charismatic outsider. They are bound to be reactionary in some sense; . . . There is always the possibility that within a large and not particularly centralized institution there may develop subcanons and revisions of periodization, to suit, say, feminists and Afro-Americans or Derrideans, or even feminist Afro-American Derrideans. What is certain is that revolutionary revisions would require transfers of powers, a reign of literary terror . . . and the business of valuing selected monuments and selected books, saved from the indiscriminate mass of historical fact, would in any case continue. (1988:126)

The "interpretive community" that Kermode invokes in the name of Stanley Fish is thus implicitly advised to resist radical canon reform of any kind, not only the reform aimed at accommodating the most recent fads of lit-crit but also those changes that would allow the repressed voices of marginal literatures, ethnic minorities, and women to be heard. With the traditionally conservative move of raising the specter of a revolutionary reign of terror, Kermode suggests that since periodization is just an "invented grid" anyway, we would all be better off—and certainly safer—with the old canon than with a new or revised one.[12] While other parts of Kermode's book, and certainly many of his other works, moderate this extreme canonicism, it is important to see the full implications of his position and its ambivalent origin in a critique—which is also a defense—of the nominalist period model.

I do not believe that Kermode's conclusions are a necessary consequence of his premises, and therefore it is possible to accept the latter yet reject the former. The inseparability of applying period labels from value judgment points to the intrinsic connections between periodization and canon formation. But if literary trends and the periods within which they function are perceived systemically and historically, then exposing the teleological and system-dynamic goals of trend formations (including the processes by which period labels are selected and conventionalized) need not lead to the nominalist defensiveness that Kermode now seems to espouse. In the introduction to an important study of postmodernism, Brian McHale (1987:4–11) argues that just because "romanticism," "modernism," and "postmodernism" are all "literary historical fictions, discursive artifacts constructed either by contemporary readers and writers or retrospectively by literary historians," it does not mean "that all constructs are equally interesting or valuable" (1987:4). Between the two extremes that Wellek originally charted out as "the Platonic idea" of a literary period or trend and its "arbitrary linguistic label" (1970:92) there lies a multiplicity of partially overlapping, fuzzy groupings which are no less aesthetically, psychologically, and historically real for their producers and consumers because their ontology is determined by the specific dynamics of literary intertext and social-historical context.

The incongruity between the history of a term and the history of a concept forms the basis for the objection to strict nominalism. The discrepancy between the extensions of the categories of a chronological period and the literary trends within it forms the core of the critique of the dateline approach. Since the 1940s, Wellek has pointed out repeatedly that there is no such period that all individual works in it can be subsumed under the period term. By now, theorists dealing with periodization within anything resembling a pluralist framework start from the premise that conventional periodizations in literary history do not reflect the entire literary production of a period but only that portion which for a variety of reasons became canonical and associated with the dominant literary grouping.[13] Wellek's contribution is unique, however, because in exposing the monolithic nature of period terms he provides the necessary transition toward a pluralistic, dynamic account of literary trends (though he never quite makes that full transition himself). In the process, Wellek also begins to examine the type of conceptual category that literary groupings constitute:

> For many years I have argued the advantage of a *multiple scheme* of periods, since it allows a variety of criteria. . . . A multiple scheme comes much closer to the actual variety of the process of history.

Period must be conceived neither as some essence which has to be intuited as a Platonic idea nor as a mere arbitrary linguistic label. It should be understood as a *"regulative idea,"* as a system of norms, conventions, and values which can be traced in its rise, spread, and decline, in competition with preceding and following norms, conventions, and values. (1970:92–93; emphasis added)[14]

A work of art is not an instance of a class, but is itself a part of the concept of a period which it makes up together with other works. *It thus modifies the concept as a whole.* ([1963] 1973:92; emphasis added)

Although Wellek describes this type of concept as a "regulative idea," the description fits exactly what John Searle (1969:33) terms a "constitutive" (as opposed to a "regulative") rule: "[R]egulative rules regulate antecedently or independently existing forms of behavior; for example, many rules of etiquette regulate inter-personal relationships which exist independently of the rules. But constitutive rules do not merely regulate, they create or define new forms of behavior. The rules of football or chess, for example, do not merely regulate playing football or chess, but as it were create the very possibility of playing such games." Searle's definition of constitutive rules may prove important for the Wittgensteinian component of my analysis of modernism. The fact that the category structure of literary trends is more like games than like etiquette may have something to do with why trends seem to follow a family-resemblance model (in the context of Wittgenstein's view of language as a game).[15]

Wellek purports here to talk about literary periods, but his "multiple scheme" could actually refer to the entire spectrum from period through movement and trend to style, if not genre proper. Implicit in Wellek's critique, though, is a challenge to the linear sequentiality of the continuum of degrees, proposing in its stead a set of multiple, simultaneous spatial schemes. Yet despite the implications of his own model, and his own admonitions against both essentialism and linear continuity, Wellek's language betrays more than a trace of an organicist reification of period as having a unidirectional life cycle—a "rise, spread, and decline"—of its own.[16]

In several ways, Wellek's views are still innovative today. First, as I have argued, is his emphasis on the need for a multiple scheme of periods.[17] Through a critique of monolithic periodization, Wellek leads to a repudiation of the chronological period model because the temporal sequences of literary production do not all belong to the same trend. Thus, numerous antimodernist and postmodernist works were written within the supposed modernist time frame. Strictly speaking, therefore, it is not the scheme of periods which is multiple, but the trends, movements, currents within each period. Interestingly, this critique seems intimately linked with Wellek's attempt to extricate himself from the confines of his own formalist and structuralist heritage. Focusing on a short and relatively neglected essay, the last collaborative effort of Jurij Tynjanov and Roman Jakobson, "Problems in the Study of Language and Literature,"[18] Wellek suggests that "what is needed (and this is implied in . . . Tynjanov and Jakobson) is a modern concept of time, modeled not on the metric chronology of the calendar and physical science, but on an interpenetration of the causal order in experience and memory" ("Evolution in Literary History," in Wellek, [1963] 1973:51). Applied to the study of modernism, this first revision of the period model is an important step toward understanding, for example, how the variety of trends from futurism to surrealism and dada can all be subsumed under one period term, "modernism."

Second, Wellek underlines the great internal divergences among the various traits of each period concept and the inseparability of the concept and its members (what he terms a "regulative idea"). This is an important step toward developing a logically rigorous yet nonreductionist account of the internal make-up of each literary trend. Wellek's description of the clusters of heterogeneous works "in the actual process of history" as constituting and modifying the concept of period, of which they are part, combines historical relativism with typological pluralism. This amalgamation is made especially clear in his discussions of baroque and symbolism:[19]

> In discussing baroque as a period term we should, however, realize that, also as a period concept, baroque cannot be defined as a class concept in logic can be defined. If it were, all individual works of a period could be subsumed under it. ([1963] 1973:92)

> A period concept can never exhaust its meaning. It is not a class concept of which the individual works are cases. (1970:120)

Wellek, however, never exactly defines that elusive "regulative idea" which both constitutes and modifies its membership.

Third—and of particular importance for an international cluster of trends such as modernism—Wellek argues that simple chronology will not do because the works that have come to be associated with one period, trend, or movement not only are located in discontinuous or at least partially incompatible points in time but are also situated in disparate social and geographic spaces. Many discussions have shown this discontinuity to be true of modernism, but the implication is always that it is due to modernism's special international and contradictory make-up. Wellek's argument turns the need for a geography of periodization into a necessary component of the general theory of literary groupings:

> Literary terms most frequently radiate from one center but do so unevenly; they seem to stop at the frontiers of some countries or cross them and languish there or, surprisingly, flourish more vigorously on a new soil. A geography of literary terms is needed which might attempt to account for the spread and distribution of terms by examining rival terms or accidents of biography or simply the total situation of a literature. (1970:91)

No small task this, and one which is of crucial importance for the Hebrew and Yiddish modernist experiments "on a new soil" that are at the center of my study. What seems to undermine the poignancy of Wellek's own call to include a spatial component in periodization is his almost eerie emphasis on terms to the exclusion of the concepts designated by these terms and their social, historical, and geographical frame of reference. It almost seems as if for Wellek the linguistic labels were all that determine "the total situation of a literature." While this metalinguistic emphasis is perhaps understandable given the terminological confusion surrounding the various -isms of literary periodization, it nevertheless creates a *Phantom Tollbooth* effect,[20] where cultural centers radiate with literary terms and disembodied signs are either waved through or detained at national borders. Thus, at the same time that Wellek underscores the significance of national struggles, waves of immigration, and the uprooting of communities for the emergence of radical differences between contemporary works of the same literary period, his language denies the very reality and referentiality of those forces.

All three of Wellek's critiques of the chronological period model—the multiple scheme, the period as regulative idea rather than logical class, and the emphasis on a geography of periodization—motivate, albeit still implicitly, a transition from chronological period terms to the (competing or successive) literary movements and trends which are active within a given period and which develop within it contradictory yet salient styles.

As I suggested above, Wellek's positions both have their origins in and form a reaction against the intellectual context of late (system-theoretical) Russian formalism and Czech structuralism, especially their models of literary dynamics. At the same time, his views are also to be understood in the context of postwar central European reactions against nineteenth-century historical relativism,[21] on the one hand, and static typology in the tradition of *Geistesgeschichte*, on the other.[22] Interestingly, Wellek's argument seems to be particularly fired up when he reacts against the "purest example" of static periodization "whose roots are a romantic belief in the homogeneous spirit of ages and a love of local color in time . . . which are . . . a synchronic counterpart of the diachronic myth of national character" (Guillén, 1971:446). Indeed, Guillén, Wellek, and many other more pluralist scholars of periodization present their alternative accounts quite self-consciously in opposition to this once-dominant trend in German literary history.[23] This reaction is quite understandable since many of these critics witnessed the classificatory bent of *Geistesgeschichte* turn into nationalist, "volkish," and racist *ideal typen*.[24] This political impetus is strongly felt throughout the work of many other European scholars, as well as in the research of Guillén, one of the few theorists of the literary trend proper.

In his seminal article, "Second Thoughts on Literary Periods," Guillén (1971:420–69) struggles to unearth a tradition of theorizing about literary trends, currents, and movements, and to elucidate—like Wellek—the basic terms for discussing this topic. But since such a tradition does not really exist within literary theory itself, he raises the examples of Bogumil Jasinowski and Claude Lévi-Strauss as two of the most important early critics of chronological periodization in general and credits them with introducing—each in a different context—the need for a shift of emphasis from period to trend. The connections between their views and those of Wellek are quite striking, although Guillén, who acknowledges his own debt to Wellek, does not explicitly link him to this decidedly continental intellectual chain.

Compare, for example, the arguments in favor of a multiple scheme of periodization and against viewing period as a traditional logical class, which Wellek developed between the 1940s and the 1960s, with Jasinowski's logical analysis of history in an article published in Paris in 1937: "Les époques consécutives ne s'excluent donc pas, comme s'excluent les membres d'une division en classes, car les unités périodologiques ne sont pas fondées sur la disjonction des caractères et ne relèvent pas du principe de contradiction dont toute la discrimination dans le domaine du discontinu . . . reste insépara-ble."[25] Period concepts, then, do not constitute classes in the strict logical and set-theoretical sense because the multiple successions of periods are not mutually exclusive. They are not based on a logical disjunction of features and do not follow the principle of contradic-tion (the law of the excluded middle).

But does a multiple scheme of periods necessarily preclude their description as logically consistent classes? Not, for example, accord-ing to Meyer Schapiro (1970:113) in his important remarks at the New Literary History Symposium on Periods: "The same object can be classed in many different ways, all logical and consistent with our knowledge of the structure of the objects. Hence many different pe-riod classifications are possible. It is the problem and the theoretical viewpoint that determine the choice of a classification, with its order of generality and its particular historical boundaries." While I would take issue with the characterization of periodization as a classification of objects, and while I would want to know more on the exact logical and methodological interrelation of such numerous period classifica-tions, I find the argument useful for an account of the heterogeneous literary trends of modernism.

Guillén, however, completely sidesteps the logical issue of cate-gory structure, which Jasinowski, Wellek, and Schapiro all raise. The problem, he argues,

> with regard to Jasinowski's view, . . . is whether a period can adapt itself to the trajectory of time as intimately as such a view assumes. In other words, the distinction between an absolute and a relative peri-odization is not simply a matter of logical stress—as if, for example, we were saying: when we focus on the dominant features of a period, differences tend to come out sharply; but if, on the other hand, we stress dialectics, and keep in mind the "dominated" traits, which are likely to recur in another period, we tend to obtain a mixture of dif-ferences and similarities. Jasinowski's basic concern, essentially, was with *temporal* (as against merely spatial) typologies, and with their peculiar nature. Our own concern should be with the extent to which periods are supposed to reflect becoming or to parallel the course of time. (1971:435)

Guillén, disregarding the importance of logical analysis in the Polish intellectual tradition of which Jasinowski is a typical representative, writes off this part of Jasinowski's argument as "simply a matter of logical stress."[26] The "failure" of period concepts to constitute a logical class in the classical set-theoretical sense, however, continues to be singled out in contemporary criticism as one of the main causes for the impossibility of theorizing about historical concepts (e.g., Perkins 1991, 1992). Since the literary object of study is so intimately dependent on logically loose, variable, and inconsistent period concepts, the argument goes, any hope for "truly theoretical" explanations of literary phenomena must be abandoned.

In fact, a rather similar critique of period concepts from the perspective of a belated logical positivism has been presented by Joszef Szili. The terms of Szili's argument echo Jasinowski's and expand on it using the framework developed by another Polish logician, Tadeusz Pawlowski, in a 1980 study of the logical structure of concepts.[27] From the historicity and changeability of period concepts, Szili (1988:35) infers the impossibility of logically defined literary concepts in general: "L'idée selon laquelle il existe une notion de littérature cohérente qui changerait tout en restant coherénte, c'est-à-dire garderait son identité tout au long de son évolution n'est qu'une illusion. Je ne pense pas à l'illusion de nos organes sensoriels, mais à celle de notre sens de la formation de notions logiques." The very historicity of period concepts prevents them, and consequently the notion of literature itself, from maintaining identity over historical change. Therefore period can be nothing but a pseudoconcept (Szili, 1988:34). As Szili acknowledges, this profound skepticism about the possibility of unified concepts in what he calls "aesthetic literature" is shared by a variety of contemporary literary approaches "within the New French criticism, some English and French Marxist theories, American deconstruction, the work of certain semioticians and the school of empirical literary science . . . centered around the periodical *Poetics*" (1988:33).

Interestingly, Szili himself is well aware of recent logical and set-theoretical frameworks, based on Wittgenstein's notion of family resemblance and on Lotfi Zadeh's (1965) theory of "fuzzy sets," which could accommodate open-ended, heterogeneous categories such as period concepts. However, given the positivist nature of Szili's theoretical expectations, this accommodation constitutes a profound disappointment:

[I]l n'a qu'à constater à la manière de Wittgenstein que la cohérence n'est fondée que sur une vague "ressemblance familiale."

Les spécialistes de la logique nous avertissent que des "notion" de la sorte appartiennent à la catégorie des notions *ouvertes,* ce qui veut dire qu'il n'y a pas de limites exactes qui séparent les objets et leurs subordonnés des autres objets. . . . Il s'agit donc d'un terme imprécis et doté de plusieurs significations ("Fuzzy"). (1988:35)

Accepting the fuzziness and open-endedness of these categories as a blessing and not as a curse would require, of course, a fundamental revision of our critical expectations. Ironically, literary critics who end up with the most skeptical, antitheoretical conclusions are often those who embrace the most positivistic, rigid views of what constitutes a theory in the first place.[28]

In discounting Jasinowski's critique of period concepts as failing to form a logical class, Guillén has in fact glossed over one of the most central—and most potentially misleading—repudiations of periodization in literary history. What Guillén considers more crucial to the issue of periodization than Jasinowski's "matter of logical stress" is what he suggestively and rather vaguely describes as "the vaunted reconstitution of becoming" (Guillén, 1971:437). Drawing on the last chapter of Lévi-Strauss's *La pensée sauvage* (1962), Guillén arrives at an analysis of literary periods as a cross between chronology and typology. Rejecting the notion of period as "an uninterrupted and homogeneous series" (what I have been referring to as the period model, or the first third of the continuum in Figure 1), Lévi-Strauss offers instead the model of "a constant leap from one order to another" (Guillén, 1971: 436). This position prefigures, despite its typically structuralist formulation, later poststructuralist and system-theoretical notions of ruptures, *glissements,* or slippage in the dynamics of literary periods. Guillén is fully aware of the importance of this tension between a linear conception of a sequence of periods and a spatialized view of a discontinuous series of leaps between multiple sequences of periods. He concludes that "[p]eriods, existing somewhere between the order of chronology and that of an atemporal typology, between diachrony and synchrony, are thus a good example of 'le caractère discontinu et classificatoire de la conaissance historique' [Lévi-Strauss, 1962:345]" (1971:437–38).

This description, in effect, articulates the conceptual map outlined in Figure 1, a map which, despite its linear distortions, points to the symptomatic location of the literary trend in-between the two poles of typology and periodization. However, when Guillén offers in the same study examples of the two poles, of "two limit-concepts . . . toward which most systems of periodization are likely to tend" (1971: 445), he fails to go all the way in either direction. Unable to transcend the monologism of the opposition between periodization and typology, which he himself so poignantly criticizes, Guillén ends up describing only the section of the continuum from period to trend. It is quite significant that when it comes to literary styles, modes, and genres, Guillén in the 1970s—like other critics exhibiting pluralism with respect to the first half of the continuum—hung on to a monolithic approach.[29] While Guillén's later work takes a decidedly Bakhtinian direction and introduces typological and historical variability to the discussion of genre, it continues to subsume the literary trend or current under discussions of periodization, while granting the theory of genres its own name and discourse (see the chapter titled "Genres: Genology," in Guillén, 1993:109–141).

Douwe Fokkema (1984:1–18), in his semiotically oriented model of literary trends, initially follows Guillén and Wellek in lumping together period and trend, and treating genre as a separate "code." However, in his application of the five codes "that are operative in virtually all literary texts" (1984:8) to questions of historical poetics, he admits that "variations in the system of genres and subgenres coincide . . . with the rise of new period codes, or rather group codes." His subsequent assimilation of genre and period to trend forms the core of Fokkema's innovative argument. Combining Guillén and Wellek's challenges to chronological periodization with the methodology of Russian semiotics—especially Jurij Lotman's (1977) development of the notion of code—Fokkema directly advocates a focus on the center of the continuum: "I would suggest that the literary historian who wishes to come to any general observations, and possibly also explanations, should work with the concept of group code or sociocode, i.e. the code designed by a group of writers often belonging to a particular generation, literary movement or current, and acknowledged by their contemporary and later readers. Together, these writers and their readers form a semiotic community in the sense that the latter understand the texts produced by the former" (1984:11). This emphasis on the sociocode is of crucial importance in integrating the critique of periodization into a socially oriented systemic approach. Since Fokkema's challenge to the period model and his use of the concept of sociocode were designed not only with twentieth-century literature in mind but also with an eye to accounting for non-Western and marginal literatures, it warrants detailed presentation.

There are several reasons why the term period code is not very appropriate. First, it assumes a unilinear development of all literature, which is wrong, even if one tacitly restricted oneself to European and American literature. Not only are there Asian and African literatures which do not participate in European periodization, but the quick succession and frequent coexistence of different avant-garde movements in twentieth-century European literature in fact forbid the term period code and suggest its replacement by group code or socio-code. Secondly, the term period code obscures the simultaneous existence of avant-garde, canonized, and popular literature . . . , produced and read by different semiotic communities. The concept of period code tends to obfuscate the fact that, apart from the succession of avant-garde literature, older types of literature are still being read. . . . The term socio-code may enable us to describe the protracted existence of codes that once were avant-garde but later became canonized or even trivial. Literary history, then, can be described with reference to more or less dominant sociocodes. (1984:11–12)

While Fokkema's actual application of these ideas to readings of modernist literature in effect denies the ideological pluralism of his critique of periodization, his position integrates—at least on the level of programmatic declaration of intent—some of the ideas I wish to develop further. Even so, Fokkema's emphasis on the concept of group results in an interpretation of the center of our continuum which is too literally sociological. In fact, only the self-conscious literary movements, circles, cenacles strictly fit his description. Clearly, not even all subtrends within modernism, one of the most movement-oriented literary groupings of all time, could be said to have had members that regarded themselves and were acknowledged by their contemporaries as belonging to one group. And, yet, one would want to account somehow for these poetically affiliated but sociologically unaffiliated modernists as well. Thus, for example, replacing "period" with "sociocode" will do nothing to remedy the marginalization of women within the canons of modernism, since they did not form a special female modernist "group code," their literary production—and its suppression—cutting across the movements and trends of international modernism. Elaborating on Joan Kelly's famous title-question, "Did Women Have a Renaissance?" (1984), Gilbert and Gubar suggest that an alternative literary history needs "to interrogate not only

'accepted schemes of periodization' [Kelly, 1984:19], but the very con-
cept of periodization in and of itself" (Gilbert and Gubar, 1991:74). The
model of marginal modernist prototypes, which I propose here, is in
part an attempt to question the very concept of periodization by dis-
rupting the all too automatic identification of biographical group mem-
bership with poetic grouping or affiliation with literary trends.

In the first chapter of their book, *Modernist Conjectures: A Main-
stream in European Literature 1910–1940,* Douwe Fokkema and Elrud
Ibsch (1987:1) briefly address some of these difficulties:

> The term "movement" pertains to a sociological process. If a group of
> writers can be clearly distinguished, with manifestoes and other col-
> lective publications, one can speak of a movement, e.g., the Futurist
> movement. If the texts produced by a movement are considered as
> literature rather than as the result of an intentional function, they can
> be said to constitute a literary current. Expanding a suggestion by
> Claudio Guillén [1971:421], we consider the term "literary current" as
> a complement, not only of "literary period" but also of "literary move-
> ment." The literary current manifests itself in texts, the movement in
> action.

But is locating the literary current "in texts" any less of a reification
of dynamic historical formations than viewing the literary movement
as a purely sociological process is a denial of its textuality? As with
some of the previous views which I have examined, the problem
seems to lie in the entrenched critical practice of bipolar thinking. As
a corrective, I wish to emphasize, quite deliberately, the terminolog-
ical metaphor of a literary trend as a way to fuse and mediate between
the current and the movement, as well as the larger oppositions of
periodization and typology, society and text.

As Fokkema and Ibsch acknowledge in their account of currents
and movements, the new focus on the literary group is indeed un-
imaginable without their immediate precursor, Guillén. However,
Georg Brandes—especially through Guillén's construction of his role
as the father of the literary current—provides all these critics with the
initial metaphor for the shift from period to trend.

Trends, Currents, Undercurrents, and the Tides of Literary History

Wellek ([1965] 1986, vol. 4, ch. 16), Poggioli (1968), and
Guillén (1971), three of the leading proponents of the shift of theoret-

ical emphasis from periods to movements and trends, trace the dynamic metaphor of the current back to Brandes's *Main Currents in Nineteenth Century Literature* (1906). But Brandes was not the only one thinking along those metaphorical lines around the same time. As Guillén himself acknowledges, Bendetto Croce ([1906]; in Guillén 1971:450–51), one of the fiercest opponents of both the theory of genres and traditional models of aesthetic periodization, speaks of currents (*correnti*) in his brief essay on romanticism:

> "Romanticism" is not a simple equivalent of the chronological partition "the first half of the nineteenth century," nor of the ethnic partition "Germanic civilization," particularly when we notice that people distinguish, within that same limit of time and within those same national limits, between *Romantic currents and non-Romantic currents, dominating currents and opposing currents.* (Translation from Guillén, 1971:450–51; emphasis added)

Integrating Croce's and Brandes's accounts, Guillén attempts to argue for the notion of current as the most powerful postromantic metaphor for literary groupings. Guillén emphasizes all those implications of the metaphor which are crucial for dynamic, diachronic, open-ended, and heterogeneous literary groupings such as modernism:

> Usually the metaphor . . . can be subdivided into "undercurrents," "crosscurrents," and so forth. . . . Musing on a splendid landscape, Brandes [1906, vol. 1:17] explored the literal level of the term in a description of the southern end of Lake Geneva: ". . . you see the Rhone rush, impetuous and foaming white, out of the lake. A few steps further and you can see its white stream joined by the gray slow waters of the Avre. *The rivers flow side by side, each retaining its colour.*" (Guillén, 1971:451; emphasis added)

Guillén further discusses the directionality and purpose implicit in the image of a current and concludes: "The notion of literary currents is frankly diachronic, dynamic, open-ended, and suggestive of relations with historical and social developments" (p. 453). But, Guillén's analysis suggests, the historical context in which Brandes's "subordination of periods to currents" (p. 459) was developed has to be bracketed if it is to apply to all historical categories of periodization. The emphasis on currents has to be freed from some of its antitheoretical, irrationalist connotations, divested of its "surrender to flux and mutability, of [its] indifference to generalizations" (p. 463). As an alternative, Guillén chooses to selectively model his account on those aspects of the metaphor of a current which can "compensate for the failure of periods to render diachrony" (p. 468). In my own account, I also selectively focus on those aspects of current which best illustrate my position. For reasons I have briefly indicated above, I have been privileging the more neutral metaphor of the literary trend. However, the concept of a current interests me deeply as well, though for different reasons than Guillén's. The metaphor offers the possibility to follow not only, with T. S. Eliot and Cleanth Brooks, "the main current," the "essential line of development coming to us out of the past, the main current as distinguished from the accidental or the peripheral,"[30] but also the cross- and undercurrents, which may remain submerged and unacknowledged yet have the power to bring about a change of tide.

CHAPTER 3

Behind the Graph
and the Map

Literary Historiography
and the Hebrew Margins of Modernism

The Limits of Literary
Historiography and Cartography

The liminal concept of a literary trend, especially as exemplified by the diverse, even contradictory, literary production of international modernism, may provide an enabling moment for revitalizing the metatheoretical discourse on literary historiography. Modernism, with its disruptions of bipolarities and its valorization of the marginal and the eccentric, could train us to look at the old questions of literary periodization and typology with a more nuanced, kaleidoscopic gaze. The metaphor of a literary trend or current, whose evolution we observed in Chapter 2, is closely associated with the literary production of modernism. It calls into question, in vivid, kinetic terms, the basic practices of traditional literary historiography.

Specifically, when the production of international modernism is construed as a dynamic set of trends, with their attendant currents, undercurrents, and countercurrents, it suddenly becomes necessary to reassess the usefulness and validity of two of the major metaphors of literary historiography: the graph, which is also known as the line of literary chronology or lineage (by which critics usually mean patrilineage); and the map, which often limits our view to national, not global, trends and marks only "major attractions" and clear-cut borders between literary movements or schools. Beyond the problems of any particular literary system, there are general conceptual problems that the trends and movements of modernism reveal about traditional practices of literary historiography. As Ralph Cohen memorably put it: "Histories of movements are all too often written without an awareness of how they move" (1991:108). In this study my critique focuses on historiographic constructions of modernism in two inter-related and marginalized poetic systems—Hebrew and Yiddish—and their partial yet multiple affiliations with the various -isms of "main-stream" international modernism. But the dominance of the graph and the map is most dramatically evident in Hebrew poetic histori-ography, where issues of literary geography and cartography have become, at least during the latter part of the modernist "era," as politicized as their nonliterary counterparts. It is therefore on con-structions of Hebrew modernist poetry that this chapter will concentrate.[1]

Any strict adherence to the two metaphorical models of literary historiography, the graph and the map, tends to produce two types of critical distortions. The first foregrounds the poetic patrilineage of individual and generational struggles as, for example, the struggle of "strong poets" with their "precursors"—in Harold Bloom's (1973) psychoanalytic formulation. In constructions of Hebrew poetry this view necessarily exaggerates Avraham Shlonsky's rebellion against Chaim Nachman Bialik, his great premodernist precursor; and Nathan Zach's generational struggle against Nathan Alterman, his early modernist predecessor. Such a linear account of Hebrew literary dynamics ignores important marginal figures; more complex, ambiv-alent affiliations; and simultaneous—rather than sequential—differ-ences among trends.

The second distortion derives from casting the dominant poets and authoritative texts of modernism as the epitome of the collective spirit of their era, the most typical or representative voices of their cultural milieu or *Zeitgeist*. Shlonsky and the *moderna* poets of the pre-Statehood Generation are seen as a product of the revolutionary Zionism of the Third Aliyah; this is Dan Miron's (1987a:116) influen-tial thesis, a thesis he has maintained even while taking the extreme nominalist position that all period and style concepts are merely ar-bitrary, artificial, and tentative labels. Similarly, *dor ha-mdina* (State-hood Generation) poetry of the fifties and sixties is often viewed as an outgrowth of the Westernizing nihilism of the period; this is Gideon Katznelson's (1968) famous position, revived by neonationalist or localist writers like Ortzion Bartana (1985) and Menachem Ben (1986).[2]

Poetry is thus denied any critical stance vis-à-vis the social and political system of which it is part, a particularly reactionary consequence given modernism's commitment (at least in some of its constructions) to a "negative mimesis"—in Adorno's (1984:7) terms—of mainstream culture.[3]

We have inherited a set of graphs and maps of Hebrew modernism that have been, and continue to be, shaped by a variety of forces within the literary system. It is important, however, to recognize that the modernist canon is still in a state of flux, that its graphs can still be replotted and its maps redrawn. By questioning the very tools of the trade employed in these historiographic or cartographic critical practices, I hope at least to draw attention to what they conceal.

Standard historical accounts of modern Hebrew literature posit a two-tiered view of Hebrew poetic modernism. It is no accident that the canonical picture of modernism in Hebrew poetry places its beginnings chronologically in the 1920s and 1930s, and territorially with the shift of the literary center from eastern and central Europe to Palestine. While the leading poets of this supposedly first "line" are sometimes described as the troika of Nathan Alterman, Avraham Shlonsky, and Leah Goldberg, they are more often depicted as a male twosome—Shlonsky and Alterman, the poets who were most self-consciously involved in the fashioning of a new poetic sociocode: the *moderna* of the pre-Statehood (Eretz-Israeli) Generation. All native speakers of Russian, these poets were acknowledged to have imported into Hebrew verse mainly Russian modernist sensibilities, especially the Russian versions of futurism (Vladimir Mayakovsky) and symbolism (Alexander Blok). The *moderna* poets were all master translators (and this is no less true of Goldberg than it is of her male counterparts) who feverishly furnished their reading public with translations of masterpieces of world literature from Shakespeare to Brecht, thereby enriching, indeed enabling, the production of a modern literature in the newly revived Hebrew language. Yet, despite the international nature of their translated literary corpus, the *moderna* poets remain associated quite exclusively in the canonical literary picture with modernist developments in the countries with which they had the most biographical and cultural contacts: Russia and France. The acknowledged influence of Russian and French versions of modernism (and the "official" historiography typically describes these affiliations as influences, often in the most crudely biographistic terms) allowed these poets to be associated in the public mind—at least to some degree—with a powerful international literary movement. This association came despite their geographical displacement from, and ideological abdication of, European cultural models. Yet, it was at the same time evident from the very first critical accounts that the poetics of the pre-Statehood Generation, in its most central line, must be construed primarily as being in opposition to the dominant intrinsic Hebrew literary line of Bialik's generation: the *moderna* needed to be liberated from the hegemony of Bialik if it were to develop its own poetic idiom.

The second acknowledged phase in the official graphs and maps of Hebrew poetic modernism is centered chronologically in the 1950s and 1960s and geopolitically around the establishment of the state of Israel. The Statehood Generation (*dor ha-mdina*) poets, as they have come to be called, are again construed sometimes as a threesome, Yehuda Amichai, Nathan Zach, and Dahlia Ravikovitch, but most often as the male duo, Amichai and Zach. They are commonly credited with (or accused of, depending on the critic's perspective) introducing into the Israeli scene the influence of Anglo-American versions of modernism, such as imagism and vorticism. The highly influential works of T. S. Eliot, Ezra Pound, William Carlos Williams, and Wallace Stevens could now be presented as literary models, translated, and increasingly read in their English original, not in the least because the anti-English sentiment of British Mandatory times was gradually being replaced by a growing Americanization of Israeli culture. Furthermore, there is a vague understanding that somehow "importing" Anglo-American modernism suited the poets' internal literary goals, such as the revolt against the dominant poetics of the *moderna*, even though standard accounts do not usually explain exactly how that was achieved. When construed as a belated imagist import, this last modernist phase, which witnessed the completion of the painful process of the linguistic revitalization of Hebrew, is at the same time viewed as parasitic on or epigonic to a mainstream international modernist trend. In the simplistic terms of literary datelines, Statehood Generation poetry increased, quite ironically, the time lag between Hebrew and European poetic developments. By the time Anglo-American modernism started informing Hebrew poetry, the imagists and vorticists, whose heyday had been in the teens and twenties, had either passed on to other things, by changing styles and ideology, or passed on altogether (Stevens died in 1955, Williams in 1963, Eliot in 1965, Pound in 1972).

Reduced to its schematic, most "representative" prototypes, this two-tiered picture of Hebrew poetic modernism depicts either a line of succession from one generation of early modernist fathers to late modernist sons (the graph) or two kingdoms feuding over the same literary territory in the poet Meir Wieseltier's (1980:405) metaphor[4] (the map): the *moderna* pre-Statehood Poets (*ha-dor ha-eretz yisre'eli*), followed or flanked by the Statehood Generation poets (*dor ha-mdina*). The more sophisticated graphs and maps associate each of the two modernist trends, as we have seen above, with one or more movements of international modernism (but never more than three of them). Schematically, again, the *moderna* is aligned with Russian futurism and symbolism (and more rarely with German expressionism); and *dor ha-mdina*, with Anglo-American imagism. But once the standard graph and map are subjected to closer scrutiny, fissures and curves emerge that disrupt the integrity of the model from the inside. Michael Gluzman (1991a) has shown how these historiographic outlines, as well as the studies that are based on them, tend to leave all or most of the female roles in the modernist family narratives empty: a patrilineage without mothers or sisters, a kingdom with two kings but without queens, princesses, or even ladies in waiting.[5]

The chronological/linear aspect of the graph presupposes that Hebrew poetic modernism is a literary period with a clearly marked beginning, middle, and end. Even within the two-tiered approach, which demarcates only two successive generations of poets, discontinuities, gaps, and partial overlaps cannot be ignored. Conventionally, the representatives of the two ends of the modernist poetic patrilineage are Shlonsky and Zach, just as their "strong" premodernist precursor is Bialik. Though it is too early to tell who will eventually emerge as their antithetical follower, it looks like Wieseltier has been groomed for the role more than others. What this patrilineage conceals, however, is the simple fact that there is no line going from Hebrew premodernism through the two purported modernist phases to postmodernism. If we take the metaphor of the graph seriously, what we come up with is not one line but rather a series of broken-off sections of distinct parallel lines, as Figure 2 shows.

Alterman's symbolist-aestheticist version of the *moderna* maintains only a family resemblance with Shlonsky's futurist-expressionist one. And Zach's neoimagism is radically different from Amichai's not only because of its strong dadaist elements; Zach also maintains an (unacknowledged) affiliation with the subversive first-person minimalism

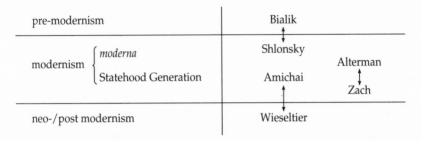

pre-modernism	Bialik ↕
modernism $\begin{cases} moderna \\ \text{Statehood Generation} \end{cases}$	Shlonsky Alterman Amichai ↕ ↕ ↕ Zach
neo-/post modernism	Wieseltier

Fig. 2. The graph model of literary historiography.

of Rachel and through her, with Russian acmeists like Anna Akhmatova and Osip Mandelstam. In contrast, Amichai's two (fully acknowledged) literary mothers are Leah Goldberg and Else Lasker-Schüler. (These differences between the two dominant strands within each mainstream modernist wave become fully visible, of course, only once the exclusionary dimensions of the modernist mappings are rectified). Similarly, while Shlonsky is forever chained to Bialik in his struggle with him—as Avraham Ha-Gorni-Green (1985) has persuasively argued—other struggles abound. Less acknowledged but aesthetically and ideologically as compelling are the antithetical links between Alterman and his premodernist precursor Shaul Tchernichovski, in a dialogic reworking of a Nietzschean/irrationalist/aestheticist literary prototype. This pattern continues into the relationship between Statehood Generation poets and neo- or postmodernists of the 1970s and 1980s. Wieseltier (1980:405), their leading spokesperson, praises Zach as the major liberator of Hebrew modernism from "the two kings wearing one crown" (Shlonsky and Alterman). However, his and other contemporary poets' attack on Amichai, on the spontaneous, intoxicated "addictive I" of Amichai's "hot/bold, fiery flow with the crowd" exhibits the stronger "anxiety of influence" (Wieseltier, 1980:416). Clearly, even within this exclusively male historiographic narrative, the graph is a radically misleading metaphor for modernism simply because (a) the members of each synchronic segment of the line are drastically different from one another in their modernism; and (b) different members of a modernist generation link themselves with different precursors, establishing a dialogic tension with those specific poets whose work is most relevant to their own.

As a corrective to the graph of literary lineage I proposed in Chapter 1 the trope of the rope or thread, which is one of the metaphors Wittgenstein (1972, vol. 1:67) uses to illustrate his concept of family

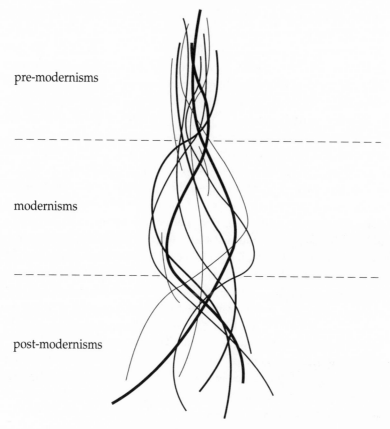

pre-modernisms

modernisms

post-modernisms

Fig. 3. The rope model of literary historiography.

resemblance: "In spinning a thread we twist fibre on fibre. And the strength of the fibre does not reside in the fact that some one fibre runs through its whole length, but in the overlapping of many fibres."

Through this figurative reorientation of literary historiography, the premodernist, modernist and neo- or postmodernist trends need no longer be construed as synonymous with the production of single great poets or major group codes. For in the Wittgensteinian configuration, both short and long, both thin and thick strands wind and overlap and make equally crucial contributions to the formation of an open-ended, twisted, yet rather strong whole, a whole whose strength derives precisely from being formed out of many uneven, twisted strands. Note that the metaphor works both synchronically—to account for the heterogeneity within the poetic trend (each marked off section of the rope on Figure 3), and diachronically—to account for the complex, interrupted or ambivalent continuities—or partial over-lap—between trends. This, I would argue, is not exclusively the case in Hebrew literary history, although there are reasons this literature may provide a particularly heightened example, and a good part of this study is devoted to showing why that is the case. Rather, I pro-pose this alternative trope as a visual enticement to reconfigure the literary trend as an open-ended category that maintains a culturally structured family resemblance among its members rather than being defined by a series of necessary and sufficient conditions.

It is similarly important to base the challenge to the cartographic model of a literary map on an examination of its own presupposi-tions. The foremost consideration, perhaps, is the problem of territo-riality. Mappings of modernist Hebrew poetry (but not, interestingly enough, of Hebrew prose!) tend to fix the locus of modernism: its site, its static territorial domain is pre-statehood Palestine and post-1948 Israel. Yet, how can Hebrew modernist poetry be tied to a local, national map when its geographical center is in the midst of one of the most radical shifts in its history, a shift whose magnitude can be matched perhaps only by the Second Temple exile?

The immediate result of limiting the map of modernism to the borders of Mandatory Palestine and the State of Israel is that the rich modernist Hebrew production outside of Israel is left beyond our purview altogether, and the intricate ties between Hebrew and Yid-dish modernism on the one hand, and Hebrew and Arabic on the other, are completely denied.[6] This static and narrow territorialist schema has made it possible for those of us involved in the produc-tion and reception of Hebrew literature to miss—or dismiss—some of the most innovative modernists in our language. Thus, within the confines of the exclusively male version of the cartographic model which I have been examining (Wieseltier's kingdom of two kings), the omitted places are all in the diaspora: David Fogel's Viennese dark gate and German concentration camp, Chaim Lensky's Leningrad prison, even the "region of grey towers along the shores of a grey river" in Gabriel Preil's New York (1960:111) are excluded from the dominant maps, unfit (until very recently) for inclusion in the canon-ical space of Hebrew poetic modernism.[7] When Wieseltier, in his extended monarchic map of the *moderna*, mentions "the exiled king," he refers to Uri Zvi Greenberg, a poet who is marginalized by an internal (ideological) exile within the territorial Zionist modernism.

However, these hegemonic claims of the local, Middle Eastern map are quite duplicitous, for there is not a single native of the land or even one poet of Middle Eastern origin among the canonical representatives of the *moderna* (even the name of their circle is a European transplant). And as for the so-called second phase of Hebrew modernists, the democratic "loose coalition" (*ko'alitzya rofefet*) of *dor ha-mdina* poets, in Wieseltier's (1980:405) terms, their most canonical paragons are native speakers of German (Zach, Amichai, and Pagis). Indeed, as we shall see, the first native Hebrew poet, Esther Raab, became a poetic alien in her own land precisely because of the literal nature of her nativism. It is altogether ironic that modernism, which on the international scene was so often associated with the cosmopolitan prototype of the exile, and in European literature was specifically typified by the diaspora Jew (James Joyce's Bloom is one salient example), should in Hebrew poetry so strongly deny its own extraterritorial dimensions.

A further distortion associated with this localist cartography, even within the terms of its masculinist model, is the marginalization or oversimplification of the Hebrew poets' complex affiliations with the various trends of international modernism. True, most mappings acknowledge the influence of Russian futurism and symbolism on the *moderna,* and of Anglo-American imagism on *dor ha-mdina,* but this is only a partial, and highly precarious, affiliation with a cluster of conflicting trends. Alterman's work, while affiliated primarily with French and Russian symbolism (a troubled and potentially contradictory blend in itself), also reveals an orientation toward later French modernist developments such as surrealism. It is precisely this surrealist moment which makes him, rather than Shlonsky, the perfect antithetical precursor for Zach: the European struggle between surrealism and dada is played out within the local context, as if it were a purely regional, Middle Eastern conflict.

The metaphor of a geographical map, with its closed national borders, masks the fact that these poets were not merely influenced by but actually saw themselves as Hebrew practitioners of and participants in these international movements, and that both their individual and their group poetics (especially, the genre of the modernist manifesto) are to be read in the triple contexts of the internal Hebrew/Yiddish literary system, the Middle Eastern versions of cultural modernism, and the international modernist affiliations.

While the limited range of the cartographic model could account for the narrow parochialism of canonical views, its two-dimensional, static spatiality explains the disregard for marginal, deviant, or dynamic forces active below the surface. The surface of this map is calibrated not by the sea level of common literary output (most of which wasn't modernist even in the heyday of modernism) but rather by the isolated peaks of the dominant literary groups. Thus, the geographical, rather than topographical, nature of this map represses the heterogeneity of literary production and conceals the coexistence of wildly divergent literary trends: for example, epigonic writers in the style of Bialik's generation who continued producing well into the 1950s. Similarly, Statehood Generation poetry needs to be seen as writing not simply within a modernist Anglo-American context but against the background of the diversified heritage of fifty years of modernist, antimodernist, and postmodernist production within English and American poetry. Most important, perhaps, the two-dimensional map veils the existence of potentially subversive marginal and subterranean forces which might threaten the level facade of the cartographic model. Both geologists and literary theorists agree, however, that such submerged forces are precisely those that are the most active in pushing for systemic change.

The distortions created by canonical models are, to be fair, not only a result of hegemonic literary politics but also a consequence of the extraordinary difficulty in nailing down any adequate and consistent picture of modernism. We have already seen what a heterogeneous and fuzzy category international modernism is. In many of its constructions, it valorizes quite self-consciously the very ruptures and contradictions that make its definition as a classically conceived literary category impossible. And, yet, the typical opening move in a critical study of modernism is first to acknowledge the vagueness, complexity, and open-endedness of the category and then to proceed to treat one segment as if it were representative of the whole. On the basis of this selective modeling, the critic then provides a list of common and distinctive features which are supposed to serve as a criterial definition of modernism in general.

Hebrew critics, like others, when they have followed the model of the map, in the tradition of classical genre theory, have tended to provide inventories of modernist traits, styles, and themes, and to ignore the historicity of the literary trend. A typical example of such an approach within Hebrew criticism (though much more sophisticated than is the norm) is Reuven Tzur's (1985) ahistorical discussion of modernism as a "mannerist," nonromantic style, active in literature at least since the seventeenth century but quite close in its poetics to medieval Hebrew poetry in Spain as well. When, however, critics of Hebrew poetry have followed the graph of the period model, they have tended to reduce modernism to periodical divisions which are often completely extraliterary and, by encompassing all of the literature produced in a certain period, are devoid of any explanatory power. In Hebrew literary histories this approach is often marked by political datelines such as the Ottoman versus the British period.[8] These demarcations rarely provide any account of the many ways in which modernism as a literary trend relates to but never fully correlates with the total literary production and consumption of the period or the extraliterary events that are central to it. The few histories or surveys of modern Hebrew poetry that exist tend to follow an undifferentiated nominalist model, listing periods in a medley of chronological, territorial, and political criteria.

Instead of presenting the canonical modernists as a homogeneous group, we need to expose the tension between the perceived prototypical features of a collective poetics (of the trend or movement) and the poetics of individual paragons, be they centrally or peripherally affiliated with the collective. If Shlonsky is our paragon for *moderna* poetry, then the futurist affiliation is in the foreground, and the symbolist one retreats somewhat to the margins. From this perspective, Alterman becomes an atypical prototype of the *moderna*. This is indeed the case when the system defines itself vis-à-vis the past: in the confrontation with Bialik, no symbolist poetics can provide a new, revolutionary alternative for the simple reason that Bialik already prefigures symbolism in his own work. However, when the Janus-faced literary system faces forward, or to be precise when the next generation seeks to enter into face-to-face confrontation with the canon, Alterman becomes the paragon of the *moderna,* and his symbolist-surrealist version of the poetics of abundance is contrasted with the neoimagist poetics of *dor ha-mdina.*

Third Circle, First Circle, Open Circle

So far I have examined the limits of the metaphors of the graph and the map within the traditional two-tiered construction of Hebrew poetic modernism. However, a handful of scholars have maintained for quite some time now that this grouping itself needs to be challenged, and that a third tier needs to be observed. These critics are known as proponents of the "third circle" (*ha-ma'agal ha-shlishi*) of Hebrew modernist poetry, a term first coined by Dov Sadan (see Hever, 1983). This third circle is third only in the order of discovery; it is first chronologically. We are dealing here then with the roots of Hebrew poetic modernism, roots which have been only partially acknowledged. Hever (1990b:93) has shown that "Dov Sadan is the one to have rebelled against the historiographic claim which limited Hebrew poetic modernism to the pre-Statehood modernism of the twenties [the *moderna*], and ignored the earlier modernist circle, which saw its beginnings in the first and second decade of this century, in the poetry of Avraham Ben-Yitzhak, Avigdor Ha-me'iri, David Fogel, Yehuda Karni, and Y. Z. Rimon."

Both Sadan's important corrective (endorsed since by several other critics) and Hever's cast of characters reveal that this third/first circle is now being returned to the canon in its exclusively male form. But let us stay for a minute with the presuppositions of this more inclusive model of a circle in order to examine what it conceals. Fogel has come to be the central paragon of this modernist circle, which Robert Alter has named the anti-*nusach* (antiformulaic) generation—the *nusach* being the maximalist style crafted by Shalom Ya'akov Abramovitch (Mendele) in prose and Bialik in poetry, which enabled the revival of Hebrew as a language of modern literature.[9] Yet when Fogel is described, even praised, as a retrospective model for the poetry of the Statehood Generation, it is most often as an unaffiliated, esoteric, or "episodal" talent. He was canonized and enshrined as a model for emulation primarily by Zach and Pagis some forty years after the publication of his first book. In manifestoes that establish the principles of the (chronologically) third modernist circle (the Statehood Generation), Zach uses Fogel's personal example to attack rather mercilessly the poetry of the second modernist trend (the *moderna*). Thus, as Zemach (1962:115) points out, here—as in the Russian formalist model—a literary son rebels against the father by embracing the poetics of an uncle. (Again, no mention of aunts and daughters.)

Indeed, Fogel offers a dramatic illustration of the importance of the marginal as a limit case that enables the extension or change of a literary paradigm. Yet his poetry also illustrates the inevitable limitations of any "extended standard" version of the traditional historiographic model. His work, and the still unfolding history of its reception, is constitutive of *glissements chronologiques* or *Epochen-schwellen*, the sliding shifts or thresholds which lead from the old to the new, often in broken motion rather than in continuous linear progression.[10] This dislocated order, however, has made it possible for the "invisible center" of the literary system—to use Russell Ferguson's memorable phrase (see his introduction to Ferguson et al., 1990:9–18)—to appropriate this once marginal writer while remaining oblivious to the more radical, and as yet culturally threatening, dimensions of his work. The first of these threatening dimensions can only be described as Fogel's radical dislodging of sexual taboos. Not only is the lovers' eros linguistically and culturally modeled on patterns of kinship,[11] but, conversely as well, parent-child relationships are described in erotic and, in the case of a son's poems to his father, homoerotic terms. Second is Fogel's equally radical (given the historical context) dissociation from Zionism and his refusal to mobilize his version of Hebrew modernism to national thematics. Third, and most important perhaps, is the submerged anti-*nusach* literary trend, of which Fogel is only one visible peak: minimalist or "minor key" modernist male and female poets, who never formed a self-conscious coterie and yet are numerically among the largest groups in Hebrew literary history. Despite its heterogeneity and multiple affiliations, this group shares an easily recognizable poetic style, once the historiographic distortions, which prevented its visibility, are corrected.

Fogel's demarginalization has so far occurred in two waves: first, in the fifties and sixties, and more recently in the eighties and into the nineties. Statehood Generation poets needed a precursor who would lend legitimacy to the minimalist poetics they adapted from Anglo-American imagism and from the more introverted versions of German expressionism. They also required a paragon who, in his poetic stance, could validate their own rejection of the dominant maximalist poets of the *moderna*. Therefore Fogel's poetics of "poverty" (Miron, 1991b:97, 99, 157) acquires a high salience, a self-imposed functional minimalism which helped it both marginalize itself and veil its affiliation with a crucial literary-historical conjuncture of trends that self-consciously oscillates between impressionism and expressionism. Ironically, then, Statehood Generation poets who "have kept discovering" Fogel[12] may have, in their selective modeling of his poetics, also helped suppress some of the most innovative and widely practiced aspects of Fogel's type of modernism.

Since the second wave of Fogel's demarginalization has still not ebbed, it is hard to tell how far it will go. The focus seems to be on a new valorization of Fogel's fiction. In the center of attention now is his newly discovered/translated/rewritten novel/diary/autobiography, which grotesquely blends realism with the fantastic. There is also a marked renewed interest in biographical criticism of his (and other "minor" writers') works. This criticism clearly serves the needs of an emerging postmodernist Hebrew fiction, with its attempts to blur genre distinctions, to blend the fantastic and the realist, and to reinstate "confessional" prose in the center of the canon.

My own intervention, as well as the work of my colleagues, is therefore part of this still ongoing process.[13] It seems that Fogel could so far be accepted into the center of the canon only if he remained an individual paragon, an unaffiliated lone giant like Paul Cézanne or Shmuel Yosef Agnon, not a prototype for a modernist literary trend few of us knew we had. Many of the women poets who developed similar or different anti-*nusach* versions of modernism at roughly the same time as Fogel are now also being "discovered" and moved to the center of the canon, thanks to the important work done by Miron and others, yet they too are discovered as individual, unrelated, and unaffiliated "female talents." The connection remains to be made between the work of each of these poets and the trend poetics of this suppressed early modernist project.

Once the links between the two canonical modernisms and their marginal precursor are acknowledged as a collective cultural practice, the mainstream poets of late Hebrew modernism (Statehood Generation) seem quite intricately linked to the group poetics of the anti-*nusach* poets, on the same Wittgensteinian model of strands in a rope that I outlined earlier. We can thus begin to trace the uneven, interrupted, yet intertwined threads leading not only from Zach's minimalism to Fogel's liminal impressionism/expressionism but also to Rachel's acmeism, although Zach has never acknowledged this connection. Other strands and links abound, and wait to be studied and fully traced in their partial, ambivalent, and multidimensional details: Amichai's (explicitly acknowledged) affiliation with the anti-modernist critique of modernism in Goldberg's poetics; and despite what I am sure would have been David Avidan's violent protestation, his poetry's affinities with Raab's radical conflation of linguistic and sexual experimentation.

The Marginal as Exemplary:
The Poetry of Esther Raab

Beyond this recovery project, it is important to note how the critique of the graph and map of modernism can affect our construction of the relationship between center and periphery, the dominant and the marginal. As I suggested earlier, canonical modernisms often cluster around deviant, atypical examples. Modernism at large is obsessed with the marginal as exemplary, in its choice of stylistic and intertextual models, in its selection of paragons, and in its thematics. Modernist Hebrew literature's preoccupation with the margins combines this general tendency with the intrinsic heritage of valorizing the eccentric or the lowly. It has inherited a whole gallery of exemplary marginal archetypes and themes from all genres of Hebrew and Yiddish cultural discourse: *ha-nistar* (literally, the "hidden one"), *ha-talush* ("the uprooted one"), *ha-helech* or *ha-noded* ("the wanderer"), *ha-meshulach* (roughly, the "homeless/holy messenger"), to name just a few common "types." Modernist and Jewish cultural trends, in their rich and complex confluences, have obviously allowed some configurations of marginality to be adopted as poetic prototypes. These same trends, however, have perpetuated the exclusion or minorization of others. Yet if we wish to see where changes in the literary system come from, we need to be able to hear precisely those minor voices. Within the minimalist poetics of the anti-*nusach,* modernist marginality in Hebrew reached its most intricate development.

I have mentioned that one of the most intriguing and subversive practitioners of such a modernist poetics of marginality was Esther Raab, the first native modern Hebrew poet. A major reason for her continuing peripheral status within the canon is, quite ironically, her being a native poet, for if immigrant culture is the norm, writing as a native is the condition that marginalizes. Raab develops her own nativist version of a modernist minimalism, or a "poetics of poverty"[14]: in her poems as well as in her interviews (for example, with Hilit Yeshurun in Raab, 1981:103), she presents both the land and the Hebrew language of early twentieth-century Palestine as models for an enticing new ideal of bareness. What was beautiful about the Hebrew of the time, she says, was that it was so impoverished or thin (*dala*) that individual words—not fixed expressions or larger units of signification—had to have real weight. Among her images of the bare, splendidly harsh landscape, the scorned biblical *atad*[15] ("bramble bush") becomes a positively charged metaphor for Raab's sparse, sexually aggressive new poetics. In the privileging of minimalism and in the poetics and politics of poverty Raab is very much like Rachel, Elisheva, the early Yocheved Bat-Miriam, and the early Goldberg. She shares this poetics with the male practitioners of what we have been calling anti-*nusach* modernism. But, more radically antitraditional and experimental than any of the other anti-*nusach* poets, she uses minimalist lexical, figurative, and thematic strategies that destabilize the canonical system on almost all levels of the text: from a symbolist distortion of syntactic word order to a feminist reversal of traditional gender roles.

Writing from a marginal position can—perhaps must—destabilize the norm of the literary and linguistic system by marking the unmarked, charging the neutral, colorizing the colorless, particularizing the universal. Writing in a newly revived language (as Hebrew was in the twenties), writing as the first native poet (male or female) in that reborn language, all the while remaining a self-conscious participant in French modernism[16] make it impossible for Raab to take anything for granted—syntactically, semantically, pragmatically, and, not least of all, prosodically. Writing as a woman in a language that is her "father" tongue (and Raab makes that a literal point that recurs in her interviews and poems), a language which genders everything, yet treats only the masculine as unmarked, as the norm, compels Raab to thematize, even politicize, the very choice of grammatical gender in her common nouns and adjectives. As a result, all nominals are potentially personified, telling—on the level of grammar—a narrative parallel to or subversive of the one told referentially. More specifically, gender and sex (both *min* in Hebrew) become linked in new and unpredictable ways.

In the gendered manner in which she marks the unmarked, Raab has become for later Hebrew modernists and postmodernists, both female and male, a latent yet influential metalinguistic model; her influence can be seen in works ranging from Amichai's "Sonet habinyanim" ("The Verb-Pattern Sonnet") and "Bikur malkat shva" ("The Visit of the Queen of Sheba") to Yona Wallach's "*Ivrit hi sexmanyakit*" ("Hebrew Is a Sex Maniac").[17]

In the opening lines of the poem "Lo ach ve-esh kirayim" ("Neither a Hearth nor a Stove Fire") Raab associates traditional female

gender roles, which the speaker rejects on the thematic level, with
nouns whose feminine gender bears the guise of masculine morphol-
ogy.[18] The female role which the speaker is refusing to fulfill is met-
onymically associated with the feminine nouns *ach* and *esh* ("hearth"
and "fire"), which do not look feminine but are.[19] Note further that this
rejected, traditionally warm and nurturing "feminine/masculine" fire
is replaced by a new kind of "masculine femininity," the cold and
piercing green and blue fire of animal eyes or a lightning bolt. *Chaya*
("animal"), which prosodically also reverses *ach* ("hearth"), is gram-
matically and morphologically feminine but referentially is usually
construed as male. The result is a jarringly new and ideologically
charged rhetoric of ungrammaticality, the likes of which mainstream
Hebrew modernism has never seen. By the middle of the poem, gender
reversals have led to a blurring of erotic, religious, and maternal love,
which in turn paradoxically enables the white doves ("yonim levanot,"
again a morphologically masculine noun) to play the traditional female
role the speaker initially rejects. The modernist, expressionist home
they build for her lover is not the proverbial nest a good wife is
supposed to build but a mystically pure heimat—warm stove and
all—inside the speaker's heart. By the end of the poem not only are male
and female stereotypes completely inverted, but the possibility of
telling internal from external, subject form object has also been called
into question.

לֹא אָח וְאֵשׁ כִּירַיִם

לְךָ אֲטַפֵּחַ –

עֵינֵי חַיָּה יְרֻקּוֹת עוֹמְדוֹת,

וּבְרָקִים כְּחֻלִּים

יוֹרוּ גִּצִּים וִיגַשְׁשׁוּ

אֶת אֲשֶׁר מֵעֵבֶר

לְבִצּוֹת הַכְּבָדוֹת הַחַמּוֹת –

וּבְרָאשֵׁי אֶצְבָּעוֹת תָּרֹן זֶה כְּבָר

צִנַּת-בֹּקֶר טוֹבָה

מַרְעִידָה

לִקְרַאת אוֹרוֹת לֹא הָיוּ עוֹד...

וְנִצְבְּרוּ הֲמוֹן יוֹנִים לְבָנוֹת
וְרִשְׁרְשׁוּ בְּרַחֲמִים וְטָהֳרָה
סְבִיב רֹאשְׁךָ הַנּוּגֶה,
וּבָנוּ לְךָ קֵן בִּלְבָבִי –
סֻכָּה תַּמָּה, כִּירָה חַמָּה,

מֵעַל יְצוּעֲךָ רֹאשׁ כָּבֵד תָּרִים,
לִבְּךָ לֹא יֵדַע עַל מָה יַעֲגַב,
הָהּ, כִּי בְּלִי דַּעַת כָּל הַלַּיְלָה
אַחֲרַי, בִּדְרָכַי הַקָּשׁוֹת,
בִּכְבָלִים לֹא יְנֻתְקוּ גְּרַרְתִּיךָ.

[Neither a Hearth nor a Stove Fire]

Neither a hearth nor a stove fire
for you will I kindle—
animal eyes green standing,
and blue bolts
tendons shall shoot and grope
that which lies beyond
the heavy hot swamps—
and at the fingertips ringing out long since
a good morning chill
quivering
toward lights not yet there . . .

But when like an abandoned child
upon my knees you'll rest—
then hoards of white doves gather round
and rustle in pity and purity
around your dejected head,
they'll build you a nest in my heart—
an innocent hut, a warm stove,

from your bed you'll lift a heavy head,
your heart won't know wherefore it is sad,
oh, for unbeknownst to you all night
after me, in my hard ways,
in unbreakable chains I dragged you.

   —Raab (1988:30; published in 1926, translation mine)

More typical of the anti-*nusach* style, the poem "Ke-tzipor meta" ("Like a Dead Bird") (Raab 1988:32; written in 1922) describes the somber but powerful bond between the female speaker and her male lover in images that on the face of it could have been written by Ben-Yitzhak or Fogel: the lover comes ("floats") toward the speaker in the last moments of sunset powerless and weary like a dead bird on a stream. What is prototypically Raab's, however, is the gender reversals that underscore the strength of their bond, a strength that is anchored in the male lover's vulnerability. The male lover is metaphorically and metonymically associated with grammatically feminine nouns: the simile of a dead bird (*tzipor meta*), the synecdoche/metaphor of his body parts—the eyes (*eynecha*) as the setting sun and the weary arms (*zro'otecha*) dripping sadness.

כְּצִפּוֹר מֵתָה עַל הַזֶּרֶם
צַפְתָּ אָז לִקְרָאתִי.
עֵינֶיךָ כָּבוֹת עָמְדוּ
וּמִבַּעַד לְזָהָב עָמוּם
רֶגַע עוֹד לָחָשׁוּ;
זְרוֹעוֹתֶיךָ עֲיֵפוֹת
רוֹעֲפוֹת עֶצֶב.
זַיִת דַּל עָלֵינוּ,
צְלָלִים חִוְרִים לְרַגְלֵינוּ.

[Like a Dead Bird]

Like a dead bird on the stream
you floated then toward me.
Your eyes dimming-blinded
and through dull gold
a moment they still glowed;
your arms tired
dripping sadness.
A meager olive tree over us,
pale shadows at our feet.

> —Raab (1988:32; published in
> 1922, translation mine)

Finally, and most dramatically, "Ani tachat ha-atad" ("I under the Bramble Bush") presents the female speaker appropriating metonymically the aggressive, phallic, and grammatically masculine thorns (*kotsim*) of the bramble bush, in the process reinscribing the *atad* as a new Israeli poetic/feminine model (a *tsabrait*[20] before the cultural iconization of the *sabra*). The syntax reflects this transgressive appropriation by creating in the enjambed first sentence (lines 1–4) a sustained ambiguity that constantly toys with ungrammaticality: the bramble's thorns (*kotsav*, literally "his thorns") can be construed as the direct object of the speaker's laughter though the verb expressing it is intransitive ("tsocheket," feminine singular of "laugh," as well as the gerund "laughing"). Most radically perhaps, the poem ends with a feminine appropriation of the cut that binds:[21] the speaker literally cuts (*gazarti:* idiomatically, "casts") the lovers' verdict (*gzar din*) or determines their fate with her sword.[22] This she does *be-echat*, a modernist portmanteau of the colloquial *bevat-achat* ("with one blow," "all at once," which is morphologically feminine) and the sacred *be-echad* (as in *hotsi nishmato be-echad*, "he died with the name of God on his lips," morphologically masculine), which is the elliptical form for the *shma* prayer, used to indicate martyrdom or a holy man's death. With this one motion Raab launches, from her forgotten corner in Petach Tikva, a new iconoclastic era in modernist Hebrew literature.

אֲנִי תַּחַת הָאָטָד

קַלָּה, זֵידוֹנָה,

קוֹצָיו צוֹחֶקֶת

לִקְרָאתְךָ זָקַפְתִּי;

אוֹר מַכֶּה עַל הַמֶּרְחָב,

כָּל קִפּוּל בִּשְׂמָלָתִי

לִי יִלְחַשׁ:

לִקְרַאת מָוֶת

לָבָנָה וּמְחוֹלֶלֶת

אַתְּ יוֹצֵאָה.

אַתָּה מוֹפִיעַ –

וַאֲנִי קַלָּה צוֹהֶלֶת
מְנִיפָה חֶרֶב נוֹצֶצֶת
וּבְעֶצֶם צָהֳרַיִם
בִּשְׂדוֹת לְבָנִים מֵאוֹר
אֶת דִּינֵנוּ גָּזַרְתִּי
בְּאֶחָת!

[I under the Bramble Bush]

I under the bramble bush
light, malevolent,
its thorns laughing
towards you
I erected;
light beating upon space,
every fold in my dress
whispers at me:
"toward death
white and dancing
you go out."
You appear—
and I light cheering
a shining sword hoisting—
and in the midst of noon
in fields white with light
I cast our verdict—
with one blow!

        —Raab (1988:31; published in
            1922, translation mine)

Both Raab's curt nativist modernism and Fogel's urbane European one are usually absent from—or completely marginalized within—the official graphs and maps of Hebrew modernism, along with the submerged anti-*nusach* modernisms of many other poets of the twenties and thirties. In recovering their project for a postmodernist reading culture it is important not to fall into the same exclusionary practices that the traditional metaphors of literary historiography and cartography implicitly endorse. In other words, their strand need not be construed as more important than, say, that of the *moderna* poets in shaping the twisted cords of Hebrew modernism. Instead, what I've been implying here, and what I'll argue explicitly in the coming chapters, is that even the poets who have come to serve as prototypes of the various trends of Hebrew, Yiddish, and indeed "international" modernism are often atypical examples of the literary production in the mainstream of their trend's "graph" or "map." Their ascent to the role of modernist prototypes is often accompanied by a selective modeling of their poetics on those features of their works which are culturally and historically salient at the time—or which can easily be made so. But, if this is the case, then atypicality can no longer be a condition that decanonizes. The slippage between modernism and marginality needs to be observed, even magnified, so that through it we can begin to see at once more inclusively and more (self-) critically.

PART TWO

Stylistic Prototypes

CHAPTER 4

Beyond Language Pangs

The Possibility of Modernist Hebrew Poetry

The challenge of writing modernist poetry in Hebrew during the first half of this century ought to have been unbearably difficult. A language that could claim almost no native writers and few native readers, that held to purist and archaist stylistic norms, that still carried the unwieldy burdens of traditional rhetoric and poetic diction (*melitsah* and *shibbuts*[1])—how could such a language become the vehicle of a modernist poetic experiment? Moreover, how could Hebrew, in the brief span from the beginnings of its linguistic and literary revival (the 1880s) to the crest of its first wave of poetic modernism (roughly, the 1920s),[2] have achieved enough stylistic flexibility to accommodate modernist needs for expressive authenticity? But Hebrew poetry managed to do just that and even escaped paying the price that a stylistic struggle of such magnitude could exact.[3]

Rather than create a stylistic crisis, Hebrew poetry's unique affiliation with international modernist movements propelled it toward breathtaking imagistic and poetic achievements. In fact, the ideology and poetics of modernism actually facilitated the achievement of certain internal stylistic goals which were crucial for the poetic redevelopment of the Hebrew language. A beneficial rapport existed between the aesthetic demands of the external modernist affiliation and the particular needs of the newly revived Hebraic tradition. Thus, for example, the *moderna* poets of the pre-Statehood Generation often employed neologisms both as a vehicle of modernist (futurist-inspired) poetics and as part of the push toward lexical innovation that was necessary for the revival of the Hebrew language. Although each of the three modernist waves in Hebrew poetry developed this rapport within different areas of expression, modernism and Hebraism (namely, the dynamics of the Hebraic literary and linguistic system) nevertheless offered all Hebrew poets a truly serendipitous conflation of purposes. It is important to stress at the outset, however, that Hebrew modernism did not simply adapt foreign influences for indigenous needs. The dynamic hierarchies of diverse stylistic and ideological prototypes within modernism were particularly adaptable to the internal needs of each of the national literatures that participated in it.[4] What remains extraordinary about the Hebrew versions of poetic modernism is the consistency with which the international modernist affiliations could be made to cohere with the peculiar historical demands of the Hebrew literary and linguistic renewal.

As opposed to mere co-option of extranational trends, modernist Hebrew poetry overcame its "language pangs" by evolving a complex rhetorical mechanism in which stylistic strategies and devices received dual but logically independent justifications: one from the external modernist literary system, and the other from the internal Hebraic system. The Russian formalist notion of motivation of the device (*motivruvka priëma*)[5] and its modifications in Benjamin Harshav's [Hrushovski's] theory of the text[6] best describe this systemic congruity between the external and internal literary dynamics. But first the problem itself needs to be presented in more precise terms.

A historicized, politicized revision of Israeli neoformalist polysystem theory[7] generates one component of my account of Hebrew poetic modernism. It may not be accidental that the Israeli polysystem model itself arose, in part, as a response to the historical conditions peculiar to Hebrew literature and language. Let me try out these particular critical tools in describing the linguistic problems that modernist Hebrew poetry inherited from Bialik and other predecessors. Indeed, Chaim Nachman Bialik very early on was keenly aware of these problems and ingeniously articulated them with unparalleled force in his essay "Chevley lashon" ("Language Pangs"). Using Bialik's analysis as a point of departure, I shall restate the linguistic condition in neoformalist terms and then go on to present the clusters of prototypical stylistic features associated with each of the three modernist Hebrew trends as historically unique responses to these conditions.

Since these stylistic developments were most crucial during the earlier stages of Hebrew modernism, I shall devote the bulk of this chapter to representatives of the first two modernist trends in (my account of) Hebrew poetry: the anti-*nusach* (antiformulaic) poets, whose retrospective paragon turned out to be David Fogel; and the *moderna* of the pre-Statehood Generation, whose activist, dominant paragon was undoubtedly Avraham Shlonsky.[8] Yehuda Amichai and the other members of the third modernist wave of Statehood Generation poets write at a time when already many of the linguistic problems are at a stage of final resolution. Still, I shall discuss some of their salient stylistic features since they have continued to benefit from the literary/linguistic rapport between international and domestic modernism.

Bialik, Automatization, Language System

What exactly were the linguistic and stylistic problems that modernist Hebrew poetry inherited from its premodernist forebears, the poets of Bialik's generation? As I indicated above, Bialik himself, with his unique sensitivity toward language, brilliantly diagnosed the central problems facing Hebrew as a language of modern literature. "The mere existence of linguistic assets alone, as plentiful as they may be, still will not suffice," Bialik asserts in "Chevley lashon":[9]

Rather [these linguistic assets] need a turning and overturning, [they require] the perpetual, cyclical motion of life. In this movement the most faithful guardian angel of language is created—routine use. The wealthiest of languages, if its assets are not commonly traded, handled and touched . . . every hour and every moment in both writing and speech, suffers a marred and miserable existence, gradually deteriorating and falling behind. Great is the power of living speech. No absurdity of grammar or logic exists which the stomach of the living language cannot digest . . . but on the other hand, a language that is not alive, its powers of digestion weakened, . . . begins to show the dry bones of its philological skeleton.

. . . .

To obliterate completely the barrier between our soul and our tongue, to put an end to all the "language pangs" all at once—all this will become possible only through a total rejuvenation of the language and a renaissance of speech and writing. There is no other way: either a complete revival or . . . a life of shame that would be worse than death. (Bialik, 1965:197–98; translated by Chana Kronfeld and Eric Zakim)

Confronting the stylistic crisis of Hebrew literature head-on with this model of a healthy linguistic economy and anatomy, Bialik's essay prefigures, as early as 1905(!),[10] two radically modern conceptions of literary and linguistic evolution: first, the Russian formalist notion of the automatization and deautomatization of discourse;[11] and, second, the Israeli neoformalist notion of linguistic/literary polysystems.[12] In the first of a series of studies devoted to the special conditions of the Hebrew language system, Itamar Even-Zohar himself stresses that Bialik already reveals a deep understanding "of the problems, deficiencies, and especially the defects of the language . . . which lacks a complete polysystem." Even-Zohar then acknowledges his own theory's indebtedness to Bialik, despite what he terms Bialik's "imprecise terminology" (Even-Zohar, 1970:292). Bialik's incisive, albeit "imprecise," metaphorical description thus provides a particularly instructive beginning to an account of the stylistic crisis which modernist Hebrew poetry inherited from its predecessors.

In his discussion of the importance that clichés have in the linguistic "economy," Bialik shrewdly uses precisely such a life-giving cliché: the metaphor of lexical coinage (*matbe'a lashon* literally, "a coin of the tongue"). By reviving the dormant metaphorical import of *matbe'a lashon* and turning it into the "currency" of a speech community's negotiations and transactions (*matbe'a over la-socher* "currency," "negotiables"; literally "a coin handed to the merchant"), Bialik demonstrates the power of *shigra* (routine use) before our very eyes. He activates, in his own discourse, that "faithful guardian angel" of the Hebrew language which the discourses of his contemporaries lack so badly. In allowing its linguistic assets to be recycled and "automatized," a language actually ensures its stylistic vitality. Through "the perpetual motion," the turning and overturning of literary and everyday use, a language system establishes its strong norms (what Bialik refers to elsewhere as *nusach*) against which all creative deviations and deautomatizations are measured.

Even-Zohar describes automatization as a "process and/or state whereby signs are (wholly or partly) dereferentialized" (1986:66).[13] Signs, be they literary, linguistic, or cultural, tend to become " 'automatic stock' for given situations, that is motorized and not controlled by free selection decisions. A large portion of communication . . . is indispensably automatic. . . . [Automatization] can be conceived of not just as an elementary feature of signs, but as a necessary condition for their efficient functioning" (1986:66–67). The linguistic economy implied by Even-Zohar's metaphor is stock market oriented, whereas Bialik's invokes the handling and touching of merchandise in the market place. But both have a strong sense of the necessity of automatization for vital linguistic function.

Bialik clearly understood the need for an all-encompassing conception of language as a system. In establishing his metaphorical anatomy of language in the second half of the passage from "Language Pangs," Bialik again revives and reifies a lexicalized figure of speech, the anatomical sense of *lashon* (tongue/language). By metonymic extension from "tongue" to "body," Bialik constructs an elaborate anatomy of the life and death of a language. In terms that would easily fit both a modernist poetics and a contemporary linguistics,[14] he stresses that a vital language system can digest and absorb any logical absurdity and ungrammaticality. "Bad" grammar and illogic present no danger to the life of the language system. On the contrary, a language becomes contaminated by allowing the normative rules, "the dry bones of its philological skeleton," to show through. Bialik goes on to prescribe a total revival of Hebrew both in writing and in speech as the only available cure, not only for the obvious nationalist ideological reasons but because—as the anatomical metaphor suggests—Hebrew must become a vital, dynamic, and interactive system which demands and receives the full development of all its strata. Only then can it function properly within the linguistic and literary domains. This antipurist, antiphilological view ultimately calls into question the conservative stance that later modernist generations attributed to the National Poet, Preserver of the *Nusach*.

Bialik's organistic account of language is clearly reminiscent of later formalist and neoformalist theories, in particular the views adopted by Jurij Tynjanov and Roman Jakobson ([1928, 1971] 1978), the founders of the systems approach to literature and language.[15] Like them he stresses the interdependence of all linguistic strata, both canonical and noncanonical, and their holistic function within the linguistic/literary body. In discussing the importance of stratification to the life of the language system, Even-Zohar also uses organistic/systemic metaphors that differ from Bialik's only in their heavily mechanistic overtones:[16]

> Similarly to a natural system, which needs, for instance, heat regulation, so do cultural systems need a regulating balance in order not to collapse or disappear. This regulating balance is manifested in the stratificational oppositions. The canonized systems . . . would very

likely stagnate after a certain time if not rivaled by a non-canonized system, which threatens to replace it. . . . This guarantees the evolution of the system, which is the only way by which it can be preserved. (Even-Zohar, 1979:295–96)

An equally important correlation exists between Bialik's views in "Language Pangs" and the neoformalist dynamic conception of language. Even-Zohar and the Israeli theorists have developed a "theory of dynamic system" similar to Bialik's as an alternative to the structuralist "theory of static system . . . usually associated with the teachings of Saussure" (Even-Zohar, 1979:289). Inspired by Harshav's [Hrushovski's] integrational semantics, Even-Zohar repeatedly emphasizes open-endedness and heterogeneity:

A semiotic system is necessarily a *heterogeneous, open* structure. It is, therefore, very rarely a *uni*-system but is, *necessarily,* a *poly*-system—a multiple system, a system of various systems which intersect with each other and partly overlap, using concurrently different options, yet functioning as one structured whole, whose members are interdependent. . . . Against a background such as [this], the term polysystem is more than just a terminological convention. Its purpose is to make explicit the conception of the system as dynamic and heterogeneous. (Even-Zohar, 1979:290).

Even-Zohar's polysystem hypothesis and Bialik's metaphor of linguistic anatomy converge at their objection to philological purism and normativism. Bialik's open embrace of any "absurdity of grammar or logic" produced by living discourse is echoed in Even-Zohar's privileging of noncanonical, nonstandard language and literature within the evolution of the polysystem: "Thus, standard language cannot be accounted for without the *non*-standard varieties; . . . the polysystem hypothesis involves a rejection of value judgments as criteria for an *a priori* selection of the objects of study" (1979:292). Finally, Bialik's complex image of Hebrew's sick linguistic body with its stagnant social economy is repeated in Even-Zohar's diagnosis of modern Hebrew as a defective polysystem or pseudopolysystem, "lacking primarily the system of colloquial speech along with its specific subsystems (standard vernacular, slang, class registers, geographical dialects, etc.)" (Even-Zohar, 1971:339).

The striking correlations between Bialik and the neoformalists may now allow us to reformulate the stylistic crisis which Bialik describes through metaphor: in the absence of strong and clear-cut norms for ordinary language use, no coherent frame of reference can exist for a literary/linguistic system. The language of literature, lacking the "faithful guardian angel" of routine use, is then forced to supply not just the deautomatization but also the prerequisite automatization of its own discourse. Thus, in order to achieve stylistic stratification the system must artificially fill in the gaps within its various stylistic registers by inventing equivalents or compensations for nonexisting slang, dialects, technical language. However, these artificial or invented modes of compensation (such as Shlonsky's well-known use of Aramaic as an equivalent for slang) do not, as a rule, become adopted by the entire speech community. Rather than perfecting the defective polysystem, the artificial registers can lead to the creation of a "pseudo-polysystem" (Even-Zohar, 1971:339).

Extricating the language of Hebrew literature from its defective or false polysystem has been, and in some ways continues to be, a long and painful process full of "language pangs." This process became uniquely productive for the modernist poets because of the coinciding emergence of the three major trends of modernism in Hebrew poetry with the general revival of the language. This conjuncture of linguistic and literary forces during the modernist era gave the "digestive powers" of Hebrew poetry enough strength to prevent stylistic starvation and emaciation.

Within Bialik's dissection of Hebrew's language pangs lies a great part of the cure: the recognition of the vital importance of change to the survival and rejuvenation of the (poly)system: "[Only] a system undergoing permanent, steady and well-controlled change is a stable one. It is only such stable polysystems which manage to *survive*, while others simply perish. Therefore, crises or 'catastrophes' within a polysystem (i.e., occurrences which call for radical change, either by internal conversion or by external interference), which can be controlled by the system are signs of a vital, rather than a degenerate system" (Even-Zohar, 1979:303–4).

It was Hebrew poetry's good fortune that at a time when the language was caught in the midst of its change-demanding crisis, it had available to it those modernist prototypes which placed a special emphasis on revolutionary change and provided a plethora of aesthetic and ideological motivations for the innovations that were necessary to the life of the language. Change and motivation go hand in hand. The Russian formalists' conception of motivation of the device formed a central tenet in their theory of literary change. The history of the novel, for example, was construed by Victor Shklovsky as "the succession of different motivations for the device of fusing short stories into larger wholes" (Steiner, 1984:58).

Clearly, however, the formalist notion of motivation cannot be adapted to the needs of a historical poetics of Hebrew modernism without some major modifications. After all, in its most well-known formulation, motivation is a rather dogmatic and reductionist concept: Shklovsky (1923:50) restricts his definition to the "extra-literary (reality-like) [*bytovoe*] explanation of plot construction."[17] Even when extended beyond the limits of prose fiction, this interpretation of motivation remains rather problematic, for it denotes "a justification of artistic convention in terms of life," terms which are always perceived as ancillary to the all-important device. Thus, Jakobson "interpreted the 'urbanism' of the futurist poets, their cult of machine civilization, as an ideological justification [motivation] of the revolution in poetic vocabulary, a Futurist's expedient for introducing new, and unorthodox word-combinations" (Erlich, 1965:195). Similarly, Boris Eichenbaum proclaimed that "Tolstoj's passion for minute psychological analysis . . . was fundamentally a matter of his . . . challenge to the clichés of romantic literature" (quoted in Erlich, 1965:196). These views, many scholars have suggested, reveal the formalists' strong modernist bias against the representational, ideational, or ethical functions of verbal art. Rather than provide a scientific model of the literary object, as some formalists purported to do, these views promoted a specific prototype of literature consistent with that presented by Russian radical modernism.

Other versions of a theory of motivation, though never fully developed, were less tendentious. By 1935 Jakobson "was ready to postulate for the 'motivation' the same autonomy which Russian Formalists claimed for the device" (Erlich, 1965:207). This change was perhaps influenced by Boris Tomashevsky's 1925 expansion of the concept to include "realistic" motivation as well as "compositional" and "artistic" ([1925] 1965: 78–87). In the reader-oriented text theory of Harshav [Hrushovski] and the Tel Aviv School, thematics, ideology, and characterization, for example, are the (realistic) motivation for the compositional device only if the reader happens to be "activating" the compositional dimension of the work. If, however, the reader is actualizing thematic or characterizational patterns, then the (aesthetic) motivations consist of compositional aspects.

While these newer developments in motivation theory have extricated the concept from a completely formalist bias, in practice they have been concerned only with part of the concept's extension. For a variety of reasons, existing contemporary discussions of motivation have dealt mainly with questions of segmentation—namely, the justification for the introduction of segments into the text sequence. There is, however, no reason to go on restricting the application of the concept in this manner. In this chapter I employ "motivation" in a much broader sense. Within this broader interpretation, I describe the workings of a dual motivation in modernist Hebrew poetry as a set of solutions to its stylistic "language pangs." In the process, some insight may also be gained concerning the applicability of modern Israeli literary theory to the modernist poetry that serves as its prototype. However, it could be argued that the polysystem theory, as it stands, will do to explain all the stylistic achievements of modernist Hebrew poetry and to render redundant the complicated dual-motivation hypothesis. I will begin by examining two such possible explanations, which are based on the concepts of system and automatization/deautomatization as traditionally construed.

The first explanation relies on the peculiar historical development of the Hebrew poetic system. Modern Hebrew poetry assimilated many extant components of its diachronic polysystem, which were kept alive by the strength of the traditional norm from the Bible to the Middle Ages. This strong norm served as a basis for the same automatization of discourse that, according to the neoformalists (as well as Bialik), is a necessary precondition for stylistic rejuvenation. This powerful conventionality engenders the required rebellion against itself, which in turn brings about a deautomatization of the poetic/linguistic code. Thus, because Hebrew poetry had a history of a strong norm, or *nusach,* it could also contain a strong modernist reaction against that *nusach.*

Although this account answers part of the question, it does not encompass all the conditions particular to the history of Hebrew. After all, from the time of the Italian Renaissance, a strong stylistic norm in Hebrew poetry actually ceased to develop, and it survived only in a dormant condition until its resurrection in Bialik's generation. (See Harshav 1993:81–132.) This inconsistent tradition might explain why modernist Hebrew poets, rather than rebel directly against the origins of their style, have always defined themselves vis-à-vis the tradition by discovering within it ever-changing complex stylistic features. These "strong beginnings" of the Hebrew canon[18] allowed each modernist generation to find in them a prototype fitting its own needs. Paradoxically, then, the influential but relatively short-lived traditional norm enabled the modernist Hebrew poets to turn their defective polysystem into a source of strength. But without help from the open-ended and heterogeneous models of their modernist affiliations it is doubtful whether the strong beginnings would have sufficed to support a major literary revival.

The difference between the polysystems of Hebrew poetry and prose could provide a second possible answer. Clearly, poetry and prose create different expectations for linguistic "fullness" and stylistic authenticity. Traditionally, poetry places fewer mimetic demands on style than prose fiction. For Hebrew poetry, polysystemic gaps in the stylistic registers of colloquial idiom and slang were simply not that critical. In contrast, Hebrew prose fiction from Uri Nissan Gnessin to Amos Oz has been caught between archaic stylistic norms inherited from the diachronic polysystem and its own aesthetic needs for a modern, expressive idiom. While the modernist poet could draw from any of the registers and historical layers of the language which fit his or her needs, the writer of fiction often had to accept a lofty and unnatural linguistic norm or struggle to compensate for the huge stylistic gap between the descriptive passages and the dialogue.[19]

This explanation has the advantage of addressing specific stylistic problems within the genres and may even help explain peculiarities of genre selection, such as the clear preference for the novella and the short story over the novel in modernist Hebrew fiction. The novel could not develop into the dominant narrative genre without the existence of a standard middle register. This register, which linguists call *ivrit beynonit* (standard Hebrew), is only now maturing into a comprehensive written style. This development has enabled the novel to rise to a position of dominance in contemporary postmodernist Hebrew fiction.

However, this explanation does not account for the problem of poetic diction. Hebrew poetry traditionally showed a strong resistance to any incorporation of "low" or "subcanonical" stylistic materials. While this tendency is probably typical of poetry in general, it was always especially characteristic of verse in the "holy tongue," where norms of ornate and lofty style have been particularly strong. Thus, it might have been expected that Hebrew poetry should have had difficulty parting with its archaist and purist tendencies, and that these tendencies in turn would have clashed with the antitradition-alism and experimentation of the modernist poetics. But this conflict did not arise, at least not in any destructive way.

Although incomplete, these two accounts introduce an important issue which the poems I discuss will soon make abundantly clear: paradoxically, there exists a strong conservative element in the ex-perimental stylistics of modernist Hebrew poetry. In the most radical innovations and reversals of past conventions there is also a return to the radices of traditional strong beginnings. We need, however, the model of a dual motivation in order to comprehend more fully the subtle modernist interplay of change and tradition, language crisis and systemic stability.

Stylistic developments in modernist Hebrew poetry are always products of a dual dynamic: the delicate balance of intrasystemic currents with intersystemic (European and American) trends.[20] The stylistic features that allowed modernist Hebrew poetry to overcome its language pangs are, therefore, a special case of this general inter-action of inter- and intrasystemic relations (see Even-Zohar, 1978:77–80; 1979:300–303).

The easiest way to illustrate these dual dynamics would be to focus on the Nathan Zach/Nathan Alterman/T. S. Eliot triad, where Alter-man represents the internal paragon against whom Zach rebels by importing and raising the salience of those aspects of Eliotesque modernism that fit his needs and marginalizing those that do not. In the process Zach would also establish for himself a role within the Israeli neoimagist trend of Statehood Generation poetry which is self-consciously analogous to that of Eliot within Anglo-American imag-ism—namely, the role of an activist, dominant paragon. But this fa-mous example could also be quite misleading. The three waves of Hebrew poetic modernism reveal, as a whole, a much more complex and subtle system of congruities or conjunctures between external and internal motivations than this paradigm of a rapport between two activist, dominant paragons might suggest.

It is often from the more ambivalent or peripheral affiliations with modernism that the unique innovations within the Hebrew literary system have emerged. Shimon Sandbank (1976) has shown in a num-ber of detailed and sensitive discussions that Fogel's expressionism is not exactly expressionist. By the same token, I would argue that Shlonsky's futurism is not exactly futurist, and that Amichai's imag-ism is not precisely imagistic.

To emphasize the decentering tendencies of modernist Hebrew poetry I chose examples from the poetry of Fogel, Shlonsky, and Amichai precisely because these poets' centrality and membership gradiences (Lakoff, 1987:12–13) within Western modernism are much lower or at least more ambivalent than those of their respective contemporaries: Avraham Ben-Yitzhak with impressionism, Alterman with symbolism, and Zach with (neo)imagism. In selecting these particular poets, I also mean to suggest that the encounter between Hebrew and European modernism did not take the form of a passive rendezvous in which both sides maintained an independent existence until, by Hebrew poetry's good fortune, a harmonious match was made. Rather, this encounter occurred as a prolonged process in which general modernist tenets were reworked and adapted to the unique needs of Hebrew poetry. The result was a highly modified series of marginal prototypes of modernism.

Three Love Poems:
Fogel, Shlonsky, Amichai

The genre of love poetry exhibits a strong traditional norm both in Hebrew (based especially on the models of the Song of Songs and medieval poetry in Spain) and in European literatures. This genre is appropriate to our discussion precisely because its conventional assets have been so "commonly traded, handled and used." Given the interdependence of automatization and deautomatization in the linguistic/literary system, it is to be expected that the impulse toward innovation and norm reversal would be vividly present in Hebrew modernist love poems. However, the poets would need to reconcile this impulse with the objective limitations of the Hebrew language system available to them. In this sense, modernist Hebrew love poems ought to offer a rather dramatic example of both the Hebrew stylistic crisis and its resolutions.

FOGEL'S "AT THE END OF DAY"

Viewed against the background of European literary developments, Fogel's antiformulaic (anti-*nusach*) generation thematically and stylistically occupies the space between premodernism and modernism proper. In many ways Fogel's poetics prefigures the features most typical of the later two modernist trends, yet it does not repudiate altogether traditional modes of expression and representation. Had he been more familiar to his contemporary readers, this would have made Fogel a perfect transitional paragon. Yet even two (poetic) generations later, for readers who are beginning to see in him retrospectively an important proleptic paragon, his transitional status is still preserved within the dynamics of literary reception and categorization. His low salience within Hebrew modernisms still causes Fogel to be described alternatively as a neoromantic, an impressionist, and an expressionist. (Compare Grodzensky, 1975:116–19; Ha-Ephrati, 1976:167–75; and Sandbank, 1976:70–82)

However, this low-key, highly individualistic poetics, with its carefully veiled subversions of realistic norms of representation and with its undercurrents of erotic radicalism, is common to a particularly large group of poets of or close to Fogel's generation—for example, Ya'akov Shteynberg, Ben-Yitzhak (Sonne), Yehuda Karni, and even more so their contemporary women poets (who are rarely included in mappings of Hebrew modernism): Esther Raab, Rachel, Elisheva, the early Yocheved Bat-Miriam, the early Leah Goldberg, and others. But the combination of their "minor-key" poetics (*shira minorit*) with a socially determined marginality coincided with a consistent avoidance of forming any literary circle or of associating with any Hebrew modernist group. While Fogel's personal canonization was probably assured only in the early 1990s, the conjuncture of poetic and social processes in the present Israeli literary system still prevents a collective label for the first modernist trend from being accepted. By selecting this example of Fogel, therefore, I reveal my own special bias: the attempt to recover his role not only as the proleptic paragon of a belated imagism but also as the avant-garde of a camouflaged or repressed early modernism.

In the early 1990s this old debate reignited the entire Hebrew press in vehement controversy over whether Fogel and his generation indeed remained forgotten until their (re)discovery by the poets and critics of the third modernist wave, the Statehood Generation. This critical struggle proves quite instructive for a theory of canon formation. Clearly, two forces are competing within the literary/cultural polysystem, each espousing a periodization of modernist trends that fits its own model.[21] The underlying problem that this debate raises is the acceptability of anti-*nusach* minimalist, yet radical, poetics within the official canon of Hebrew poetry.

This minimalism must be regarded, in part, as a reaction against the stylistics of overstatement, which Fogel associated both with the older Bialik generation and with the younger *moderna* of the pre-Statehood Generation. In what amounts to a radical reinterpretation of Hebrew poetic history, Fogel claimed that in spite of Shlonsky's famous feud with Bialik, very little divides the schools each represents. In Fogel's judgment, an overabundance of literary allusiveness characterizes both "the *nusach* poets . . . who filled their pockets with the prepackaged treasures of our language, a biblical, midrashic, mishnaic *nusach*, but who lack any individual style" and the "literary acrobats" among the linguistic innovators of Shlonsky's generation. For Fogel the *moderna* poets are merely formalist *nusach* poets in modernist guise: "The trite *melitsah*,[22] that regurgitation of ready-made verses, which every empty, talentless *maskil* ["enlightenment-Jew"] used to show off with, that *melitsah* which we have already buried once is now rising again before our very eyes, albeit in a slightly altered shape and a more modernist form, as befits the needs of our times."[23]

Fogel's harsh words, whose publication was delayed until after Shlonsky's death in 1973, contributes a new perspective to the internal stylistic norm shift in Hebrew poetry. This bitter attack on both the premodernists of the Revival (*ha-tchiya*) Generation and the *moderna* poets was delivered by Fogel in a lecture tour of Poland in 1931, about eight years after the publication of his first book of poetry, *Before the Dark Gate* (*Lifney ha-sha'ar ha-afel*) (1923). Shlonsky's first volume of poetry, *Dvay* (*Distress*), was published in 1924, one year after Fogel's, so a chronologically determined generation gap between these two rival modernist paragons cannot really exist. Thus, the famous rebellion of Shlonsky's modernist group against Bialik's premodernist *nusach* must now be seen alongside the almost contemporary struggle between two contradictory prototypes of modernism: the maximalist, extroverted style of the *moderna* poets in Palestine; and, the minimalist, introverted style of the European antiformulaic (anti-*nusach*) poets.

How then does Fogel avoid what he regards as the stylistic pitfalls of his predecessors and near contemporaries, while working within the limitations of the defective polysystem of Hebrew? "Binetot ha-yom" ("At the End of Day"), the love poem I have chosen to discuss, shows Fogel resisting almost completely the temptations of linguistic innovation on the one hand and allusive *melitsah* on the

other. Instead, he offers a functional deployment of the limited re-
sources at his disposal, turning their very limitation into an organiz-
ing stylistic feature. Not surprisingly, perhaps, these resources are
quite traditional. It is their functional, nonornamental use that con-
stitutes a stylistic innovation.

בִּנְטוֹת הַיּוֹם –
הֵן תַּבִּיט אֲהַבָתִי הַחֲשָׁאִית
לִיגוֹנֵי עֵינָיִךְ הַתְּכֵלִים,
אֲהַבָתִי הָאִלְּמָה.

אוּלָם בְּבֹא אֵלַי
הַלַּיְל הָרָךְ –
מַה יַעַרְגוּ שְׁנֵי שָׁדַי הַקְּטַנִּים,
הַחִוְרִים,
אֵלַיִךְ, דּוֹדִי.

וּפֶתַע אָז אִתֵּר מִיצוּעֵי
וּבְיָדַי אֲאַמְּצֵם אֶל חָזִי.
חָרְדָה אֶלְחַשׁ
לִדְמִי הַלַּיְל:
אֲהַבְתִּיו, אֲהַבְתִּיו.

גַּם רַחְמִי יִרְעַד חָרֵשׁ
בְּגַעְגּוּעָיו אֶל הַיָּלֶד.

[At the End of Day]

At the end of day—
my secret love will look[24]
to the blue agonies of your[25] eyes,
my mute love.

But when the soft night
comes to me
how my two small,
pale breasts will yearn,
unto you, my beloved.

And suddenly then I will leap from my bed
and with my hands I will clench them to my chest.
Anxious I will whisper
to the stillness of the night:
I loved him, I loved him.

And my womb will shudder quietly
in its longing for the child.

—Fogel ([1966] 1975:96; published in 1923;
translated by Chana Kronfeld and Eric Zakim)

The most salient examples of Fogel's strict functionalism are the poem's selective use of biblical syntax and biblical allusion. Syntactically, the poem maintains a subtle oscillation in its use of verb forms between the biblical aspectual system and the modern tense system. This oscillation, the product of interrupted diachronic processes of language change, could easily have resulted in serious obstacles to literary style. In Fogel's hands, however, it becomes a means for making the poetic Hebrew phrase at once more precise and more pliable. Moreover, the indeterminacy of tense and aspect proves to be an excellent vehicle for achieving that purposeful hesitation between premodernism and modernism, the low and ambivalent membership gradience which Fogel maintains through a delicately balanced fluctuation between impressionism and expressionism, stasis and action, observable reality and subjective space.

A brief outline of the overall stylistic functions of syntactic patterns in the poem can provide a context for Fogel's dual motivation of tense and aspect. The beginning of the poem, and the beginnings of all stanzas, establish an expectation that the text will develop a sustained, conventionally structured plot. The different phases of the action occur at defined times—*Bi-netot ha-yom . . . / Ulam be-vo . . . / Ha-la'yil ha-rakh* ("At the end of day . . . But with the coming . . . / Of the soft night")—between two specified agents (the female speaker and the male addressee), leading up to a climax, or turning point—*U-feta az 'itar* ("And suddenly then I (will) leap(ed)"), and winding down in an anticlimax—*cheresh* ("quietly"). However, several syntactic choices undermine these "action-filled" expectations, imbuing the poem with a static, "nounlike," and atemporal quality. The most obvious examples are the use of adverbial gerundives—*Bi-netot ha-yom* ("At the end of the day"), *be-vo . . . / Ha-la'yil* ("with the coming . . . / Of the night")[26]—rather than inflected verb forms, and the predominance of noun phrases, adjectives, and stative verbs and adverbials in the poem. Of the inflected verbs, only one, *ahavtiv* ("I (have) loved him") is not morphologically marked for the future but is written as a morphological past. This is also the only transitive verb in the entire poem. Yet, this one perfective, transitive verb, while semantically expressing the focal emotion of the poem—love—is clearly not an action verb at all.

The rest of the inflected verbs—*tabit* ("(will) look(ed)"), *ya'argu* ("(will) yearn(ed)"), *'itar* ("I (will) leap(ed)"), *a'amtsem* ("I (will) clench(ed)"), *elchash* ("I (will) whisper(ed)"), *yir'ad* ("(will) shudder(ed)")—can be read in two different ways. They are either aspectual, describing habitual, imperfective action which the speaker experiences (in a future converted to the present or the past), or they are marked for tense, projecting a desired, unattained, and perhaps unattainable future event. An aspectual reading is more appropriate for the first half of the poem, partly because the gerundive (*be* + infinitive) could easily mean "whenever"; the second half of the poem, coming after the adverbial *l-feta* ("suddenly"), lends itself more readily to a tense-marked reading denoting a specific—albeit fantastic—future action. The fact that both the temporal and atemporal verbs use an identical morphological future blurs the distinction between projected and actual event. This indeterminacy is supported by other stylistic manifestations of the speaker's agitated state of mind. She expresses her yearnings for her lover in the second person—*elecha, dodi* ("unto you [masculine], my beloved")—only to realize through an implied autoerotic experience that both the lover and the child she wants to have by him remain absent. In lieu of the lover, she then addresses the night, which in the course of the poem turns from a metonymic substitute for the man—*be-vo elay/Ha-la'yil ha-rakh* (literally, "with the coming to me/Of the soft night")—into the speaker's only real companion and the addressee of her whispered words—*elchash/Li-dmi ha-la'yil* ("I (will) whisper(ed)/To the stillness of the night"). The lover can now only be invoked in the third person—*Ahavtiv* ("I (have) loved him")—the finiteness of the perfective verb suggesting, perhaps, that the love story is indeed a matter of the past.[27]

Fogel makes effective use of the very inconsistencies and incompleteness within the Hebrew syntax of his time, a Hebrew that was still by and large not a fully revived, spoken language. This limitation of the Hebrew polysystem allows Fogel to capture the subtle fluctuations and purposeful hesitations which always stand at the perceptual center of the work of this transitional paragon, a hesitation between impressionist, atmospheric shades of a discrete moment in space and time, and the expressionist, internalized reality of the speaker's state of mind. In the process, the use of biblical syntax in a modernist Hebrew poem receives a dual, mutually reinforcing motivation. Intersystemically, as we have seen, the duality serves modernist expressive needs by emphasizing both the phases of an action rather than its real time and the convertibility of one "tense" into another: future into past, past into future and present. Intrasystemically, the functional revitalization of the aspectual system provides a much needed compensation for gaps in the tense system of modern Hebrew. For example, the absence of a present progressive with its vividness and immediacy of depiction is compensated for by the use of conversive verb forms that highlight the duration of an action. In this manner, a modernist desire to privilege the act of perception by focusing attention away from the objective time coincides with an internal Hebraic need to fill lacunae in the language system. Fogel's uncanny sensitivity to both linguistic and modernist needs has, perhaps, more than anything else made the stylistic achievements of his poetry so unique.

But Fogel's use of biblical syntax is innovative also in what it does not do. Unlike premodernist poets before him, he does not employ biblical syntax for the purposes of lending his text authority or complying with traditional demands for poetic decorum. Nor does he use nonbiblical syntactic patterns merely to challenge that authority and decorum. Fogel's treatment of language and style demonstrates a poetic in which both the archaic and the modern layers can be approached simply as linguistic and cultural assets. A poet is free to pick and choose from these assets, regardless of their authoritativeness, simply in order to achieve specific expressive effects. The tension between temporality and atemporality is one such example. It gives syntactic concreteness to the transitional pose so typical of Fogel's lyrical "I," between the "receptive stance of the impressionist mode and the introspective stance accompanied by 'active contemplation' which characterizes the expressionist mode" (Sandbank, 1976:51–52).

Fogel's use of biblical allusion not only exhibits the same functionalist approach as his syntax but also reveals his sensitivity to the diachronic evolution of the Hebrew tense and aspect system. The connection between the poem's patterns of biblical allusion and its oscillation between biblical aspect and tense lies in the linguistic nature of the biblical text that the poem evokes, the Song of Songs (specifically, 3:1–5 and 5:2–8). Talmy Givón has shown in his study of biblical syntax that the Song of Songs marks the "endpoint of the change," within biblical Hebrew itself, in the tense-aspect system and is therefore "the most progressive dialect-level evident in the Old Testament" (Givón 1977:188).[28] As a result of this change, all instances of the imperfect in the Song of Songs semantically and pragmatically have come to designate "IRREALIS or HABITUAL" aspects of an action (p. 248, note 21). "The PERFECT [compare *ahavtiv* in line 14 of our poem] has become the main *past* narrative *tense*, covering both continuity and anterior functions; the PARTICIPLE has become the sentential/nonpunctual/continuous/habitual aspect" (p. 233). These are precisely the "nounlike" and fantastic implications of verb construction in Fogel's poem, implications which are motivated intersystemically by adopting salient modernist subversions of romantic and naturalist conventions of representing reality and human relationships.

The syntactic function of the allusion is independent of any specific intertextual relations that may obtain between Fogel's poem and passages from the Song of Songs. In fact, the poem's language never specifically evokes those passages. Only the dramatic situation of "At the End of Day" identifies for the reader a particular allusive pattern to Song of Songs 3:1–5 and 5:2–8. The only direct and unambiguous textual marker in the language of the poem that points to the Song of Songs is the word *dodi* ("my beloved," homonymous with "my uncle").[29] Saliently located at the end of a stanza in the very center of the poem, this word alone lays bare the entire allusive device. But even *dodi* does not refer the reader specifically to the two evoked passages from the Bible; the word presents itself instead as a general biblical love epithet. There are, after all, numerous examples of its use throughout the Song of Songs, as well as in normative Hebrew love poetry of all ages. The "world" created within the poem, rather than its language, establishes the network of intertextual links between Fogel's love poem and particular biblical models. Within the poem's dramatic situation, the female speaker, alone in bed at night, in an agitated state of mind, narrates an actual or make-believe nocturnal erotic encounter with her lover. The hesitation between reality and the imagination, wakefulness and dream, that accompanies the dramatic situation is realistically motivated by the woman's agitation. But it is reinforced aesthetically both by the poem's modernist expressive goals and by the evoked biblical texts, which provide traditional normative support for these modernist goals. Once the two biblical texts are evoked, however indirectly, they become necessary to our understanding of the motivation of the allusive structure in Fogel's poem.

The two biblical passages, both dramatic monologues of a female speaker, present essentially the same narrative material in two different versions. The first evoked text, Song of Songs 3:1–5, describes the Shulamite's wakeful nighttime fantasy (*'al mishkavi ba-leylot bikashti et she-ahava nafshi* "By night on my bed I sought him whom my soul loveth"), whereas the second, 5:2–8, relegates the events to her dream (*ani yeshena ve-libi er* "I sleep, but my heart waketh").[30] Furthermore, the first version (3:1–5) clearly empowers the female speaker/protagonist and presents her as the initiator of the action: she misses her lover and decides to go looking for him; when she cannot find him she enlists the help of the watchmen; finally and quite literally she gets hold of her beloved and brings him home to her mother's bedroom. The second version (5:2–8), while erotically more explicit, depicts the woman in a more reactive and disempowered light. Although she responds to the lover's requests with coy resistance, it is he who leaves her. She cannot find him anywhere and falls victim to the abuse of the watchmen who catch her wandering about. Wounded and love sick, she can only go on waiting—and dreaming.

Like these two passages, Fogel's "At the End of Day," which is the third in a series of eleven "maiden poems" (*shirey ha-na'ara*),[31] is narrated from the female lover's point of view. The poems in this series, like the passages from the Song of Songs, alternate between a passive and an active rendering of the female role in the lovers' encounter.[32] Indeed, all eleven "maiden poems" need to be examined as one conjoined poetic unit in order for the full force of the allusive pattern to emerge. Through such a sustained allusion, Fogel's modernist goals receive a surprising reinforcement from the most traditional of sources, the biblical canon. The modernist goals most amenable to a stylistic analysis involve the subversion of two traditional norms of representation, the first concerning reality and the imagination, and the second pertaining to love and erotica.[33]

Both the passive and the active versions of the Shulamite's poem in the Song of Songs maintain a subtle hesitation between reality and fantasy not unlike that which Fogel strives to capture in his depiction of the young woman's agitated state. Specifically, both the modern poem and the two biblical "songs" it alludes to are characterized by a fundamental uncertainty of perception: does the text present the story of a nocturnal love encounter or is it all a projection of the speaker's unfulfilled yearnings for just such an encounter? Similarly, in all three texts an autoerotic experience—"by night on my bed" (Song of Songs 3:1)—or erotic dream—"I sleep, but my heart waketh" (Song of Songs 5:2)—may constitute the "event" which the poems obliquely describe. In Fogel's poem, what is presented syntactically as the narrative climax (in stanzas three and four) may in fact be a highly suggestive linguistic correlative to the speaker's own sexual climax: *U-feta az itar mi-yetsu'i / U-veyaday a'amtsem [et shaday] el chazi. . . . / Gam rachmi yir'ad* ("And suddenly then I (will) leap(ed) from my bed / And with my hands I (will) clench(ed) [my breasts] to my chest / breast. . . . / And my womb (will) shudder(ed)"). A very similar reading could be provided for the metaphorical depiction of the Shulamite "opening to" her lover, her fingers dripping with sweet smelling myrrh "upon the handles of the lock" (Song of Songs 5:5–6).[34] It is, therefore, the bold eroticism and radical metaphoricity of the paradigmatic text of traditional Hebrew love poetry which reinforces Fogel's modernist exploration of a female erotic perspective.

This brings us to the final, and perhaps most intriguing, aspect of Fogel's subtly radical use of biblical allusion: the repudiation, through metaphor and metonymy, of conventional distinctions between familial and romantic constructions of love and intimacy, a repudiation of tradition which seeks and finds for itself a model within that selfsame tradition. Throughout Fogel's poetry there is a striking sustained similarity between those poems that describe parent/child attachments and those whose theme is love between man and woman. Aharon Komem (1982:24, 29ff) was the first to point out an intriguing conflation of motifs, images, and tones in all the different kinds of love in Fogel's poetry. Especially striking are the analogies between the poems which feature the daughter and the erotic love poems to a young adolescent girl. "These two realms [the daughter poems and the erotic poems], which reveal a kind of radical reevaluation (*sidud ma'arachot*) of Fogel's attitudes toward the world and of our attitudes toward his poetry, . . . maintain a special interrelation between the poetic materials, the overall position, as well as much beyond that" (Komem 1982:24).[35]

The stylistic mechanism through which this "radical reevaluation" is effected involves a subtle reworking of biblical material. At the center of "At the End of Day" stands the lone allusive marker *dodi*. It appears at first to be simply a biblical epithet, but almost imperceptibly Fogel uses it to activate the entire metaphorical system embedded in the Song of Songs, EROTIC LOVE AS KINSHIP: the woman is a sister-bride (*achoti kala*); the male lover is (homonymously and figuratively) an uncle (*dod*); and alternatively the man is like a brother unto the woman, a brother "that sucked the breasts of (my) mother" (Song of Songs 8:1).[36] In other narrative metaphors in the Song of Songs, the desired consummation of the love relationship is depicted figuratively as the "uncle" coming home to "mother" (3:4; 8:2); elsewhere the Shulamite arouses her lover under the apple tree, in the same location where his mother gave birth to him (8:5). While these metaphors' literal kinship meaning has been largely forgotten through the automatization of routine use over the centuries, the larger context of Fogel's poetry revives and reifies them. Seen as an instance of the EROTIC-LOVE-AS-KINSHIP metaphor, the ending of "At the End of Day" acquires a radical reading: the female speaker describes an autoerotic orgasm through the maternal image of the womb trembling with yearning for a child: *Gam rachmi yir'ad cheresh / Be-ga'agu'av 'el ha-yeled* ("And [literally, "also"] my womb will shudder quietly / in its longing for the child").

Fogel's use of allusive systems such as this, which at first appears quite marginal, prefigures strategies that have become the hallmark of later Hebrew modernists' prototypical style: the subversion of traditional attitudes through the literalization and resuscitation of traditional figurative concepts. This tense cooperation between tradition and innovation, so characteristic of modern Hebrew poetry, emerges as an integral part of the dual-motivation thesis. Through the effective use of radical components within the Hebrew literary canon, Fogel, and other modernists after him, managed to overcome stylistic difficulties and achieve many of their modernist goals.

Fogel's invocation, via classical allusion, of the entire history of a genre and a device becomes quite typical of later modernists as well, and especially of Shlonsky and Amichai. "At the End of Day" draws not only on the biblical origins of the conventions of love poetry but also on the diachronic developments leading up to neoromantic interpretations of these conventions in the poetry of Bialik's Revival (*ha-tchiya*) Generation. In fact, an argument can be made for seeing "At the End of Day" as a critical response, from an individualistic, early modernist perspective, to Bialik's "At Dusk" ("Im dimdumey ha-chama"). In his reevaluation of traditional poetics, Fogel not only positions himself subversively within the classical canon but also challenges genre conventions that became established during the previous generation of the nascent national literature.

SHLONSKY'S "YOU ARE HEREBY"

Hebrew literary historiography commonly describes the intrasystemic struggle between modernism and premodernism in Hebrew poetry as an intertextual wrestling match between two dominant modernist and premodernist paragons: Shlonsky and Bialik. Avraham Ha-Gorni-Green in a study aptly titled *Shlonsky ba'avotot Bialik (Shlonsky in the Bonds of Bialik)* (1985) calls this view into question. Other scholars have also observed that the stylistic relationship of Shlonsky's *moderna* to its intrasystemic predecessors, the poetry of the *ha-tchiya* generation, is marked by a powerful ambivalence. (Compare Tzur, 1985, and Shavit, 1981, 1988.) The resistance to the strong pull which the traditional literary norm had on the pre-Statehood Poets needed to be motivated by an equally powerful intersystemic modernist affiliation. Russian futurism offered a cluster of salient prototypes such as revolutionary ideology and an attack on the literary institutions of the past. These prototypes provided Shlonsky with the required antitraditional "destructive" motivation; at the same time, the urgent needs of Hebrew as a defective polysystem in a state of crisis offered a compelling mission and a "constructive" motivation for many of the same futurist, antiromantic poetic practices. For the purposes of my argument, this conjuncture of intersystemic and intrasystemic motivations becomes particularly exemplary in Shlonsky's use of allusion and neologisms.

הֲרֵי אַתְּ

עֶרְיָה הִיא – מְקֻטֶּרֶת אֵד וְזֶבֶל.
תּוֹבַעַת וְנוֹשֶׁפֶת אֶת חֻמָּהּ.
שָׂדֶה – וּמִנְּחִירֶיהָ טַל וְהֶבֶל.
כַּלָּה – בְּהִינוּמָה. וְיְחוּמָה.

מַה פֶּרַע שְׂעָרָהּ, וּמַה צָּמֵחַ.
נָכוֹנוּ רְגָבֶיהָ לְהַדְשִׁיא.
וַיּוֹשֶׁט לָהּ אֶת פֶּלַח הַיָּרֵחַ
הָעֶרֶב כְּטַבַּעַת-קִדּוּשִׁין.

הֲרֵי אַתְּ מְקֻדֶּשֶׁת לִי בְּדֶשֶׁא,
בְּרַחַשׁ שַׂרְעַפּוֹת וְדַרְדָּרִים,
הֲרֵי אַתְּ מְזֻבֶּלֶת לִי בְּדֶשֶׁן,
בְּגֶלֶל שֶׁל צֹאנִים וַעֲדָרִים.

נוֹבַבְתְּ לִי בַּשִּׁבֹּלֶת וּבַשָּׁיִת,
שׁוֹבַבְתְּ לִי חָרוּלִים וְגִבְעוֹלִים.
יָבוֹאוּ, יִבְעָלוּךְ חוֹרְשַׁיִךְ
וְזֶרַע בָּךְ יָקִימוּ לִיבוּלִים.

יְחַמְתְּ לִי, וָאָבוֹאָה אֶל הַקֹּדֶשׁ.
רָחַמְתִּי בָּךְ הַמְּתֹם וְהָרְוָיָה.
הֲרֵי אַתְּ מְגֻדֶּשֶׁת לִי בִּגְדֶשׁ,
שָׂדֶה לְעֵת דּוֹדִים. הַלְלוּ-יָהּ!

You Are Hereby

She is naked—steaming from mist and dung,
Demanding and puffing in her heat—
A field—and from the nostrils: dew and vapor—
A bride—in a veil. An aroused woman.

How wild-looking is her hair, and how long-grown.
Her dirt-clods are ready for the grass.
And he hands her a slice of the moon
This evening as a wedding ring.

You are hereby sanctified unto me by grass,
By a whisper of thoughts and thistles.
You are hereby manured unto me by fertilizer,
With the dung of flocks and herds.

You produced for me the sheaf of wheat and the thorn-bush,
You renewed for me brambles and stalks.
They will come, your plowers will husband you
And they will establish in you a seed for crops.

You were hot for me, and so I came to the holy-place.
I felt compassion for your wholeness and your plenty.
You are hereby overflowing unto me with abundance,
A field at the season of lovers. Hallelujah!

—Shlonsky (1947:8; translated by Eric Zakim)

In "Harey at," the intertextual links to traditional sources are much more explicit than in Fogel's poem. In fact, they are flaunted in the poem's very title. And, in the end, they leave their mark on the diction and syntax of every line. The most salient feature of the allusive pattern in the poem is the marker *harey at* ("you are hereby"), which constitutes the title and reappears at the beginnings of three lines highlighted in the center and at the end of the poem. This marker evokes the traditional speech act performed by the bridegroom during the Jewish marriage ceremony, *harey at mekudeshet li . . . ke-dat moshe ve-israel* (literally: "you're hereby sanctified unto me . . . by the religion of Moses and Israel"). However, the juxtaposition of the title and the first line indicates, semantically as well as prosodically, that the traditional allusion is pointedly used for antitraditional purposes:[37]

HAREY At (you are hereby)
ERYA Hi (she is nude/genitalia)

Harey and *erya* bring together, in a rearrangement of almost identical sounds, the boldly contrasting realms of the sacred and the profane, the spiritual and the physical, contrasts which are highly prototypical of Shlonsky's poetics of allusion. The poem contains a bold allusive juxtaposition not just between the title and the first line but also within the first line itself. This contrast recurs in all other stanzas of the poem: between the naked agricultural body of a (personified) fertilized field, "steaming (perfumed) with mist and dung" (*mekuteret ed va-zevel*), and the norms of traditional Hebrew love poetry represented by the covert allusion to the beloved in the Song of Songs (3:6), rising out of the desert, "perfumed with myrrh and frankincense" (*mekuteret mor u-levona*). In addition, within the diachronic context of Hebrew love poetry, Shlonsky's reinterpretation of *harey at*, especially given his metaphorical rendering of the beloved as a field (identified explicitly in line 3), clashes with the forceful norm of the earlier *ha-tchiya* generation poetry.

It is impossible to conceive of Shlonsky's "Harey at" without in some way involving Shaul Tchernichovski's pantheistic epithalamium, "Harey at mekusemet li" ("You Are Hereby Bewitched unto Me") (1929; in Tschernichovski 1950:492). Shlonsky, then, is struggling to extricate himself from both the religious norm (*ke-dat moshe ve-israel*, "according to the law/religion of Moses and Israel") and its humanist/pantheist critique by Tchernichovski (*ke-dat oto parpar . . . be-sod kol shirat ha-adam*, "according to the law/religion of that butterfly . . . with the secret of all human poetry"). The poem combines the ideological motivation provided by the anticlericalism of socialist Zionism, a salient aspect of which is the rejection of traditional Jewish attitudes toward sacred rituals such as the marriage ceremony, with its concomitant modernist rejection of traditional and romantic notions of beauty and propriety. In this way the poem celebrates an iconoclastic secularization of traditional Mosaic values at the same time that it rejects a neoromantic religion of nature.[38] The alternative that Shlonsky offers is itself ideologically motivated: it reifies the religious and sexual metaphors which are an integral part of the left-wing Zionist idealization of agricultural labor. As in the beginning of the poem, the ideological conversion of the sacred first into the natural realm and ultimately into the realm of labor is aesthetically motivated through the spectacular prosodic conversions of a focalizing sound pattern and untraditional rhyme scheme which are placed in the center of the poem (lines 9 and 11):

mEku DESHE t (sanctified)—Mosaic religion

BE   DESHE (with grass)—Tchernichovski's pantheism

BE   DESHE n (with fertilizer)—socialist "religion of labor"

These prosodic patterns are, of course, typical of the modernist functional activation of rhyme and rhythm as opposed to a convention-dictated employment of a metrical scheme. The focalizing sound pattern and the asymmetrical rhyme are the means for establishing semantic relations among *mekudeshet, be-deshe,* and *be-deshen.*[39] By elevating *deshen* ("agricultural fertilizer") to an alternative for both traditional Judaism and pantheism, the poem bestows religious significance on the new pioneer values of labor and return to the land. This radical valuation actually has quite a specific parallel in the revolutionary and iconoclastic poetics of Russian futurism: from V. Khlebnikov's image of the modernist poet shooting arrows at the gods to his glorification of the garbage and maidenry of the "steaming fields" (1976:55, 99). The coincidence of futurist ideology and the values of the "labor religion" (*dat ha-avoda*)[40] in Shlonsky's poetry is far from accidental since the same Russian revolutionary socialism fed the roots of both.

Shlonsky's well-known tendency toward neologism also reveals a complex system of congruities between internal and external needs.

Statements made by Shlonsky in a series of manifestoes of the *moderna* supply the explicit poetics for his neologistic bent. They present the futurist view of language from a decidedly Hebraic perspective, fraught with ironic allusions to traditional Jewish texts and traditional Jewish practices. Although these pronouncements were made about twenty-five years before the publication of "Harey at," they nevertheless directly prefigure the poem's umbrella metaphor of an antitraditional woman. This woman, however, started out as the "word," and only later became the "field." "The word (under the rule of the *melitsah* of the language) just as a woman (under the patriarchal rule of society) is not free: she is dependent on her husband for her livelihood; . . . we have rebelled: 'free love! civil marriage!' Our *melitsah*—a kosher humble daughter of Israel—has accepted the tradition: matches are made in heaven. 'By the law of Moses and Israel' " (1923:189–90; in Harshav [Hrushovski], 1973:154–55). Instead of this religious linguistic bondage, Shlonsky advocates "civil ceremony, free love between words without arranged marriages of ancestral-proud style, without a dowry of associations, and mainly: without a religious *chupa* (too much family purity in our language!!). Each coupling of words—a promiscuous surrender, a one-night stand" (1923: 190; in Harshav [Hrushovski], 1973:154).

The same new value system of free love and antitraditionalism which characterized early labor ideology in Palestine generates the materials of the umbrella metaphor for a rebellious, modernist style. In the poem "Harey at," both anticonventional and "permissive" conceptions of love similarly serve as the source of materials for a metaphor, except that here the tenor is the pioneer/laborer's relationship to his land. The pioneer sexually possesses (*bo'el*), plows, and plants in the nakedness of the feminized field who demands her satisfaction from him, "puffing in her heat" (line 2).

As in Fogel, and as we shall see later on, in Amichai as well, the same "free love between words," which rebels against the norms of love poetry, simultaneously and perhaps paradoxically also preserves the traditional model. The poem "Harey at," in fact, resurrects the agricultural/natural component within the imagery of the Song of Songs itself and modifies it to fit modernist ideological needs. Whereas in the biblical poem the worlds of agriculture and sheepherding serve as vehicles for the tenor of the lovers' relationships, here the terms of the metaphor are reversed: free, unruly love serves as a vehicle for the tenor of a new commitment to the field and the land. However different, the context of the evoked biblical text is mobilized in support of even the most antitraditional of Shlonsky's modernist stances.

The neologisms themselves are new words coined from existing roots or portmanteaux, blends of two separate roots. Many of them are presented in morphological patterns with the stress on the penultimate syllable—a typical compensation device in *moderna* poetics for the paucity of such Russian sounding, "soft" (*mil'eyl*) forms in Hebrew: *péra*—a portmanteau of *pere* ("wild") and *paru'a* ("disheveled"); *gélel*— "dung"—rather than the common *milra* equivalent, the plural form *glalím*; *rachámti*—a portmanteau of *rechem* ("womb") and *rachamim* ("pity," "compassion"); *megudéshet*—a portmanteau of *gdusha* ("heaping full") and *mekudeshet* ("sanctified" or "sacred"). These neologisms and others like them appear on the surface to be lexical innovations. As such they are consistent with those modernist prototypes which view the language of poetry as a productive process of signification rather than with the opposite modernist prototype which denies the very possibility of signification. However, on close examination, it turns out that all the neologisms in the poem are actually resuscitated forms which are found at least once in traditional sources.[41] For example, a form such as *novavt* in line 13, which at first strikes the modern Hebrew speaker as odd if not incomprehensible, appears in the Bible, within a context strikingly similar to that of the poem: *ve-tirosh yenovev betulot* ("[Corn shall make the young men cheerful]/And new wine the maids") (Zechariah 9:17). Similarly, the uninflected noun *yichuma* in line 4 (note that it isn't the feminine possessive of *yichum*!) appears in the liturgical poetry of Ha-Kalir[42] in the sense of "woman," investing Shlonsky's text with the stock identification of femininity with unbridled eroticism (from *yichum*, "sexual arousal," "heat").

With all their stress on lexical innovation, the Russian futurists themselves also viewed neologisms as a process of "delving into the root."[43] Mayakovsky's description of Khlebnikov's poetic practice might easily apply to Shlonsky: "He created an entire 'periodic table of the word.' Taking the word in its undeveloped unfamiliar forms, comparing these with the developed word, he demonstrates the necessity and the inevitability of the emergence of new words. . . . Khlebnikov is simply reversing the process of word formation" (in Brown, 1976:15).

Clearly, Shlonsky is less radical in his practice of lexical innovation and experimentation than Khlebnikov and the other futurists, in part because he must limit his selections to those neologistic devices which best serve the intrasystemic goals of revitalizing the Hebrew language. Paradoxically, this very tension between innovation and tradition points to the major congruity between the needs of European modernism and the demands of the internal system within Shlonsky's poetry. According to Shlonsky's own account, neologisms are viewed by the Russian futurist poets as a way out of the impasse for a literature which is trapped between "the domestic grayness of the realists" and the "symbolists' flight to the heavenly clouds" (cited by Yaffe, 1966:159). Shlonsky continues: "Now a change has taken place in the concepts, perceptions, and interests of the generation, and of necessity this requires a change in the verbal stock. Therefore we must renovate the language, produce new words, coin expressions which have never occurred before" (cited by Yaffe, 1966:159–160).

This acute need to renovate the language becomes for Shlonsky not just a matter of modernist disappointment in realism and symbolism. It is necessary in order to help Hebrew extricate itself from the status of a defective polysystem, to fill in the gaps in the lexicon and the stylistic registers, and to work toward the establishment of a highly differentiated, stratified system which all types of discourse can then draw on. These goals, unmentioned in Shlonsky's modernist manifesto, nevertheless form an integral part of his generation's implicit poetics. Ironically, the rebellious, modernist desire to shatter the archives of petrified traditional language serves a constructive collective goal of reviving and preserving the old-new Hebrew tongue.

AMICHAI'S "JACOB AND THE ANGEL"

While many of the intrasystemic linguistic factors in the modernist process of dual motivation have become less critical in the poetry of the Statehood Generation, its major poets, and perhaps especially Yehuda Amichai, have continued to maintain a complex modernist/Hebraist rapport. Actually, in this generation the correlation between dual motivations and the tension of innovation and conservation becomes most poignant.

The Hebrew which Amichai and his contemporaries feel free to employ in their poetry is more stratified than the language of any of their predecessors, especially as regards stylistic registers. Colloquial Hebrew and slang, as well as the innovative discourse of army, Kibbutz, and children's Hebrew, are being allowed for the first time into poetry in any sustained manner. At the same time, these poets of the

1950s and 1960s continue to conduct an elaborate intertextual dia-
logue with the cultural and linguistic norms of biblical Hebrew. Their
affiliations with Euro-American (neo)modernism is yet again both
mediated and enabled by a radical rewriting of traditional Hebrew
texts. Yehuda Amichai's famous iconoclastic love poem *Jacob and the
Angel* will serve to illustrate this third phase in the complex history of
Hebrew-modernist stylistic rapports.

יַעֲקֹב וְהַמַּלְאָךְ

לִפְנוֹת בֹּקֶר נֶאֶנְחָה וְתָפְסָה
אוֹתוֹ כָּךְ, וְנִצְּחָה אוֹתוֹ.
וְתָפַס אוֹתָהּ כָּךְ, וְנִצַּח אוֹתָהּ,
הֵם יָדְעוּ שְׁנֵיהֶם תְּפֶס
מֵבִיא מָוֶת.
וּוִתְּרוּ זֶה לָזֶה עַל אֲמִירַת הַשֵּׁם.

אֲבָל בָּאוֹר הָרִאשׁוֹן שֶׁל שַׁחַר
רָאָה אֶת גּוּפָהּ.
שֶׁנִּשְׁאָר לָבָן,
בַּמְּקוֹמוֹת שֶׁבֶּגֶד הַיָּם
אֶתְמוֹל כִּסָּה.

אַחַר כָּךְ קָרְאוּ לָהּ פִּתְאֹם מִלְמַעְלָה,
פַּעֲמַיִם.
כְּמוֹ שֶׁקּוֹרְאִים לְיַלְדָּה מִמִּשְׂחָקָהּ
בֶּחָצֵר.
וְיָדַע אֶת שְׁמָהּ וְנָתַן לָהּ לָלֶכֶת.

Jacob and the Angel

Just before dawn she sighed and held him
that way, and defeated him.
And he held her that way, and defeated her,
and both of them knew that a hold
brings death.
They agreed to do without names.

But in the first light
he saw her body,
which remained white in the places
the swimsuit had covered, yesterday.

Then someone called her suddenly from above,
twice.
The way you call a little girl from playing
in the yard.
And he knew her name, and let her go.

> —Amichai (1962, 1977 ed.:260;
> translated by Bloch and Mitchell in Amichai, 1986:40)

In this poem three internal frames of reference function simultaneously (Harshav [Hrushovski], 1982a), each introducing its own register and set of intertextual relations. The first constitutes the literal frame of an erotic encounter between a man and a woman. This event motivates the introduction of the stylistic conventions of love poetry. Here belong, for example, the connotative uses of *yada* ("know") in the biblical sexual sense (lines 4 and 15), as well as the exploitation of the erotic sense of "death" in European poetry, as a periphrasis for orgasm, in line 5. The second frame of reference, of children at play, constitutes a metonymy for the first literal frame (a girl for the woman, a boy for the man). This frame motivates a somewhat restrained connotative use of children's Hebrew, where, for example, *le-natse'ach* ("getting the upper hand in a scuffle") means to force the other "to the mat," to make him or her give up or "cry uncle." Thus the sexual athletics of the couple's erotic encounter is read, within this frame, as a naive, if militant, struggle. The metonymic relation of this frame to that of the lovers is laid bare at the end of the poem when the woman-cum-child is called "suddenly from above (from upstairs)" (*milema'la*) as when a child is called in from play.

The third frame of reference is supplied by the title (and almost only by the title). It maps onto the sexual and child-play frames the outlines of the biblical story of Jacob's struggle with the angel. This action, of course, motivates the introduction of all the local biblical and religious allusions in the poem, such as the play on *ha-shem* ("name" and "God"). Notably, however, there is no trace of biblical diction or syntax in the poem, even though word connotations do activate optional biblical senses of terms.

Quite typically of Amichai's poetry, these three frames of reference are linked through linguistic rather than traditional poetic means. The masculine attribute "angel," which in this poem is made to apply to a woman, is anchored in colloquial metaphor, where *mal'ach* could apply to a woman (in the sense of "a wonderful person") or a child ("a beautiful, peaceful, and pure creature"). Amichai introduces into the poem the weighty associations of the biblical story of Jacob's struggle with the angel, with all its national and transcendental implications, in order to describe a one-time erotic encounter (the literal frame).[44] He domesticates and thoroughly demystifies these materials through the second, metonymic frame of child's play. And thus he also effects the sanctification and elevation of both the erotic and the childlike domains.

This practice can easily be characterized in terms of certain modernist prototypes, such as the drive to deflate and secularize the eternal and spiritual, and, conversely, to remystify and valorize the transient and the physical. However, within the specific intrasystemic conditions of Hebrew poetry at the end of the 1950s, the poem enlists an additional stylistic motivation for its three-tiered structure: to grant legitimacy to the literary use of relatively new registers of modern Hebrew such as slang, colloquial idiom, and children's language. This internal motivation is subtly strengthened by Amichai's (still quite minimal) use of military Hebrew. For example, the occurrence of the rare form *tefes* (from *t.f.s.*, "to grab," "hold on to") in line 4, can refer to the catch that holds the clip of cartridges. Similarly, at the end of the poem we find a nonliterary allusion, to the lyrics of a popular song of the Sinai campaign era, "Hu lo yada et shma" ("He Did Not Know Her Name").[45] This noncanonical allusion deflates and restrains the metaphysical pathos of the search for meaning in a name which is no longer God (*ha-shem*) but is instead an interpersonal code for transitory love.

Finally, as in both the Fogel and the Shlonsky poems, the modernist nontraditional biblical allusion in "Jacob and the Angel" serves to highlight an obscure but implicitly dominant aspect of the biblical text itself. Amichai's love encounter guides us to look anew at the biblical story of Jacob and the angel. We find in Genesis, through the prism of this poem, an intriguing erotic moment in the encounter between God and man, an encounter which, as we know, left Jacob/Israel injured in a very sensitive spot.

In tracing the ways in which modernist Hebrew poetry overcame its language pangs I have attempted to outline a systematic rapport between internal and external literary and linguistic needs, and their social and ideological context. Filling in the gaps in the defective polysystem of Hebrew was made easier by—rather than achieved in spite of—the pursuit of general modernist goals. However, in the actual poetic texture this rapport turned out to be part of a complex rhetorical strategy for achieving yet another delicate balance, a balance between two well-known principles in Hebrew literary history— innovation and tradition. That modernism was intimately associated not only with radical change but also with the conservation of tradition was perhaps true of the international movement as a whole. In the context of the revival of Hebrew as a language of modern poetry, this potential modernist feature gains special salience. Radicalism in the Hebraic literary and linguistic framework has, after all, always been associated with a return—of one sort or another—to the never fully lost radices of the traditional canon.

CHAPTER 5

Theories of Allusion and Imagist Intertextuality

When Iconoclasts Evoke the Bible

Mi amar le-mi u-matay ("who said unto whom and when") is the standard opening of a Bible quiz in an Israeli school, and the standard "lead-in" of many Israeli jokes. It is also a familiar reminder that traditional attitudes toward biblical quotation and allusion are still very much alive. Just as schoolchildren commit entire biblical passages to memory, so do university students (of literature as well as the Bible) learn to identify the *mekorot,* the biblical sources quoted or alluded to by writers of all periods. While Talmudic, liturgical, and rabbinic allusions are becoming harder and harder for the general reading public to identify, biblical references still form a vital part of the Israeli's "system of associated commonplaces," in Max Black's (1962:40) terms.[1]

Still, these cultural practices do not explain why Israel has emerged as a center for the theoretical study of allusion as a general literary device, nor do they account for the specific innovative views of allusion which these theories take. In this chapter I look into some of the internal dynamics of the third trend of modernist Hebrew poetry (the Statehood Generation) as it correlates with some relevant imported prototypes and paragons of Anglo-American imagism and I examine how together they helped shape contemporary Israeli theories of allusion. As in the case of the "language pangs" of earlier generations, theories of literature remain closely linked to modernist literary practices. Specifically, I find a strong link between the interactional view of allusion that has gained prominence in Israel (especially in the work of the Tel Aviv School of poetics and semiotics)[2] and the iconoclastic use of biblical and liturgical allusion in modernist Hebrew poetry of the Statehood Generation (*dor ha-mdina*). I further find that this poetry's special use of biblical allusion is in turn correlated not only with "indigenous" literary, linguistic, and ideological developments but also with Anglo-American modernism (especially as spearheaded by T. S. Eliot's famous views of tradition and the individual talent).[3] After describing the basic relevant theoretical concepts against the background of the poetic practice and its modernist prototypes, I test my initial claims by examining in some detail two exemplary poems of the Statehood Generation which employ one and the same biblical allusion: Yehuda Amichai's "Be-khol chumrat ha-rachamim" ("To the Full Extent of Mercy") and Nathan Zach's "Kemo chol" ("As Sand").

A correspondence between the theory and practice of intertextuality is not without precedence in Hebrew literary history. The pervasiveness of allusions to the Bible and other traditional sources in all phases of Hebrew poetry from the Middle Ages on has at times been paralleled by rhetorical manuals on the values of allusion and by a variety of traditions of allusive exegesis from midrash to source criticism. I shall briefly mention one such precedent, the medieval use of allusion in the Hebrew poetry in Spain, because it alerts us to the complex and potentially problematic nature of the diachronic and synchronic correspondences between the explicit and implicit poetics of allusion, and because it presents the strongest phase in the formation of the norm for poetic allusion within the Hebrew literary system.[4]

Even a poetry bound by a prescriptive or normative poetics of a convention-oriented literary school,[5] such as medieval Hebrew poetry in Spain, allows for tensions between the stated rhetorical requirements (Benjamin Harshav's [Hrushovski's] "explicit poetics") and the principles embedded in the individual works ("implicit poetics"). Dan Pagis has in a series of brilliant studies made this point emphatically (primarily, Pagis, 1970, 1976, 1991). The implicit poetics of allusion in this poetry ranges very widely from the neutral use of biblical language which does not echo any specific biblical text to the *remizah* or *shibbuts* system, in which the biblical text is a necessary component of any semantic construal and structural cohesion of the poem (Pagis, 1970: 70–77).[6] The explicit poetics of the period, however, with its emphasis on linguistic embellishment and the separation of form and content, resulted in the emergence of the decorative and semantically neutral *shibbuts* as the paradigm for medieval Hebrew poetry; so much so that in generations to come *shibbuts* sometimes becomes synonymous with a mosaic structure (*Mussivstil*)[7] and sometimes with the *melitsah*.[8]

All evidence points to the fact, as Pagis suggests, that the medieval reader had a good sense of the implicit contemporary poetics as well as of the prescribed paradigms. The reader could "recognize the [biblical] verses but would also know when it was right to ignore the biblical context" (1970:71) and when appropriate to invoke it. Only modern readers lose their way and fail to distinguish the explicit poetics of the period from the implicit one and end in imposing anachronistic paradigms on the medieval text. If these habits of misreading sound disturbingly like some source criticism of modern literature, it is only because they are.[9] At one extreme, in Pagis's diagnosis, is the critic

> who sometimes claims to have fulfilled his exegetical task by supplying marginal notes [to identify] each and every [biblical] verse. At the other extreme is the exegete who is close to a homilist [*parshan she-hu karov le-darshan*]. He believes that almost every biblical fixed expression has to drag in with it into the world of the poem connotations of an entire [biblical] verse or even of an entire chapter. Suffice it for the medieval poet to say about his patron, "If he pays no heed to my offering," and this type of exegete already suspects [the poet] of seeing himself as Cain, his brother's killer.[10] (1970:70; translation mine)

Even if medieval poetry points to the inherent difficulties of correlating critical and poetic principles of allusion, the example is an instructive one. It underscores the need to reconstruct the kinds of allusion that serve as prototypes for the poets, readers, and critics of the period and trend, and to account for the ways in which these prototypes raise the salience of some aspects of the allusive practice while suppressing others. A critical history of allusion needs to offer a descriptive and analytic account of what is perceived as central and what is perceived as peripheral in a given period or trend. It must therefore be wary of reduplicating the prescriptive requirements of the explicit poetics of that period or trend, while acknowledging its own historicity and tendentiousness. This caution becomes especially crucial as we approach late modernist treatments of biblical allusion because here the prescriptive element is often suppressed in the explicit poetics and in the critical theory, which now claim to be descriptive of all "true" poetry.

With this quest for a set of prototypes in mind, I must trade in the advantages of historical hindsight for the uncertainties of the still unfolding story of biblical allusion in late modernist Israeli poetry, explicit poetics, and theory.[11]

A shift from the tradition of *shibbuts* to the practice of *remizah* has been perceived as the essential change in the critical and poetic treatment of allusion. Whereas in the Middle Ages *shibbuts* and *remizah* are distinguished by the object of representation (the language of the biblical text in *shibbuts,* the "world" or thematic elements of the biblical text in *remizah*), modern treatments focus on the difference in function between the two modes. *Shibbuts,* and the critical tradition of source identification, is seen as a device for establishing the poet's erudition (*beki'ut*) and for lending his or her poetic expression authority and beauty. That many *shibbutsim* in fact go beyond this goal is clear. But it is also important to note that common modern conceptions choose to disregard the potential complexity of the *shibbuts* in order to render the alternative notion, *remizah,* not just functionally distinct from *shibbuts* but also implicitly superior to it. It is not surprising, therefore, that when theories of allusion began to be developed in Israel in the late 1960s, they were theories of *remizah* (still to be defined) and not of *shibbuts.* These theories provide structural and linguistic (rather than thematic and philological) accounts of allusion as a dynamic, interactional literary device which of necessity involves a reinterpretation both of the source text and of the target text. This is the case even though the modern poetic practice still accommodates uses of allusion which are *shibbutsim* according to the new interpretation—namely, ones which clearly do not require an intertextual alteration of one text by another.

How did the original binary distinction between *shibbuts* and *remizah* acquire its new sense as well as its normative import? I can only suggest one transitional link. When one looks at Hebrew literary criticism of the forties and fifties, as well as at the explicit poetic pronouncements of some of the antimodernists among the writers of the period, an interesting duality emerges. While the focus is clearly on biblical *remizah* and not *shibbuts,* what seems to be meant is *remizah* in the premodern sense, a reference "which depends on the situation described in the Bible" and not on the exact biblical wording (Pagis, 1970:75). Shimon Halkin's classic work, *Modern Hebrew Literature* (1950), for example, deals thematically (in Chapter 10) with biblical allusions as religious motifs in modern Hebrew poetry, and Ya'akov Fichman's influential *Dmuyot kdumim (Figures of Antiquity)* (1948) opens with the essay entitled "Ha-mikra ke-nose' le-shira" ("The Bible as a Topic for Literature"). The need for a vindication of the Bible as a source for allusions in a secular, often antireligious society continues to be felt even today in the critical literature.[12] It was especially strong in pre- and early statehood days, and it was thematic rather than structural in focus, as required by the antimodernist prototype dominant within the critical establishment of the time.

The shift from "motif criticism" to structural and textual analysis and from philology to linguistics in the 1960s was preceded by the emergence on the scene of the poets of the Statehood Generation, whom I have described as the third trend of Hebrew poetic modernism. These developments, as will become clear later on, were intricately related and mutually enriching. One result of these changes was the reinterpretation of *remizah,* the already privileged pole of the dichotomy, to accommodate the new contemporary paradigm of radical allusion.

The most impressive progress in the Israeli theories of allusion was made in the 1970s, most notably in the work of Ziva Ben-Porat.[13] The critical foundations for these new views were laid, however, many years before, in the unusual lexical-psychological analyses of allusion by the prolific and original scholar Dov Sadan.[14] Ben-Porat, in a joint article with Harshav [Hrushovski], the founder of the Tel Aviv School of poetics and semiotics, where the major work on allusion has been done, acknowledges her school's debt to Sadan:

> Sadan emphasized the subconscious associations in the language of poetic creation, the wealth of *possible connotations which words in poetry carry from the history of the language, their allusions to other languages and to classical texts, as well as the conventionality of idioms, expressions and topoi.* With an unformulated theory of poetic language, akin to I. A. Richards's on the one hand and Curtius's on the other hand, and with a technique and knowledge reminiscent of some of Leo Spitzer's studies . . . Sadan used his enormous knowledge of Hebrew writing of all periods to produce a series of observations about the language of poetry, *free from any ideological preconceptions. This endeavor influenced some of the younger interpreters of poetry. It matched well the techniques which the younger critics in the 1950s and 1960s learned from Anglo-American New Criticism* (Ben-Porat and Harshav [Hrushovski], 1974:5–6; emphasis added).

Remarkably like the manifestoes of the Statehood Generation poets, Ben-Porat's and Harshav's [Hrushovski's] seemingly objective account of Sadan's work is in fact an act of self-description. Despite the vast differences in methodology and technique, Sadan can serve as the proverbial grandfather of the new theorists because his work offers both an alternative paradigm and an appropriate context.[15] Note, for example, that in the italicized sentences above, the study of allusions to classical texts is associated with the investigation of other aspects of the language of poetry, such as connotation, collocation (fixed expressions), and figurative language. It is not presented as an investigation of sources and influences in their traditional conception. This indeed proves to be both the needed legitimation for the rebellion against source criticism and the context in which the new theories of allusion had their first rather localized developments.

Gideon Toury and Avishai Margalith (1973), accordingly, discuss *remizah* and *shibbuts* within a rigorous analysis and taxonomy of deviant uses of collocation in modern Hebrew language and literature.[16] The identification of the sources in their work is merely a precondition for the description of significant systematic deviations from those sources. A few years earlier, Itamar Even-Zohar (1969/70) developed a different aspect of the same association between allusion and the creative use of collocation within his account of Hebrew as a language which, given its special history, has a "defective polysystem."[17] Even-Zohar describes the allusive activation of ancient literary collocations as one of the ways in which Hebrew literature compensates for what its language lacks. It is important to note here that his emphasis is not only on the ways in which literature compensates for its linguistic deficiencies but also on the ability of the literature to turn this deficiency into an advantageous aesthetic function. Thanks to the allusive use of ancient collocation, the poet can both "replace polysystemic variation and contrast and . . . give rise to the multiplicity of meaning often resulting from the conscious manipulation of the polysystem" (p. 444, English summary). Thus, allusion begins to be conceived of as a special use of language (like collocation), with specific semantic and pragmatic functions (like ambiguity and multiple meaning).

Note also that the collocational approach to allusion assimilates the medieval sense of *shibbuts* into the modern notion of *remizah:* it focuses on linguistic rather than thematic or situational similarities between the modern and the ancient text. From this point on, Israeli theories no longer distinguish thematic from linguistic allusion, as befits a poetics which has replaced the form-content distinction with a distinction between materials and patterns. (Compare Harshav [Hrushovski], 1976:2–6.)

A truly integrationist[18] view of allusion appears in the most important treatment of the topic outside Ben-Porat's: Meir Sternberg's (1982) theories of quotation and repetition (see also Sternberg, 1976, 1977). Combining linguistic and mimetic perspectives, Sternberg presents allusion as a special form of reported discourse. (Since his treatment of allusion is subsumed under the more general topic of quotation and since he uses mainly prose fiction for his model, I shall confine my discussion to brief remarks on his article "Proteus in Quotation-Land: Mimesis and the Forms of Reported Discourse," 1982.) Allusion, Sternberg acknowledges, is a form of covert quotation, like parody, imitation, pastiche, and free indirect style.[19] But what interests him is not a structuralist taxonomy of types of quotation in which allusion, for example, will be defined by the features which distinguish it from its counterpart in a binary opposition. (In that respect his theory goes against Gerard Genette's (1982) taxonomy of "transtextuality.") Instead, Sternberg seeks to contextualize allusion within the general complex phenomenon of reported discourse, stressing what he calls "the Proteus Principle": "the many-to-many correspondences between linguistic form and representational function" (p. 112). Emphasizing "the interplay of unity and variety in quotation" rather than the distinctive features of each type of quotation (p. 112), Sternberg allows us to see the allusive process as one of the cases in which "two discourse events enter into representational ('mimetic') relations." These relations differ from ordinary representation (of the world through language) "only in the represented object, . . . [which is] the world of discourse as opposed to the world of things" (p. 107). "In this general sense," Sternberg continues, "all reported discourse—from the direct through the free or the plain indirect to the most summary or allusive quotation—is a mimesis of discourse" (p. 107).

This emphasis on intertextuality evokes poststructuralist French and American theories. Yet there are several significant differences between these notions and the Israeli conception of intertextuality. Since Julia Kristeva (1969) first articulated the belief that intertextuality is the underlying condition of all textuality, poststructuralist and especially deconstructionist critics have actually suppressed the issue of allusion as a literary device and privileged the general condition of intertextuality: "Every text is absorption and transformation of a multiplicity of other texts" (see English excerpts and discussion in Ducrot and Todorov, 1979:339). But these approaches confront a logical and methodological difficulty when they move from the level of theory to that of interpretation. As Jonathan Culler has shrewdly observed (1981:103–7), if every text takes shape as a mosaic of citations, and it is only through these intertextual codes that literature can function, what sense is there in the isolated study of specific allusions to specific texts? The study of intertextuality, by the poststructuralist account, ought not to be "the investigation of sources and influences as traditionally conceived" (p. 103). This is an idea that the new Israeli theorists of allusion, who have rebelled against traditional Hebraic source criticism, would certainly embrace.

But the concept of intertextuality, as Culler goes on to argue, proves difficult to work with. While such critics as Kristeva declare that intertextuality is all-encompassing and that it includes "anonymous discursive practices, codes whose origins are lost, that make possible the signifying practices of later texts" (Culler, 1981:103), they proceed in practice to identify and interpret specific allusions in specific texts and to claim that one allusion is more contextually relevant than another. This practice leads to a troubling inconsistency within the critical system: "The attempt to demonstrate the importance of intertextuality leads one to focus on the other discourses identifiable in and behind a discourse and to try to specify them . . . [but] a situation in which one can track down sources with such precision cannot serve as the paradigm for a description of intertextuality, if intertextuality is the general discursive space that makes a text intelligible" (p. 106).

Do the new Israeli theories of allusion face a similar dilemma? Isn't this inconsistency a necessary consequence of the concept of intertextuality? A full answer to this question would involve an examination of the concept of intertextuality and cognate concepts in the general theories of the text developed by the Tel Aviv School. I shall only outline the issue in broad strokes. In an article titled "An Outline of a Theory of the Literary Text," Even-Zohar (1972) introduces intertextual relations as "indispensable for any explicatory model of *intratextual* relations" (quoted from the English summary, p. iii). Yet, this is different from claiming, with Barthes, that intertext is the "impossibility of living outside the infinite text—whether this text be Proust or the daily newspaper or the television screen" (1975:36). The Israeli theorist does not feel compelled to make an ontological commitment to intertextuality as the defining feature of human existence simply because it is one of the defining features of human texts. This difference becomes dramatically clear when it comes closest to disappear-

ing—in the general statement of Harshav's [Hrushovski's] integra-
tionist semantics (Harshav [Hrushovski], 1982:158, emphasis added):

> Language is not an independent vehicle for conveying meaning. It is
> rather used to (re-)orient the understander in a "network of informa-
> tion" ("*World*," *which includes all previous texts as well*). . . .
>
> [A] speaker of language uses language as well as the "World" to
> convey his intentions. . . . This is true even for such highly abstract
> texts as philosophy, which cannot be understood without previous
> philosophical texts or such notions as "time," "space," etc. And it is
> certainly true for newspapers, which cannot be understood without
> newspapers (or newscasts) of previous days.
>
> . . . Semantic theory must overcome the "First-Sentence fallacy"—
> the analysis of a sentence as if it stood alone. There are no first sen-
> tences in language.

How does Barthes's intertextual newspaper differ from Harshav's
[Hrushovski's]? For Harshav [Hrushovski] and the Tel Aviv critics, to
begin with, the relativism of linguistic meaning, as it is expressed in
the intertextuality of discourses in general, is not a source for critical
or ontological anxiety. Quite the contrary. The inherent dependence of
an understander's meaning on imperfect, convention-shaped concep-
tions is readily accepted, even welcomed, because the products of these
dependencies are patterns such as allusion, metaphor, and ambiguity.
Therefore, Harshav [Hrushovski] goes on to say, "theory must not shy
away from the diffuse, ambivalent, multidirectional, imprecise, po-
tential-filled nature of language—which is its great strength in inter-
acting with a multifarious and changing "World." One should not
confuse method with ontology, the neatness of a theoretical apparatus
with a schematic neatness in language" (pp. 158–59).

It is therefore clear that an understander's interpretation of a text
always already depends on previous interpretations of other texts and
that the world these texts refer to is, for a given understander, always
only a "World"—namely, a network of information and not an ob-
jective referential reality. And yet, given these general conditions of
textual understanding, some "semantic stuff" may be organized in
patterns which refer to the "World," while others may be restruc-
tured over "discrete bodies of text" (Harshav [Hrushovski], 1982:159)
in patterns that connect one specific text to another. The difficulty
pointed out by Culler, then, does not exist for Harshav [Hrushovski]
and the Tel Aviv School, not only because for them intertextuality
does not mark an ontological crisis but also because they do not

expect meaning to reside in the words or sentences of a text. Meanings are instead observed as "open-ended networks of constructs, forming bridges between given pieces of language and the world (or language) outside of it" (p. 157). The fuzziness of the borders of such units of meaning does not mean that there is no border, no distinction between what is inside and what is outside the unit. All it means is that the distinction, in order to be valid, has to take into account the fluidity and interpenetration of semantic categories. The model of modernism I present in this study is also to be understood within this general conceptual scheme.

Whereas poststructuralist theories of intertextuality in Western Europe and the United States have moved toward greater generalization and comprehensiveness, Israeli theories have clearly evinced a growing specificity. While attempting to supply a general model for the actualization of an allusive pattern by an understander, the most developed Israeli theory of allusion to date offers a systematic account of allusion as a well-defined literary device rather than of intertextuality as a general textual condition. It is also characteristic that Ben-Porat's accounts of allusion are presented not only in theoretical studies (1973, 1976) but also in applied analyses and interpretations (1973, 1978a). Another project by Ben-Porat is a large-scale empirical study of Israeli readers' actualizations of literary allusions and of the distribution of allusions in Israeli high school matriculation-examination reading lists (1978b, 1979).

As the emphasis on the process of actualization suggests, Ben-Porat's theory of allusion, as well as the studies in descriptive and historical poetics which derive from the theory, hinges on the conceptual framework of the integrational semantics developed by Harshav [Hrushovski] (1982a, 1982b, 1979). The most abstract and most generalized formulation of Ben-Porat's account, in an article entitled "The Poetics of Literary Allusion" (1976), employs not only Harshav's [Hrushovski's] concept of the actualization, or "realization," of an allusion by a reader but also the principle of maximal patterning of elements from both texts (Harshav [Hrushovski], 1976). Additional components of Ben-Porat's theory echo, as the self-referential acknowledgment to Sadan predicted, both New Critical ideas—especially Richards's (1936) interaction theory of metaphor—and recent developments in linguistics and semiotics.

Against this background, the major operative concepts of Ben-Porat's theory of allusion can now be introduced. A functionalist, understander-oriented theory, it defines literary allusion as "a device for simultaneous activation of two texts." This activation "is achieved through the manipulation of a special signal: a sign (simple or complex) in a given text characterized by an additional larger 'referent.' This referent is always an independent text. The simultaneous activation of the two texts thus connected results in the formation of intertextual patterns whose nature cannot be predetermined. According to this definition the literary allusion differs from allusion in general (i.e., 'a hint to a known fact') with regard to the nature of both the sign and the referent, as well as the end product and the process of actualization" (1976:108). The constitutive features of all literary allusions which help distinguish them from mere hints are the independent existence of both texts, called the *alluding text* and the *evoked text*, "the presence of a directional marker or in short [a] *marker* in the alluding text, the presence of elements in both texts which can be linked together in unfixed, unpredictable intertextual patterns, and the process of actualization which reflects in its stages the efforts to reconstruct the fuller text" (Ben-Porat, 1973, abstract).

The actualization of a literary allusion by a reader is a four-step process. First, the recognition of a marker in a given sign; second, the identification of the evoked text; third, the modification of the initial local interpretation of the signal (the sign and the marker); and, finally, the activation of the evoked text as a whole in an attempt to form maximum intertextual patterning. Ben-Porat also offers a basic typology of literary allusions based on the initial distance or proximity of the mutually activated texts. Initially unrelated alluding and evoked texts result in metaphoric allusions, whereas initially related texts yield metonymic allusions.

Ben-Porat's theoretical account of literary allusion has already made an important contribution to the interpretation of complex and divergent modern allusive texts. She herself has employed the conceptual framework outlined above to provide insightful analyses of intertextual patterning in, among others, Zach's "Dantes, lo" ("Dantes, No"),[20] in a group of Hebrew poems which evoke the *Odyssey* (1979:37–41), and in Eliot's "The Love Song of J. Alfred Prufrock" (1976:118ff). Miri Baruch, in her book on Zach, *Ha-romantikan ha-mar* (*The Bitter Romantic*) (1979), devotes a chapter to the properties of allusion in Zach's poetry, combining an early version of Ben-Porat's theory with a compositional model which is relevant to the analysis of allusion offered by Menakhem Perry (1972).

It is no accident that it is relatively easy to apply Ben-Porat's system to a descriptive and historical poetics of allusion in Israeli poetry[21] and in particular to the poetry of Zach. Nor is it accidental that Ben-Porat has chosen an Eliot poem as her non-Hebrew example of an alluding text and the *Odyssey* as her classical example of an evoked text. Her theory, like its less extensive precursors, is motivated by an indigenous implicit paradigm of radical allusive practice and an imported, prototypical, explicit poetics of radical modernist credos.

The emergence of the new Israeli theories of allusion is a response to two factors: the shift in the intrinsic (Hebraic) paradigm of allusion in the poetry of the Statehood Generation and the shift in the dominant extrinsic modernist model from a Russian and French one (the symbolist and futurist tendencies of Nathan Alterman's and Avraham Shlonsky's *moderna*) to the Anglo-American prototypes of imagism and vorticism. More specifically, I find a three-way correlation, which may in fact be a causal relationship, among the following complex descriptions: (1) the theoretical account of allusion as a dynamic, unpredictable, and simultaneous interaction of two texts, which mutually modify or criticize each other; (2) the practice of radical allusion in the neoimagist poetry of the 1950s and 1960s, prototypically represented by iconoclastic intertextual patternings of secular, mundane alluding texts with biblical or other religious evoked texts; and (3) Anglo-American modernist views of intertextuality and literary history, especially those clustered around Eliot's prototypical text, "Tradition and the Individual Talent" (in Eliot, [1920] 1960), where literary tradition is described as a dynamic, fluid hierarchy which maintains a simultaneous, mutually modifying relation with the new contributions of the modern individual poet.

In order to observe the correspondences among the three domains, I present in Table 1 a schematic breakdown of five features which are prototypical of the special uses of allusion in late-modernist Hebrew poetry and their characterization within each domain. Note that on several occasions the poetry duplicates the theoretical characterization. While this is only one segment of a rather complex and fluid process, it nevertheless indicates a general tendency.

The examples cited in the domain of Statehood Generation poetry, as well as the generalizations about the poetic use of allusion, could of course be replaced by many others. I have deliberately limited my examples to the early work of two very different but equally

Table 1. Radical Allusion: Modernism, Israeli Style

Key Feature	Israeli Theories of Allusion	Statehood Generation Poetry	Eliot/ Modernism
Simultaneity	simultaneous activation of alluding and evoked text	same as theory— e.g., "Ya'akov ve-ha-mal'akh" ("Jacob and the Angel"), Amichai	simultaneous existence of past and present literature
Dynamism	dynamic interaction of alluding and evoked texts in the four-step actualization process of intertextual patterning	narrativelike extension of allusive situation—e.g., "Talita kumi" ("Talita Get Up"), Zach	dynamic hierarchy of existing literary "monuments"
Mutual Intertextual Modification	(a) radical/ obligatory modification of alluding text by evoked text	elevation of the mundane alluding text through a sacred evoked text—e.g., "Shimshon" ("Samson"), Amichai	individual talent molded by literary tradition
	(b) (optional) modification of evoked text by alluding text	deflation of sacred/lofty evoked text through a secular/mundane alluding text— e.g., "Ve-hi tehilatekha" ("And That Is Your Glory"), Amichai	individual talent can alter/ restructure literary tradition
Deviance	allusion as a type of deviant use of collocation	iconoclastic punning on biblical/religious evoked text— e.g., "El male rachamim" ("God Full of Mercy"), Amichai	tradition is maintained through the reversal/ criticism of tradition

(continued)

Table 1. *(continued)*

Key Feature	Israeli Theories of Allusion	Statehood Generation Poetry	Eliot/ Modernism
Unpredictability	results of intertextual patterning cannot be predetermined	same as theory—e.g., "Et se'aro shel Shimshon" ("Samson's Hair"), Zach	only the new/surprising work can cause the restructuring of the hierarchy of literary history

NOTE: The examples from Hebrew come from the following collections: "Ya'akov ve-ha-mal'akh," "Shimshon," "Ve-hi tehilatekha," and "El male rachamim" in Amichai (1962, 1977 ed.:260, 259–60, 71–72, 69–70); "Talita kumi" and "Et se'aro shel Shimshon" in Zach, (1960, no pagination). For a discussion of Amichai's "El male rachamim," see Sokoloff (1984:127). For a discussion of the dynamics of the allusive situation in Zach's "Talita' kumi," see Perry (1972), and see discussions of "Et se'aro shel Shimshon" in Baruch (1979:83–90).

dominant poets of this generation, Amichai and Zach, and have chosen only allusive processes that involve biblical or other religious evoked texts. In examining the new norm for allusive practices, the discussion of Amichai and Zach poems that follows should help explain why iconoclastic references to biblical texts have become so prototypical of this trend's radical modernist allusions and why these examples are foregrounded in the center of the canon.

The Israeli critics themselves have acknowledged the correlations among dominant theory, normative poetic practice, and imported modernist model. As far as I know, however, this acknowledgment was never specifically applied to allusion, nor was it ever much more than a general programmatic statement. Thus, for example, Ben-Porat and Harshav [Hrushovski], in their account of the background for the emergence of their school's theoretical orientation to literature, state: "A parallel shift [to the one that was occurring in criticism] took place in Hebrew poetry. There was a revulsion from what was felt to be "rhetorical" and empty versification, towards a "precise" poetic language and a poetry of the individual, modeled after T. S. Eliot and English modernism" (1974:7).

These statements do not reveal the extraliterary, sociological factors, which in the close intellectual community of Israel always loom large and which as a rule are quite important in the dynamics of canon formation within literary circles and movements. One such factor is simply that the founder of the Tel Aviv School of Poetics, Harshav

[Hrushovski] (under one of his numerous pen names, H. Benjamin), was also cofounder (with Zach and Amichai) of the *Likrat* circle, the core of what later became known as the Statehood Generation of Hebrew poets. Another "anecdotal" noncoincidence is the fact that Zach, who also formulated the explicit poetics of the group and published, among other things, a fifteen-point manifesto of the poetry of the 1950s and 1960s (Zach, 1966a), is also a scholar of modernist English poetry, especially of imagism, and the works of Pound and Eliot (see, for example, Zach [1976] 1981). Thus, in the manifesto, in addition to many intrinsically motivated processes (for example, reaction against what was conceived of as the over-poetic, excessively figurative, and rhetorical *moderna* poetry of the pre-Statehood Generation), the fifteen points are—quite self-consciously—styled in the manner of Pound's imagist manifestoes and Eliot's programmatic articles.[22]

Interestingly, both Zach's explicit poetics and subsequent theoretical developments adopt Eliot's view of tradition and intertextuality but transform Eliot's clearly normative statements into the descriptive language of fact. Because of its lasting impact both on the explicit poetics of the Israeli neoimagist poets and on the theories of allusion that appeared a decade later, it is worthwhile quoting Eliot's famous mixture of description and evaluation in "Tradition and the Individual Talent":

> [T]he historical sense involves a perception, not only of the pastness of the past, but of its presence; the historical sense compels a man to write . . . with a feeling that the whole of the literature of Europe from Homer and . . . the whole literature of his own country [have] a simultaneous existence and compose a simultaneous order. . . .
>
> No poet . . . has his complete meaning alone. His significance, his appreciation is the appreciation of his relation to the dead poets. . . .
>
> [W]hat happens when a new work of art is created is something that happens simultaneously to all the works of art which preceded it. The existing monuments form an ideal order among themselves, which is modified by the introduction of the new (the really new) work of art among them. ([1920] 1960:49–50)

One influential idea that Eliot expresses here and elsewhere and that I have not included in the schematic presentation of the salient features above is the assertion that difficulty is a necessary and not an altogether unwelcome consequence of the simultaneous view of tradition which supports the allusive new poetry. "I am alive to a usual objection to what is clearly part of my programme for the *metiér* of poetry. The objection is that the doctrine requires a ridiculous amount of erudition (pedantry)" (p. 52). Eliot along with Pound and other modernists—as well as latter-day critical followers such as George Steiner (1972:18–47)—legitimize the use of such "difficult" erudition in modernist poetry and so does Zach, their Israeli interpreter. Zach (1966a, point 15) claims the "right to compose individualistic poetry in a difficult, hermetic style, so long as you are dealing with a true work of art." Zach's example is Avot Yeshurun, but as Baruch (1979: 69) points out, Zach might have been talking about his own poetry and his own use of allusion. This is where Amichai's and Zach's use of allusion differ radically and where a central feature of the Anglo-American imported model is a source of internal contradiction between two dominant paragons within the Hebrew literary system.

Before we take a closer look at the differences that emerge from the three-way correlation between theory, poetic paradigm, and modernist model, I would like to note an interesting similarity between Israeli theory and praxis of allusion and the Russian approach to intertextuality.[23] As Elaine Rusinko (1979) points out, Russian theories of allusion have also been developed in order to deal with a body of poetry which shares explicit and implicit poetic prototypes with Anglo-American imagism. The acmeist poetry of Anna Akhmatova and Osip Mandelstam presented interpretive needs, in their use of allusion, which, according to Rusinko, led to the development in the Moscow-Tartu circle of subtext theories that sound surprisingly like some of the Tel Aviv theories. This is perhaps not only a result of the similarity in the modernist poetics and the acknowledged influence of Eliot on both literatures and theories. A more direct route from the Moscow-Tartu circle to the Tel Aviv School is charted by the emigration to Israel of two of the major Russian allusion scholars, Omri Ronen and Dmitri Segal, whose work is described extensively in Rusinko's article (for example, Ronen, 1977; Segal, 1975). Finally, the theories may be linked by the common formalist heritage. But that is a topic for a different study.

The theory of allusion needs to be taken one little step further to bring it to a fuller agreement with the poetic practice. In a footnote to her theoretical article, "The Poetics of Literary Allusion," Ben-Porat stops short of allowing the allusive interaction to be fully bilateral:

> It is very probable that the creation of intertextual patterns affects and enriches the evoked text . . . as well. Even if the evoked text preceded the alluding text by several hundred years, a simultaneous activation

is possible for the reader of both. Consequently, familiarity with the later text . . . can change or modify the interpretation of the evoked text. . . . In [the figure describing the components of the allusive process], however, we can only trace the effect of the intertextual patterning on the interpretation of the alluding text, since this is the text being read and reconstructed at the moment. In the actual reading process the reader may shift his attention to the effect of the intertextual patterning on the evoked text. But by doing that he has for a moment changed the roles: [the evoked text] becomes for him [the alluding text]. The problems involved in the legitimacy of manipulating such an ahistorical (and intentionally impossible) allusion in interpretation need not concern us here. (1976:114, note 9)

But it does need concern us here. The prototypical poetic paradigm of allusion for the Statehood Generation, and especially for Amichai and Zach, places, as we shall see, special significance on the mutual reinterpretation of the two texts activated in the allusive process. The question of anachronism does not arise, nor does the need to reverse the roles of the alluding and evoked texts, because this reinterpretation occurs beyond the initial phase of identifying marker, alluding and evoked texts, at a stage when there is no reason to suppose that simultaneity does not also entail, as Eliot suggested, a mutual alteration and restructuring of the textual materials.

We can now approach the first poem under discussion, Amichai's "Bekhol chumrat ha-rachamim," an untranslatable title which I render as "To the Full Extent of Mercy."

בְּכָל חֻמְרַת הָרַחֲמִים

מְנֵה אוֹתָם.
אַתָּה יָכוֹל לִמְנוֹת אוֹתָם. הֵם
אֵינָם כַּחוֹל, אֲשֶׁר עַל שְׂפַת הַיָּם. הֵם
אֵינָם כַּכּוֹכָבִים לָרֹב. הֵם כַּאֲנָשִׁים בּוֹדְדִים.
בַּפִּנָּה וּבָרְחוֹב.

מְנֵה אוֹתָם. רְאֵה אוֹתָם
רוֹאִים אֶת הַשָּׁמַיִם דֶּרֶךְ בָּתִּים הֲרוּסִים.
צֵא מִן הָאֲבָנִים וַחֲזֹר. לְאָן
תַּחֲזֹר? אֲבָל מְנֵה אוֹתָם, כִּי הֵם
מְרַצִּים אֶת יְמֵיהֶם בַּחֲלוֹמוֹת
וְהֵם מְהַלְכִים בַּחוּץ, וְתִקְווֹתֵיהֶם שֶׁלֹּא נֶחְבְּשׁוּ
הֵן פְּעוּרוֹת, וּבָהֶן יָמוּתוּ.

מְנֵה אוֹתָם.
מֻקְדָּם מִדַּי לָמְדוּ לִקְרֹא אֶת הַכְּתָב
הַנּוֹרָא עַל הַקִּיר. לִקְרֹא וְלִכְתֹּב עַל
קִירוֹת אֲחֵרִים. וְהַמִּשְׁתֶּה נִמְשָׁךְ בִּדְמָמָה.

מְנֵה אוֹתָם. הֱיֵה נוֹכַח, כִּי הֵם
כְּבָר הִשְׁתַּמְּשׁוּ בְּכָל הַדָּם וַעֲדַיִן חָסֵר,
כְּמוֹ בְּנִתּוּחַ מְסֻכָּן, כְּשֶׁאֶחָד הוּא עָיֵף
וּמְכֶּה כִּרְבָבָה. כִּי מִי דָן וּמַה דִין
אֶלָּא בִּמְלֹא מוּבַן הַלַּיְלָה
וּבְכָל חֶמְרַת הָרַחֲמִים.

To the Full Extent of Mercy

Count them.
You can count them. They
aren't like sand on the seashore. They
aren't like the numerous stars. They're like lonely people.
On the corner and in the street.

Count them. See them
seeing the sky through ruined houses.
Leave through the stones and return. Where
will you return? But count them, for they
do their time in dreams
and they walk around outside, and their unbandaged hopes
are open, and they will die of them.

Count them.
Too soon they learned to read the terrible writing
on the wall. To read and write on
other walls. And the banquet in stillness goes on.

Count them. Be present, for they've
already used up all the blood and some is still missing,
as in a dangerous operation, when one is worn out
and beat like ten thousand. For who's judge and what's judgment
unless it's in the full sense of night
and to the full extent of mercy.
                    —Amichai ([1962] 1977 ed.:253; translation mine)

In a typical move, the speaker of Amichai's poem issues a series of instructions to an unidentified addressee, who may be either the reader or a rhetorical objectification of the poetic persona. But despite the syntax of speech, the diction of the opening line is just enough too formal—for a poet who makes a point of using "only a small part of the words in the dictionary" (from "El male' rachamim" ["God Full of Mercy"] in Amichai, [1962] 1977 ed.:69–70) for the address to be taken literally. *Mene* ("enumerate," "count") is much more formal than the colloquial *sfor* ("count"), as is the use of the imperative rather than the future for commands. And, indeed, we soon discover that *mene* is part of a marker which triggers intertextual patterning not with one evoked text but with the recurring biblical narrative type-scene of the divine promise to make the children of Israel as countless (*lo' yimanu*) as the sand on the seashore and like the numerous stars in the sky (lines 3–4). The familiarity and generality of this complex marker (complex because it triggers the activation of more than one discrete evoked text) makes the speaker's series of commands and assertions readily interpretable. The interpretability does not seem to suffer from the fact that the alluding text explicitly negates the message and the tone of the evoked narrative pattern and its most famous manifestation—God's promise to Abraham and his descendants (Genesis 15:5, 22:17). Furthermore, the negation of the biblical injunction against counting people itself constitutes another marker, evoking the story of David's temptation by Satan to count his people and the terrible devastation that befell the country as a collective punishment for his sin (1 Chronicles 21). The two evoked texts, the promise and the punishment, are in direct conflict, but they are both activated through the same sign, *mene*.

With the transition from instruction to description in lines 3–4, it is no longer God's injunction that is being negated but his figurative language. The two stock similes of the evoked texts of the promise are exposed when they are taken literally: the fact that these people are few enough to be counted proves that "like sand" is not a correct (literal) similarity statement. The speaker's unadorned use of syntactic repetition ("they aren't like x, they aren't like y, they are like z") emphasizes his obsession with literal fact and his rejection of simile and hyperbole. This rejection is especially emphatic since the final, affirmed "like" statement is not properly a simile at all, nor even a literal similarity statement. They *are* lonely (or few, single; *boded* can mean both) people. The final line of the first stanza sparsely but insistently establishes the replacement of the figurative by the literal, hyperbolic promise by minimalist reality.

In this first activation of allusive material, Amichai's poem already reveals a prototypically modernist intertextual process: the deflation of the traditional and sacred source (namely, the values associated with the evoked text) and, simultaneously, a heightening of the valuation of the mundane and disillusioned "World" that is the reference of the alluding text. Like the rejection of the nationalist-religious idea of being chosen through doing battle with God (in "Jacob and the Angel"), biblical promises of plenitude are renounced here in favor of the world of lonely, separate people who are victimized by their own dependence on impossible dreams and empty promises. Their hopes are like open wounds that will eventually kill them (line 12). It is these people, Amichai says, who are entitled—after all the waiting and hoping—to the full severity of mercy. This oxymoronic *inclusio* starts and ends the poem with a linguistic rather than a literary allusion based on the deviant use of the collocation *be-khol chumrat ha-din* (idiomatically, "to the full extent of the law"). The oxymoronic semantic potential of *chumra* ("severity," "rigor") and *rachamim* ("compassion," "pity," "mercy") is reversed, first prosodically by revealing that the two share the same consonantal root in a different order (ch.m.r.—r.ch.m.) and second, thematically by redefining true mercy and compassion as the refusal to give false hope, hence as "rigor" or "severity." This, then, is the full reversal of the biblical promise, which according to Amichai is full of (dangerous, misleading) hope but empty of mercy. (See his "El male' rachamim" ["God Full of Mercy"] in Amichai, [1962] 1977 ed.:69–70.)

The ease with which the Hebrew reader can mutually activate the multiple alluding and evoked texts in this short segment of the poem is part of the poem's antimodernist ideological and thematic import. Like the very identification of the marker, this import is laid bare in the text in an antielitist identification with the lonely rather than the chosen people, and, on a thematized level, by using antielitist allusions, namely markers that every native speaker of the language can identify and activate. With this accessibility as the primary goal, and the critique of the Eliot-Pound prototype of elitist allusion perhaps an implicit target as well, the poem can now allow the allusion hunters among its readers the treat of more subtle and intricate intertextualities. But not before the entire poem has been supplied with an allusively naive surface.

Still, then, on this first level of the readily accessible allusive pattern, the second half of the poem appears to put in the foreground one central marker, which is so well known it has become a cliché. The reference to the "writing on the wall" is not meant to be dug up by scholars. It is right there in the explicit language of the third stanza, as are the reversals of the meaning of the evoked text and its associated commonplaces. Belshazzar and his lords could not read the writing on the wall which foretold their doom (*mene mene tekel u-farsin*, "God has numbered the days of your kingdom, has weighed in the balances and decided to cut off [root p-r-s] your kingdom from you and give it to Persia [again, root p-r-s]," Daniel 5). Hence, people who fail to see the warning signs of disaster are, according to the cliché, those who cannot read the writing on the wall. In the alluding text, however, the marker reverses the marked by asserting what the Bible negates (just as "count them" reversed a biblical negation). Knowing the destructive divine intentions, being able to read the writing on the wall, is not much help. Aware of their own disastrous fate and that of others, they can only continue this mock-feast-turned-Last-Supper in stillness (line 16). The Hebrew *bi-dmamah* implies absence of sound and of motion, total inertia, at the same time that it echoes phonetically the blood (*dam*) of the extended metaphor of wounds, surgery, and blood donors developed in the second and fourth stanzas.

I turn now to the context of the reconstructed poem, where the more subtle allusive interactions are to be found. The repeating first line functions as a rather latent "allusive junction" (to adapt Harshav's [Hrushovski's] concept)—namely, a complex marker which can be linked to more than one evoked text or block of texts. As such it can trigger an intertextual activation and mutual modification not only of the alluding and evoked texts but within and among the evoked texts themselves. The conflation and interpenetration of the promise of the Pentateuch with the epitome of prophetic threat or curse in Daniel results in our increased perception of the promise as jeopardy and affliction. It also serves to place the reference of the alluding text not on an exclusively Jewish level but within a more universal and existential framework; the destruction of Belshazzar's kingdom, a metaphor for the human apocalypse in general, causes us to read even the usually Judaic promise in more universal terms.

We have come full circle from a simple, explicit challenge to the validity of the biblical promise to the actualization of the promise as curse and punishment, a writing on the wall, a warning which will not prevent the disaster. The careful reader of this unorthodox version of the biblical promise will discover that the conflation of promise and punishment, blessing and curse, is already present in the Bible. The marker thus causes an interaction even between the missing parts of the evoked text. This unpredictable element of the allusive interaction can be discerned in the exact language of Amichai's initial marker for the biblical promise. In these exact words the promise occurs only once in the Bible, in the context of another highly symbolic narrative which our system of associated commonplaces has turned into a stock metaphor for persecution and for the Holocaust as well. I am referring of course to the binding of Isaac. The first time in which God combines the similes of sand on the seashore and stars in the sky, and the only time in which the verse appears verbatim as in the poem is in Genesis 22:17, a few narrative minutes after the disaster of the binding of Isaac (the *akedah*) almost happened.

The discovery of this association of promise and curse within the Bible itself is much more evident a theme in Zach's poem "As Sand."

כְּמוֹ חוֹל

כְּשֶׁאֱלֹהִים בַּתַּנַ"ךְ רוֹצֶה לְהַבְטִיחַ,
הוּא מַרְאָה עַל כּוֹכָבִים.
אַבְרָהָם יוֹצֵא מִפֶּתַח אָהֳלוֹ בַּלַּיְלָה
וְרוֹאָה אוֹהֲבִים.
כְּמוֹ חוֹל עַל שְׂפַת הַיָּם, אוֹמֵר אֱלֹהִים,
וְהָאָדָם מַאֲמִין. אַף כִּי הוּא עַצְמוֹ מֵבִין
שֶׁלּוֹמַר כְּמוֹ חוֹל, הִיא רַק לְשׁוֹן כִּבְיָכוֹל.
וּמֵאָז נִשְׁאֲרוּ הַחוֹל וְהַכּוֹכָבִים שְׁלוּבִים
בְּרֶשֶׁת הַדִּמּוּיִים שֶׁל הָאָדָם. וְאוּלַי לֹא כְּדַאי
לָעֲרֹב כָּאן אֶת הָאָדָם. לֹא עָלָיו דֻּבַּר אָז שָׁם.

וַהֲרֵי נֶאֱמַר בִּמְפֹרָשׁ כְּמוֹ חוֹל, וּמֵמֵילָא מְדֻבָּר
גַּם עַל הַיְכֹלֶת לִסְבֹּל. אוֹ שֶׁמָּא אֶפְשָׁר לַחְשֹׁב שֶׁהַכֹּל
הֻתַּר אָז וְאֵין עוֹד, בְּפֵרוּשׁ אֵין עוֹד, גְּבוּל.

כַּחוֹל עַל שְׂפַת הַיָּם. וַהֲרֵי אֵין שָׁם מִלָּה עַל מַיִם. וּבְפֵרוּשׁ
מְדֻבָּר שָׁם עַל זֶרַע. אֶלָּא שֶׁכָּךְ הוּא מִדַּרְךְ הַשָּׁמַיִם
וְאוּלַי גַּם מִדַּרְךְ הַטֶּבַע.

As Sand

When God in the Bible wants to promise
He points to stars. Abraham strolls
from his tent at night
and sees lovers. As sand on the sea shore,
the Lord says. And man believes,
even though he understands that to say
as sand is merely a way
of speaking.
And from that time on,
sand and stars have been intertwined in
man's net of images. But perhaps
we shouldn't speak here of man.
He wasn't mentioned there and then—

and yet it is said explicitly *as sand*,
from which we might infer
the capacity for enduring. On the other hand,
it's possible to believe
that everything is then set free
and there are no more—explicitly
no more—boundaries.

As sand on the sea shore. But then, water
is never mentioned. God does, however,
speak of seed. Which only goes to show
the ways of heaven
and possibly, those of nature.

—Zach (1965; translated by Everwine
and Yasni-Starkman, 1982:17)

   The differences in the poetics of allusion between these two con-
temporary Israeli poets is all the more evident because both the cen-
tral evoked text and the general attitude toward it seem to be similar
in both poems. Whereas for Amichai the allusion to the biblical prom-

ise is a means toward the expression of a message about contemporary life and human expectations, which is not intrinsically linked to the biblical stories, Zach turns the biblical text, or more precisely the language of the evoked text, into his theme. Ben-Porat, who discusses other poems by Zach in her studies of allusion (for example, 1978b), refers to this intrinsic linking of the theme or fictional world of Zach's alluding texts and that of his evoked texts as "metonymic allusion." In this type of allusion, she argues, the marker functions as a device to point to preexisting contiguities between the alluding and evoked texts. She distinguishes this type of allusion from what she calls "metaphoric allusion," where, as in Amichai's poem, the two texts are not initially linked at all, but the sequence of the poem ultimately points to ways of turning the evoked text into a metaphor for the world depicted in the alluding text. It is not certain that this part of Ben-Porat's argument in fact works, and not only because the Jakobsonian dichotomy of metonymy and metaphor is probably too rigid to be useful here. The typical structure of allusion employed by Zach, in contradistinction to Amichai, involves not only an initial linkage with the materials of the evoked texts but a thematization of allusion as a linguistic and literary device, one which Zach both uses and mentions, to invoke a common logical distinction, but one for which he ultimately has little respect.

What in Amichai's poem is an occasional and implied reference to the figurative language used in the biblical promise becomes in Zach's poem the central tool for emptying the evoked text of any promise of meaning. When God in the Bible wants to perform the speech act of promising, an act—John Searle (1969:57–71) reminds us—which has a whole list of constitutive rules and sincerity conditions, he does what couldn't ever constitute a sincere promise: he points to stars (the Hebrew *mar'eh 'al* deliberately uses child language to emphasize the unattainability of promising someone "the moon and the stars"). But Abraham, naive, literal-minded, and trusting as always, already sees in his fertile imagination the first enactment of the promise, as lovers religiously fulfilling the command *peru urvu* ("be fruitful and multiply"). This is Zach's initial retelling of the biblical scene, the reinterpreted marker which now begins to undergo a series of revolutions and reversals in the text sequence in a sophisticated but ostensibly nonsensical parody of the rabbinic exegesis of biblical allusions (note the use of Talmudic connectives throughout the second half of the poem). The strategy seems to be the exact reverse of the one employed by Amichai; whereas the markers in the first half of the poem were to a large extent readily identifiable, the second half is most deliberately obscure and mostly so in places where it uses terms like "explicitly" or "absolutely." The surface structure is one of a nonsense string; ideas and pseudomarkers are concatenated by mere phonetic association; rhyme (both internal and traditional end rhyme) does not point to a meaning relation between its constituents; the rhyme appears to be the only connection: *chol, khol, li-sbol, ha-kol.* In none of the famous evoked texts of the promises are these terms associated. The same is true for the pseudononsensical concatenation of *mayim-zera-shamayim-teva* (water-seed-heaven-nature, the internal rhyme in the Hebrew being deliberately "bad").

Yet once Zach has achieved his primary meta-allusive goals, namely the illusion that biblical promise, language, metaphor, and even speech act have all been emptied of their meaning, and once, furthermore, the reader is told that the system of commonplaces associated with the evoked text—namely, the tradition of rabbinic exegesis—also consists of empty logical connectives which point to no inherently valid argument (second stanza), Zach has in fact allowed a significant amount of meaning to escape through the cracks in his persona's cynical mask. We understand, for example, that not only is the expressibility of language being challenged but so is the very existence of God. In line 7, man (but also Adam) realizes that to say "as sand" is only a manner of speaking. But the term used for "manner of speaking," *ki-vyakhol,* is also one of the euphemistic names for God ("the So to Speak"). This allusive junction causes the metaphors of the promise to interact with the euphemism for God, with the result that the literal meaning of *ki-vyakhol* ("as if" or "not really") is being sarcastically revived and applied to God's existence.

Let me illustrate Zach's use of a "difficult" or nonsensical allusive facade as a cover for a meaningful intertextuality with one last example. In the parody of Talmudic exegesis presented in the second stanza, an apparent nonsequitur is offered as a mockery of rabbinic attempts to justify, after the fact, the discrepancy between the plenitude of biblical promise and the misery of historical Jewish existence. Since the words *chol* ("sand") and *li-sbol* ("to endure," "suffer") rhyme, and since the text of the promise explicitly mentions *chol,* then *li-sbol* must be pseudologically implied. Zach is clearly poking fun here at the tradition of far-fetched midrashic interpretation, evident especially in the repeated use of *be-ferush* and *bi-mforash,* which idiomatically mean "explicitly" or "clearly" but literally mean "(located) in the interpretation"—namely, not in the text. Yet, when one meticulously traces all the uses of the metaphors of the promise in the Bible—as in a traditional allusion hunt for the *mekorot*—it appears that Zach's pseudononsensical claim is quite literally true. We have already seen the conflation of promise and suffering in the story of the binding of Isaac, the text in which the heavenly and earthly metaphors of plenitude occur for the first time. More surprising, however, in all the historical books of the Bible the metaphors of the promise have had their context of application reversed quite consistently. They have been appropriated for exclusively dangerous, militant descriptions and most often occur in the portrayal of the enemy. When Joshua fights the Canaanites (Joshua 11:4), it is they who are like the sand on the seashore; when Gideon fights the Midianites, their camels and their army are like sand on the seashore (Judges 7:12); the only time in 2 Samuel in which the metaphor is applied to a Judean (17:12), it is still ironically the enemy: Absalom's army is described by the adviser of this would-be usurper of David's reign as sand on the seashore.

In this manner Zach manages here as in other poems to bring across his favorite radically modernist message about the meaninglessness of language and the futility of the divine and creative word; and at the same time he continues subterraneously the very same tradition of ingenuous biblical exegesis whose allusion hunt and far-fetched methods of interpretation he so sarcastically parodies.

This duality in the rhetorical strategies of Zach, and its mirror image in Amichai, brings us, once again, to a fundamentally conservative moment in this iconoclastic allusive poetry of antitradition. Both Zach and Amichai, as well as the other poets who stand at the canonical center of the Statehood Generation, can be described as coming out of the tradition:[24] they are the harshest critics of the delusions of transcendent hope which tradition gives (Amichai) or of the illusion of meaning which its sacred language maintains (Zach). The one wishes to exalt the mundane and the secular, while deflating the traditional and sacred; the other wishes merely to thematize the tautological nature of all language and all thought. In this sense both place themselves outside of the indigenous tradition and in the mainstream of international modernism. But as reinterpreters and retellers of biblical, Talmudic, and liturgical allusions, in fact even as vociferous critics of the biblical God, they cannot help but identify themselves as evolving out of the same tradition which they so consistently fight. In this sense, Amichai and Zach and the other ambivalent Hebrew modernists are in the end familiar figures. They are the last in a long line of God's critics whom, like Job and Levi Yitzhak of Berdichev, the tradition has managed to pull into the mainstream.

PART THREE

Paragons from the Periphery

CHAPTER 6

Yehuda Amichai
On the Boundaries of Affiliation

In a complex early poem of the 1950s, "Through Two Points Only One Straight Line Can Pass" ("Derekh shtey nekudot over rak kav yashar echad"),[1] Yehuda Amichai combines geometrical theorems with astrological tales and images of love in a metaphysical style reminiscent of John Donne.[2] Yet the poem was set to music by a popular singer and became quite a hit in Israel in the 1970s, underscoring the popular success of Amichai's poetry. This poem, like quite a few others by Amichai, participates in a unique tradition—blending Middle Eastern and Eastern European custom—of blurring the distinction between poetry and song, of treating *shira* (poetry/song) as part of everyday experience.[3] Amichai's popular success (and the critical displeasure that it often elicits) also lies in the background of his ambivalent relation to literary modernism.

This ambivalence marks a contradictory set of orientations in Amichai's poetics. One orientation places antielitism at the center of his poetics; Amichai reduces both God and the sacred muse to life-size, sometimes bite-size, dimensions, and succeeds in generating a truly popular poetic voice able to reach people in the work-a-day world. Yet an opposite orientation within his poetry embraces much of the poetics of Anglo-American modernism, including the difficulty of classical allusion, highly figurative language, and syntactic fragmentation. These imported modernist prototypes in Amichai's poetry seem to deny or at least clash with the possibilities for a truly accessible populist poetics. Amichai does not simply oscillate between these two orientations; rather, he harnesses together both the popular

and the difficult within a systematic, unified poetics that problema-
tizes trend affiliation in general and the boundaries of modernism in
particular. Thus, while Amichai is the most central poet Israeli mod-
ernism has produced, he remains on the margins of his poetic trend
affiliation. How do these two contradictory orientations, simplisti-
cally construed as modernist and antimodernist, coexist, and how do
they combine in the actual poetic practice?

In the poem "Ve-hi tehilatekha" ("And That Is Your Glory") the
picture of God as a *garagenik,* a mechanic lying on his back under-
neath a world that keeps breaking down as if it were a lemon of a car,
creates a quotidian image that is at once populist and iconoclastic:

מִתּוֹךְ: וְהִיא תְּהִלָּתֶךָ

אֱלֹהִים שׁוֹכֵב עַל גַּבּוֹ מִתַּחַת לַתֵּבֵל,
תָּמִיד עָסוּק בְּתִקּוּן, תָּמִיד מַשֶּׁהוּ מִתְקַלְקֵל.
רָצִיתִי לִרְאוֹתוֹ כֻּלּוֹ, אַךְ אֲנִי רוֹאֶה
רַק אֶת סָלְיוֹת נְעָלָיו וַאֲנִי בּוֹכֶה.
וְהִיא תְּהִלָּתוֹ.

From: And That Is Your Glory

Underneath the world, God lies stretched on his back
always repairing, always things get out of whack.
I wanted to see him all, but I see no more
than the soles of his shoes and I'm sadder than I was before.
And that is his glory.

—Amichai (1962, 1977 ed.:71–72;
translated by Bloch and Mitchell in Amichai, 1986:11–12)

Framed by its title and refrain, the poem also alludes to an obscure
piece of liturgy for the Days of Awe that the average reader cannot
identify since it is not found in the abbreviated versions of the *mach-
zor,* the holiday prayer book many synagogue goers use. Amichai
alerts the reader to the allusive context by including a parenthetical
remark next to the title—"(from a liturgy for the Days of Awe)"—but
does not tell us where to find it, nor who the liturgical poet is. Fur-
thermore, the title and refrain require not only the identification of
this allusion but also a scholarly "excavation" of the rare paradoxical
meaning of *tohola* ("fault," "imperfection," as in Job 4:18) alongside

the normative sense of *tehila* ("praise," "glory"). The combination of the domestication of God and an intertextual, etymological critique constitutes Amichai's typical stance (see Arpali 1986:114–119). This bivalent position has led critics and readers alike to observe that Amichai's poetry is at once easy and difficult, accessible and elusive, familiar and strange. (See Tzvik, 1988:12–14, 29–30.)

Ironically, this simultaneous use of contradictory poetic beliefs is commonly associated with the conceptual structure of the category *modernism* in general. But Amichai's particular form of ambivalence leads him in part away from the modernism of his—and his generation's—Anglo-American prototypes. This further complication adds two interesting questions to an investigation of Amichai's poetics. First, how can the very ambivalence toward the modernist prototypes embedded in his poetry point to Amichai's own modernist affiliation? And, second, what use is it to talk about his modernism if the very turning away from one of its trends can itself be seen as a modernist practice? A closer examination of what it means for Amichai to be or not to be affiliated with Hebrew and international modernism might help shed some light on the particular ways in which he has come to serve as a paragon of his generation while remaining—in many important ways—on its margins.

The poetry of the entire third modernist wave of the Statehood Poets demonstrates an ambivalent position toward these complex trends. The explicit poetics (manifestoes, public proclamations) of Amichai's generation proclaimed it to be a late modernist, neoimagist grouping. However, the implicit poetics, reconstructed from the poets' actual works, contains many principles which subvert or go beyond the modernist stance, whether they are a reaction against the *moderna* of the pre-Statehood Generation or a partial withdrawal from—and modification of—the newly imported Anglo-American prototypes. These contradictory trends, though, are manifested much more fully in Amichai's own poetry than in the poetry of his fellow central poets of the Statehood Generation, in particular Nathan Zach, who along with Amichai and, somewhat later, Dahlia Ravikovitch is often identified as the core poet of this generation. Precisely for this reason Amichai's poetry and poetics offer an intriguing challenge to any attempt to view modernism on the model of marginal prototypes.

Modernism was always a self-referential literary movement, although this fact does not make self-reference itself into a sufficient condition for modernism.[4] The choice of affiliation among modernists

was usually quite deliberate and often entailed the compulsion either
to join or to form groups of like-minded artists, in what Douwe Fok-
kema (1984:11–12) has termed the "sociocode of modernism." Each
group would then usually provide public declarations of its explicit
poetics to distinguish itself from other groups. Not only do the icon-
oclastic manifestoes of Filippo Tommaso Marinetti and the Italian
futurists before the First World War set the stage for this type of
writing, but the futurists remain perhaps the most salient example of
the self-conscious, manifesto-publishing literary group; after the war
that role falls to the dadaists, who made the manifesto into a full-
fledged literary genre that embodies—again self-referentially—its
own necessary and imminent destruction. These modernist groups
were intent on supplying the readers as well as the critics with pro-
grammatic credos stating their aesthetic and ideological goals, goals
they often deviated from—in significant, even systematic, ways—in
the implicit poetics of their literary practice.

Amichai's generation of Hebrew modernist poets, led by the ac-
tivist paragon Zach, follow this familiar pattern, and perhaps because
of the trend's belatedness, their explicit poetics often read like self-
referential allusions to the famous "high-modernist" manifestoes.
Given all this, Amichai's participation in the formation of Statehood
Generation groupings remains highly ambivalent. He was a founding
member of *Likrat*, the modernist group whose magazine published
the neoimagists' works and manifestoes in Israel during the early
1950s. But Amichai himself never actually signed any public credos
and never wrote any manifestoes; to this day he regards himself as
only a marginal member of the *Likrat* group. His only credo, as he
once told an interviewer, is his noncredo: *ha-ani ha-lo ma'amin she-li*
("my nonbelieving I" or "my 'I don't believe' ").[5]

Amichai's ambivalent relation to *Likrat* is acknowledged even by
Zach, a cofounder of the group and its self-appointed spokesperson
throughout its various transformations. Even though Amichai never
publicly articulated a binding set of aesthetic principles for his own
poetry, Zach, always quite keen on the manifesto as a metapoetic
genre, points to Amichai as a salient prototype of Statehood Gener-
ation poetics. In Zach's major manifesto of 1966, titled "On the Sty-
listic Climate of the Fifties and Sixties in Our Poetry" and better
known as *tet-vav ha-nekudot* (the fifteen points), Zach (1966a) provides
a checklist of necessary and sufficient conditions for the poetry of his
generation. Zach's list is revealing precisely because this type of def-

inition cannot work for modernism or for that matter for any literary trend. With perhaps a touch of self-irony, Zach finds himself at once citing Amichai as the internal paragon, the most salient example of the third trend of Hebrew poetic modernism, and also acknowledging Amichai's deviation from the various strictures of the fifteen points.

In point (a), Zach prescribes: "Opposition to the quatrain,[6] because of its excessive symmetry and static nature." Zach then continues by citing an example from Amichai that, he claims, successfully breaks the "squareness" of the line. But Amichai clearly and consistently prefers the quatrain, especially in his early poetry, to which Zach refers in the 1966 manifesto. Zach is then forced to qualify his very first principle by saying that Amichai finds ways to break the static symmetry of the quatrain, especially through the use of enjambment, even while continuing to write stanzas in quatrains. Zach encounters similar trouble when he states in point (d) that free verse should be embraced as a rule for the generation's poetic goals. But he immediately qualifies the prescription by saying that Amichai's rhythms continue to be free even though, in this early period, they are often based on more or less regular tonic-syllabic metrical schemes. Zach cannot minimize the importance of Amichai within the neomodernism of the 1950s and 1960s, but he is forced to acknowledge that Amichai's implicit poetics provides a limit case for the explicit poetics that he, Zach, is trying to establish as the mainstream of the trend. While Amichai's poetry has since undergone many changes, his work continues to present complex challenges to any orthodox notions of literary affiliation.

Solutions to these challenges become especially elusive because Amichai rarely thematizes the aesthetics of poetry in his poems, or at least he never presents his poems as overt statements of metapoetic pronouncement. This fact in itself points to Amichai's ambivalent modernism since poems about poetry have often been considered by poets and readers alike as a quintessential modernist gesture; modernist poets have made poetry, modernity, metaphor, or poetic language in general the subject of their poems. From Paul Verlaine's "Ars Poétique" to Wallace Stevens's "Of Modern Poetry," modernists have used their poems to explore the aesthetic, philosophical, and even the most technical metapoetic questions about their work. In the entire corpus of Amichai's work, by contrast, only a handful of poems actually thematize the poetic process; and even these few present themselves as if they don't.

However, while Amichai shuns the metapoetic use of poetry, he does compensate for it with a meditative concern for language, ordinary language, especially the kind that is traditionally considered quite unpoetic. Grammatical constructions, everyday trite phrases, and word etymologies are commonly thematized by the speaker in Amichai's poetry. But despite this concentration on the possibilities of language, Amichai's speaker never presents himself as a poet contemplating the possibilities of poetic language; for Amichai, language never goes beyond the quotidian, the realness of the everyday and colloquial. Rather than make metapoetic assertions, Amichai's speaker consistently takes on the character of an ordinary human being thinking about ordinary language. His demystification of the written word and the concomitant privileging of ordinary discourse explain why for Amichai the poem about language replaces the poem on poetry, just as journalistic interview—with its emphasis on colloquial speech, dialogue, and direct communication between people—replaces the manifesto as metapoetic genre. The poet, Amichai said during a visit to the University of California at Berkeley in 1986, is the lowest of the low; but that, he added, is the greatest achievement a poet could possibly strive for. In typical Amichai fashion, which refuses to take on any elevated role for the poet, Amichai has always claimed that he writes poetry because he is too lazy to do anything harder. For the poet, as for the reader, poetry should be easy because it is ordinary language—not any privileged poetic diction—which is magical, inexhaustible, and, if one only pays attention, infinitely complex.[7]

The privileged and complex status accorded to ordinary language is brilliantly exhibited in the early poem "Sonet ha-binyanim" ("The Verb-Pattern Sonnet") (Amichai, 1962, 1977 ed.: 64–65). In this poem, Amichai offers a spectacular, utterly untranslatable account of life as changing grammatical constructions. The universal second-person addressee in the poem is caught within the structure of language, within the morphology of Hebrew verb forms, making the rocky journey from active to passive action, with a final, self-fulfilling stop in the reflexive. But the point is not the modernist and postmodernist cliché about the trap of the sign. Neither is this poem merely a series of puns on the traditional names of the patterns created by Hebrew verbs. Rather, through sustained verbal play with the correlation between the name of a pattern and its thematic, human significance Amichai seems to suggest, with perfect seriousness, a maximalist view of the power of dry, ordinary language. The triconsonantal roots and the verb patterns "built" around them[8] are the very core of the grammar of the Hebrew language. In this grammar—its precision, nuances, and modulations (Amichai often uses the adjective "precise," *meduyak,* derived from the same root as "grammar," *dikduk,* as a poetic—even romantic—compliment)—Amichai finds true poetry, material for the late modernist revival of the Hebrew sonnet. Taking a few basic roots through the dizzying transformations that make up Hebrew verb patterns, he also tells the story of a human life. The following verbs and paradigms diagram the transformations that constitute the journey of a life within the poem (X representing a consonant variable that can be filled by any lexical root in Hebrew):

Verb	Paradigm	Function
LIXOX	KAL	active
XAXUX	PA'UL	passive
NIX'AX	NIF'AL	middle voice/agentless
XAXEX	PI'EL	active
XU'AX	PU'AL	passive
MAX'IX	HIF'IL	causative
MOX'AX	HOF'AL	passive
MITXAXEX	HITPA'EL	reflexive

סוֹנֶט הַבִּנְיָנִים

לִכְתּוֹב, לִשְׁתּוֹת, לָמוּת. וְזֶה הַקַּל.
וּכְבָר אַתָּה פָּעוּל, אָהוּב, כָּתוּב.
עַד שֶׁעוֹשִׂים אוֹתְךָ: אַתָּה נִפְעָל:
נִבְרָא, נִשְׁבָּר, נִגְמָר, נִמְצָא וְשׁוּב

עֲלִילוֹתֶיךָ מִתְחַזְּקוֹת כָּל-כָּךְ
עַד לַפְעֵל: נַגֵּן, דַּבֵּר, שַׁבֵּר.
עוֹלָם הַמַּעֲשִׂים כֹּה יְסַבֵּךְ:
פָּעַל, שָׁבַּר, קִבַּץ, בְּלִי חוֹזֵר.

אַתָּה מַפְעִיל: הָאֲחֵרִים עוֹשִׂים
וְשׁוּב מָפְעָל בְּחִלּוּפֵי נִסִּים,
מַשְׁגִּיחַ וּמֻשְׁגָּח, מַלְהִיב, מָלְהָב.

וְרַק בַּסּוֹף אַתָּה חוֹזֵר אֶל עַצְמְךָ
וּמִתְבָּרֵר וּמִתְלַחֵשׁ, הַכֹּל מֻחְזָר,
בְּהִתְפָּעֵל וְהִתְקַפֵּל עַד שֶׁנִּגְמָר.

The importance of the poetic function of conjugation does not rest on the accuracy of the grammatical insight. After all, it is a gross oversimplification to assert such an automatic, predictable correlation between verb pattern and syntactic-semantic function in Hebrew. The main point of the poem is how "mere" grammar can be made to tell such a fascinating meditative story about life's processes. Drawing attention to the linguistic medium and orienting the reader toward the signifier rather than the signified are inherently modernist gestures; through a particularly modernist defamiliarization of semantic features within Hebrew, the poem forces the native reader to perceive grammar in a new, philosophically charged way. But the way Amichai expresses his point—the abandonment of standard thematic presentation in favor of an expressive thematization of grammar that follows a mimetic paradigm—both upholds and subverts basic modernist tenets at the same time. The valorization of language, its ability to express meaning and convey ontological truth, goes against the modernist concern with language's inability to signify (a position which Zach represents consistently).

Amichai's view that poetic language is no more creative and insightful than grammatical forms and the discourse of ordinary people becomes a central feature in another early poem, "El male' rachamim" ("God Full of Mercy") (Amichai, 1962, 1977 ed.:69–70). In this famous poem, however, Amichai speaks self-consciously about the relations of poet to language, especially concerning the problems of difficulty within a modernist poetic discourse. At one important and yet subdued moment in the poem, the speaker says of himself: *ani she-mishtamesh rak be-chelek katan min ha-milim she-ba-milon* ("I who use only a small part of the words in the dictionary"). This simple declaration reveals Amichai's ambivalent attachment to modernism. The speaker here objects to the poetics of difficulty so common to many modernist trends, from German expressionism to Anglo-American imagism and vorticism. He is just another member of the speech community, whose experiences with humans and with God have taught him the superiority of simple literal language to lofty poetic diction. Those experiences have taught him, as the title and first three lines suggest, to take the trite metaphor *el male rachamim* (God full of mercy) literally, thereby unmasking its inverse meaning: "God full of mercy, / If God weren't so full of mercy / There would be some mercy in the world and not just in him" ([1962] 1977 ed.:69; translation mine).

In his later work Amichai goes even further, radically challenging the very distinction between various forms of language—ordinary, poetic, scientific—and between linguistic action and real-life action. In the poem "Ba-yom she-bo nolda biti lo met af ish" ("On the Day My Daughter Was Born No One Died") Amichai obscures the typographic distinction between poetry and prose.

בַּיּוֹם שֶׁבּוֹ נוֹלְדָה בִּתִּי לֹא מֵת אַף אִישׁ

בַּיּוֹם שֶׁבּוֹ נוֹלְדָה בִּתִּי לֹא מֵת
אַף אִישׁ בְּבֵית הַחוֹלִים וְעַל שַׁעַר הַכְּנִיסָה
הָיָה כָּתוּב: "הַיּוֹם הַכְּנִיסָה לַכֹּהֲנִים מֻתֶּרֶת."
וְזֶה הָיָה בַּיּוֹם הָאָרֹךְ בְּיוֹתֵר שֶׁל הַשָּׁנָה.
וּמֵרֹב שִׂמְחָה
נָסַעְתִּי עִם יְדִידִי אֶל גִּבְעוֹת שַׁעַר הַגַּיְא.

רָאִינוּ עֵץ אֹרֶן חוֹלֶה וְחָשׂוּף מְכֻסֶּה רַק אִצְטְרֻבָּלִים אֵין סְפֹר. וּצְבִי אָמַר שֶׁעֵצִים הָעוֹמְדִים לָמוּת מַצְמִיחִים יוֹתֵר אִצְטְרֻבָּלִים מִן הַחַיִּים. וְאָמַרְתִּי לוֹ: זֶה הָיָה שִׁיר וְלֹא יָדַעְתָּ. אַף עַל פִּי שֶׁאַתָּה אִישׁ הַמַּדָּעִים הַמְדֻיָּקִים, עָשִׂיתָ שִׁיר. וְהֵשִׁיב לִי: וְאַתָּה, אַף עַל פִּי שֶׁאַתָּה אִישׁ חֲלוֹמוֹת עָשִׂיתָ יַלְדָּה מְדֻיֶּקֶת עִם כָּל הַמִּתְקָנִים הַמְדֻיָּקִים לְחַיֶּיהָ.

On the Day My Daughter Was Born No One Died

On the day my daughter was born not a single person
died in the hospital, and at the entrance gate
the sign said: "Today *kohanim* are permitted to enter."
And it was the longest day of the year.
In my great joy
I drove with my friend to the hills of Sha'ar Ha-Gai.

We saw a bare, sick pine tree, nothing on it but a lot of pine cones. Zvi said trees that are about to die produce more pine cones than healthy trees. And I said to him: That was a poem and you didn't realize it. Even though you're a man of the exact sciences, you've made a poem. And he answered: And you, though you're a man of dreams, have made an exact little girl with all the exact instruments for her life.

—Amichai (1980:44; translated by Bloch and Mitchell in Amichai, 1986:131–132)

The poem takes the form of a reported conversation between the speaker, an aging poet whose wife has just given birth to their daughter, and his scientist friend, Zvi. Within this dialogue, the poem builds an important analogy between the aging poet, who is still producing both poems and babies, and, on the hills at the outskirts of Jerusalem,[9] some dying pine trees that, as a matter of botanical fact, produce more pine cones than young, healthy trees; interestingly, the analogy is built as a traditional poetic simile. But in the dramatic situation of this poem, the poetic qualities of the simile are attributed to the spontaneous speech of Zvi, the scientist, who knows the right botanical facts about trees, and not to the conventions of the literary institution within which the reader ultimately finds this simile—namely, the poetic text. This reversal—on the level of theme—of the traditional roles of poetic and nonpoetic discourse is echoed closely in the generic structure of the text.[10] The poetic first stanza gives way to prose as the spontaneous speech of the scientist subverts the lyrical ruminations of the old poet. There is no sense here of a professionalization of language or poetry, or any sense of a necessity for difficulty in poetic discourse; the point of this poem is expressed clearly, meaningfully, and prosaically by a scientist, who within traditional terms is the opposite of the poet. Thus, an egalitarian view of the poetic language is effected, a view which is much more characteristic—within the Anglo-American models of Statehood Generation poetry—of the work of the antimodernist critics of elitist modernism: W. H. Auden, George Orwell, Philip Larkin, and others (see Lodge 1981: 3–16).

Amichai's redefinition of the poet's status may be motivated by specific reactions to traditional poetic models within the Hebrew literary system as well as to international modernist movements generally. In Chaim Nachman Bialik's premodernist verse, the poet is seen not only as a prophet but also as a mother, giving birth to the tear/poem/prophecy; clearly, Amichai's poetic persona, especially in a poem like "El male' rachamim" works against precisely this type of poetic model. But Amichai's poet equally distrusts the poet qua linguistic magician, a view that continues to predominate in the work of the *moderna* poets of the first wave of Hebrew modernism. Ironically, the motivations for Amichai to reject the elitism of a Pound, with all its subsequent links to fascism and antisemitism, also cause him to deny the special powers that had been attached to the Hebrew poet within a Jewish nationalist or socialist framework.

Shimon Sandbank (1976:173–214) and other critics, by showing the influence of Rainer Maria Rilke and Auden on Amichai, have pointed out the poetic complications that arise from these combinations of disparate influences and reactions. The specific qualities that can be associated with Rilke and Auden in Amichai's work demonstrate the ways in which selective modeling of modernist and antimodernist prototypes helps form Amichai's particular style of ambivalent modernism: Rilke as the paragon who represents Amichai's orientation toward protomodernist poetics; and Auden representing his tendency toward an antimodernist critique. Instead of creating a homogenized unity from the combined models of his predecessors, Amichai maintains the individual strands of each and uses the differences between them as a source of tension that informs his own discourse strategies. Thus, Amichai's need to maintain a rhetorical impression of accessibility remains consistent with the Auden prototype, while his emphasis on innovation, surprise, and reversal of conventional meaning stays true to the Rilke one. Amichai's use of Auden and his use of Rilke are closely interwoven and not in the least because, as Sandbank (1976) has shown, Auden himself, though critical of Rilke, was also greatly influenced by him.

Amichai's combination of readability and elusiveness, familiarity and surprise, is perhaps best illustrated by his unique use of metaphor. The long autobiographical *poema* "Travels of the Last Benjamin of Tudela" is an important but often neglected poem that reflects on many of the issues that Amichai faces as both a modernist and an antimodernist poet. It offers many excellent examples of Amichai's ambivalence through his use of metaphor. Metaphor, in effect, is the overarching principle of the poem's organization: a fragmented, simultaneous journey of the adult protagonist into "everything that I had," a nonlinear spiritual autobiography which is also "an autobiography of the world."[11] This journey to the past of the speaker and of his culture is modeled, metaphorically, on the travels of Benjamin of Tudela,[12] Amichai self-consciously placing himself at the end of this generic tradition. This parodic point of departure is significant, for in its intertextual cycles the very possibility of presenting a life—or a literal journey—in linear fashion is denied, at the same time that it is attempted again and again.

In the middle of the second strophe, as the speaker attempts for the first time to describe his childhood and capture what it was like to see the world through the eyes of a toddler, there appears a complex catalogue of similes which forces the adult perspective onto the child's:

מִתּוֹךְ: מַסְעוֹת בִּנְיָמִין הָאַחֲרוֹן מִטּוּדֵילָה

אַךְ כְּבָר אָז הָיִיתִי מְסֻמָּן לִכְלָיָה כְּתַפּוּז
לִקְלוּף, כְּשׁוֹקוֹלָדָה, כְּרִמּוֹן-יָד לְפִצּוּץ וָמָוֶת.

From: Travels of the Last Benjamin of Tudela

But even then I was marked for annihilation like an
     orange scored
for peeling, like chocolate, like a hand grenade for
     explosion and death

—Amichai ([1968] 1975:97;
translated by Bloch and Mitchell in Amichai, 1986:60)

The fragmented catalogue of similes is prototypical within modernist trends like expressionism and imagism in its focus on the simultaneous, paradigmatic aspects of language rather than on linear, syntagmatic, and logically coherent sequence. Furthermore, a striking semantic and stylistic distance between the frames of reference of the tenor and the first two versions of the vehicle within the catalogue enhances the initial incongruity of the two lines. The selection of the colloquial *shokolada* and *tapuz,* rather than their more formal equivalents, *shokolad* and *tapu'ach zahav,* for "chocolate" and "orange," respectively, contrasts with the grand and tragic *mesuman li-khlaya* ("marked for annihilation"). The switch mid-metaphor to metonymy with the third vehicle (a hand grenade) further complicates the figurative structure of the catalogue; the hand grenade—the instrument of death—is like the victim, implying perhaps that the child is destined not just to be killed but also to kill.

What first appears fragmented and distant—and ultimately modernist in its apparent incongruity and lack of cohesion—actually becomes closely integrated by intricate image schemas that mitigate or bridge the semantic distance between the terms of the metaphor. Various thematic and linguistic clues absorb the vehicles into a quasi-literal frame and thus, subverting modernist tendencies, make the metaphor simple and visually accessible despite its radical novelty.

For example, the visual and associative cohesion within the vari-

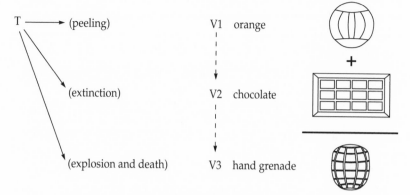

Fig. 4. Amichai's composite image schema (T = Tenor; V = Vehicle).

ous versions of the vehicle—orange, chocolate, and hand grenade—
reveals a composite visual collage that links the entire metaphoric
process (see Figure 4). The mapping of one image (the chocolate bar
divided into little squares) onto another image from the same domes-
tic realm (the orange scored for peeling) produces a visually realistic
motivation for the unexpected, deadly member of the catalogue (the
hand grenade). The hand grenade is "simply" a "mapping" of the
chocolate bar onto the orange scored for peeling, an inviting looking
chocolate orange. From a child's point of view, the adult's powerless-
ness before the inevitability of death is given shocking sensual im-
mediacy. In typical fashion, Amichai enhances the accessibility of this
metaphor through the use of junction words, polysemies which ap-
ply—in a different sense—to the domain both of the tenor and the
vehicle: the verb k-l-h ("finish off") is used with reference to both
chocolate and life. The poetic message seems to be that ordinary
language, not the poet's privileged sensibility, brings together the
mundane and the philosophical. Even more poignant is the use of
rimon yad as a junction term, returning it to the literal meaning ("hand
grenade" in Hebrew literally means "pomegranate of the hand");
thus, for one ironic moment the hand grenade becomes yet another
food item on the list.

The larger context of these charged lines enhances the realistic
motivation for the use of such radical figures of speech. The items in
the catalogue are, for the most part, selected from the immediate
experiential field of a child but seen from the war- and death-fearing

perspective of the adult. Hence the semantic distance between vehi-
cles in this catalogue of similes is simply a realistic expression of the
simultaneity of these two points of view, the child's and the adult's,
so common to the genre of autobiography. In the end, the combina-
tion of surprise and simplicity, or of the attempt to present the novel
and surprising as simple and readable, produces a uniquely cohesive
metaphor. Amichai's metaphors follow this same bifurcated pattern
of ease and difficulty throughout his poetry: at first, a wild, often
playfully violent conflation of heterogeneous semantic material but—
after a second look—a combination so natural that we begin to won-
der why no one has made it before.

We have seen in Chapters 4 and 5 similar effects created by Ami-
chai's uses of intertextuality to critique both the internal tradition of
decorous pastiche and the elitist classicism of Anglo-American mod-
ernist allusion. In "Two Hopes Away" Amichai again plays with
the combination of simplicity and complexity in one of his most favorite
intertextual domains: the biblical allusion. "Two Hopes Away" is part
of a quatrain cycle entitled "The Right Angle." All the quatrains in the
cycle are conceived with geometric precision as belonging in the right
angle "between a dead man and his mourner" (Amichai, 1962, 1977 ed.:
153; 1986:29). Death, war, and fire imagery become recurring motifs.
The quatrain "Two Hopes Away," the title poem for Amichai's second
book of poetry (1958), centers on the survivors and victims of the War
of Independence. But in several of the other quatrains in the cycle
Amichai extends this frame of reference to include those who survived
or perished in the German death camps of the Second World War.
Within this thematic setting Amichai introduces an allusion to the
epiphany of the burning bush in Exodus 3:

מִתּוֹךְ: בְּמֶרְחַק שְׁתֵּי תִקְווֹת

בְּמֶרְחַק שְׁתֵּי תִקְווֹת מִן הַקְּרָב, חָזִיתִי שָׁלוֹם.
רֹאשִׁי הֶעָיֵף מָכְרָח לָלֶכֶת, רַגְלַי חוֹלְמוֹת חֲלוֹם.
הָאִישׁ הַשָּׂרוּף אָמַר: אֲנִי הַסְּנֶה שֶׁבָּעַר וְאָכַל, גַּשָׁה הֲלֹם,
מַתֵּר לְךָ, הִשָּׁאֵר נְעָלֶיךָ עַל רַגְלֶיךָ. זֶה הַמָּקוֹם.

From: Two Hopes Away

Two hopes away from the battle, I had a vision of peace.
My weary head must keep walking, my legs dreaming apace.

The scorched man said, I am the bush that burned and that *was*
   consumed:
come hither, leave your shoes on your feet. This is the place.

—Amichai (1962, 1977 ed.: 153;
translated by Bloch and Mitchell in Amichai, 1986:28)

The most striking feature about this traditional allusion is, of
course, its antitraditional nature. The antitraditionalism of the allu-
sion is generated by a series of role reversals between the sacred and
the secular. The speaker of "Two Hopes Away" is a weary foot sol-
dier, hallucinating about peace a reified "two hopes away" from the
battle.[13] His is a thoroughly antiheroic epiphany, for he is no Moses,
and there is no God speaking from the burning bush. Rather, the
symbolic bush is replaced by the literally burnt/burning comrade.
But while there is no miracle, the very trial by fire makes the burnt
man—like Tiresias in Eliot's Fire Sermon in "The Waste Land"—into
the true oracle. There is no transcendent, sacred authority present
before whom the surviving soldier must remove his shoes, as he feels
compelled to do. Instead—and this is the point of the deflation of the
miraculous and of the sacred—it is he and his fellow soldiers that are
sacred; the power of the epiphany resides in them. In a play on words
that highlights precisely this reversed function of the sacred and the
profane, the speaker says, "This is the place," meaning also "this is
God," since *makom* is one of the common euphemistic names for the
deity. The divine promise of rescue from the enemy in the verses of
the evoked biblical text that follow the burning bush narrative is
deflated by its contrast with the emphasis on human suffering. More-
over, the human and divine roles are completely reversed, with the
poetic epiphany deeming the ordinary human victim the only truly
sacred authority.

Amichai's celebration of the ordinary and deflation of the sacred
becomes the larger ideological framework within which he articulates
a critique of modernism. But the anticlassicism of this particular al-
lusion is also an example of Amichai's rejection of the elitist, inten-
tionally difficult, use of allusion in Anglo-American modernism. How-
ever, this rejection does not allow Amichai to remove completely the
label of modernist. In a move that is also typically modernist, Amichai's
almost obsessive use of biblical and liturgical allusion demonstrates
that a poet can effect the simultaneous activation of two texts and their
implied contexts, thereby overcoming the linear confines of language.
Moreover, the poet can produce intricate, innovative, and iconoclastic

deviations from the norms and conventions set by those evoked texts, and yet appear perfectly lucid and completely accessible to the general reader or professional critic. Hovering on the borders of poetic affiliation, embracing modernism yet escaping it, Amichai seeks for the poet a state of syncategorematic existence, a state between ontological and aesthetic categories, a state he calls *beyna'yim* or "interims":[14]

מִתּוֹךְ: בֵּינַיִם

אֵיפֹה נִהְיֶה כְּשֶׁהַפְּרָחִים הָאֵלֶּה יַהַפְכוּ פֵּרוֹת
בַּבֵּינַיִם הַצָּרִים, כְּשֶׁפֶּרַח שׁוּב לֹא פֶּרַח
וְהַפְּרִי טֶרֶם פְּרִי. וְאֵיזֶה בֵּינַיִם נִפְלָאִים עָשִׂינוּ
זֶה לָזֶה בֵּין גּוּף לְגוּף. בֵּינַיִם עֵינַיִם בֵּין עֵרוּת לְשֵׁנָה.
בֵּינַיִם עַרְבַּיִם, לֹא יוֹם, לֹא לַיְלָה.

From: Interims

Where will we be when these flowers turn into fruit
in the narrow interims, when flower is no longer flower
and fruit not yet fruit. And what a wonderful interim we made
for each other between body and body. Interim eyes between
waking and sleep.
Interim dusk, neither day, nor night.

—Amichai (1989:35; translation mine)

CHAPTER 7

David Fogel and Moyshe Leyb Halpern

Liminal Moments in
Hebrew and Yiddish Literary History

David Fogel and Moyshe Leyb Halpern—what could these two radically different poets possibly have in common?[1] Even a cursory familiarity with their poetry is sufficient to establish the divergence of their poetic styles: the minimalist, introverted, and deceptively plain Hebrew free verse of *Ayefim anachnu, / nelkha-na li-shon* ("Weary are we, / let us go to sleep") (Fogel, [1966] 1975:253) versus the raucous, flagrantly rebellious, rhythmically and figuratively rich Yiddish poetry of *Mayn umru fun a volf un fun a ber mayn ru / Di vildkayt shrayt in mir, di langvayl hert zikh tsu* ("My restlessness is of a wolf, and of a bear my rest, / Riot shouts in me, and boredom listens") (Halpern, [1919] 1954:152; translation in Harshav and Harshav, 1986:401). However Fogel and Halpern are perhaps more alike than they initially appear; their respective rhetorical impressions may prove subversively misleading. (While the once symbiotic literary systems of Hebrew and Yiddish did, indeed, continue to maintain complex contacts during the modernist era,[2] my inquiry focuses on the roles of these two poets within the dynamics of modernism in their respective literary systems. The point of comparison, therefore, is intra- rather than intersystemic.)

Within the model of marginal prototypes outlined in Part 1, Fogel is portrayed both as a retrospective paragon for the third trend of Hebrew modernism, the Statehood Generation neoimagist poets, and also as one of the few acknowledged representatives of a repressed prototype of marginal modernism, the antiformulaic first wave of Hebrew modernism comprised primarily of non-Zionist male and

Zionist female Hebrew poets. Halpern was construed as a proleptic paragon for the introspectivists in New York, the generation of modernist Yiddish poets that followed his own; and, from a synchronic perspective, within his own group, the aestheticist/impressionist poets who made up *di yunge* ("the young ones"), Halpern was seen as a deviant paragon. He was the "odd man out," "the mischievous rebel within this movement of self-declared rebels" (Wisse, 1980:36). Both poets offer dramatic illustrations of the importance of limit cases and transitional prototypes for the formation and crystallization of literary trends in general and modernism in particular.

There is, however, a more concrete point to be made about the relationship between the poets' marginal prototypicality and the periodization of modernism in Hebrew and Yiddish poetry. Both Fogel and Halpern published their first books of poetry at the time of the beginnings of modernism within their "indigenous" poetic systems.[3] Yet this time period is already considered the height of modernism within the mainstream of the central and eastern European literary systems to which each poet maintains strong links.[4] The "international time lag," so characteristic of the intercultural dimensions of modernism in general, places Fogel and Halpern, particularly in their early poetry, at a crucial literary-historical conjuncture: on the fuzzy boundaries between pre- or protomodernism and modernism proper, or, more specifically, in a self-conscious oscillation between impressionist and expressionist literary prototypes. Their poetry and poetics elaborate and thematize this oscillation in incompatible, even contradictory, ways. Yet the salience of *glissements* between premodernism and modernism in their work is itself a decidedly modernist tendency within their specific literary and cultural contexts.

In order to understand the social and cultural background for Fogel's and Halpern's modernist hesitation on the threshold of modernism, some light needs to be shed on the manner in which each poet either resisted the allure of or was excluded from the dominant trends of contemporary literary systems. For Fogel, a famished, uprooted perpetual wanderer through Europe's modernist centers, the very decision to become a Hebrew poet was an act of self-marginalization and self-modernization.[5] Unlike his near contemporaries, the *moderna* Hebrew poets, who participated in shifting the center of Hebrew literature from Europe to prestatehood Palestine and were actively involved in the politics and praxis of labor Zionism, Fogel was never truly committed to or actively involved in any branch of Zionism.

Throughout his life he remained ideologically, though not aestheti-
cally, alienated from the linguistic-national Hebrew revival. Robert
Alter has argued persuasively in *The Invention of Hebrew Prose* (1988:
72) that Hebrew was to become for Fogel, as for other antiformulaic
writers, a road into international modernism, "a calling card that gave
them entry to the great polyglot salon of European culture, as if to say:
We belong here as equals, and we are proud to display our original
address."[6] Yet Hebrew, as well as Yiddish, poets would always re-
main in a remote corner of this great polyglot salon; they would
hardly have been able to engage in very much modernist mingling,
given that while they could understand the language of the other
guests, no one could comprehend theirs. The examples of Fogel and
Halpern, the great neglected paupers of Jewish literature, call into
question the possibility of transgressing socially and economically
determined marginality and achieving equality even within those
prototypes of international modernism which purport to privilege
exile, periphery, and multilingualism.

Fogel's Hebrew diary,[7] which spans roughly ten years in the young
poet's life (1912–22) and breaks off significantly just before the pub-
lication of his first book of poetry, expresses his total alienation from
any of the collective settings that cultivated Hebrew letters during
that period, be they traditional/religious or modern/Zionist. On the
day after Yom Kippur in 1912, feeling like an exile in his hometown
of Satanov (having been deported back there from Vilna, where he
had been studying Hebrew), Fogel writes: "Yesterday I was in the
synagogue but nothing at all from the prayers left an impression on
me" (1990:272). A couple of weeks later, having stolen across the
border to Lemberg [Lvov], the Galician capital of Hasidic Jewry, he
describes his anguish in the form of hatred for the community to
whose children he must teach Hebrew in order to survive: "I hate
Lemberg and its Jews with their sidecurls down to their shoulders"
(1990:275). In Vienna in 1913, on the eve of the Zionist Congress, he
expresses an acerbic optimism, couched in language that blatantly
precludes identification with Zionism as the possible source of that
optimism: the Zionist Congress is a source of joy simply because it
provides temporary employment to the starving young poet. Able to
work for a living (as a porter or doing odd jobs for the Jewish National
Fund), Fogel receives a short-lived break from his usual hunger:
"[The Congress] has removed to some extent the philosophy of hun-
ger from me. And I'm hoping to be rid of it [the philosophy of hunger]

at least for this month: Days of the Zionist Congress, days of profit. . . . Yes, the last period has been so terrible in its famine, I've been so hungry that my hair started falling out. . . . Just as in the novel by Knut Hamsun. Yes, those were the days" (1990:299). The sarcastic reference that elevates hunger to a philosophy and its "aestheticiza-tion" in Hamsun's influential novel *Hunger*[8] are very much in the spirit of traditional Yiddish humor. They also suggest a self-conscious critique of the romantic stereotype of the tormented poet-philosopher who needs to suffer and starve in order to attain a higher level of spiritual creativity.

Interestingly, around this time Fogel contemplated emigration to Eretz Israel but in a context that could not be less enthusiastic: "[S]ometimes when my patience dwindles, I would like to run away from here even to the bottom of hell (*she'ol tachtiya*) or to the end of the world (*le-afsey tevel*): to America, to Argentina, to Brazil, to Eretz Israel, it makes no difference where, just to run away, not to be here" (1990:291). It is not accidental that Fogel lists Eretz Israel here as the last item in a catalogue of escape routes metaphorically located in hell or at the end (literally: zeros, nullity) of the world. Indeed, sixteen years later his attempt to escape poverty and isolation by emigrating to Palestine would fail miserably. Feeling like a refugee in Tel Aviv even more than in any of the European capitals he had wandered through, Fogel would leave Palestine merely one year after his emi-gration, more isolated and despondent than when he came, never to return.

Yet the same diary also evinces the extraordinary single-minded-ness and zeal with which Fogel carried out his plan to mold himself into an unaffiliated modernist Hebrew poet: he starts from his sys-tematic study of Hebrew in Vilna (what he nostalgically refers to as his "Vilnaese metamorphosis," *ha-gilgul ha-vilna'i*[9]) through his self-styled apprenticeship in German and western European literature, all the while struggling with hunger, unemployment, homelessness, and the early stages of tuberculosis. As Alter (1988:75) points out, even the geography of his wanderings almost seems part of this literary self-education: "He sojourns briefly in Vilna, then Odessa, Lemburg, and beginning in 1912, in Vienna, as if on an inadvertent pilgrimage of the major way stations of Hebrew literature in Europe." Yet it would be critically naive to portray Fogel's social and ideological isolation, and his lifelong indigence, as poetic choices, calculated steps in a plan for self-modernization. Ultimately, Fogel's death at the hands of the

Nazis in 1944 underscores how involuntary his "victimhood" was throughout his life.

Similar dangers need to be avoided in characterizing Halpern's inability to find a well-paying job or to cooperate with the Yiddish literary and political establishment of New York—and the horrible destitution this entailed for him and his family—as a willful modernist retreat to the margins.[10] The sustained ambivalence and sarcastic tone of Halpern's poetry, as well as his journalistic and personal writing, have perpetuated the critics' tendency to equate his poetics of rebellion with a biographical refusal "to settle down." Furthermore, the blurring of the borders between self-directed criticism and social protest, a central thematic tension in Halpern's work, tends to be interpreted reductively within a critical tradition that is highly biographical: the poet, unable to care for his wife and child, tries to blame his inadequacies on the general social and political condition only to realize in the end that he himself is to blame. This is a gross oversimplification of the social and poetic critique so inexorably intertwined in Halpern's work and expressed with vivid rhetorical ambivalence even in his early personal correspondence.

In a letter dated July 23, 1917, to Royzele Baron, who was later to become his wife, Halpern describes his social and economic hardships through a series of metapoetic images that oscillate typically between ruthless self-irony and biting social protest:

> Perhaps it is only the lyrical poet who coquettishly shows off his suffering like a clown toying with the bells on his cap, or like a pauper who jingles the few coins in his pocket so others would believe he has golden riches?
>
> For, after all, there still exists the light of day, not only night. And I'm not yet old enough to say that everything is nothing. But the truth is that the lighter the day, the darker my hope becomes. And not because everything is nothing, but rather because everything is a lot! And if there is something which is nothing—then I am it, I alone who have been wandering around for ten years already, together with ten million other people, like one huge hunk of raw meat, in the lumbering *garbage can:* New York. (Quoted in Greenberg, 1942:67; translation mine; italics in the original).[11]

The first simile of poet and clown pitilessly questions the poet's transformation of his suffering into aesthetic material by exposing the poem as manipulative exhibitionism. The deflating image of the bells on his clown's (jester) cap (*vi a payats mit di gleklekh fun zayn mitsl*) renounces any pretense to lasting aesthetic value. This theme recurs throughout Halpern's poetry: a fierce self-critique of the poet's social helplessness and inevitable complicity in an oppressive structure by aestheticizing his own suffering and that of the oppressed working classes.[12] Yet the second simile in the letter, which is presented in typically disjunctive-interrogative syntax as a hypothetical alternative to the first, is already much more ambiguous with respect to the poet's responsibility: *oder vi a kabtzn vos klingt mit di etlekhe groshn in keshene kedey mentchen zoln gloybn az er iz raykh in gold?* ("or like a pauper [beggar] who jingles the few coins in his pocket so others would believe he has golden riches?"—literally, "that he is rich in gold?"). The first part of the image appears to reiterate the first simile and still depict the poet as a beggar who uses his destitution to increase his appeal. Once we get to the end of the sentence, however, the meaning seems, almost imperceptibly, to have been reversed: the poet now describes himself as a proud pauper who hides his poverty by jingling the few coins in his pocket as if they were a golden treasure. Characteristic also of Halpern's later poetry, these two contradictory readings are made possible by the lexical ambiguity of *kabtzn*, meaning both "beggar" and "pauper," and by the "associative concatenation" of syntax, which shifts the situation mid-sentence.[13] The result is a simultaneous condemnation and exoneration of the poet's marginality.

The second paragraph evokes a similar tension between two opposing views of the poet at the social and economic periphery of his community. The first view is expressed through a sardonic allusion to old Solomon's proclamation: "Vanity of vanities; all is vanity" (Ecclesiastes 1:2). The young poet cannot hide behind the nihilism of "everything is nothing"[14] precisely because, within the social context of the immigrants' struggle to survive in an urban consumer society, "everything is a lot." At this point Halpern appears to conclude, as expected, that "if there is something which is nothing—then I am it," internalizing the blame as well as the value system which treats people as commodities and a lack of assets as evidence of personal worthlessness. But within the apposite sentence which expands on this personal nothingness, the relative clause completely reverses the direction of the argument: the poet who starts out saying "I alone [am nothing]" ends up describing his lonely (*aleyn*, oscillating here between an adjectival and an adverbial use) wandering—and that of millions of others—in the lumbering garbage can (the Yiddish is brutally expressive and quite untranslatable here: *umgelumpertn mist-kastn*) called New York. The final simile also sustains two different readings, and again this duality is made possible through a combination of syntactic ambiguity and lexical polysemy. In one sense the poet is saying: I have been wandering all alone, like a big lump of live flesh or raw meat (*lebedike fleysh*) in this dirty (garbage-can-like) metropolis, and there are millions of others just like me. In another sense he is also saying: together with (as one with) (*in eynem*) millions of others who share my destitution and isolation from mainstream society, we form one huge hunk (*eyn groys shtik*) of raw meat, discarded by the affluent culture and thrown into the lumbering urban garbage can, New York City. Not only does this final twist place the responsibility for poverty and marginality away from its victims, it also suggests, in the image of the unified human mass of raw/live meat/flesh, the potential for insurgent power which is latent within it.

Halpern: Deviant Paragon, Proleptic Paragon

In his mature poetry, especially in the genre that Benjamin Harshav (1990:107) has aptly named "political talk-verse," Halpern achieves a systematic blurring of the borderline between the poetic speaker's critical introspection into his personal marginality and "an existentialist-anarchist slashing at life in general and at American capitalism in particular" (1990:107). This self-styled genre, and the peculiar thematic ambivalence associated with it, is already dominant in his first volume of poetry, *In New York*. This book established Halpern as the deviant paragon among his contemporaries, *di yunge*, and as a proleptic paragon for the introspectivists, who reacted against them. As Kathryn Hellerstein points out in the introduction to her volume of translations from Halpern, *In New York: A Selection* (Halpern, 1982:xiii), "[T]he struggle between the poet's responsibility to self and to community culminates in the final and most ambitious poem of the book, 'A Night,' where the protagonist dreams himself into a collective, historical voice, with which he tells simultaneously the stories of the poet and of his people." An early version of "A Nakht" appeared in 1916, in the *yunge* anthology Halpern coedited with Menachem Boreysho, *East Broadway* (1916:20–60). Four years later a new group of introspectivist poets published their own poetic credo in the journal *In Zikh,* blasting Halpern—as one of the leaders of *di yunge*—but at the same time formulating artistic principles for which "A Nakht"—as well as many of Halpern's earlier and later poems—serves as a latent but rather obvious example.

Halpern's poem provides a particularly intriguing reworking of the materials and techniques first introduced in his letter to Baron. The poem takes significant steps to subvert the aestheticist harmonies of *di yunge* and to offer an overtly expressionist, apocalyptic alternative to their poetry of "quietude."[15] "A Nakht" is often taken to be an antiwar epic, in which the pacifist Halpern declares the impending ruin of Europe. Ruth Wisse writes that the poem was "[s]et equally against both sides of the war [World War I], . . . [and] concentrated on the destruction itself. The result was a fevered work of apocalyptic doom in which all of European civilization disintegrates with the Jews in its midst" (Wisse, 1988:95). Wisse's remark most likely captures the circumstances of the poem's composition; however, as a reading of the poem, it presupposes the very distinctiveness of the personal and the collective that Halpern's work disrupts. Wisse's reading therefore remains an essentially premodernist interpretation of the articulation of the relationship between personal fate and historical condition: the death of the speaker is seen as a microcosmic reflection of the macrocosmic destruction of an entire civilization. David Roskies offers a different, and more appropriate, description of the poem as "the *conflation* of two nightmares, one personal the other historical" (1984:95, emphasis added). If the poem's figurative language, syntax, and manipulation of point of view are taken seriously and if the location of "A Nakht" at the end of an architectonically structured book whose title is *In New York* is systematically explored, then the poem emerges as an "experimental verse narrative" (Hellerstein in Halpern, 1982: xiv) which—much like Eliot's "The Waste Land"—forms a new modernist poetic prototype. As in "The Waste Land" and other radically modernist long poems, the poetic world view of Halpern's "A Nakht" emanates from the structure of the text.

In an important but often neglected article, Seth Wolitz (1977) has argued that in its conception and organization, Halpern's first book, *In New York,* projects this type of modernist world view. The book's organization brings together three distinct levels of meaning within each poem. Thus, as the book moves from beginning to end, each poem acts within all three separate continua, creating a rather complex systematic structure that multiplies levels of meaning within any particular poem along several different paths throughout the book as a whole. These three levels, while related in that they can be seen within each poem, are actually quite distinct:

1. natural time—one day in the life of a foreigner, from morning to night,
2. the life of the *Poète Maudit* from childhood to death,
3. the generational epic repetition of the ejection from the Garden of Eden into the exile of Israel. (Wolitz, 1977:62)

These three architectonic levels are articulated through the arrangements of poems in the book. The book is divided into five sections, starting with morning/childhood/the Garden of Eden (in the first section called "In Our Garden") and ending with night/death/exilic apocalypse (the last section of the book, comprising the twenty-five part poem, "A Nakht").[16]

Contrary to Wolitz's claim, however, this three-tiered organization hardly effects a harmony of symbolist "correspondences," of the kind *di yunge* would have appreciated. Instead, the mixed-up simultaneity of all three levels, the mélange of voices and masks, and the fragmented iterability of all points of view create the cumulative, "jagged, episodic narrative" (Hellerstein, in Halpern 1982:xiv). While individual early poems incorporated by Halpern into this new book in 1919 may preserve some of the aestheticist, impressionist, and symbolist norms of the *yunge* model, the later poems, such as "A Nakht," and the overarching structure of the book as a sustained composite narrative introduce into Yiddish poetry new expressionist and postsymbolist prototypes.

When "A Nakht" is read as the culmination of the book-length portrait that Wolitz aptly calls a *neshome-landshaft* (soulscape) of *In New York,* it can no longer be construed according to premodernist, realist norms as a vision of the destruction of Europe and its Jews (although this theme is certainly an important part of the work). Rather, the poem is both a projection and an interiorization of that vision, an expressionist montage of the war theme on top of other fragments of personal and collective existence. The vision is split spatially between eastern Europe, the speaker's bedroom in New York, and a mythopoetic Middle East; it takes place simultaneously in the present, in an undetermined series of historical-mythical pasts, and in a mock-apocalyptic future. Nonlinear space and time are all refracted within the speaker, who is both asleep and wide awake, and whose identity is divided between the detached third-person narrator, the elegiac first-person participant in individual and historical destruction, and the discordant *mentshele,* the humunculus as "brilliant master of ceremonies," whose nihilistic hokum is "more chilling than the barbarism he describes" (Wisse, 1988:96–97). Halpern transforms typical Yiddish discourse strategies into a highly intricate art form: the dialogic monologue, the question as indirect speech act, the ironic quotation, and the digressive, associative concatenation of syntax (Harshav, 1990:98–116). All of this takes place within a decadently rich prosodic framework, which for *di yunge* was part of a serious attempt to turn literary Yiddish into a refined instrument of high-brow culture, but which in the context of "A Nakht" has a chilling, morbid effect.[17] Section XX offers an untranslatable thematization of this contrast between prosodic and semantic structure in the *danses macabres* of fragmented victims and the disembodied acts and tools of victimizers.[18]

The early letter to Baron expressed the inseparability of a personal sense of responsibility for the poet/pauper's nothingness and a collective protest against the system that discards its human resources as so much raw meat in the garbage can called New York. Now, in "A Nakht" the kaleidoscopic objectification of the personal and social perspectives is refracted in a series of harrowing narrative elaborations that systematically erase distinctions among all the realms involved in the narrative.

פֿון: אַ נאַכט XX

שטעלט מען זיך אָפּ אויף אַ שנייאיקן פֿעלד,
לאָזט מען מיך איבער אַליין.
קומט אויף אַ קוליע, פֿאַרבונדן דעם קאָפּ,
דאָס מענטשעלע ווידער צוגיין.

רופֿט עס מיך קעניג, און נויגט זיך פֿאַר מיר,
און פֿרעגט נאָך מײַן ווונטש, מײַן באַגער.
זאָג איך אים: – זעסט דאָך אַז איך בין אַליין,
און רירן זיך קאָן איך ניט מער.

טוט ער אַ ווונק – קומט, פֿון זעלנער געיאָגט,
אַ נאַקעט סקעלעט פֿון דער ווײַט.
הייבט עס די פֿיס, ווי בײַ נאַכט אין אַ שענק
אַ מויד צווישן שיכורע לײַט.

הייבט עס די פֿיס און עס טאַנצט אַרום מיר,
טאַנצט עס און זינגט מיט געברום:
– אַזוי זאָל זיך דרייען דער טויט אַרום דיר
אין אייביקן רעדל אַרום. –
. . . .

קומען אָן ביימער פֿון איטלעכער זײַט,
וויגן זיך טויטע אויף זיי.
וואַרפֿט זיך אַרויף אויף די ביימער דער ווינט,
וואַרפֿט אויף די טויטע מיט שניי.

שטעלן די טויטע זיך אויס אין אַ ראָד
אַזוי ווי מען שטייט פֿאַר אַ טראָן:
– געטאָן זאָל זיך דיר ווערן דאָס אייגענע בייז,
וואָס אונדז איז געוואָרן געטאָן.

אויף אייביק פֿאַרוויסט זאָל פֿאַרבלײַבן די ערד,
וווּ דו האָסט געשפּונען דײַן טרוים.
זאָל הענגען דאָרט, אָן אַ פֿאַרוואָס, אַלע נאַכט
אַן אַנדערער אונטער דײַן בוים.

און שטרעקסטו דײַן האַנט אַ פֿאַרבענקטער אַהין –
געליימט זאָל דיר ווערן דײַן האַנט.
דערשטיקט זאָלסטו ווערן אין מיטן פֿון וואָרט,
ווען דו וועסט דערמאָנען דאָס לאַנד.

און שטאַרבנדיק זאָלסטו אַרומוואָגלען אויך,
און קיינמאָל געשטאָרבן ניט זײַן,
דערפֿאַר וואָס דו שלעפּסט מיט דײַן קעניגס-טרוים אונדז
אָן אויפֿהער, לאַנד-אויס און לאַנד-אײַן. –

הער איך די טויטע מיך שילטן אַזוי,
וויין איך און שעלט זיך אַליין.
פֿאַלט פֿון די טויטע דאָס אמן אויף מיר,
אַזוי ווי אַ שטיין נאָך אַ שטיין.

קומט אין אַ ליידיקן וואָגן געשפּאַנט
אַ פֿערד, ווי דער שניי אַזוי ווײַס.
הענגט אים געפֿרוירן דאָס בלוט פֿונעם מויל,
גלאַנצט אויף זײַן גריווע דאָס אײַז.

שטרעק איך צום מענטשעלע אויס מײַנע הענט,
קוקט עס מיך אָן אַזוי קאַלט.
זע איך דעם וואָגן פֿאַרזונקען אין שניי,
זע איך דאָס פֿערד ווי עס פֿאַלט.

טראָגט זיך אַ קול דורכן ווינט, דורך דער נאַכט,
רופֿט עס – אָהאַי! – און – אָהאַ! –
קוק איך זיך אום, אין דער ווײַט, אין דער ברייט
איז שוין מער קיינער ניטאָ.

From: A Night, XX

So they stop on a snowy field,
and leave me behind alone.
Along comes on a crutch, head bandaged,
that Little Man again.

It calls me king, it bows low,
asks my every wish and desire.
I tell him:—you see I'm alone,
and can't move anymore.

He winks—and along comes, chased by soldiers,
a naked skeleton from afar.
Lifts its legs, like a woman at night
in a bar among drunken men.

Lifts its legs and dances around me,
dances and sings in a growl:
—Death should go around you like this
with its eternal wheel.—

. . . .

Trees come closing in from every side,
cradling corpses in their limbs.
The wind turns against the trees,
charges at the corpses with snow.

The corpses line up in a circle
as if standing before a throne:
—may the same evil be done to you,
that has been done to us.

Forever barren may the earth remain,
upon which you have spun your dream.
May there hang every night, without a reason why,
another man from your tree.

And if you should stretch out a longing hand over there—
may your hand be struck numb.
May you choke to death in the middle of your word,
when you mention the name of this land.

And dying you'll go on wandering,
and never be dead and done,
for you drag us along with your royal dream
without end, land in, land out.—

As I hear the dead cursing me so,
I cry and curse myself.
The corpses' last Amen drops on me,
like stone after stone.

Hitched to an empty wagon
a horse comes along, white as snow.
From its mouth the blood hangs frozen,
on its mane gleams the ice.

I stretch my hand out to the little man,
it stares back at me so cold.
I see the wagon sinking in snow,
I see the horse as it falls.

A voice carries through the wind, through the night,
it calls—Ahoy!—and—O ho!—
I look around me, far and wide,
and there is no one there anymore.

                    —Halpern (1919, 1954 ed.:215–17; translation mine)

As the metapoetic dimension of this section suggests, "[T]he dead cannot forgive the survivor the rhetorical web of deceit that has been spun around them, and they curse their would-be elegist" (Wisse, 1988:96). But it is the gallows humor, the wink of the naked skeleton, the sarcasm of the *mentshele* that ties the critique of the poet's aestheticization of horror to its brutally unadorned depiction:

פֿון: אַ נאַכט XV

אָנגעוווירן האָט דײַן ברודער,
נעבעך, ביידע הענט אין שלאַכט.
קען ער זיך שוין מער ניט קראַצן –
נעמט אים ניט קיין שלאָף בײַנאַכט.

From: A Night, XV

Your own brother, poor thing
lost both his hands at war.
Now he doesn't sleep at night
since he can't scratch himself anymore

—Halpern (1919, 1954 ed.:
200; translated by Wisse, 1988:96)

The Yiddish poet Malka Heifetz Tussman, herself an important liminal figure whose career spans several modernist trends, in referring to Halpern's ironic multiple voices and the unique role humor fulfilled for him, described this rhetorical strategy as "laughing on the wrong side of the mouth" (literally: "laughing with lizards," in the wonderful Yiddish idiom, *lakhn mit yashtsherkes*), "a tortured, automatic laughter" in which Halpern "[a]t once ridicules both the world and himself, for he is the world" (quoted by Hellerstein in Halpern, 1982:xiii).

This connection between self-ridicule and "world-ridicule" and the thoroughly expressionist motivation given to it ("for he is the world") may help explain the significance Halpern's poetic and rhetorical innovations had for his supposed rivals, the younger poets of the introspectivist group, of which Heifetz Tussman was an important member. One of the introspectivists' major principles, formulated in their first manifesto of 1919 (*In Zikh*, [1919] 1920; translated in Harshav and Harshav, 1986:774) reads: "The world exists and we are part of it.[19] But for us, the world exists only as it is mirrored in us, as it touches *us*. The world is a non-existent category, a lie, if it is not related to us. It becomes an actuality only *in* and *through* us. This general philosophical principle is the foundation of our trend. We will try to develop it in the language of poetry." As Yankev Glatshteyn ([1919] 1920), the leading introspectivist poet, was later to acknowledge, this general philosophical principle had already reached significant development in the poetry of their predecessor, the odd man out among *di yunge*:

Halpern. In other words, from Halpern's implicit poetics, from the poetic principles embedded in and inferred from his actual literary practice, the introspectivists derive an important tenet of their explicit poetics, even before they had published any poetry as a group.[20]

Halpern's closeness to the introspectivists can also be seen in the social, political, and anti-aestheticist elaboration of this principle in the introspectivists' theoretical and critical writings. Later on in the same introspectivist manifesto the poets declare the inseparability of the personal and the collective, the emotional and the social:

> For us, then, the senseless and unproductive question of whether a poet should write on national or social topics or merely on personal ones does not arise. For us, everything is "personal." Wars and revolutions, Jewish pogroms and the workers' movement, Protestantism and Buddha, the Yiddish school and the Cross, the mayoral elections and a ban on our language; . . . we write about ourselves because all these exist only insofar as they are in us, insofar as they are perceived *introspectively.* (Translated in Harshav and Harshav, 1986:779)

As Harshav correctly observes, "This is not an escapist, ivory tower poetry" (1990:178). The introspectivists' ideas echo precisely the kaleidoscopic refraction of levels of history and personal experience in the *neshome-landshaft* (soulscape) of Halpern's speaker. Yet when the composers of the first introspectivist manifesto single out paragons from among their precursors, Halpern is not one of them. Instead, they mention Halpern as a run-of-the-mill member of *di yunge,* whose poetry has lost its relevance and vitality.

In rejecting the aestheticist ossification of their immediate predecessors,[21] the introspectivists turn, in keeping with the formalist model, to the avuncular path, to a contemporary of *di yunge* who was associated with a faction one critic has called the "sober" poets: "As with the older writers, here too there is an exception—namely, H. Leyvik. Leyvik is only in part one of the Young Generation. From the first, he introduced so much that is individual—and even profound—that there can be no talk of his stopping, of his having already completed his poetic mission [like the rest of *di yunge*]. We regard him, too, as being close to us" (in Harshav and Harshav, 1986:783). Only in Glatshteyn's series of essays in the first two numbers of the introspectivist journal *In Zikh* ([1919] 1920) is Halpern mentioned explicitly alongside Leyvik as an exception to the destructive and deadening influence of *di yunge,* epitomized by Mani Leyb's aestheticist poetics of "quietude" (see Wisse, 1988:21–44ff): "Among his [Mani Leyb's] small, helpless imitators, linguistic "Mani Leybism" has spawned a dead language without the slightest breath of the spoken word. Except for two—[Leyvik] with his simplicity and Halpern with his vulgarity, vitality, and mobility—the language of all other *Yunge* is colorless and lifeless, despite the plaudits so many have heaped on them for having given us a finer linguistic tool."[22]

These attempts to find an appropriate paragon within the rejected paradigm point to a perception of heterogeneity within the poetic voices and styles of this earlier paradigm. In part this situation results from the unusually sophisticated theoretical (and not only programmatic) orientation of two of the main introspectivists: Avrom Glantz-Leyeles and Glatshteyn; it is also a function of the anomalous proximity of one "generation" of Yiddish modernist writers to the other and their intimate knowledge of each others' internal struggles and rifts.

Wisse (1988:ch. 3) offers a fascinating description of the tensions within *di yunge* and the ways Mani Leyb, Halpern, and Leyvik represented different aestheticist/symbolist prototypes. She reveals a three way split within *di yunge:* the core of the group centered on Mani Leyb and his poetics of quietude; the "sober faction," eventually led by Leyvik, who criticized Mani Leyb's and David Ignatoff's "slippered smugness, their dustiness, their spitting into the alien cold" (Leyvik, 1919:33); and the "ironic faction" of Halpern and Moyshe Nadir, whose work for the humor magazines and whose German (rather than Russian) influences made them "[s]keptical of both the efficacy of art and the possibilities of a refined literature in an immigrant vernacular" (Wisse, 1988:52–55). In terms of the prototype model, it seems that this struggle was inevitable among the various strands. From the start this heterogeneous group maintained only a tenuous family resemblance among its members: the competing contemporaneous prototypes of (Germanic) poetic impressionism, aestheticism (or art for art's sake), symbolism (of a Russian model), and decadence. By 1918 Halpern, the poet most closely associated with the German rather than the Russian models, was already shifting into a dominantly expressionist prototype which made him a proleptic paragon for the introspectivists. Halpern's newly found salience as an artistically unaffiliated and politically committed *poète maudit* at the very time—indeed during the same years—that the introspectivists were trying to establish themselves may explain why his status as a paragon was never fully recognized until after his death.

Because of the poetic closeness between Halpern and the introspectivists, it may be possible to conclude that the proximity of the publication of Halpern's first book to the appearance of the innovative *in zikh* manifestoes was not a mere coincidence. This is not to say that the individual introspectivist poets owe all their inventiveness to Halpern nor that the publication of *In New York* is directly responsible for the introspectivist credo. Clearly, as the *in zikh* group itself always declared, these new modernist poets saw themselves as part of the broad range of movements that made up international Euro-American modernism. They themselves constituted a heterogeneous cluster—like their predecessors who acted as "high-modernist" prototypes—each poet working to reverse major strands within *di yunge* poetics. The generational tension was construed primarily as a struggle between expressionism and the earlier poets' impressionism; as Anglo-American modernisms (imagism, vorticism, and objectivism) reacting against *di yunge*'s aestheticism; and, to a lesser extent, as futurists rejecting their predecessors' symbolism and decadence. It is, therefore, understandable why Glatshteyn, the introspectivist who was much closer to the expressionist/futurist prototypes than the Eliotesque Glantz-Leyeles, would be among the first to acknowledge Halpern's role.

Halpern's poetry and poetics do not fit well into the framework of *di yunge*, not simply because of the growing pessimism and complexity of his work, as Wisse suggests (1980:40), nor because he was always the outsider and rebel, as standard critical anthologies describe his marginalization from the group. Rather, Halpern's poetry stands between impressionism (one of the *yunge* prototypes) and expressionism (one of the introspectivists' prototypes), using expressionism to criticize impressionism. Like Fogel, Halpern straddled the jagged spaces between premodernism and modernism "proper," a straddling which in its transitional, intercategorical status becomes itself prototypically modernist.[23]

While this transitional status applies primarily to what philosophers of science have termed "the context of justification," namely what can be descriptively surmised from the poetic works and programmatic discourse, I think it pertains to "the context of discovery" as well, the circumstances under which these works were produced and received. Halpern's early published work in *Shriftn, East Broadway*, and especially *In New York* may indeed have helped the young introspectivists form their poetic principles as well as supplied them with "ammunition" for their later struggle against the dominance of *di yunge*. The tremendous impact of *In New York* is widely acknowledged. As Wolitz points out (1977:56), the book was considered "a major landmark in [Yiddish] literature." Wolitz goes on to cite A. Tabachnik's statement that *In New York* "is one of the few epoch-making books in Yiddish literature" and Itzik Manger's exclamation that this is "one of the greatest poetry books of modern poetry in general." Glatshteyn's own homage to *In New York* is characteristically expressed in silence, in the way he chose "to structure his inaugural volume of poems" (Novershtern, 1986:138).

When the general labels "impressionism" and "expressionism" are applied to modernist groupings in marginal literatures such as *di yunge* and the introspectivists, the problematical nature of determining trend affiliation is underscored. As I have suggested, *di yunge* also aligned themselves with symbolism (especially through the imported Russian paragon of Alexander Blok) (Boaz, 1971:160–74), while the introspectivists explicitly pledge allegiance also to Anglo-American imagism (*In Zikh*, [1919] 1920:25).[24] This blurring of affiliations at the international margins of a trend is symptomatic of the center of the category as well. Numerous general critical discussions of impressionism in mainstream literatures associate it with symbolism (Mains, 1978; Paulk, 1979) as well as with decadence and naturalism (Scott, 1976). Similarly, the term *expressionism* has been used imperialistically, referring at times to all the modernist trends in the first quarter of this century (Furness, 1973). It is possible nevertheless to use these labels, however tentatively, within the particular conjuncture of modernist and premodernist tendencies in Yiddish poetry in North America from the 1910s to the 1930s. Specifically, we need to explore the extent to which the vacillation of the literary system on the threshold of modernism can be illuminated through the perspective of the contrasting prototypes of impressionism and expressionism. Only within this specific conjuncture can Halpern's special role as deviant and proleptic paragon be understood.

Irving Howe and Eliezer Greenberg ([1969] 1976:39–40) have argued for a clear distinction between the first *modern* Yiddish group in North America, *di yunge*, and the first *modernist* one, the introspectivists:

> While *Die Yunge* validated the idea of the poem as autonomous creation and brought into the narrow precincts of Yiddish poetry some awareness of modern European literature, they cannot be said to have been "modernists" in any strict sense of the term. For self-conscious

experimentation with form and theme, we must turn to a new group of Yiddish poets who began to make their presence felt shortly after the First World War, . . . the *In Zich* or introspectivist group.

The question of whether literary impressionism (or any of the other trends associated with *di yunge*, such as symbolism, aestheticism, and decadence) can be excluded categorically from modernism depends on how precisely the category is delimited. The single criterion offered by Howe and Greenberg, that modernism involves "self-conscious experimentation with form and theme," remains too vague and latently evaluative to be useful. Undoubtedly, Mani Leyb, Ignatoff, not to mention Leyvik, and most certainly Halpern conceived of their poetic coterie as experimenting with styles and materials that had never before been used in Yiddish poetry. That their poetry was perceived as such in the initial stages of its critical reception can be seen from reviews that refer to *di yunge*'s poems as formless, sloppy, and ridiculously "beautiful";[25] perhaps, most amusingly, this self-evaluation can be surmised from *di yunge*'s own metapoetic self-parody published in their satirical review, *Der Kibitser* (April 15, 1908, p. 4; translation by Wisse, 1988:18).

Call us *Yunge*
Call us *Goyim*
As you will.
Write reviews, write criticism
To your fill.
No! We'll not perform
Tradition's dance.
Our two-step is the modern
Decadence!
From the void
From airy nothing
From the abyss
Lacking form, without much grace
Or artifice,
Our verse, too proud perhaps,
And happenstance
Will tunefully accompany our
Decadence!

Clearly, when contrasted with the high-modernist, free-verse models of the introspectivists, *di yunge* poetry seems quite traditional. But, typical of the dynamics of literary movements in general, when compared with the rhetoric and thematics of their predecessors, the sweatshop poets of the turn of the century, they emerge as modernist experimenters. Furthermore, neither impressionism nor aestheticism, symbolism nor decadence, was wholly and unambivalently embraced by any of these poets, not even by Mani Leyb. Hence, in a way Halpern's stormy and ambivalent affiliation with *di yunge* makes him a marginal prototype of the group as a whole.

As this kind of marginal prototype, Halpern has a role within the Yiddish literary system similar in significant ways to Fogel's within Hebrew poetry. From their (different) marginal vantage points, Halpern and Fogel launched poetic/critical explorations of the limits of impressionism. In the process, they pushed the impressionist prototype to its outer boundaries, to the place where, turning back on itself, impressionism becomes expressionism. Although interartistic analogies are quite politically and methodologically problematic, especially where examples of "great artists" are concerned, such a "larger-than-life" example leaps out at us from the center of the mainstream artistic canon: the postimpressionist painting style of Paul Cézanne, who took impressionism so seriously he made it reach beyond itself, and in the process became the great deviant paragon whose work is now taken to be one giant prolepsis of all the high-modernist trends that were to follow. That the margins of peripheral literatures may be filled with small Cézannes is one of the most ironic—and ultimately encouraging—quirks of literary dynamics.

Focusing as it does on the competing models of impressionism and expressionism, Maria Kronegger's (1973:14) common characterization of impressionism in its poetic manifestations becomes particularly useful for our purposes:

> Impressionism is born from the fundamental insight that our consciousness is sensitive and passive; . . . consciousness faces this world as pure passivity, a mirror in which the world inscribes or reflects itself. As detached spectator, the individual considers the world without having a standpoint in it. Reality is a synthesis of sense-impressions. . . . What we actually see is a vibration of light on matter in dissolution.

Literary impressionism, especially in its German models, which are most relevant for both Halpern and Fogel, is often associated with the creation of a mood (the notorious *Shtimung* of *di yunge*). This description refers to a mental state which forms the organizing principle of the text rather than the dynamic act of an interpretative narrator/

speaker. Yoseph Ha-Ephrati (1976:144–75) developed a theory of lit-
erary impressionism which shows how these three principles cohere:
the passive nature of consciousness, reality as a synthesis of sense
impressions, and the mood as organizing principle of the text.[26] Ac-
cording to Ha-Ephrati, literary impressionism consists of the attempt
to create the illusion that the world is rendered as it is perceived by
an observer who is part of that world at a certain moment, without
any conceptualizing or editorializing mediation between the reader
and the fictional observer (who may or may not be the lyrical "I" of
the poem). In other words, the impressionist text, in order to create
the illusion of immediate sense perception, cannot afford to be per-
ceived as self-conscious, to draw attention to its fictionality, or to
create an ironic distance between the observer/perceiver and the im-
plied author or reader. It is on this technical, perceptual basis that *di
yunge's* much criticized flight from political engagement is to be un-
derstood, as well as the gallery of passive observers who populate the
poetry of Fogel and his antiformulaic generation.

The prototype of an expressionism which also informs the work of
these Yiddish and Hebrew poets can be traced back to the program-
matic assertion first made in the German expressionist manifesto of
Kazimir Edschmidt during a lecture in Berlin in 1917 and adopted
two years later by the Yiddish introspectivists in North America.[27]
Edschmidt's statement reads: "The world is there. There is no sense in
repeating it." Instead, reality needs to be created anew within the
soulscape of the artist; the artist then becomes the new human who is
no longer a character but a real human being, a human being "en-
tangled in the cosmos."[28] The *in zikh* credo contains an analogous
passage: "The world exists (*iz do*) and we are part of it. But for us the
world exists only insofar as it is reflected in us (*es shpiglt zikh op in
undz*), as it touches (moves) us" (*In Zikh*, [1919] 1920:5).

We can see from these descriptions that expressionism differs from
impressionism precisely in its ambition to give purely "internal" or
"subjective" events the effect or status of "objective" or "factual"
reality. Of greatest importance for the political and ideological dimen-
sions of the two credos—those dimensions which define the ambiv-
alence of these poets' marginality—is the proliferation of mimetic,
even ethical, motivations for the introspective, expressionist practices.
Thus, for example, in their manifestoes, the introspectivists, like ex-
pressionists elsewhere, continuously insist that their kind of poetry,
their kind of rhythms, and their kind of subject matter are more

"realistic," more "true" and "authentic," than any premodernist, non-experimental rendering of external reality. *Di yunge's* impressionism has to be replaced because it is "unreal" and "untrue." The first introspectivist manifesto argues for the truth of the "introspective manner" (in Harshav and Harshav, 1986:774), while declaiming the mendacity of the *yunge* method:

> [T]he poet must *really listen* to his inner voice, observe his internal panorama—kaleidoscopic, contradictory, unclear or confused as it may be. From these sources, he must create poetry which is the result of both the fusion of the poet's soul with the phenomenon he expresses and the individual image, or cluster of images, that he *sees within himself* at that moment.
>
> What does take place in the poet's psyche under the impression or impact of any phenomenon?
>
> In the language of our local poets, the "Young Generation" (*Di Yunge*), this creates a *mood*. According to them, it is the poet's task to express or convey this mood. How? In a concentrated and well-rounded form. Concentration and well-roundedness are seen as the necessary conditions, or presuppositions, that allow the poet's mood to attain universal or, in more traditional terms, *eternal*, value.
>
> But this method, though sufficient to create poetic vignettes or artful arabesques, is essentially neither sufficient nor true. From our point of view, this method is a *lie*.
>
> Why?
>
> Because the mood and the poem that emerge from this conception and this method must inevitably result in something cut-off, isolated, something which does not really correspond to life and truth. (In Harshav and Harshav, 1986:775)

This attempt to reject a competing poetic paradigm by scientifically refuting its truth claims points to a curiously antimodernist element within this prototypically modernist literary program: both Yiddish introspectivism and German expressionism evince a return to mimetic, representational criteria as a justification for a radically non-representational poetic technique.

Halpern's expressionist critique of impressionism, while evident already in his first book, reaches its fullest development in his later poetry, no doubt because of the influence of the new introspectivist model which he inadvertently may have helped launch. In his later poetry, with its radical disruptions of the traditional strophic and prosodic structures that were irresistible for him as a younger poet, Halpern's intergenerational role becomes most complex.

The first section of Halpern's "Zunfargang oyf Beymer" ("Sunset on Trees") offers an interesting ars-poetic thematization of the introspectivist critique of impressionism and its particularly aestheticist *di yunge* interpretation. Published posthumously in 1934, the poem is divided into two sections, with the same repeating refrain. The second section of the poem (stanza 2 and the refrain) calls into question the whole poetic project—be it impressionist, realist, or modernist—by describing the poet's work as an impossible mystification of "the real thing," a harmful, aestheticizing mimesis of human emotions. In what seems half oath, half curse, the speaker forbids the poet in him to "stretch out his hands/ to that which people call happiness," implying that he can only wreck its wholeness. By severing the pain of real people from its concrete social setting and framing it aesthetically within the formal relations of the poetic image, the poet puts their already precarious existence in jeopardy: "sorrow that dances on a golden tightrope—over a river that copies the sky." The point of departure for this total reassessment of "the crying [that] people call song" is a more localized, almost technical critique—in the first section of the poem—of one of the most conventional scenes of poetic and artistic impressionism: "sunset on trees."

פֿון: זונפֿאַרגאַנג אויף ביימער

הימל. זונפֿאַרגאַנג אויף ביימער,
און ווינט און פּחד מיט טרויער באַצירט,
און דאָס ייִנגל אין מיר דעם מענטש דעם גרויען
האָרכט צו זען די האַנט וואָס פֿירט
די זון, זאָל זיך לייגן שטאַרבן.
און דער קינסטלער אין מיר קוקט אויף זײַנע פֿאַרבן
וואָס זענען גאָלדיק און בלוי און רויט –
און זײַן לעבן ווינט ווי דער אייביקער טויט
וואָס איז שיין און ליכטיק אין אָוונט שײַן,
ווי אַ קינד וועון די מאַמע וויגט עס אײַן.

זאָל זיך בויגן מײַן קאָפּ דער גרויער –
זאָל זיך בויגן מײַן קאָפּ דער גרויער.

From: Sunset on Trees

Sky. Sunset on trees,
and wind and dread decked out with grief,
and the little boy in me to the man the gray one
listens to see the hand that leads
the sun, to lie down and die.
And the artist in me looks at his paints
which are golden and blue and red—
and his life weeps like the eternal death
that is beautiful and bright in the evening shine
like a child when his mother rocks it to sleep.

Let my gray head bend down—
let my gray head bend down.
          —Halpern (1934, vol. 2:130–31; translation mine)

The poem's title and first two lines, with their strictly nominal elliptical syntax and omission of articles, invoke a stock subject for impressionist poems and paintings: a static visual "freezing" of a sunset. The process of sunset in nature is rendered as a "synthesized sense impression" of a moment of "retinal contact" between sky, sunset, and trees, seemingly without the mediation of an interpretive consciousness. The injection of dread and grief into the scene in line 2 could still be considered impressionist, in its impersonal objectification of a *Stimmung*. But the equivalence of emotional and meteorological entities in the zeugma "and wind and dread . . . with grief," especially the near-oxymoronic personification of *batsirt* ("decked out," "adorned") when combined with "grief" or "sadness" (*troyer*), begins to call into question the possibility of being a detached spectator of a natural scene. In the third line, the poem turns inward to a self-conscious contemplation of the lyrical "I" and with it to a total rejection of impressionism. Abandoning an impressionist rendition of a sunset, Halpern makes the possibility of such an artistic rendering the topic of his introspection. Through this thematization of poetic technique and artistic affiliation, the mind of the dramatized observer, rather than being a passive, reflective medium, becomes the only measure of reality.

Significantly, at this point the syntax turns radically expressionistic, and the interplay of visual perspective and poetic point of view becomes more and more intricate. Translated literally, the second sentence (lines 3–5 in the Yiddish) reads:

And the little boy in me the man the gray one
listens to see the hand that leads
the sun, (should) lie down to die.

While the deferral of the predicate *horkht* ("listen to," "hear") is
slightly more grammatical in Yiddish than it would be in English,
the effect of the enjambed lines with no punctuation marks is still
remarkably jarring. Read according to lineation, the text creates a
series of equivalences between subject and object, the little boy and
the gray old man, listening and seeing, cause and effect, sunset and
death. Halpern, a talented painter in real life, is not content to ed-
itorialize about the contrast between the static, impressionist pre-
modernism of the first two lines and the dynamic, figurative expres-
sionism of the painter's/poet's hand leading the sun. Instead, the
perspective is internalized and multiplied, quite literally, by focusing
on the little boy inside the speaker (*in mir*) listening to the aging adult.
The little boy fails to recognize the old man as himself because the
older persona is an outer, objectified self. That outer self is perhaps
the impressionist–*di yunge* artist/poet who comes to the sunset with
the ready-made symbolic "reading" of death and old age, and im-
poses it on the natural sunset scene under the illusion of capturing the
moment "as it is." It is not the sense impression synthesized by the
passive, nonreflective artist but his very hand "that is leading (leads)
/ the sun, to lie down to die" because—as in the most traditional
versions of the pathetic fallacy—his own head is old and gray and
about to "set." This ironic critique of impressionism as veiled roman-
ticism concerns poetry as much as painting, as the synaesthesia cre-
ated by the irregular Yiddish word order shows: *horkht tsu zen* ("lis-
tening to see").

Halpern rejects the premodernist symbolic senses of sunset and the
impressionist mood which pretend to be passively recorded by the
artist as "retinal" imprints of the natural sunset on his unreflective
consciousness. Yet he does so only to arrive at those same senses and
mood again through the circuitous route of introspection. An intrigu-
ing parallel to the first section of this poem is found in the same
introspectivist manifesto quoted above, in the very section that criti-
cizes impressionist renditions of sunsets:

[The premodernist poet] uses too many ready-made images and ma-
terials pre-prepared for him ahead of time. When the poet, or even
the ordinary person [*azoy a mentch*] looks at a sunset, he can see the

strangest things, which appear on the surface perhaps to be completely removed from the sunset. The image which is reflected in his soul is removed by a whole chain of fast-flying associations from that which his eye sees. (*In Zikh*, [1919] 1920:9; translation in Harshav & Harshav, 1986:776)

Halpern engages precisely this type of fast-flying chain of associations, depicted in rapid centrifugal motion, during the second half of this section of the poem. Here the expressionist mode is laid bare quite explicitly: the "cognitive reference point" (Lakoff, 1987:41, 45, 89) for the scene is no longer the realist sky or the aestheticist painting of the sky, but the expressionist gauge of reality, "the artist in me"; the objects for self-conscious introspective examination cease to be the ready-made clichés (imposing death on the sunset) but are instead the beautiful raw materials of expression: not structured color strokes capturing the golden, red, and blue hues of the natural scene, but blotches of paint on the artist's palette. Halpern no longer uses a literal sunset "standing in" for a metaphorical death but an inextricable combination of traditional poetic oppositions: life and death, childhood and old age, metaphor and literal meaning, external and internal reality. Only once the poem completes this kaleidoscopic view of the artistic subject (as both persona and theme) from all its contradictory inner and outer angles can the (little boy within the) speaker come to terms with his external, adult self and accept with stark simplicity the analogy between his graying head and the setting sun: "Let my gray head bend down—let my gray head bend down."

Fogel: Retrospective Paragon, Repressed Paragon

In the case of Fogel, even more than Halpern, the critique of impressionism and the ambivalent affiliation with expressionism are crucial to the poet's special role as marginal prototype within the literary system. Yet since only one of Fogel's roles—as retroactive paragon for the Statehood Generation poets—has received any degree of recognition, and only in the context of late modernist affiliations, the issue of Fogel's struggle between impressionist and expressionist models retreats into the background; there is little discussion or even awareness of the issue in the critical literature. Fogel's poetry was retroactively construed according to the needs of Hebrew poetry in the 1950s and 1960s, at a conjuncture of the new acceptance of imported Anglo-American, neoimagistic poetics and the rejection of the old dominance of futurist-inspired, maximalist poetics of pre-Statehood *moderna.*

Moreover, the two Statehood Poets who have had the greatest stake in turning Fogel into a retrospective paragon, Dan Pagis and Nathan Zach, were also engaged in a struggle to extricate themselves from the dominant modernist prototypes of their native German and shift to the Anglo-American models, which offered them, politically and aesthetically, greater freedom and more room for innovation. It is therefore not surprising that Pagis, in his erudite critical edition of Fogel's poetry, argues with uncharacteristic zealousness against those critics who "have found in the open-ended structure of Fogel's poetry and in their radical images traces of German expressionism" (Fogel, [1966] 1975:42). Interestingly, Zach, in his influential book-length manifesto-cum-literary-criticism, *Zman ve-ritmus etsel Bergson u-va-shira ha-modernit* (*Time and Rhythm in Bergson and in Modern Poetry*) (1966b), argues with Pagis on this point and clearly outlines Fogel's connections to German expressionism:

> Dan Pagis' argument . . . that Fogel never heard of German Expressionism, and therefore was not influenced by it in his early poetry, an argument based mainly on the fact that "in the poet's diary there is no trace of any impression made upon him by the new trends in poetry, or that he was at all familiar with them," is not very convincing. . . . The influence of German poetry on Fogel's poetry is, in my opinion, crucial. This is a general stylistic influence and therefore there is no sense in listing specific lines or images which are common to him and to the German poets, even though this could have been done as well. (1966b:56)

Zach's own tendentiousness is revealed, however, when in the same book, as in other of his essays of the 1960s, he self-consciously dehistoricizes Fogel even though, as the quotation above attests, he is keenly aware of the historicity of Fogel's modernism.

In this discussion, Zach uses a mélange of Fogel's poetry and T. S. Eliot's criticism in order to lend legitimacy to the cause of free verse in the poetry of Zach's own generation and to reject the rich meters of Nathan Alterman and Avraham Shlonsky's *moderna:* "A poem by Fogel which is written in such [free] rhythm, proves how right is T. S. Eliot when he asserts that 'there is no freedom in art,' and that the artist who expresses himself through the rhythms of free verse must be no less, even at times more sensitive than those who employ the 'mechanism of repetition,' or at least of the more mechanical ones among them" (1966b:50).

But when Zach reads a Fogel poem, the poem functions only as an exemplary text for the poetics of Zach's own generation rather than as an ambivalently expressionist poem maintaining a dialogical relation with other German and Hebrew modernist models of its time, such as impressionism, decadence, and symbolism. The poem Zach reads, "Le'at olim susay" ("Slowly My Horses Climb"), is the first poem in Fogel's first book (and the only collection of poems published during his lifetime, *Lifney ha-sha'ar ha-afel* [*Before the Dark Gate*], 1923):

לְאַט עוֹלִים סוּסַי
עַל מַעֲלֵה הָהָר,
לַיְלָה כְּבָר שׁוֹכֵן שָׁחוֹר
בָּנוּ וּבַכֹּל.

כְּבֵדָה תַחֲרֹק עֶגְלָתִי לִרְגָעִים
כַּעֲמוּסָה אַלְפֵי מֵתִים.

זֶמֶר חֲרִישִׁי אֶשְׁלַח
עַל פְּנֵי גַלֵּי הַלַּיְל,
שֶׁיַּעֲבֹר לַמֶּרְחָק.

סוּסַי מַאֲזִינִים וְעוֹלִים לְאָט.

[*Slowly My Horses Climb*]

Slowly my horses climb
up the mountain slope,
night already dwells black
in us and in all.

Heavy my wagon will squeak at times
as if laden with thousands of dead.

A silent song I'll send
upon the waves of night
that will pass into the distance.

My horses listen and climb slowly.
—Fogel ([1923] 1966, 1975 ed.:73;
                        translation mine)

Zach, who treats the reader to a stunning analysis of the prosodic, syntactic, and musical aspects of rhythm in this poem, prefaces his analysis with a six-point "summary" of the general characteristics of Fogel's style evident in this poem. Predictably, these six points echo several included in his own fifteen points (1966a), the manifesto of his own Statehood Generations's poetry published in the same year as his book:

1. laconic, selective diction,
2. open-ended structure, composed of image-stanzas whose narrative links are fairly loose,
3. the poet's avoidance of innovative or overstylized figurative language (his metaphors are more natural and evocative than those of Shlonsky and Alterman thanks to their more concretized sensual import, the natural appearance of his landscapes, the astute distribution of the figures over the entire poem and the avoidance of cerebral or excessively wordy-artificial constructions),
4. traditional diction which stays away from neologisms, linguistic acrobatics, and purely phonetic decorativeness,
5. renunciation of originality as a value unto itself, . . .
6. despite what appears here as simplicity and naturalness of language (and indeed such "naturalness" does exist here too!), the careful eye detects in Fogel's poetry a remarkable inventiveness and maneuverability. (Zach 1966:52b)

These points—all astute observations and evaluations of Fogel's poetics—exclude most of the stylistic and thematic features that are salient within the particular historical prototypes of the first trend of Hebrew modernism. But these are precisely the characteristics that make Fogel a representative of a repressed trend of Hebrew poetic modernism, a trend whose recovery has only just begun. Ironically, then, the Statehood Poets who "have kept discovering" Fogel since the late 1960s, in a selective modeling of his poetics aimed to serve their own historical needs, have also helped suppress some of the most radical aspects of Fogel's type of modernism. Furthermore, by turning him into an individual paragon, the Statehood Generation poets ignore the fact that a rather large number of individuals, many of them women, developed similar antiformulaic versions of modernism at roughly the same time as Fogel, even though they never formed a self-conscious coterie.

What Halpern's "A Nakht" achieves within the expanded structures of an experimental narrative poem—of an entire book of poetry, in fact—Fogel accomplishes in the confines of what Greenberg has aptly called a *kamer-lid*, a chamber-music poem.[29] "Slowly My Horses Climb" establishes, with lexical and rhythmic economy, the concrete situation: horses slowly climbing up the mountain slope as night descends, as if the mimetic rhythm of the horses' slow trot also punctuates the imperceptible stages of the process of nightfall. This is the sparse functionalism that Zach finds so remarkable. However, what happens next is typical of almost all of Fogel's poems that start out with the impressionist impetus of capturing the nuances of an external scene or act at the instant of its becoming, without any projection of the observer's consciousness. The poem subverts the concreteness of the situation—indeed, the very ability to discern concrete and abstract, literal and figurative—at the moment that the situation is established; this subversion occurs in Halpern's sunset and night poems as well. The color black, an apparently redundant, unadorned epithet of night, actually becomes a radical, ungrammatical, but functional adverb, a move Zach describes as the "salvation of the color black by turning it from adjective to adverb" (1966b:52). Zach argues that this shift creates a syntactic analogy among the first three stanzas (1966b:52). But this shift is not just syntactic; the grammatical transformation of black into an adverb is the first step in the movement of the night inward, into the undefined, systematically blurred plural consciousness of speaker, horses, and "all": *layla kvar shokhen shachor / banu u-vakol* ("night already dwells black / in us and in all"). This one simple step, defining the locus of the night's "black dwelling" inside the poetic "us" as well as the surrounding "all," transforms the passive and flat impressionist *Stimmung* into an expressionist "entanglement in the cosmos,"[30] where it is no longer possible to tell where subject ends and object begins. Michael Gluzman (1993a:138) has astutely observed:

> As a "substance" that dwells within the speaker, the night is not only an external temporal marker but also an inner quality. Moreover, the

opposition between foreground and background is also destabilized as a result of the complex relationship between subject and object, since it is unclear whether the night foregrounds the speaker or whether the speaker foregrounds the night.

Just as the structure of Halpern's long poem revealed night as an internal property, a mental state of being *"in* New York," Fogel's poem transforms within its texture—through the enjambed last line of the first stanza—the descriptive element into an expressive one.

Typically, the framing stanzas (one and four) employ a present tense, *beynoni* (which in Hebrew can mark a present progressive or habitual action or state as well as an adjectival form): *olim, shokhen, ma'azinim, ve-olim* ("climb/ing," "dwell/ing," "listen/ing," "and climbing"). The adverbial use of *kvar* ("already"), therefore, enhances the sense of a change, a perfected, albeit stative action. Moreover, the chiastic structure of the beginning and end of the poem—*le'at olim* and *olim le'at* ("slowly climbing" and "climbing slowly")—emphasizes the difference within the sameness in the poem's concrete situation. After the expropriation of the night from the domain of external reality, the act of listening (*ma'azinim*) to the imperceptible objectified song (poem?) is added to the scene. The reader is reduced to the aural perspective of the horses, who, pulling the wagon along uphill, are deprived of seeing their load. Thus, the simile "as if laden with thousands of dead"—its hyperbole seemingly so out of line with Fogel's poetics of understatement—can be construed as a literal hypothesis (though surreal) rather than a figurative comparison. Neither the horses nor the reader may ever know what is really in the wagon since the poem seriously questions the very possibility of knowing what is actually there in any described moment of reality.

This "epistemological ambivalence" (Gluzman, 1993a) is maintained through one of Fogel's major linguistic achievements (described in detail in Chapter 4): the development of late biblical fluctuations between grammatical tense and aspect into a refined stylistic merging of impressionism and expressionism. Fogel's verbs produce a consistent hesitation between the factual and the hypothetical, "realis" and "irrealis," action and stasis. Remarkably, these innovations, important within both the intrinsic and the international literary/linguistic systems, are hardly ever mentioned in discussions of Fogel by poets and critics of the Statehood Generation. The reason is quite clear: both the internal function of perfecting the defective polysystem of literary Hebrew and the general poetic function of providing a *glissement* between two crucial periodological and typological models are important only when the system is conceived in its historicity. By the time Zach, Pagis, and their colleagues arrive on the scene, the problems addressed by Fogel's poetics have been solved or displaced by others. Yet only by acknowledging this linguistic achievement can we understand the specific ways in which Fogel and the other anti-formulaic poets allowed Hebrew poetry a way out of the *nusach* and into modernism.

In the second and third stanzas of "Slowly My Horses Climb" the verbs appear in the ambiguous future/imperfect form which allows them to be construed either as an uncompleted action (captured impressionistically in the process of its becoming) or, quite the reverse, as an "irrealis," fantastic, or surreal situation. The image of thousands of dead becomes an expressionist projection of the speaker(s)'—or listener(s)'—state of mind. Ironically, the one "realis" grammatical tense in this stanza appears only in the surrealist image of the thousands of dead on one wagon, as if the emotional reality of the wagon's macabre load—and its analogue, the introverted version of the night—were the only sure thing left in the scene. It is precisely this kind of a reversal of mimetic norms of representation and romantic norms of poetic self-expression that Halpern's critique of impressionism also achieves.

The third stanza thematizes the very impossibility of separating the (ir)reality of the scene from the poet's expression. It is typical, as Eric Zakim has argued convincingly (1996),[31] that a metapoetic musical resolution supplants the visual concreteness of the discrete images: "A silent song I'll send / upon the waves of night / that will pass into the distance." Since we already know that the night is "in us and in all," the song that the speaker sends out into the distance is simultaneously also introjected, sent inside himself and his listeners. That this song is silent both disrupts its reality claims and matters not at all since the entire process of perception has been turned inward. Thus, it says little about Fogel to assert, as the few critics who have bothered to read his poems closely are prone to do, that most of Fogel's early poetry "is a poetry of night and darkness, or a poetry of evening and sunset: the night 'dwelling dark' is analogous to the wagon of dead bodies, . . . to the very stance 'Before the Dark Gate.'—This is the central motif of this poetry, and its various images are meant only to create one multi-faceted poetic situation: standing face to face with death." (Luz, 1964:189–90, 214). The expressionist critique of impressionism is meant, among other things, to make just such a static motif hunt completely meaningless because no night, evening, or sunset in Fogel—as in Halpern—can have any stable, general meaning outside of the particular disruptions which constitute it uniquely in each text.

This point is made even more emphatically in Fogel's seminal poem "Be-leylot ha-stav" ("On Autumn Nights"), a salient example of the transition from impressionism to expressionism in the first modernist Hebrew trend of antiformulaic poetry.[32]

בְּלֵילוֹת הַסְּתָו
נוֹפֵל בַּיְּעָרִים עָלֶה לֹא-נִרְאָה
וְשׁוֹכֵב דּוּמָם לָאָרֶץ.

בַּנְּחָלִים
יִקְפֹּץ הַדָּג מִן הַמַּיִם
וְהֵד נְקִישָׁה לַחָה
יַעַן בָּאֹפֶל.

בַּמֶּרְחָק הַשָּׁחוֹר
נִזְרָעוֹת דַּהֲרוֹת סוּסִים לֹא-נִרְאִים
הַנְּמַסִּים וְהוֹלְכִים.

כָּל אֵלֶּה יִשְׁמַע
הַהֹלֵךְ הֶעָיֵף
וְרַעַד יַעֲבֹר אֶת בְּשָׂרוֹ.

[On Autumn Nights]

On autumn nights
there falls in the forests an unseen leaf
and lies still to the ground.

In the streams
the fish will jump from the water
and an echo of a moist thump
will answer in the darkness.

In the black distance
gallops are sown of unseen horses
that are melting away.

All these
the tired wanderer will hear
and a quiver will pass through his flesh.
—Fogel ([1923] 1966, 1975 ed.:113; translated by
Chana Kronfeld and Eric Zakim)

On first reading, the poem seems to be a paradigmatic example of impressionistic static observation. Three discrete images each occupy a stanza (leaf, fish, horses) and present the verbal equivalent of a series of "retinal imprints," each of which freezes one fleeting and nuanced moment in nature. The final stanza observes, in detached and precise fashion, the physical effect made by these "synthesized sense data" on the human observer.

However, when readers pay careful attention to the linguistic texture of each stanza, as the impressionist technique demands, and when they take seriously the implicit invitation—which this poetic prototype carries with it—to focus on the most fleeting and delicate of movements, they realize that the text, in typical expressionistic fashion, presents the most subjective, imperceptible internal qualities as if they were objective sense data. In fact, none of the finely detailed scenes can be concretized by any of the perceptual means privileged by an impressionist mode of writing or painting.

In the first stanza, the leaf is not only unseen but also invisible (*lo nir'eh*) and cannot in principle be visually perceived; this single, invisible leaf falls on many fall nights (simultaneity of time) and in many forests (simultaneity of place). The omnipresent, invisible leaf then lies down to the ground *dumam*—not only without sound but also without motion. The possibility that any observer might actually have sense impressions of an objective, external scene is negated at the same time that it seems to be asserted and with respect to every one of the senses and reality principles involved: sight, sound, motion, time, and place.

The possibility of impressionist concretization is further problematized in the second and third stanzas. As Zakim has shrewdly suggested (1995), each image forms only a sense trace around which the scene "fills out." Thus, the first half of the second stanza is impossible to perceive since it depicts a single, specific fish jumping out of the water in many different streams. The second half of the stanza, which can be perceived in terms of singular identity, is only a synaesthetic echo (*hed . . . ba-ofel*, "an echo . . . in the darkness") of another synaesthetic trace of an action (*nekisha lacha*, "a moist thump"). As the images recede into the horizon (from the illusion of a close-up view of a leaf to the explicit remoteness of "In the black distance"), their "impossibility," by any premodernist standards, becomes pronounced on all levels of the text: the predicate *nizra'ot* ("are sown") stands in ironic, almost grotesque, contrast to the haunting insubstantiality of its subject (*daharot*, "gallops"), and its self-erasing, syntactically and semantically misleading modifiers. The metaphorical "seeds" are the auditory traces of horses which, like the leaf of the first stanza, are both unseen and invisible (*lo nirim*); and these invisible horses, not the sound of their hoofs, are melting away, or—as Zakim has cogently observed—surrealistically, literally, melting and walking (*ha-nemasim ve-holkhim*).[33]

The sustained negation of all realist and impressionist concretizations of the three scenes places their referents in the soulscape of the weary traveler of the last stanza: his weariness, his experiences on the road—of which we can see and hear nothing—and, ultimately, his very mode of existence as a *helekh* (literally, "a walker") mark him as the poem's shifting, transitional center of consciousness. These are the conditions that not only affect our perception of the scenes but actually give them their identity.

When the Israeli poets of the fifties and sixties rediscovered Fogel in their own poetic image, they were only doing what poets—and critics—always do when they struggle for hegemony over a dominant literary regime: they made him their own. In a similar if less self-conscious way the introspectivists tacitly adopted Halpern's implied poetics as a model in their own battle with *di yunge*. Both Halpern and Fogel pointed to a future even as they wrestled with the burdens of the poetic past within their respective literary traditions. From their displaced or decentered vantage they could begin to create a modernist poetic expression that in its richness—both as individual voice and as paragon for later generations—played cruelly on the irony of each poet's personal and physical destitution.

Remapping modernism in Yiddish poetry to include marginal prototypes and deviant paragons like Halpern is important for a critical examination of the paths taken in the literary history—fast becoming the archaeology—of Yiddish culture. But within Hebrew poetry, a more rigorous understanding of the role played by marginal prototypes like David Fogel is vital for the future of the literary system, not just for excavating its past.

CHAPTER 8

The Yiddish Poem Itself

Readings in Halpern, Markish,
Hofshteyn, and Sutzkever

In earlier chapters I have looked at ways in which the production and reception of modernist Hebrew poetic trends, or of the total oeuvre of individual Hebrew poets, exemplify and challenge the model of marginal prototypes I have developed here. Chapter 7 goes on to open Yiddish poetry to this examination by developing a comparative perspective. It unfolds the partially parallel narratives of marginalization and liminal modernism in the work of the Yiddish poet Moyshe Leyb Halpern and the Hebrew poet David Fogel. In this chapter my focus will be on the individual poem rather than the total oeuvre of a poet as a locus of decentered exemplariness. The question to be addressed, in the process of subjecting these texts to close reading, is one of thematization and implicit poetics. To what extent do these poems, construed in the historical context of their multiple/partial trend affiliations, reveal a concern with their own marginality and modernism? And if they do, how do the different articulations and contextualizations within each text affect the theoretical model presented here?

The poems I have chosen, including another by Halpern, demonstrate some of the tense polyphony characteristic of all formations of modernism in Yiddish poetry. Modernist Yiddish poetry, perhaps even more than the Hebrew poetry of this movement, provides salient examples of marginal prototypicality for a number of reasons. First and foremost, perhaps, is the status of Yiddish as a literary system poised on the edge of complete annihilation. This perspective from the precipice, while it makes the process of reading these wonderfully rich poems exceedingly painful, might also allow access to cultural, linguistic, and aesthetic processes that would normally be imperceptible. But the challenge is to read "the Yiddish poem itself" closely and rigorously even when the poets themselves died of hunger and neglect (Halpern), were murdered by Stalin (Markish and Hofshteyn), or survived the Nazi genocide (Sutzkever). We must repair not only the ravages of historical erasure but also the damages of a sentimentalizing, nostalgic *Yiddishkayt*. And let the poetry be heard. Second is the condition of being a language without a land. The development of modern Yiddish literature involves the construction of a collective identity that cannot be reduced to the Eurocentric model of the nation-state. In this, Yiddish modernism discloses a heightened, literalized articulation of marginal modernism as deterritorialized literature at the same time that it calls into question standard literary models of nationalism, colonialism, and cultural identity. Third, while the historiography of its many sociocodes (groups, journals, shifting centers) remains to be written, Yiddish modernist poetry exhibits in intensified fashion the modernist obsession with forging an aesthetic through constructing a literary group identity. To what extent then do these individual poems, written in some cases by the same poets who participated in the collective composition of the group's manifestoes, reveal an implicit poetics, and if they do, how is the dialogic tension between the explicit and implicit poetics to be accounted for within a family-resemblace or prototype model of literary trend? But it is best perhaps to allow the poems to speak.

Some notes on the texts. The readings in this chapter include five poems by four major Yiddish modernists: Halpern, Perets Markish, Dovid Hofshteyn, and Avrom Sutzkever, who represent three of the shifting centers of modern Yiddish literature: New York, the Soviet Union, and Israel. The English translations provided try to remain as close to the original as possible to give a literal sense of lexical and syntactic composition. The translations should enable the reader of English to follow the stylistic analyses of the Yiddish texts. In addition, a transliteration of the Yiddish is provided for each poem to help non-Yiddish speakers follow the discussions of sound patterns and to illustrate the special emphasis modernist Yiddish poetry attaches to prosodic virtuosity.

Moyshe Leyb Halpern (1886–1932)

מײַן שרײַעדיקײַט

מײַן שרײַעדיקײַט איז אײַנגעשלאָפֿן איבער מײַנע הענט
ווי אַ קראַנקער אין מיטן גאַס אין אַ ווינטערנאַכט אויף אַ שטיין,
דאָס ליכט פֿון דער לבנה אויף אַזוינעם איז געל ווי אויף אַ טויטן,
און בלויז דער ווינט וואָס פֿליט אין דער פֿינצטער פֿון שילד צו שילד –
איבער די אַלטע קליידער-געשעפֿטן – זעט אים –
און די וועלט איז דאָך אַזוי אומענדלעך-רײַך אין פֿענצטער,
וואָס לײַכטן אַרויס אין דער נאַכט – אַנטקעגן רעלסן
בײַ די ברעגן פֿון ים,
פֿון ברעג אַרונטער,
פֿון פֿאַלאַצן מיט גאָרטן און צוים אַרום זיך –
און דאָרט איז וואַרעם לײַב אונטער זײַד –
און געלער און ברוינער קוכן צווישן פֿינגער און ציין ווי פּערל קליינע,
בעת די אויערן הערן ליבע-רייד פֿון מאַן אָדער פֿרוי,
און פֿאַראַן ווײַן-פֿלעשער מיט אַזוינע לאַנגע שמאָלע העלדזער שיינע
און מיט זילבער פֿון אויבן און מיט גאָלד
און בלומען פֿאַר אַזוי פֿיל איבעריק געלט
אויף הערצער – וואָס זענען אפֿשר זייער גוט – ווײַל זיי האָבן ליב.
נאָר ווי פֿרעמד און ווי אָפּגעשיידט זיי זענען פֿון דעם אין מיטן גאַס.
לויט זייער פֿרײלעכקײַט איז ער אין גאַנצן נישטאָ,
אויסגעטראַכט בלויז. אויסגעטרוימט פֿון אַ שרעקנדיקן אין דער פֿינצטער
אין אַ נײַער דירה ערגעץ
איינער אַליין
די ערשטע נאַכט,
שלאָפֿט ער ניט – הערט ער דעם ווינט – מיינט ער, ווער ווייסט וואָס
עס טוט זיך דאָרט ערגעץ אין דרויסן.

Mayn Shrayedikayt

Mayn shrayedikayt iz ayngeshlofn iber mayne hent
vi a kranker in mitn gas in a vinternakht oyf a shteyn,
dos likht fun der levone oyf azoynem iz gel vi oyf a toytn,
un bloyz der vint vos flit in der fintster fun shild tsu shild—
iber di alte kleyder-gesheftn—zet im—

un di velt iz dokh azoy ummeglekh-raykh in fentster,
vos loykhtn aroys in der nakht—antkegn relsn
ba di bregn fun yam
fun breg arunter,
fun palatsn mit gortn un tsoym arum zikh—
un dort iz varem layb unter zayd—
un geler un broyner kukhn tsvishn finger un tseyn vi perl kleyne,
beys di oyern hern libe-reyd fun man oder froy,
un faran vayn-flesher mit azoyne lange shmole heldzer sheyne
un mit zilber fun oybn un mit gold
un blumen far azoy-fil iberik gelt
oyf hertser—vos zenen efsher zeyer gut—vayl zey hobn lib.
Nor vi fremd un vi opgesheydt zey zenen fun dem in mitn gas.
Loyt zeyer freylekhkayt iz er in gantsn nishto,
oysgetrakht bloyz. Oysgetroymt fun a shrekndikn in der fintster
in a nayer dire ergets
eyner aleyn
di ershte nakht
shloft er nit—hert er dem vint—meynt er, ver veyst vos
es tut zikh dort ergets in droysn.

My Screamingness

My screamingness fell asleep in my arms
like a sick man in the middle of the street on a winter night on a
    stone,
the light of the moon on someone like that is yellow as on a dead
    man,
and only the wind which is flying in the dark from signboard to
    signboard—
over the old garment stores—sees him—
and the world is after all so impossibly rich in windows,
that shine out in the night—facing rails
by the shores of the sea
from the shore down,
from palaces with garden and fence all around them—
and there flesh is warm under silk—
and yellow and brown cake between fingers and teeth like little
    pearls,
while the ears hear love-talk from man or woman,
and there are wine bottles with such long slender beautiful necks
and with silver on top and with gold
and flowers for so much superfluous money
upon hearts—which are perhaps very good—for they love.
Yet how alien and how cut off they are from that someone in the
    middle of the street

judging by their cheerfulness he is not there at all,
just imagined. Dreamt up by a fearful (man) in the dark
in a new apartment somewhere
all alone
the first night
he does not sleep—so he hears the wind—so he thinks, who knows
    what
is going on somewhere out there.

—Halpern (1934, vol. 2:166–67; translation mine)

"My Screamingness" was published posthumously in 1934 in the
second of a two-volume edition of poems from Halpern's later period
(1924–32). Although this volume includes mostly unpublished manu-
scripts, "My Screamingness" survives as one of Halpern's major po-
ems and one which apparently occupied the poet for some time. A
significantly different, longer, and altogether more transparent ver-
sion of this poem appears in the first volume of the same edition and
is dated 1927.[1] The present version, with its carefully structured free
verse, its systematic avoidance of traditional rhyme (the type of
rhyme which always was a great temptation for Halpern), and espe-
cially with its virtuoso manipulation of tensions between rhythm and
syntax, bespeaks a new, perhaps never fully developed phase in the
tightly wrought modernist poetics Moyshe Leyb concealed under his
rogue's mask.

The "screamingness" of the title and first line is an untranslatable
neologism in Yiddish (shrayedikayt), a noun formed from the gerund.
It expresses a unique combination of the angry pain of "outcry" (ge-
shray or the verb shrayen) and the ruthless, garish vulgarity of "loud-
ness" (shrayedik is a dead metaphor similar in sense to "garish" or
"loud" as in "a loud tie"). This combination of pained outcry and
flaunted loudness summarizes better than many longer descriptions
the "Moyshe Leybism" of the multifaceted persona that we meet in so
many of Halpern's poems. The screamingness of the poetic "I" is
given two contrasting personifications. First, it is implicitly described
as a baby crying itself to sleep in a parent's arms (line 1). Then it is
seen as a sick derelict asleep on a stone during a cold winter night
(line 2), harshly reversing the soothing, warm implications of the first
line. Interestingly, this reversal is effected through an extended simile,
a figure of speech which according to traditional views serves to point
out similarities rather than create contrast. By implication, the cold
stone in this simile becomes the ironic equivalent of the parental/

poetic cradling arms. Furthermore, sleep itself is no longer the calming, peaceful rest of one whose needs have been satisfied; it is a state of deathlike petrification. In line 3 the metaphor of sleep as death is developed further by utilizing the flexibility of gender in Yiddish: *likht* usually means "light" when feminine, and "candle" when it is—as here—in the neuter, although the two may be used interchangeably. Thus, invoking the traditional Jewish custom of lighting a candle by the deathbed, the line can also read: "even the (beautiful, romantic) moonlight looks like deathbed candlelight when it touches someone like that sick man."

The sick derelict becomes, as the poem unfolds, an expressionist juncture of orientations: for the speaker he serves as an objectified version of his screaming artistic self, while at the same time presenting society's attitudes toward the artist and toward the poor and the homeless. A link between the personal and the social themes of the poem, the "screamingness"-cum-sick-man, provides both a metaphor for the inner turmoil of the lyrical "I" and a metonymy for the distress of poverty during the depression. This link is made explicit in the 1927 version of the poem mentioned above, in which Halpern's own shocking economic hardship is directly identified with the sick derelict's state: the screaming self is openly described as a hungry artist (*a kinstler a hugeriker*) (Halpern, 1934, vol. 1:215). The scene of the sick man, introduced initially only as a simile (line 2), takes over completely as if it were part of the literal frame and has an elaborate, concrete, and seemingly nonfigurative situation spun around it. With this development, the first-person point of view as well as the objectified screaming "I" totally disappear: the scream falls silent when it falls asleep.

Two dynamic elements, the wind and the light, develop the situation by moving the scene from the static image of the sick man asleep in the street to other more affluent parts of the city. There is an interesting division of labor between the two elements: the wind appears in the context of the poorer parts of the city (lines 4–5) and is associated with the absence of light (it is "flying in the dark . . . /Over the old garment stores"), and the light is associated with the richer sections (line 6, lines 10–17) and is the one to show the way out, to shine on the escape route. Thus, *loykhtn aroys* in line 7 means both literally "shine out" and idiomatically "show (shed light on) the way out"; *fentster*, "window(s)" (line 6), is contrasted with *fintster*, "darkness" (line 4), and is a traditional metaphor in Jewish literature for light, liberation, and hope.[2] Here, however, windows are explicitly and ironically associated with being rich (line 6). Irony is maintained through ambiguity: "the world is . . . impossibly rich in windows" can mean either that there are an infinite number of windows (ways out, sources of hope) for the screaming, impoverished artistic self; or it can have the contrary meaning, that it is only in(side) windows (of palaces such as are described in lines 10–17) that the world's impossible, unattainable riches lie—for the rich to own and enjoy.

The transition, with the wind, from the inner city (lines 4–5) to the glittering suburbs along the coast (lines 8–10) appears to inject an optimistic chance for change, literally to outline an escape route from homelessness and illness; yet the ambiguous diction and syntax undercut the very possibility of such a solution. All the terms used to depict the escape route—the windows shining on the way out, the railway tracks, the coastline—also describe a series of barriers which cut off the destitute artistic self from the better world. The windows have impossible (*ummeglekh*) riches locked up inside them; the word for "railway tracks," *relsn* (line 7), also means "railings," and even "the shoreline," *breg*, means, in addition, "edge" or "border." Furthermore, this shoreline is high up, above the observer's reach since the light is shining out from the hilly shore down (line 9). The 1927 version of the poem may explain this enigmatic passage. Between 1927 and 1929 a very sick and hungry Halpern stayed in Los Angeles. And, indeed, the physical and social landscape of a hilly coastline dotted with the rich estates of partying "beautiful people" seems to fit the Los Angeles that Halpern observed but was never part of, in the late twenties, just before the Great Depression.[3]

While the list of ways out is only implicitly revealed to be a catalogue of barriers, the final item (and the subject of the next ten lines) quite explicitly shuts the outsider out. Line 10 uses the word *tsoym*, which in addition to the meaning "fence" is the generic term for any type of barrier. It provides a summary of the preceding catalogue and indicates, in its blatant juxtaposition with *gortn* ("garden"), a switch in tone from implied irony to unveiled sarcasm. The sarcastic depiction of the "beautiful people" in their fenced-off high palaces (lines 10–20) is especially rich in expressive uses of syntax, rhythm, and rhyme.

The sense of constant movement and the ironic undercutting of the illusion of progress which accompanies it are served by the syntax of the first section of the poem. The descriptive section which covers the bulk of the text (lines 3–17) is all one long sentence, interrupted by sets of dashes which follow intonational rather than grammatical patterns.

Numerous enjambments and fluctuations in line length contribute further to the dynamic, innovative structure. Rhyme is almost completely absent in its traditional location at the end of lines, while line beginnings, instead of having the conventional "content" words (nouns, verbs) are almost exclusively occupied by grammatical formatives—conjunctions and prepositions. As a result, a flowing speech rhythm is achieved, of the kind that was rare in the poetry of *di yunge* aestheticists of Halpern's generation. This flowing rhythm is also flexible enough to accommodate the many syntactic ambiguities and to allow the speaker to weave his ironic or sarcastic commentary into the description.

This flexibility is especially evident in lines 11–19, where the text alternates between a detailed description of the scene's aesthetic and sensual beauty, and a sarcastic editorial deflation of whatever romantic connotations that a rich and beautiful type of existence might evoke. On the one hand, "teeth like little pearls" (line 12) and "wine bottles with such long slender beautiful necks" (line 14) are metonymic descriptions of the beautiful people in terms of their beautiful objects (pearls), and of the beautiful objects in terms of the people (the women's long and slender necks). On the other hand, the very use of metonymy as the central device for depicting this precious beauty has a deflating effect. It creates an interchangeability between the people and the objects. The fragmentary, modernist impetus of the metonymic description is enhanced by the use of synecdoche—a metonymy based on part-whole relationships—in lines 12–13; people are represented only by lists of their body parts: fingers, teeth, ears. The ears are being talked to about love while the fingers and mouth are busy consuming "yellow and brown cake." The critical tone becomes increasingly evident in the closing description (lines 16–19). The interplay of the two meanings of *hertser* in Yiddish ("hearts" and "chests"), together with the enjambment of lines 16–17, create a sarcastic double entendre: an image of people wearing rich flowers on their chests, as tokens of their devotion to beauty and love, but who really have money on their mind. Similarly, when their ability to love is asserted (line 17), the transitive verb *lib hobn*, "to love," receives no object. Instead we have—for the first time in the entire poem!—a period, typographically indicating just how narcissistic their love is and how "cut off they are from that someone in the middle of the street" (line 18). Expressionist syntax is in this manner rendered strictly, rigorously functional; experimental modernism is made to provide an urgent and most precise form of social critique.

Now that the image of the sick man in the street has returned, we expect the poem to complete the circle by going back to the first-person point of view of the beginning. The young Halpern may have chosen to do just that. The Halpern of "My Screamingness" prefers simplicity to symmetry, using the closure of the poem to provide a realistic motivation for the title and initial image. The word "imagined," *oysgetrakht,* in its bivalent location at the end of a sentence and the beginning of a line, offers the semantic transition to the final section of the poem. For the palace people, the sick derelict is not a metonymy for poverty, nor is he a metaphor for a screaming artistic self; he simply does not exist (line 19). In their cheerful disregard, any type of existence which is uncomfortably different from their own is characterized as imaginary. But *oysgetrakht* (literally, "thought up") self-consciously refers also to the poet's imagination, which is responsible for this fiction, this metaphor of artistic outcry as a sick derelict.

Although the final section is presented in the third person, it is clearly a metapoetic objectified version of the lyrical "I" of the beginning. However, unlike the earlier objectification, this one is blatantly literal and personal. The colloquial diction and speech rhythm of the last five lines supply a balancing counterpart to the highly figurative, structurally intricate first section. Thus, the conclusion of the poem simply tells us how the image of the sick man and, by implication, of the poet's screamingness came into being. The loneliness of the poet in an apartment that is not yet home (line 21), the night, his sleep-lessness, the sound of the wind—all combine in the waking dream where the screaming self is created in the poet's image.

Perets Markish (1895–1952)

ווייס איך ניט, צי כ'בין אין דר'היים,

צי אין דער פֿרעמד –

איך לויף!...

צעשפּיליעט איז מײַן העמד,

ניטאָ ז'אויף מיר קיין צוים,

כ'בין קיינעמס ניט, כ'בין הפֿקר,

אָן אָן אָנהייב, אָן אַ סוף...

מײַן גוף איז שוים,

און ס'שמעקט פֿון אים מיט ווינט;

מײַן נאָמען איז: "אַצינד" . . .

צעוואַרף איך מײַנע הענט,

דערלאַנגען זיי די וועלט פֿון איין עק ביזן צווייטן,

די אויגן כ'לאָז געווענדט,

פֿאַרטרינקען זיי די וועלט פֿון אונטן ביז אַרויף!

מיט אויגן אָפֿענע, מיט אַ צעשפּיליעט העמד,

מיט הענט צעשפּרייטע, —

ווייס איך ניט, צי כ'האָב אַ היים,

צי כ'האָב אַ פֿרעמד,

צי כ'בין אַן אָנהייב, צי אַ סוף . . .

[Veys Ikh Nit Tsi Kh'bin in D'reym]

Veys ikh nit tsi kh'bin in d'reym,[4]
tsi in der fremd—
ikh loyf! . . .
Tseshpiliyet iz mayn hemd,
nito z'af mir keyn tsoym,
kh'bin keynems nit, kh'bin hefker,
on an onheyb, on a sof . . .

Mayn guf iz shoym,
un s'shmekt fun im mit vint;
mayn nomen iz: "atsind" . . .
Tsevarf ikh mayne hent,
derlangen zey di velt fun eyn ek bizn tsveytn,
di oygn kh'loz gevendt,
fartrinken zey di velt fun untn biz aroyf!

Mit oygn ofene, mit a tseshpiliyet hemd,
mit hent tseshpreyte—
veys ikh nit, tsi kh'hob a heym,
tsi kh'hob a fremd,
tsi kh'bin an onheyb, tsi a sof.

[Don't Know if I'm at Home]

Don't know if I'm at home,
Or if I'm afar—
I'm running! . . .
My shirt's unbuttoned,
There are no reins on me,
I'm nobody's, I'm unclaimed,
Without a beginning, without an end . . .

My body is foam,
And it reeks of wind;
My name is: "Now" . . .
If I throw out my hands,
They'd give the world a smack from one end to the
    other,
My eyes if I let roam about,
They'd guzzle down the world from the bottom up!

With eyes open, with an unbuttoned shirt,
With hands stretched out,
I don't know if I have a home,
Or have a-far,
If I'm a beginning, or an end.

—Markish (1918–19; reprinted in Harshav [Hrushovski], Sutzkever, and Shmeruk,
    1964:375–76; translation mine in collaboration with Bluma Goldstein)

In his essay "In the Ways of Jewish Poetry" (1921), Markish writes: "The spirit of human creativity and the spirit of the revolution are so intermingled that it is hard to tell which . . . generates which" (quoted from the Hebrew translation in Harshav [Hrushovski], 1973:117). This combined spirit finds an expression in "Don't Know If I'm at Home" with the forcefulness and the conviction of a poetic credo. Written during the tumultuous times of the Russian revolution, the poem belongs to a group of early programmatic statements in which Markish asserts a new stance for the poet. The joyful aggressiveness with which the speaker in this poem interacts with the world around him is reminiscent of Russian futurist and other modernist manifestoes of the period, with which the young Markish was strongly—though not exclusively—affiliated. Underlying these early poems is Vladimir Mayakovsky's dictum: "The revolution of content—Socialism-Anarchism—would be impossible without the revolution of form—Futurism" (Mayakovsky, 1918, in Harshav [Hrushovski], 1973:56). This belief not only gave poetry in general a sense of indispensability but also allowed Markish and the other Yiddish poets in revolutionary Russia to integrate their Jewish modernist experience with the cultural and political collective one. Radicalism became for them the unifying factor that rendered the different dimensions of their expression—political, poetic, and ethnic—consistent rather than contradictory.

In the spirit of Mayakovsky's futurism, but in terms which foreshadow Markish's own involvement with expressionism, the poem presents the general theme of poet versus world through an extended modernist metonymy: it focuses on the speaker's body (hands, eyes) as representing the poet's new dynamic grip on reality. This portrait of the poet as "new man" is not without its self-irony. The speaker is seen running around with no definite goal, hands waving wildly, eyes turning in his head—a disheveled and violent image, echoing the prototypical descriptions of the *geyer* or *meshulekh*, the Jewish holy tramp, the privileged, valorized marginal character of Jewish cultural discourse. The revolutionary modernist poet is thus seen not only as free and unencumbered (lines 5–6) but also as abandoned and poor. *Hefker* (line 6) is a complex notion implying lawlessness and recklessness on the one hand, and neglect and abandonment on the other. In the background one hears the expression *hefker-mentch*, "derelict," as well as the humorous saying *hefker petrishke* (literally, "ownerless parsley"), which stands for "anything goes." But unlike the devastating social and self-criticism of Halpern's beggar/clown or sick derelict (Chapter 7), in fact unlike the macabre depiction of the poet's destitution in Markish's later work, the liberating, celebratory tone is unmistakable.

The combination of the new image of the liberated modernist poet with the traditional image of the wandering Jew uprooted from his or her cultural tradition runs throughout the poem as a personification of a modernist marginal prototype of poetic and social existence. The new "native of the world" who does not need a home is also the poor homeless tramp who has severed ties with the past; the revolutionary poet who unbuttons his shirt and reeks of the wind in celebration of his new "organic" and "naked" aesthetics is also the disheveled derelict whose smell is probably not pleasant (the Yiddish in line 9 uses the impersonal colloquial expression *es shmekt fun im*, "it smells from him," which usually implies a rather foul odor). Perhaps the clearest examples of ambivalently modernist images are those that involve the speaker's hands and eyes (lines 11–16). They depict the new poet's sense of power and aggressive creativity: rather than record reality passively, he has the ability to reach into it, even beat it up (in line 12).

In the description of the hands, the same verb, *derlangen*, means both "to reach" and "to deal a blow." Similarly, in the description of the eyes, the verb *fartrinken* (line 14) can mean both "to booze up" and "to drown or flood." Thus, the poet simultaneously takes reality in and ex-presses it, flooding it with his own inner visions. However, to these complex images Markish still manages to add that other dimension of the wandering pauper and thereby to "Judaize" and ironize his own radical modernism. In sharp contrast to the poet's aggressive blow to the world, the stretched-out hands (line 16) echo a beggar's pose. Similarly, the eyes, which are a simultaneous source of artistic impression and expression, are also seen as roaming about (line 13)—a synecdoche for their wandering owner. Furthermore, the verb *fartrinken* has in colloquial Yiddish an additional sense which fits very well the prototype of the penniless, homeless poet: it denotes idiomatically spending all one has on drink, as well as drowning one's troubles in alcohol.

Despite its undercutting effect, the image of the poor wanderer does not destroy the poem's rejoicing in the new. This celebration is especially evident in the playful reversal of conventions, both linguistic and poetic, as well as in the poem's tone and diction. Even though it is a poetic self-portrait, the poem deliberately deviates from the lyrical strategies that are traditionally associated with this mode. Instead of a static, descriptive profile of the lyrical "I" reflecting after the fact on his experiences and emotions, we get the impression of a breathless, spontaneous, and hurriedly edited "instant replay" of the poet in motion and action.

The focus on the dynamic perception of a present moment is, of course, not just a mark of the modernist mode of presentation. It is also one of the poem's major themes, foregrounded in exclamatory futurist fashion at its center (line 10)—"My name is: 'Now.' " Markish's flaunted statement of an abstract concept (*Atsind* can also be translated as "the Now") in the center of a poem whose genre is traditionally descriptive and concrete is no accident. Even though the line is weakly metaphorical, the diction reveals a clear preference for the more abstract and declamatory *atsind* (rather than the colloquial and concrete terms for "now," *itst* or *yetst*). This selection is especially salient on the background of the blunt slang and colloquial idioms used everywhere else in the poem. A few years after the publication of this poem, when Markish was organizing the Yiddish expressionist movement, he generalized this practice as an explicit poetic principle:

"Jewish poetry has left behind its back the descriptive stage and is approaching the threshold of the liberated idea-word, the sublime philosophical thought" (in Harshav [Hrushovski], 1973:120).

While the center of the poem foregrounds the speaker's concern with time, the beginning and end of the poem reveal a preoccupation with space. But whereas the speaker joyfully contracts time to a dynamic, ever shifting present, without past or future, his rejection of linear space proves more complex. The spatial statements in the first and last stanzas differ significantly. Whereas in the first stanza the speaker asserts that he does not have a beginning or an end (line 7), by the end of the poem he is asking whether he himself is a beginning or an end. Conversely, while in the first line the speaker questions his being at home, in the last stanza (line 17) he questions the very fact of his *having* a home. This chiastic representation of the speaker's orientation in space, the fusion of having a property and being an entity, are typical of the expressionist poetics which opposed the very dichotomy of inner and outer reality. In the first stanza the speaker already sees himself as boundless, "Without a beginning, without an end" (line 7), but his view of the world around him is still scientifically and aesthetically the premodern one; he accepts the distinction between here and there, near and far, familiar and foreign. In the Yiddish all these conventional oppositions are captured in the two fixed expressions: *in der heym* ("at home," line 1), as against *in der fremd* (roughly, "away from home," "in foreign parts," line 2).

However, in the process of the poem the speaker himself changes; his epistemology grows into his (already modernist) aesthetics and (revolutionary) politics. He grows to view not only himself but also the world around him as having no beginning and no end. Once he realizes that his hands can reach from one end of the world to the other (line 12) and that—homeless little tramp though he is—he can still give that huge world a good smack, the distinction between far and near, being at home and being away from home, no longer holds. Moreover, since he is free to act in this world and to change it, even those foreign parts can belong to him. The revolutionary socialist and the radical modernist views converge to produce the new, oxymoronlike notions: of possessing that which is (according to the old view) alien and unpossessible; and of giving up ownership of that which is considered inalienable and possessible.

The reversal of the "normal" way of looking at the world and at a human being's place in it is reflected also in the violation of linguistic norms. Markish uses the term *fremd* as if it were a concrete, possessible noun (something like "afarness," the place where one feels far from home). Normally, *fremd* is an adjective, and nominal uses occur only in expressions such as *in der fremd* (line 2, "away from home"). Thus, the locution *kh'hob a fremd* (loosely translated as "I have a-far") is both grammatically and conceptually jarring; it reconciles the wandering tramp with his modern surrogate—the revolutionary poet—by reinterpreting for both the notions of home and of ownership, of beginning and of end. Ultimately, however, not just the norms of language and perception are called into question but even the promise of modernism and modernity. The poem's end, after all, asserts only the speaker's "I don't knows," not any positive credo, in his mock-heroic echo of Jesus' "I am Alpha and Omega, the beginning and the end, the first and the last" (Revelation 22:13).[5]

Dovid Hofshteyn (1889–1952)

די קריִע גייט —
און ברעגן נעמען ברייט
דעם וואַסער-יאָד
אויף אַקסלען ווייך-באַוואָקסענע,
און לאָזיעס בוקן זיך
פֿאַר זונען-פֿרייד...

און לאָזיעס איינע וועלן די פֿאַרהיילטע דראָפֿן
אין פֿרישן טייַד באַניַיען,
און איינע וועט עס אונטערשוועענקען,
מיט וואָרצלען זיי פֿאַרכאַפֿן
און פֿירן אין די וואַסער-לענגען...

נאָר העל איז זונען-פֿרייד!
אויף טייַד אויף פֿרייַען קריִען גייט!
און שטענגלעד בוקן זיך:
מיר זייַנען גרייט, מיר זייַנען גרייט...

[Di Kri'ye Geyt]

Di kri'ye geyt—
un bregn nemen breyt
dem vaser-yokh
oyf akslen veykh bavoksene,
un lozes bukn zikh
far zunen-freyd . . .

Un lozes eyne veln di farheylte drapn
in frishn taykh banayen,
un eyne vet es untershvenken
mit vortslen zey farkhapn
un forn in di vaser-lengen . . .

Nor hel iz zunen-freyd!
oyf taykh oyf frayen kri'ye geyt!
un shtenglakh bukn zikh:
mir zaynen greyt, mir zaynen greyt . . .

[The Ice Floe Is Moving]

The ice floe is moving—
And banks, magnanimous, are putting
The water-yoke
On soft hairy shoulders,
And twigs are bowing low
To sun-joy . . .

And some twigs will renew their healed-over scratches
In the fresh river,
And some will be washed away,
Roots seized
And led into the water-reaches . . .

Yet bright is the sun-joy!
On the river onto freedom the floe is moving!
And young stems are bowing low:
We are ready, we are ready . . .

           —Hofshteyn ([1912] 1919:27; translation mine)

Dovid Hofshteyn was one of the central figures of modernist Yiddish poetry in the Soviet Union. Together with Leyb Kvitko and Markish he formed "the lyrical triumvirate of the Kiev Group" (Liptzin, 1972:203), which for a while was the leading force in Yiddish modernism in Russia. Although he was raised in a rural area of the Ukraine, Hofshteyn received a sophisticated formal education in

Kiev, where he became prominent in literary Jewish life after the revolution. Even though Hofshteyn often tried to follow the party line, he never quite managed to rid his poetry of the forbidden cultural and biblical associations. In 1948 he was seized, and after years of torture he was executed on August 12, 1952, the same day that saw the collective murder of many of the greatest Yiddish writers in Stalinist Russia, including Markish and Kvitko.

Hofshteyn's is a low-key, lyrical, and introverted modernism. Innovations are never flaunted in his poetry, and those aspects which are most daring and unconventional are often also latent or implied. This tone is especially true of the early poetry, from which my selections are taken. The romantic images of a pantheistic, glorified nature are in the foreground, while the modernist tone is lurking underneath, undercutting the traditional view and adding contemporary "antipoetic" dimensions to it. In this sense, Hofshteyn's poetry participates in the same "minor key" liminal modernism that Fogel and the other antiformulaic Hebrew writers engaged in.[6]

In "The Ice Floe Is Moving," the impression of traditional symmetry turns out on examination to be quite misleading. Although the beginning and end of the poem are made to create the illusion of a regular rhyme scheme (aa, da), no regular scheme in fact appears. Instead, functional rhyme is used throughout, namely rhyme that appears only to convey meaning relations between the rhyming elements. Similarly, while the meter consists of seemingly regular iambs, the number of feet per line varies constantly, according to the requirements of meaning and speech rhythm, rather than in accordance with any symmetrical form. (Note, for example, how the meter emphasizes the center of the poem in line 7).

This poem, written in 1912, describes a natural phenomenon which must have been quite a familiar sight for a boy growing up in the northwestern Ukraine: The floe, the ice field covering the river during the winter, has begun to melt and is floating downstream, carrying with it the promise of spring and rejuvenation. However, a half-implicit metaphor, which encompasses the first stanza, introduces quite different feelings into the scene. The riverbanks putting the water-yoke on their shoulders bring to mind the Russian *burlaki*—the barge haulers, who would often be prisoners, wild and despondent forced laborers on a chain gang. Thus, the poem's quietly subversive tone is already established here by combining two images of opposing semantic and aesthetic import. The explicit, literal image of the floating ice floe invokes the conventional associations of spring with joy and renewal (lines 5–6). The implicit, figurative situation of the prisoners (the riverbanks) hauling a barge (the ice floe) stresses those aspects of the natural scene which the conventional depiction usually fails to mention: the hard labor involved in pulling the water-yoke with its cargo of an ice field and the efforts needed to keep these waters under control (within the banks). The melting of the ice signals here the dangers of flooding, the violence inherent in nature, no less than the renewed joys of sunshine.

The two opposing images are combined into one complex scene. The banks are indeed wild-looking like the *burlaki* (*bavoksene* in line 4 means "overgrown," not just "hairy"); but they are softly so (*veykh*). Unlike the prisoners, the riverbanks put the water yoke on their shoulders of their own free will, with a broad, magnanimous gesture. Finally, this combined image does not overshadow the literal scene but rather adds concreteness to it: *breyt* (line 2) can refer metaphorically to the banks' open and generous gesture, but it also literally describes the width of the river. Similarly, *bavoksene* (line 4) may refer to the wild and hairy look of the metaphorical *burlaki*, but it also describes the vegetation along the banks.

The second stanza is the only one to use the future tense, placing the speaker in a position of knowing things to come. This ironic distance of the speaker from the scene undercuts the romantic tone of the "rites of spring" in lines 5–6. Two different fates are described for the twigs, and by extension for all those awaiting rejuvenation: some will be "renewed" in the fresh water, in a scene that echoes purification rites; others, less fortunate, will be swept away and uprooted. A closer look reveals, however, more than a touch of irony in the first case, and more than a glimpse of hope in the second. Again, in Hofshteyn's subtle modernist poetics, opposites are presented only in order to be merged. Renewing (*banayen*) old scratches can indeed here mean having them cleansed and refreshed by water, but it must mean also a reopening of old wounds. This ironic twist is most effectively felt in the Yiddish syntax because the word *banayen* (line 8, "renew") comes as a rhythmic surprise at the very end of a sentence with inverted word order, and with it comes the reversal of all romantic expectations.

The second prediction is indeed ominous. The Yiddish uses an impersonal sentence, with an unspecified and nonreferential "it" as the subject which is doing all the capturing, uprooting, and carrying.

Moreover, even though the scene has clear references in nature, its human connotations for the relations between oppressor and oppressed are undeniably present: the common metaphor of uprootedness and the reference—through the verb *farkhapn* (line 10, "capture," "seize," "kidnap")—to the practice in czarist Russia of kidnapping Jewish youths for military service. However, the violent fate predicted for the twigs, or the human parallel they may represent, is carefully mitigated. The twigs will, after all, be led to the water-reaches (*vaser-lengen* in line 11), an expression coined by Hofshteyn which connotes adventure, openness, and freedom.

Just as pain and submission were the price for maintaining the romantic dreams of cyclical renewal, so are freedom and the opening of new horizons a compensation for the violent upheaval of change. The second stanza, with its image of the raging river on the verge of spring, makes the problem of freedom and submission more explicit in the thematic structure of the poem. Two competing models for development in nature and in humanity seem to emerge as the poem's correlated aesthetics and politics: the old model, coupling pantheism with self-imposed servitude and seeking to maintain the present order (stanza 1); and the new model, combining freedom and change with the dangers of violence and destruction (stanza 2).

In the third stanza the speaker directly expresses his feelings about the natural scene and more implicitly about the issues of social renewal and change. Again, the emerging view is a combination of the old model and the new, of romanticism and radical modernism. Each line is a short exclamation, reaffirming in a modified but enthusiastic way the joys of spring. A detailed contrast is established between the first stanza, with its one long sentence, and the third, with its brief, excited one-liners. The first three lines of the third stanza repeat asymmetrical lines in the first stanza (in lines 12 and 6, 13 and 1, 14 and 5) with several significant changes. For example, now the ice floe—not just the riverbank—is portrayed as a prisoner, albeit one that is sailing to freedom (line 13). *Frayen,* rather than *frayhayt,* is chosen for "freedom" to emphasize its complementary relationship with *freyen zikh* ("to rejoice"). Consequently, although the sun-joy is reaffirmed (line 12), the stems are no longer bowing low to it. Their readiness for liberation is indicated in the fact that their bow is not directed at any particular authority but rather is expressed in their speech act (line 15). Clearly, the romantic reading of the twigs awaiting the renewal of spring is still possible. But the emphasis on freedom (in line 13) gets a strong, though subtle, reinforcement in the last line. The only words actually spoken in the poem, "We are ready, we are ready," echo the prayer uttered before drinking each of the four glasses of wine during the Seder celebration on Passover eve, the feast commemorating liberation. Since Passover is also the spring festival, the allusion offers a combination of the natural theme of spring with the social and national theme of freedom.

Finally, the Yiddish word for ice floe offers a juncture of the double perspective the poem maintains. *Kri'ye* is homophonous with the Hebraic term used in Yiddish to describe the custom of tearing clothes as a sign of mourning. Death and rejuvenation, mourning and joy, imprisonment and liberation, are seen as complementary dimensions of the same experience. Thus, an ostensibly premodernist poem about the traditional theme of the coming of spring is revealed to be an excited—though not an anxiety-free—annunciation of the imminent social and aesthetic revolutions: communism and modernism.

כ׳האָב דערזען זי ביַים טיַיך
אונטער צוויַיגן,
אונטער גרינעם, מיט הימל פֿאַרלאַטעטן דאַך.
אין אַ פּאָר צענדלינג טריט,
אויף דעם ערדישן שוויַיגן
האָט געשטומט דאָרט אַ שטיין,
אַ פֿאַרעקשנטער גליד
פֿון מיַין אורלאַנדס צעזייטן, צעשטויבטן געביין...

כ׳האָב דערזען זי אין נאַקעטער פֿרייד פֿון איר ליַיב,
אין צעפֿלאַסענער קרוין פֿון די דופֿטיקע האָר,
כ׳האָב דערהערט פֿון די טיפֿן פֿון אוריונגע יאָר:
— אָט אָ-די רופֿט מען וויַיב!

[Kh'hob Derzen Zi Baym Taykh]

Kh'hob derzen zi baym taykh
unter tsvaygn
unter grinem, mit himl farlatetn dakh.
In a por tsendling trit,

oyf dem erdishn shvaygn
hot geshtumt dort a shteyn
a far'akshnter glid
fun mayn urlands tsezeytn, tseshtoybtn gebeyn . . .

Kh'hob derzen zi in naketer freyd fun ir layb,
in tseflosener kroyn fun di duftike hor,
kh'hob derhert fun di tifn fun uryunge yor:
—Ot-o di ruft men vayb!

[I Saw Her by the River]

I saw her by the river
Under branches,
Under the green, sky-patched roof.
Several dozen steps away,
Upon the earthly silence
There a stone was mute
A stubborn limb
From my old country's bones, scattered and turned to dust . . .

I saw her in the naked joy of her flesh,
In the disheveled crown of her fragrant hair,
I heard from the depths of age-young years:
—This is what one calls a wife!

                    —Hofshteyn ([1912] 1919:55–56; translation mine)

As in "The Ice Floe Is Moving," the central artistic concern of this poem is the relation of contrasting elements. The poem consists of two images which together form one scene: a naked woman by the river, and—"several dozen steps away" (line 4)—a dusty old stone. Despite the spatial contiguity of the two images within the "world" of the poem, there are striking contrasts between them in structure, theme, point of view, style, and genre. The image of the naked woman is clearly in the foreground, but it is given in two discontinuous strokes in the first part of each stanza (lines 1–3, 9–10). The depiction of the stone which "interrupts" the woman image is also given in five lines, but it is presented in one continuous segment (lines 4–8). This digression from what appears to be the main human focus of the poem creates a tension between the two images. However, when the alternating images are examined in detail, it turns out that despite their opposing tendencies each image also contains elements of its counterpart. Contrast and similarity are finally brought together in the last two lines of the poem, where the historical (associated with the stone) merges with the personal (associated with the woman).

At the beginning of the poem, the image of the woman is presented as a vivid, concrete experience of the lyrical "I" ("I saw her"). The verb *derzen* ("to see all at once," "to discern") as well as the other occurrences of verbs indicating sense perception in the poem (lines 9, 11) use the prefix *der*, which emphasizes the perfective and sudden aspect of the action of seeing (*zen*) or hearing (*hert*). While these verbs have the force of immediacy, they also draw our attention to the fact that the speaker is reconstructing a personal past experience, rather than "objectively" or impressionistically observing a present one.

The tension between syntax and diction in the first three lines adds another dimension to the hesitation between immediacy and perfectiveness. Syntactically, the woman is the object of description, and the river, green branches, and blue sky are just the natural backdrop expressed in a series of prepositional phrases. However, these prepositional phrases constitute the bulk of the sentence and are semantically the most informative part. In fact, in this first part of the image, reference to the woman is limited to a single pronoun (*zi*, "she"), giving her no concrete character or shape. As in the postimpressionist paintings that this scene echoes, the distinction between foreground and background is either deliberately blurred or altogether reversed. Furthermore, like other more famous modernist images of women by the water,[7] Hofshteyn's poem deflates the familiarly romantic or decorative conventions associated with bathing scenes in the artistic tradition such as Tintoretto's *Susanna and the Elders* and Renoir's *Bathers*. It is interesting to note that this image-oriented poem, like other early modernist poems in Yiddish and Hebrew, draws much more directly on the history of art than of literature, embracing a postimpressionist modernist prototype and conveying meticulously the possibilities of applying this artistic model to poetry. At the same time, however, the contrastive structure of the image, the emphasis on physical juxtaposition rather than symbolic interpretation, and the lexical and syntactic economy reveal an orientation toward a contemporary poetic modernist trend to which Hofshteyn owes a great deal: Russian acmeism.

The third line, with its surprising metaphor of "the sky-patched roof," foreshadows the contrastive structure that is to become the poem's central device. The realm of social reality is introduced ironically through a description of a natural scene. The branches and the treetops form a roof over the woman's head; but rather than stress the beauty of the sky patches that show through the treetops, the speaker invokes an image of a poor, dilapidated house, in which "sky-patched" is a sarcastic euphemism for "full of holes." (*farlatete*, "patched up," evokes a semantic field of poverty and refers primarily to the mending of tattered clothes.) Conventional expectations would be that this figurative depiction of nature in human terms enhance or parallel the theme of free, erotic beauty which the woman later comes to represent (lines 9–10) or that it supply the appropriate backdrop for the anticipated love scene: a lovers' nest, a natural haven, or a canopy of trees and sky. Instead, the text suggests a moldy (green), leaky (sky-patched) roof. Interestingly, the contrasts between the vehicle (leaky roof) and the tenor (treetops and sky), and between the metaphor as a whole and the initial image of the woman, result in the ultimate inseparability of these contrasting domains. This inseparability, in turn, is essential to Hofshteyn's modernist artistic credo: there can be no clear distinction between the natural and the social, the human and the inanimate, the past and the present. Thus, the woman is first seen "under branches" (line 2), merging into a natural backdrop; but the same natural backdrop is also a human and a social one, as the syntactic parallelism indicates: "Under branches/Under the green . . . roof" (lines 2–3).

The speaker makes the transition to the second image by "measuring" its distance from the first image—"several dozen steps away"—or, more literally, "in a couple of tens of steps," where "in a" is used in a spatial context in the same way that it may be used temporally in expressions such as "in a couple of minutes." As in the beginning of the poem, the reader is introduced to the image (line 4) through the point of view of the speaker. But unlike the abrupt "I saw (all at once)" of the first line, here the speaker approaches the stone more gradually, as though step by step (and note that in the Yiddish word order is manipulated so that the stone is "arrived at" only at the end of line 6).

Whereas the metaphor in the first image was concealed as part of the concrete natural scene (the sky-patched roof of trees), the image of the stone flaunts its nonliteral nature in two sets of metaphors of two lines each. The first centers around silence, or more precisely the active and willfull refraining from speech. Thus, the Yiddish for "earthly silence" (line 5) reads literally "the earth's refraining from speech" (*erdishn shvaygn*), and the stone's being mute (line 6) is expressed in the Yiddish by an intransitive verb derived from the adjective *shtum* (mute), resulting in something like "there a stone muted." Silence thus becomes an active means for expressing protest, anger, and pain. On this background the stone itself can insert—in the second metaphor—the veiled theme of Jewish dispersal and survival. Ironically, this metaphor (lines 7–8) first turns the stone into a part of a living body, "a stubborn limb," only to describe later on the dismemberment and death ("turned into dust") of the rest of the organism. Around the same time Bialik coined his famous Hebrew metaphor *peger avanim* ("a corpse of a stone"), which also personifies an inanimate object only to indicate its death.[8]

The speaker's personal experience of the woman's erotic and life-producing beauty is perceived as dependent on his ability to come to terms with the collective heritage of pain and destruction. But even as the stone is becoming a collective symbol, the speaker refers to it as a limb from "my old country's bones." The national experience of age-old collective suffering is personified and personalized in this half-dead body toward which the speaker feels the same attachment that he has to the vibrant, beautiful body of the naked woman.

The ability to recognize the living limb in the stone, the links to history within the present experience, and the message inscribed in the silent objects provide the central experience of the poem. Only once these links are established do the present moment and the beautiful woman it depicts come to life. It is almost as if the anatomical metaphor of the stone provides the bones (*gebeyn,* line 8) and the woman's naked joy forms the flesh or skin (*layb,* line 9) of one and the same living organism. Note that in the Yiddish the woman's flesh and the country's bones are juxtaposed in parallel position at the end of successive lines (lines 8 and 9). The majestic, Venus-like image of the woman is, in this context, reinterpreted in quite untraditional terms: she is indeed "natural woman," Venus and Eve, royal because unruly (line 10); but she is as much one with human history (line 11) as with nature.

Thus, only in the second stanza is the actual union of the historical and the personal, the painful and the beautiful, achieved. The structure reflects this resolution of opposites, for only here do we find a fully symmetrical scheme couched in the traditionally harmonious quatrain. When the first image of the woman by the river is continued so vividly in lines 9–10, it is perceived not only as a contrast but also as a complement to the image of the stone.

The last two lines of the poem make explicit this complementarity of nature, humanity, and history when the silence of the stone is replaced by speech; the age-old ancestral country (*urland*) by the oxy-moronic neologism "age-young years" (*uryunge yor*); and the distant "her" (*zi*) of the first line by the familiar exclamation: "This is what one calls a wife!" While this ending, like others by the young Hof-shteyn, may sound a little heavy-handed, it provides an interesting and intricate metaphorical reading which in retrospect may organize the whole poem: a modernist variation on the traditional Jewish motif of the wedding in the graveyard.[9] When the speaker is symbolically calling the woman a wife (line 12), he is invoking the bridegroom's speech act at a wedding ceremony. In times of communal strife, such as are described in lines 7–8, the destruction of the people (the bones of the ancestral country) symbolically warrants a graveyard cere-mony. Thus, the woman is being called a wife in a cemetery of sorts, "a few dozen steps away" from memorial stones (*shteyn* can also refer to tombstone) and the skeletons or remains (alternative meaning of *gebeyn*, line 8) which have turned to dust (*tseshtoybtn*, line 8). But this figurative graveyard wedding ceremony is not enacted to ward off the dangers of death or disaster, as in the folkloristic tradition. Rather, it functions aesthetically and socially as a corollary to the "marriage" of the living and the dead, the young and the old, change and tradi-tion. Politically, it bespeaks the Yiddish modernists' attempt to join the national Jewish heritage with the unbridled revolutionary present.

Thus, the veiled traditional motif of the wedding among the graves allows Hofshteyn's emergent political radicalism to cohere and—a more difficult task—to grow naturally out of his traditional cultural roots. This need to reconcile change and tradition, the cosmopolitan "I" with the national "we," eventually became the identifying mark of Hofshteyn's poetry. Tragically, the Stalinist oppressor could not, in the end, tolerate this mark of dialectical pluralism.

Avrom Sutzkever (b. 1913)

הירשן ביַים ים-סוף

דער זונפֿאַרגאַנג האָט זיך פֿאַרעקשנט מיט העזה
צו בליַיבן אין ים-סוף ביַי נאַכט, װען עס קומען
צום פֿאַלאַץ פֿון װאַסער – די אומשולדיק ראָזע,
די אײדעלע הירשן צו שטילן דעם גומען.

זיי לאָזן די זיַידענע שאָטנס ביַים באָרטן
און לעקן אין ים-סוף די רינגען פֿון קילקײט
מיט פֿידלענע פּנימער לאַנגע. און דאָרטן
געשעט די פֿאַרקנסונג ביַי זיי מיט דער שטילקײט.

געענדיקט – אַנטלױפֿן זיי. רױזיקע פֿלעקן
באַלעבן דעם זאַמד. נאָר עס בליַיבן פֿול יאָמער
די זונפֿאַרגאַנג-הירשן אין וואַסער און לעקן
די שטילקײט פֿון יענע, וואָס זענען ניטאָ מער.

Hirshn Baym Yam-Suf

Der zunfargang hot zikh far'akshnt mit hoze
tsu blaybn in yam-suf bay nakht, ven es kumen
tsum palats fun vaser—di umshuldik rose,
di eydele hirshn tsu shtiln dem gumen.

Zey lozn di zaydene shotns baym bortn
un lekn in yam-suf di ringen fun kilkayt
mit fidlene penimer lange. Un dortn
geshet di farknasung bay zey mit der shtilkayt.

Ge'endikt—antloyfn zey. Royzike flekn
balebn dem zamd. Nor es blaybn ful yomer
di zunfargang-hirshn in vaser un lekn
di shtilkayt fun yene, vos zenen nito mer.

Deer by the Red Sea

The sunset insisted impudently
On staying in the Red Sea at night, when there come
To the palace of water—the innocent rosy,
The graceful deer to quench their thirst.

They leave their silken shadows on the shore
And lick in the Red Sea the rings of coolness
With fiddle-long faces. And there
Takes place their betrothal to the silence.

Finished—they run away. Rosy stains
Animate the sand. Yet there remain woeful
The sunset-deer in the water and lick
The silence of those, that are no more.

    —Sutzkever (1963:71; published in 1949; translation mine)

"Deer by the Red Sea" is an Israeli Yiddish poem. Like so many of the other poems Sutzkever has written since coming to Israel in 1947, it offers a surprisingly harmonious hybridity of the most Israeli in milieu and experience with the most uniquely Yiddish in idiom and expression. "Deer by the Red Sea" is a hybrid text also in its trend affiliation, a typical example of what Harshav has cogently described as Sutzkever's "Neo-Classical Modernism" (in his introduction to Sutzkever 1991:4). The poem's prosody, which first appears anachronistically traditional, in fact offers a modernist functionalism applied to a tightly symmetrical metric scheme. Each stanza contains four lines of four amphibrachs each. However, the amphibrach is also the least conspicuous of meters in Yiddish because it coincides with the penultimate stress pattern of normal speech. Frequent changes in syntactic rhythm (sentence length, enjambment) and the unpredictable location of caesuras in the metrical line[10] combine to establish a speech rhythm alongside the symmetrical traditional meter. Similarly, the rhyme scheme is completely regular, but within its limits we find several modernist innovations such as rhyming across word boundaries (yoMER/nitoMER, lines 10 and 12) and the equivalence of voiced and voiceless consonants for the purposes of rhyme enrichment (Es KUMEN/dEm GUMEN, lines 2 and 4).

On the literal and concrete level, the poem presents a closely observed natural scene: deer drinking water by the Red Sea at sunset (or, to be more precise, when the sun has already set and its reflection lingers on in the water). Silence, shadows, reflections, and rosy-red colors dominate the delicate scene. One gets the impression that with some luck a quiet and careful nature observer might witness just such a scene near the Red Sea, in the southern tip of the Israeli desert.

However, several puzzling elements prevent the literal interpretation from being fully realized and suggest instead a figurative, if not a surreal, situation. How can deer drink seawater? How come the sun sets in the Red Sea when (for an Israeli observer) the sea is in the south, not the west? Once such hesitations are created, the surreal elements in the beginning and end of the poem are put in the foreground: the unnaturally prolonged sunset (staying in the water at night, lines 1–2) and the reflection of the deer in the water without any real deer nearby to produce it (lines 11–12).

How, then, is the initial literal impression maintained despite the violations of verisimilitude? Among other devices, the diction is especially functional for this effect, presenting a carefully noncommittal and periphrastic vocabulary. Note, for example, that the deer are never explicitly said to be drinking Red Sea water. Instead, they quench their thirst in "the palace of water" (line 3), or they "lick in the Red Sea the rings of coolness" (line 6). Thus, the description seems simultaneously to be true to nature and to blur the borderline between the probabilities of external reality and the possibilities of poetic imagination.

This fusion of the levels of reality is perhaps most evident in the subtle linguistic treatment of color terms in the poem. The central color images consist of different kinds of red: the colors of the sunset and of the water in the sunset, the innocent rosy deer (line 3) and later their rosy images as they disappear into the distance (lines 9–10). Thus, the scene is not represented by the expected contrast of white sand and blue sea but rather—like an impressionist painting—by the fleeting shades and nuances of the moment captured. This foregrounding of reds clearly surpasses, however, the requirements of simple concreteness. As the English translation indicates, the very name of the sea invokes this color. In the Yiddish text the sea is called by its normal Hebrew name *yam suf* (the Sea of Reeds), but the other, more poetic name, *ha-yam ha-adom* (the Red Sea) is definitely in the background. Thus, the sunset and its reflection in the water allow the Red Sea, in reality the bluest of seas, to be seen as literally red. This reification of a label that otherwise has no literal reality reveals two qualities common to all of Sutzkever's poetry: its emphasis on the power of words to create realities and its special sensitivity to the role of the Hebraic component in Yiddish.[11] David Roskies has passionately and carefully articulated the correlation between Sutzkever's valorization of art and language and the survivor-poet's "desire to impose meaning on chaos" (Roskies, 1984:254). Through the implied echo of a Hebrew name, the materiality of red—and its mythopoetic qualities—become both equally palpable, equally (sur)real.

Another reality created through words and anchored in a particularly Hebraic mythopoesis concerns the multiple meanings associated with deer in this poem. The first appearance of the deer relates their rosiness to innocence (line 3). They are thus seen as fawns, baby pink and virginal—qualities which become especially significant in the second stanza with its erotic figurative situation. The deer's second—and most striking—characteristic is expressed in the adjective *eydl* (line 4), one of the richest in meaning and connotation in the Yiddish language. Among these meanings are: graceful, of noble birth, kind, spiritual, vulnerable, delicate, and abstract. To these meanings one should add the traditional Hebraic contexts in which deer (and fawns or gazelles) appear repeatedly as metaphors for the lover (Song of Songs, medieval Hebrew poetry in Spain) and the soul (Psalms). Most significantly, deer are emblems both of the nation (see below) and of natural and artistic beauty. Sutzkever's poem seems to utilize all these metaphorical potentials, concentrating on the deer's associations with love, natural beauty, and art, but injecting them with the (shadowy, reflected) national image of "those, that are no more" (line 12). The special use of the multiply ambiguous adjective *eydl* in conjunction with *hirshn* (deer) makes many of these associations possible. In addition to the senses listed above, *eydele hirshn* is also the plural of a name of a specific kind of deer, *eydlhirsh*, the European and Asian red deer. Like the Red Sea, then, this conventional name is given literal veracity while at the same time enhancing the all-pervasive presence of the color red. The red deer literally become one with the sunset and the water, in anticipation of their symbolic union within the poem's figurative situation.

This quite elaborate figurative situation or event accompanies the literal scene from the very beginning of the poem. In it, a bold and impudent sunset ventures to stay in the palace of water at night, just when a delicate and discreet affair is to take place: noble and innocent visitors (the graceful deer) take off their silken clothes (shadows), and in a scene of delicate erotic initiation, they are betrothed to their mate or mates. There is some unclarity about the mate's identity in this metaphorical ritual. The second stanza, in which the climactic moment is described, explicitly names the silence as the bride (*shtilkayt*, "silence," is feminine singular in Yiddish, whereas *hirshn*, "deer," is masculine plural). However, within the figurative situation, the silence seems to be a metonymy for the water (the deer drink the silence) or for an as yet unnamed entity found in the water in the quiet of night. Thus, in lines 6–7 the drinking itself has nuptial connotations, with the "rings of coolness" echoing wedding bands and the deer's "fiddle-long faces" invoking the klezmer music of a Jewish wedding. Finally, in lines 11–12, the secret spouses are revealed. Both the silence and the water turn out to be metonymies linking the flesh-and-blood deer with their ethereal mates, the "sunset-deer" who "remain woeful" in the water. These mysterious sunset-deer are quite easily explained realistically within the concrete situation as the real deer's reflection in the sunset-red water. And yet the world which this poem creates defies the simplicity of such an explanation because within it the sunset-deer are really present while the flesh-and-blood ones "are no more." We witness, then, at the end of this poem the final fusion of real and imaginary, of the object described and its reflection or shadow, of nature and its representation in art.

The literal and the figurative situations which were developed in the first and second stanzas combine in the third to form one intricate pattern. At first, the two realms can still be kept apart to some extent; literally, the deer, no longer thirsty, have finished drinking and are seen running away. In the air at dusk their figures look like rosy stains on the sand (lines 9–10). At this point the reader is reminded, of course, of the initial violation of verisimilitude (the deer drinking seawater) and must turn to the figurative situation. Here, the language clearly refers to a postorgasmic state ("to finish" in Yiddish and Hebrew slang means to have an orgasm). Through their sexual initiation, the deer have introduced into the barren and stagnant desert new elements of vitality, fertility, and dynamism (*balebn,* line 10, means "to animate" both in the sense of "fill with life" and "impart motion, activity"). The image of a revitalized desert is again created through the use of the color image, and it invokes the national rather than sexual connotations of the deer (as in the biblical *ha-tsvi Israel,* "the deer Israel"). Significantly, however, the desert and the flesh-and-blood deer that bring it to life remain in the background. It is not, in the final analysis, just a national turn that the poem has taken, even as references to the destruction of European Jewry become undeniable. But the last two lines add to the poem's emphasis yet another metaphorical potential of the deer image—that of the artistic object: the sunset-deer. For Sutzkever, art is neither holding up an objective mirror to reality (after all, these are sunset-deer) nor a purely abstract expression of an inner reality (they are reflections of "real" deer). Instead, "Deer by the Red Sea" offers a complex blend of representation and expression typical of Sutzkever's attempt to unite what he calls "the world of truth and the world of lies."[12]

The "real" flesh-and-blood deer "are no more," but in their disappearance, they have produced something of meaning—ethereal and intangible as it may be—which has a lasting reality all its own. The poem ends with the imagined literary deer mourning the loss of the real ones. This ultimate reversal can also be taken as a statement about the need to cling to the reality of the aesthetic process, of the sunset-deer, in a world that destroys its flesh-and-blood ones.

CONCLUSION

Marginal Prototypes,
Prototypical Margins

My friend tells an old Yiddish joke about a rabbi who comes into the synagogue during the Days of Awe, prostrates himself in front of the Holy Ark and says: "Master of the universe, forgive me for I am nothing." A few minutes later, the *chazn* (cantor) walks in, prostrates himself in front of the ark of the Torah and says: "Master of the universe, forgive me for I am nothing." After yet a few more minutes, in comes the lowly *shammes* (synagogue sexton), who prostrates himself in front of the ark and says: "Master of the universe, forgive me for I am nothing." Hearing this, the rabbi sits up, pokes the *chazn*, and, pointing to the *shammes*, says: "Look who's a nothing!" (*ze nor ver s'iz a gornisht*).[1]

I wish to use this story, to enlist it, for the conclusion of this study of marginal modernist prototypes in order to sound a cautionary note. Discussions of marginality face an almost unavoidable temptation to treat the "minor" condition of a literature or a writer as an achievement, a nothing which is something, a status attainable only by an elite consisting of the "marginally correct"[2] (those who currently qualify as "marginal," "peripheral," "decentered," "ec-centric," in a culturally acceptable way).[3] Like the rabbi in this story, who excludes the lowly *shammes* from the class of "true nothings" while signaling in gesture and tone the *chazn's* privileged inclusion, contemporary critics may be engaged in a classist appropriation of the marginal. Reading this joke as a parable on marginality in the hands of a powerful center, we can see the rabbi reinscribing the self-effacing, common *gornisht* of Yiddish slang as the Jewish mystic's highest achievement, the rare and blissful state of spiritual *ayin*—a nothing that is everything, a void that is plenitude.[4] We might also focus on the elitist duplicity of the rabbi's self-deprecation, a duplicity that reveals itself fully in the scornful use of the presentative *ze nor* (roughly, "just see") in the punchline of the Yiddish original, *ze nor ver s'iz a gornisht*. Both perspectives expose how those in the know, by setting the terms of the discussion, deny the margin's right to its own marginality, perhaps the only property that truly belongs to it. As long as exclusionary practices figure so dominantly in canon formation, the process of "revising" or "reforming" the literary canon runs the risk of duplicating or "re-circulating the domination"[5] it has set out to subvert.

In particular, this note of caution may be useful for Hebrew literary studies today. With the recent burgeoning of scholarly, biographical, and publishing interest in works by historically marginalized authors (David Fogel, Dvorah Baron, Chaim Lensky, and early modernist women poets and critics), Hebrew literary historiography appears to be entering a more inclusive phase. Moreover, the relative visibility of contemporary Hebrew writers whose marginality is due to "extraliterary" factors such as ethnicity, gender, or politics contributes to the creation of a seductively misleading impression: that this is an open, nonexclusionary contemporary canon, a canon which is actively and vigorously revising its own literary history, allowing in those who only yesterday were marginalized or ignored altogether.

Yet these recent revisionary moves, important as they are, mark only the first steps in a long overdue process, a process that is itself not independent of the cultural power dynamics it is struggling to alter. It is we, the academic elite (which, truth be told, amounts to close to nothing—*gornisht*—in its power outside the literary system), the publishers, the literary public-relations people, and the canonical writers, who all participate in creating what Russell Ferguson has aptly termed "the invisible center" of the literary-cultural system.[6] And this invisible center, not the marginal voices themselves, gets to decide how far the canon is going to open up, what will now become central, what will retreat to the margins, and who will still remain beyond the pale.

The invisible center—which, to quote Ferguson (in Ferguson et al., 1990:9) again, "whenever we try to pin it down, always seems to be somewhere else"—has a vested interest in periodically revising the canon, both diachronically and synchronically. A controlled influx of "counternarratives" into mainstream culture is "essential to its health and survival. . . . The vital, independent cultures of socially subordinated groups are constantly mined for new ideas with which to energize the jaded and restless mainstream of a political and economic system based on the circulation of commodities" (Ferguson, in Ferguson et al., 1990:11). Phrased in semiotic rather than economic system-theoretical terms, this is precisely the role of the periphery in literary dynamics according to the Israeli neoformalist model of Itamar Even-Zohar, which I discuss in Chapter 4: the margins provide a much needed deautomatization of a literary norm whose continued atrophying dominance would have destabilized the system.

My account, like those of Ferguson and Even-Zohar, intentionally brackets the impossibly muddled question of the role of intrinsic aesthetic value in canon formation. This is not to say that I believe poetic greatness to be purely a matter of convention, nor that I claim poetic marginality to be independent of issues of aesthetic inferiority and epigonic repetition. Clearly some works have maintained a dominant position in the canon because they have been consistently experienced as possessing great aesthetic power.[7] I believe a discussion of modernist marginalities can be conducted separately from squabbles over intrinsic aesthetic value.[8] It is well and good to equate canonicity with greatness by pointing to the really good poets who are placed at the center of the canon. But what is one to make of the really good poets who are not? If, as this study argues, even at the very center of the international modernist canon various trends often cluster around marginal, minimally representative, or even completely unaffiliated and atypical prototypes, then both modernism and marginality—as well as the methodological concept of a prototypical example itself—need to be historicized and contextualized. This need suggests the dual role of my own concluding remarks: to alert us to the temptation of regarding any partial representation (the present one included) of Hebrew and Yiddish literary marginality as if it were the whole picture; and, while illustrating those aspects of the marginal that are now culturally more visible, to offer a glimpse, if even that, of the invisibility that still remains.

Figure 5 is therefore not a model of marginality which I would advocate but rather a schema of those cultural formations of marginality which are now visible within the literary system I am most familiar with, Hebrew. But although the particular formations will be different for other literatures, the structure will be similar. In its schematic structure, Figure 5 reappropriates for the margins the same

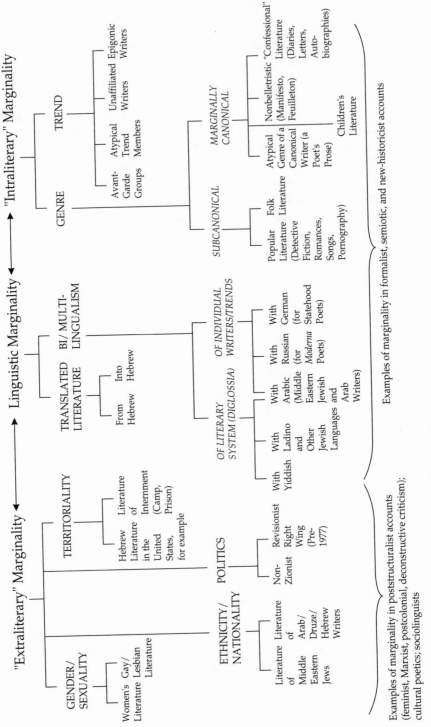

Fig. 5. Formations of marginality in modern Hebrew literature.

cartographic metaphor that this study criticizes in the historiography of the center (see Chapter 3); and it coordinates different types of marginality with the theoretical contexts within which they are most often discussed. Moving for once from right to left as in Hebrew, the intraliterary marginalities of genre and trend, as well as the linguistic marginality of translated works or bi- and multilingual writers, are the formations of marginality which the more "scientific" literary theories have dealt with (within a Russian formalist, a semiotic, or an Israeli neoformalist context).[9] The "extraliterary" formations of marginality, which underscore the minor status of the writers' social and political affiliations, are typically (though not exclusively) the focus of poststructuralist discussions.

That these formations always crisscross and combine is perhaps most dramatically illustrated by the example of the Hebrew poet Avot Yeshurun (1904–92). This great and difficult poet, whose struggle with the literary canon straddled at least three successive literary trends, received his long overdue recognition only on his deathbed in the form of the prestigious Israel Prize. His position as the odd man out had its start, as Michael Gluzman has shown,[10] in a critical stance on the margins of the *moderna*. As the *moderna* was losing its hegemony, Yeshurun developed into a peripheral paragon for some Statehood Generation poets who occasionally used his divergence from the dominant poetics of his contemporaries as a justification for their own generation's rebellion against the Shlonsky/Alterman prototypes of modernism. In order to recover Yeshurun's poetics for Hebrew literary history, a project which has only just begun, the marginality of his work needs to be reconstructed in its diverse yet intersecting dimensions: a poetics of antipurist trilingualism which returns the Hebrew literary system to its earlier diglossic stages (injecting a richly allusive, historically stratified Hebrew with a heavy dose of Yiddish and Arabic); a poet who starts out as an atypical modernist trend member (of the *moderna*) and continues, over the next two literary generations, to be both an unaffiliated modernist and a sidelines paragon for avant-garde groups, maintaining, thanks to his (biological and literary) longevity, a critical position on the margins of both the Statehood Generation and the neo- and postmodernism of the 1970s and 1980s; most important perhaps, a poet who throughout this long period (but in particular until the 1960s) was consistently condemned and spurned by the "invisible center" for the radical nature of his political, ethical, and linguistic critique of Zionism. Thus, for this one poet, the relevant formations of marginality in Figure 5 would include all of the following: under "linguistic marginality," both bi- and multilingualism of individual writers and of the literary system; under " 'intraliterary' marginality/trend," unaffiliated writers, atypical trend members, and avant-garde groups; and under " 'extraliterary' marginality/politics," the critique of Zionism.

Figure 5 records only those formations of marginality that have been operative within the changing conditions of modern Hebrew literary history and that can be defined as marginal against the background of what has served internally as the norm. For example, "exile" does not appear as a single formation on the chart simply because it is the underlying normative condition of many of the other formations. Indeed, exile has been constitutive of the production of most Hebrew literature for a good part of its history. It is not surprising, therefore, that during the periods when exile, uprootedness, and immigration are the norm, being a native poet can be a condition that marginalizes—to wit, the modernist canon's blindness to the great poetry of the first native Hebrew poet in the modern era, Esther Raab.[11] It is thus ironic, though by no means accidental, that patriotic nativists like Raab occupy the same marginal position in the canon as poets who have dissociated themselves from the Zionist project (Fogel) or who actively critique its ethical foundation (Avot Yeshurun).

The need to historicize and contextualize all formations of marginality is further underscored when a parameter such as exile is considered in the framework of international modernism. Given the normative status of exile within the modernist Hebrew literary system, one might have expected Hebrew poetry to have become one of the most instructive examples of decentered, deterritorialized writing. In the ways in which it associates exile with modernism, bilingualism, cultural intertextuality, and issues of national and personal identity, Hebrew poetry captures some of the most representative features of both international modernism and marginal literatures. But these facts in themselves are not sufficient to make Hebrew poetry salient as a marginal modernist prototype. In valorizing Jewish exile, in turning the uprooted, bilingual Jew into the metonymic representation of the modernist human condition par excellence, discussions of modernism, marginality, and minor literature have tended to universalize the Jewish "example" out of existence. It is much simpler to use the Jew—not the literature written in the Jew's language—as paradigm or as loose trope for all that is other in a privileged, modernist, antithetical, universally marginal sense. But in this tropological embrace (from James Joyce's Bloom as "modernist man" to Lyotard's post-modernist declaration, "We're all jews"), the literality of Jewish cultural discourse is blatantly denied.[12]

As a corrective to this universalizing mood, this study has been intently focused on the particular formations of privileged and un-privileged marginality *in*, not *of*, modernist Hebrew poetry. When our view is limited to the specific conditions of the Hebrew literary system, as it is in Figure 5, the formation of exile which has the capacity to marginalize is internment, or exile within exile (as in the case of Lensky writing Hebrew poetry in a Russian prison[13]). Just like exile, exterritoriality in general does not appear as a formation of marginality in modernist Hebrew poetry until quite recently, for the simple reason that it was the normative general condition of writing in Hebrew prior to the shift of the literary center to Eretz Israel. Yet this condition too cannot be generalized, for within the necessarily duplicitous model of a cartographic historiography not all exterritorial writing is similarly normative. When the territorial displacement is geographically dissociated from any of the canonical centers (in Europe or Israel), we find marginalized or even completely excluded foci of literary production. For example, this is the case with Hebrew literature in the United States, an ironically asymmetrical condition given the centrality of American modernism to the Hebrew literary system in its Israeli formation.

Examples such as these illustrate my (decidedly programmatic) claim that modern Hebrew poetry can call into question contemporary theories of the margin. In particular, modernist Hebrew poetry may make us rethink the assumptions that underlie views of marginality within the left-hand ("extraliterary") portion of Figure 5, views which often presuppose a rather simplistic colonial model of nationalism and minority literature, and which identify exile with the need to write in the language of the occupier—but which, like Deleuze and Guattari in their famous book (1986), focus on centrally canonical prototypes such as Franz Kafka using German in Czechoslovakia.[14] At the same time, contemporary theories of marginality that work within a colonial model may, quite ironically, become increasingly applicable for one marginal sector within contemporary Israeli literature—namely, the Hebrew literary production of Arab and Druze writers such as Anton Shammas and Na'im Areydi.[15] Thus, it is quite likely that, in the transition from modernism to neo- and postmodernism, the Hebrew literary system will also "normalize" its formation of marginality and, in the process, gradually lose what Deleuze and Guattari (1986) have so problematically described as a "truly minor" status (see Introduction).

Much more even than Hebrew poetry, marginal prototypes within Yiddish modernism provide a profound challenge to current conceptions of decentered discourse. Yiddish, the quintessential landless language, always has exile and exterritoriality as its normative conditions, ironically even when it is written—as in the case of Avrom Sutzkever—in Israel, against the grain of the dominant Israeli Hebrew literary system. Modernist Yiddish poetry, in its unparalleled diversity and richness, is perhaps one of the strongest counterexamples to any geographical or chronological model of literary historiography. In its elaborate, self-conscious groupings, its jointly authored manifestoes, and its sophisticated explicit poetics, Yiddish poetry presents a striking illustration of what Fokkema (1984:1–18) has termed the "socio-code" of modernism. And yet this radically experimental impressionist, expressionist, futurist, and imagist poetry was produced in the absence of any one hegemonic territorial—or "colonial"—center. Rather, it appeared on the international margins of multiple, partially overlapping modernist centers: in the United States, Poland, and Russia. Like many other decentered modernisms, perhaps earlier than some, Yiddish poetry reached its apex during the years between the two world wars, one brief historical moment before it was destroyed by Nazism and Stalinism. It conducted its modernism not, as Deleuze and Guattari mandate, as "a minor practice of a major language" (Ferguson et al., 1990:61) but defiantly and self-consciously in a language that was marginalized and was considered inappropriate for sophisticated modernist production both within the international literary community and within an increasingly militant Hebraist Jewish culture.

This book has addressed only a few peripheral paragons of this rich marginal modernism, hinting in a few places at the work that remains to be done. The historiography of Yiddish modernist poetry needs to be taken beyond the graph and the map, exposing not only its complex links to mainstream Euro-American trends but also the exclusionary practices which its own canon has maintained. Specifically, we need to explore the persistent marginality of women's poetry in a literature that could produce, as early as 1928, a 390-page-long anthology of *Yiddishe Dikhterins* (Yiddish women poets).[16] This is a project that has only just begun, yet again the scholarly tendency has been to look at individual contributions rather than at the liminal roles that women poets consistently play in the transitions from one Yiddish modernist phase to another.[17] Similarly, the intricate relationship between Hebrew and Yiddish modernist poetry during a period when both literatures are emerging from their mutually dependent, diglossic state still remains to be explored. We need to understand more systematically the different formations of marginality that have affected the reception of bilingual (Hebrew-Yiddish) modernist poets like Uri Zvi Greenberg and Gabriel Preil, formations which have enabled a belated canonization of Greenberg as a post-1977 poet laureate but have yet to allow Preil, a Hebrew poet in New York, anything but peripheral access to the canon. Literary historiography needs to build a critical reading of its own practices into the discourse of the profession, to expose and resist the drive to erase some forms of marginality ("Look who's a nothing!") while privileging others.

Notes

Introduction

1. Quoted from the script, published as *Monty Python's The Life of Brian (of Nazareth)* ([1979] 1992:46).

2. Beyond the parabolic reading, *The Life of Brian* may also participate quite literally in the discourse on the margins of modernism in thematizing the Eurocentric tendencies of modern "Judeo-Christian" appropriations of "indigenous" Middle Eastern cultures. Brian, a British-named half-Roman, is a deflated stand-in for the historical Jesus but nevertheless gets to be the lead character in the film. He is depicted as a de-Orientalized "Judeo-Roman," who is oddly unfamiliar with the cultural practices of his society. In a hilarious parody of the obligatory chase scene in action movies, Brian almost gets caught by Roman centurions because he is unable to haggle over prices in the marketplace. The "real" Jesus is only heard sermonizing from afar at the very beginning of the movie, never commanding the foreground of the frame, structurally analogous in his insertion into the narrative to Dennis, the bearded man in the corner who mumbles "I'm not." The movie audience is restricted to the point of view of the group of bickering onlookers standing at a distance, calling one another "big nose." We can never hear the nonparodic, non-Westernized Jesus. He remains mere background, a completely marginal figure, an inauthentic double of a double.

3. Dada was launched by the expatriate Jewish Rumanian poet Tristan Tzara (1896–1963), né Samuel Rosenstock (his assumed last name means "trouble" in Hebrew, and he indeed meant it). Other eponymic tales abound, both about Tzara's first and last name, and about the name of the movement. Tzara's famous manifestoes of 1916–1921 were collected and translated by Barbara Wright in Tzara ([1977], 1992). But the liminality and polylingualism of Rumanian Jewish modernism (Marsel Janco, Dan Pagis, Paul Celan, in addition to Tzara) remain largely unexplored. I am grateful to Yehudit

Shendar and Michael Taub for their important input on Janco, dada, and the Rumanian-Israeli modernist connection.

4. So how come the principles of Russian acmeism (such as "A = A") sound so much like the Anglo-American imagism we all canonized a long time ago?

5. Akhmatova is mentioned only once in the entire book and then only as a source reporting "the literary youth in [the Soviet Union] to be 'wild' about [Mandelstam's] prose"; see Donald Fanger, "The City of Russian Modernist Fiction" in Bradbury and McFarlane ([1976] 1981:476). Marina Tzvetayeva is nowhere to be found. Marianne Moore and H. D. are mentioned only in lists of poets but do not receive individual critical attention. Else Lasker-Schüler gets seven words, three of them her name. Virginia Woolf and Gertrude Stein are the only women modernists to be discussed in any detail. This marginalization of women modernists, I submit, is quite the norm in general discussions of modernism. It is avoided only in volumes devoted exclusively to women's literature or to corrective literary history, such as Bonnie Kime Scott's groundbreaking anthology *The Gender of Modernism* (1990).

6. My critical reading of these theoretical materials has greatly benefitted from an ongoing research dialogue with Michael Gluzman. He discusses theories of marginality in the context of canon formation in the introduction and conclusion of his Ph.D. dissertation, "Suppressed Modernisms: Marginality, Politics, Canon Formation" (1993a).

7. The dichotomy of center and periphery itself may be an example of the numerous cross-generic connections so common in modernism between literary affiliations on the one hand and critical/theoretical trends on the other. It is born of the ambivalent affair between the theories of Russian formalism and the practices of Russian futurist poetry.

8. Originally published in *Kafka: Pour une littérature mineure* (1975). An abbreviated version of their essay appears in Russell Ferguson et al. (1990: 59-69).

9. See Lloyd (1987), especially pp. 19-26; and Lloyd (1990:381-82) in JanMohamed and Lloyd (1990).

10. The idea of the minor as oppositional is developed in JanMohamed and Lloyd (1990:369-393). This volume contains several important essays on minority discourse that would be denied status as "truly minor" by the theoretical framework that the editors of this very book adopt from Deleuze and Guattari. This is just one illustration of the urgent need for the theory of the minor to catch up with critical practice.

11. In his 1990 interpretation of Deleuze and Guattari, Lloyd seeks to neutralize the exclusionary impact of their typology by distinguishing "minor" from "minority" writing. But note that he still implicitly correlates only minor writing (namely, in a major language) with the progressive anticanonical stance, whereas minority literature is associated only with the possibility of "fulfilling a major function," namely replicating the conservative processes of the canon. The other (logical and empirical) possibility of a minority literature fulfilling a minor, oppositional function—in its own "minority lan-

guage"—is not addressed because it would refute Deleuze and Guattari's linguistic imperative:

> Any definition of "minor" writing is obliged to take into account its oppositional status *vis-à-vis* canonical or major literature thus described. For this reason, a too hasty identification of "minority" with "minor" literature will inevitably be inaccurate, and Deleuze and Guattari are thus far correct to remark in their study of Kafka that it is perfectly possible for a literature of minorities to "fulfill a major function." . . . Deleuze and Guattari are equally correct to seek to differentiate a literature of minorities written in a "minority" language from a minor literature which would be that of minorities composed in a major language. For "minor literature" is so termed in relation to the major canon, and its characteristics are defined in opposition to those which define canonical writing. (Lloyd, in JanMohamed and Lloyd, 1990:381)

12. Michael Gluzman, unpublished ms. I discuss this criterial definition and the model of categorization it invokes in Chapter 1, in the context of the failed search for a definition of modernism. Let me just suggest here that an intensional definition of a politicized, historicized concept of minor writing—that is, a definition based (logically) on necessary and sufficient conditions or (linguistically) on a checklist of distinctive features—is probably the wrong way to go. It would be like trying to account for context-dependent metaphor by using transformational grammar. More important perhaps, this type of definition tends to replicate the same neoclassical Eurocentric classificatory drive that the privileging of the minor aims to undo. For two independent critiques of this classificatory drive, see Foucault ([1970]1973) and Lakoff (1987).

13. In conversation. For a discerning analysis of Kafka's radical readings of Jewish cultural tropes in their central European context, see Goldstein (1992:40–65).

14. On the role of Vienna and Berlin among the shifting centers of modern Hebrew literature, see Silberschlag (1985:29–43) and Nash (1985:44–58) in Abramson and Parfitt (1985).

15. See especially Robert Alter's essay "The Power of the Text," in Alter (1991:67–92). On Kafka's resistant, modernist recasting of the Hasidic narrative model, see Goldstein's innovative early essay (1968). On Kafka's numerous intertextual links with the bilingual Hebrew-Yiddish writer Y. L. Peretz, see Jofen (1984). Deleuze and Guattari do acknowledge Kafka's ties to the Yiddish theater, but they underscore the performative, not the literary, nature of that cultural link (1986:25). For an account that stresses Kafka's textual, almost exegetical, preoccupation with the cultural function of the Yiddish theater, see Goldstein (1992:46–47); and see also Beck (1971).

16. Alter (1991:40) describes the haunting scene, related in a postcard from Kafka to Robert Klopstock (sent from Berlin on October 25, 1923), in which a terminally ill Kafka struggles through the unbelievably difficult Hebrew of Brenner's novel *Shkhol ve-khishalon* [Breakdown and bereavement] ([1902]1972), a page a day.

17. The resistance to the idiom of a hegemonic culture as a formation of minor writing is discussed by Michael Gluzman in an unpublished ms.

18. Yosef Ha-Ephrati was the first to provide a rigorous reading of Ben-Yitzhak's new poetics in the dual contexts of Hebrew and international literary trends, especially the oscillation between impressionism and expressionism. See Ha-Ephrati (1976:162–175).

19. This volume of Canetti's memoirs is aptly titled *Das Augenspiel* (1985). See especially Part 2, "Dr. Sonne," pp. 99–176. Translated into English by Ralph Manheim as *The Play of the Eyes* (1986:89–162). All quotations are from the English translation.

20. I am referring to Bialik's astonishingly proto-modernist essay, *Chevley lashon,* a punning title which I translate as "Language Pangs." See detailed discussion in Chapter 4. Benjamin Harshav has argued persuasively for a sustained and complex analogy between modernism, the revival of Hebrew, and what he has termed "the Jewish revolution" (in Harshav, 1993). Let me stress that for Ben-Yitzhak, as for the other anti-*nusach* (antiformulaic) modernists, the choice to write in Hebrew cannot be explained simply as an extension of Zionist nationalism. Ben-Yitzhak's intensely critical association with institutional Zionism is described with vivid candor by Leah Goldberg ([1952] 1988: 42–43).

21. See Leah Goldberg's adoring memoir of Ben-Yitzhak, *Pgisha im me-shorer* [Encounter with a poet] (Goldberg, [1952] 1988). As a major poet of the dominant *moderna* group in Palestine, and as the founder and chair of the Department of Comparative Literature at the Hebrew University in Jerusalem, Goldberg, in her moving memoir-cum-literary-criticism, went a long way toward establishing Ben-Yitzhak's minor-key modernism in a canon then shifting from the domination of a maximalist version of futurist/expressionist affiliation (Goldberg's own *moderna*) to a more minimalist/imagist one. Thus, Goldberg's recovery of Ben-Yitzhak for the Hebrew canon needs to be seen alongside Nathan Zach's and Dan Pagis' rediscovery of Fogel as what I will call a "proleptic paragon" for the late-modernist project of their own Statehood Generation. It is significant, however, to note the subversive element of Goldberg's role in undermining the hegemony of her own (predominantly male) literary group and in pointing in a direction of privileging the minor modernisms which Zach and Pagis were to follow a few years later.

22. In her poem "Avraham Ben-Yitzhak," Leah Goldberg valorizes this refusal somewhat equivocally, using religious—significantly, Catholic and monastic—imagery. The first two stanzas read:

מִתּוֹךְ: אברהם בן-יצחק

הִנֵּה פָּנֶיךָ בְּהִלַּת-סֵרוּב.
עַל פְּזֵ הַיּוֹם מְסֻגֶּרֶת-עֵץ כַּהֶה
שֶׁל הַחַלּוֹן כָּלְאָה אֶת מֶרְחַקֶּיךָ.

עַל מִצְחֲךָ הָרָם וְהַזָּחוֹחַ
נוֹגַהּ אוֹר צוֹנֵן שֶׁל הַסָּפֵק
כְּעַל תְּמוּנוֹת קְדוּמוֹת שֶׁל אַפִּיפְיוֹרִים.

From: Avraham Ben-Yitzhak

Here is your face in a halo of refusal.
Upon the gold of day the dark wooden frame
Of a window has locked in your distances.

On your high and proud brow
The cold light of skepticism shimmers
As on age-old portraits of popes.

—Goldberg ([1952]1988:232)

The poem was first published in *Al Ha-Mishmar* 10:2865 (December, 1952). It was written, however, in 1938–39. See Goldberg ([1952] 1988:7); translation mine.

23. From "Ashrey ha-zor'im" ("Happy Are the Sowers"; in Ben-Yitzhak, 1992:20). The various versions we have of the poem date from 1925 to 1928. The second line in the Hebrew displaces the idiom of productive accomplishment *yarchiku lekhet* ("will go far, will achieve a lot") with its non-idiomatic deflation *yarchiku nedod* (literally, "will wander far"). These lines, as well as the rest of the poem, read as a parodic rejection of *shibbutz*, the pre-modernist traditions of mosaic-like allusions to sacred texts. At the same time it also rejects the authoritative plenitude of New Testament allegory, sermon, and parable. Note, for example, the iconoclastic conflation of Psalms (126 and 127) with the Sermon on the Mount and the parable of the sower. On the poem's intertextual engagement with Christian sources as well as its internal critique of Zionist politics, see Hever (1993:144–155). Dan Pagis' reading of the poem emphasizes meta-poetic aspects such as the total renunciation of aesthetic ornament—a perspective that fits Pagis' own poetic project: to turn Ben-Yitzhak, posthumously, into a model for the minimalist poetics that he and the late modernists of the 50s and 60s (Amichai, Zach, Ravikovitch) were struggling to legitimize. See Pagis' entries on Ben-Yitzhak in *The Modern Hebrew Poem Itself* (Burnshaw et al., [1965] 1989:50–53).

1. Modernism through the Margins

1. Because of my comparative perspective I have focused here on cross-cultural differences. Others abound. Among those, the more specific sources of complexity and contradiction include individual differences among poets affiliated with the same modernist trend, the internal heterogeneity of the oeuvre of a single author, and the tensions between a poet's—or a group's— explicit poetics and their actual poetic practices.

2. Jonathan Culler (1982) offers the following comparison between traditional and deconstructive descriptions of literary group terms such as modernism (although his examples are typically drawn from romanticism): "The critical tradition has worked by transforming a difference within into a difference between, construing as distinctions between modes and periods a heterogeneity at work within texts. . . . Deconstructive readings characteristically undo narrative schemes by focusing on internal difference" (1982: 248–49).

3. See Zadeh (1965); for applications of fuzzy set theory to the semantics of natural language, see McCawley (1981) and Lakoff (1987:21–22, 138–39). The concept of meaning horizons was developed within Benjamin Harshav's integrational text semantics. See Harshav [Hrushovski] (1984; 1982a; 1982b; 1979).

4. Even a recent study by Astradur Eysteinsson titled *The Concept of Modernism* (1990), while analyzing quite brilliantly the critical and historical circumstances that led to the formation of various critical opinions on modernism, hardly discusses the metatheoretical requirements for an adequate account of the concept's internal structure.

5. Compare, for example, Fillmore (1975), Rosch and Lloyd (1978), and Lakoff (1987).

6. See also Głowiński (1976) on the need to historicize both genre and period models. Polish structuralists realized this as early as the mid 1970s.

7. As evidenced by the recurrence of references to *Epochenschwellen* (literally, thresholds of epochs) or to *glissements* between periods or trends in continental theories of periodization. See, for example, Gumbrecht and Link-Heer (1985a) and Orecchioni (1972). As Fohrmann (1988:277) shrewdly notes: "Mostly one prefers to . . . begin in terms of centers and epochs; but one is soon obliged to deal with borders and temporal limits to explain the so-called transitions, and one eventually comes to notice that the whole genre or epoch—when it is perceived accurately—is nothing but a single transition."

8. A systematic critique of these attempts at definition is found in Eysteinsson (1990:8–50).

9. On the controversy over the number of "waves" in Hebrew modernist poetry, see the discussion in Chapter 2.

10. See Wittgenstein (1958:17–20, 87–88, 125, 145, 152; 1972, Part 1, Sections 67–73, 77, 108), Rosch [Heider] (1973), Rosch (1975; 1977), Rosch and Lloyd (1978), Rosch and Mervis (1975), and Rosch, Simpson, and Miller (1976), Fillmore (1975; 1982; 1985), Lakoff (1972; 1987), Lakoff and Johnson (1980), Lakoff and Kövecses (1987), Lakoff and Turner (1989), Even-Zohar (1969/70; 1971; 1972; 1978; 1979; 1986; 1990), and Harshav [Hrushovski] (1976; 1979; 1982a; 1982b).

11. For commentary on this section, see Baker and Hacker ([1980] 1985: 134–136).

12. Barsalou's examples include lists of various kinds, like "things to sell at a garage sale." Far from being trivial for literary purposes, the concept of an ad hoc category is proving fruitful, for example, for the understanding of novel poetic metaphors, as Yeshayahu Shen (1988) has shown.

13. In addition to Rosch's own work (see note 10), see Lakoff (1987:40–45, 56–57, 59–63, 467–68ff) and the articles in Holland and Quinn (1987).

14. In this belief I differ from some of the major proponents of prototype theory and am perhaps more influenced by Wittgenstein's position that contexts are never completely stable. On some of the tensions between prototype theory and its purported roots in Wittgenstein's concept of family resemblance, see Givón (1986).

15. I developed this concept within an outline of a prototype theory of metaphor in Kronfeld (1983).

16. This view can serve, in a way, as a critique "from the margins" of the ahistorical, platonic concept of an "ideal type" [*Idealtyp*] in whom all the representative features of an era are harmoniously combined. For a well-documented attack on this concept, so popular at one time in German discussions of periodization, see Weisstein (1973a:77–78).

17. For this last point I am grateful to Robert Alter.

18. See, for example, Shklovsky ([1925] 1990:189–205) and Tynjanov ([1929] 1971).

2. Theory/History

1. In his influential book, *The Theory of the Avant-Garde* (1968:17–25). And see also the discussion in Guillén (1971:466–67, note 62) and (1993:290–91, 297–98).

2. In 1973, Ulrich Weisstein (1973a:85) writes: "Even today, the favorite kind of annalistic periodization is the display of literary wares according to centuries. The catalogues of our colleges and universities literally bulge with titles like 'English Seventeenth-Century Literature' or 'Deutsche Literatur des 19. Jahrhunderts.' It is seldom realized that such labels and the content of the academic package do not necessarily coincide. And yet, when as comparatists we speak of the nineteenth century, we scarcely think of the calendar years 1801–1899." Unfortunately, these observations are as true today as they were in 1973. Weisstein finds a "partial abstraction from chronology without repudiation of the chronological framework" in the "more differentiated alignments according to strictly historical viewpoints, such as the reign of a monarch and the duration of a war or a political alliance" (1973a:85–86). I am not at all sure that from a literary point of view, these "alignments" are necessarily more differentiated than the purely annalistic ones.

3. See, for example, Leenhardt (1972). Using an analysis of Heinrich Wölfflin's "grammar of styles" of the Renaissance and the Baroque as his point of departure, Leenhardt concludes: "Chaque époque n'est donc pas un degré, une étape vers une forme plus accomplie, vers un perfectionnement du genre; elle produit elle-même sa propre perfection, et c'est pour cette raison que toute périodisation doit nécessairment se fonder sur une typologie, laquelle implique la perfection de chaque type" (1972:28).

4. See, for example, Hausenstein, *Vom Geist des Barock* (1921) and discussion in Hermand and Torton Beck (1975:50). Typology is explicitly associated with an antihistorical intensional approach in René Wellek's first discussion of the subject, in a seminal paper delivered in 1940: "According to this theory, advocated, for instance, by Herbert Cysarz, periods are merely *abstract types,* not time sections in a historical process. We can therefore speak of Greek romanticism or medieval classicism, as we mean only that this or another work of art *shows certain characteristics* which we traditionally have come to call "classical" or "romantic" or "realistic" (1941:83, emphasis added). For a

critique of Cysarz's typological approach and its underlying view of period as essence (*Wesensform*), see also Weisstein (1973a:77, 198–99), Milch (1950), and Hermand and Torton Beck (1975:48, 57, 59, 135, 165). Cysarz takes stylistic typology to an extreme, not only "forming pseudo-concepts such as Hellenistic Romanticism or Expressionist Gothic" but also transferring "stylistic concepts to the human sphere, so that a Gothic or Baroque man ultimately emerges" (Weisstein, 1973a:198–99). Cysarz expounds these views in "Das Periodenprinzip in der Literaturwissenschaft" (1930) and *Literaturgeschichte als Geistesgeschichte* (1926). His ideas are usually considered an extreme development of the typological tendencies of German *Geistesgeschichte*, which in the twenties and thirties came to be associated with nationalist and racist ideas of the eternal German literary spirit. Thus, for example, Joseph August Lux, in 1925, writes about the "thousand-year-old German romanticism." For Lux, the gothic, baroque, romantic, and expressionistic are all "equally important manifestations of the eternal romantic mode in which the Germanic spirit was most fully realized." See *Ein Jahrtausend deutscher Romantik*, discussed in Hermand and Torton Beck (1975:51–52). On the connection between *Geistesgeschichte* and modern European racism, see (Heilke, 1990).

5. On the distinction between cenacle, school, current, and movement, see Poggioli (1968:20–21ff).

6. On partonomy as a taxonomic system based on part-whole relation see Andersen (1978).

7. The term "trend" is favored over "movement" or "current" in typological rather than periodological accounts, perhaps because the dynamic metaphorical sense is less transparent.

8. As Poggioli observes, this "circumstance did not escape T. S. Eliot, who, in his essay on a specific group of seventeenth-century poets, after asking to what extent the so-called metaphysicals formed a school, immediately added in parentheses, 'in our own time we should say a 'movement' '" (1968:20–21). On the origin of the dynamic metaphors of movement, trend, and current, see my discussion of Georg Brandes later in this chapter.

9. These are the terms in which the question is often explored by the innovative research groups on historical poetics that have been active in central and eastern Europe since the 1970s. See, for example, the work of the Institute for Literary Studies of the Hungarian Academy of Sciences, as described in the Soviet-Hungarian Symposium on Literary Epochs, published in *Neohelicon* 15(1)(1988); the work of Jan Fischer and the research group on periodization at the Institute of Romance Studies in Prague; and the research group at the Institute for Literary Research in Warsaw, in particular the work of Michał Głowiński and Janusz Sławiński. See Głowiński's account of Polish structuralism (1975) and his protest, nearly twenty years later, that these important contributions remain unrecognized because they were not written in English, or "one of the so-called congressional languages" (Głowinski 1994: 895–97). See also Nadezhda Andreeva-Popova's (1985) summary of her group's research (at the University of Sophia, Bulgaria). However, as Popova suggests, while these theories examine literary trends both as part of an

epochal system and as a component of a stylistic system, their main focus is not on the structure of the trend itself but rather on transitions from one trend to another. This, as I argue below, is the tendency of most system-theoretical approaches to literary history. It leaves the questions regarding the category structure of the literary trend itself largely unanswered.

10. This was also H. P. H. Teesing's influential thesis (1949:111).

11. "The Term and Concept of Symbolism in Literary History" in Wellek (1970:90–121); and "The Concept of Baroque in Literary Scholarship," "Postscript 1962," "The Concept of Romanticism in Literary History," "Romanticism Re-Examined," "The Concept of Realism in Literary Scholarship," all included in Wellek [1963] (1973).

12. Kermode's metaphors underscore not only political stability but also economic security as the payoffs of conserving the elite canon. Note the references to the "business" of "valuing selected monuments and selected books" (1988:126).

13. Compare Guillén's argument in "Second Thoughts on Literary Periods": "[W]e do not mean by period simply a section of time. We mean a critical concept that is applicable to a section of historical time and to its dominant structures and values" (1971:464). More recent examples include David Lodge's emphasis on the oscillation between modernism and antimodernism in the first half of the twentieth century. See Lodge (1981:3–16). On the discontinuities of literary periods and the simultaneous coexistence of diverse periodological features, see Claus Uhlig's important book, *Theorie der Literarhistorie* (1982). John Frow (1986:vii) describes these discontinuous and simultaneous periodizations as "the multiple temporalities of texts within complex sets of intertextual relations." For a discussion of the relations between canon formation and periodization, see the various articles in von Halberg (1984) and "Canon and Period" in Kermode (1988:108–27).

14. For a critical view of the selective application of "the life-cycle analogy" to models of periodization, see H. W. Janson's persuasive argument (1970).

15. On the games that Wittgenstein himself plays with the language-as-game simile, see C. W. K. Mundle's commentary (1970:190–93 and 244–45). The usefulness of the family resemblance model to the analysis of periodization as well as to the description of trends or schools is briefly suggested in Robert Fogelin's commentary (1976:123). J. P. Stern, in an essay titled "From Family Album to Literary History" (1975), uses Wittgenstein's concept of family resemblance to develop a diachronic model of the history of a genre or a theme. He focuses primarily on Wittgenstein's rope analogy in an attempt to describe the intertwining of a literary strand with a historical one. Unfortunately, the result is a revalidation of both the dateline approach and a dressed up version of *Geistesgeschichte*.

16. Wellek's position, and that of other theorists working largely within the heritage of Russian formalism and Czech structuralism, often reveals vestiges of essentialism, possibly through the influence of Wilhelm Dilthey and Wölfflin on their models of literary evolution. On the impact of Dilthey's philosophy and Wölfflin's poetics on later conceptions of "the growth and decline of cultures as biological phases of an organic development of

mankind," see Hermand and Torton Beck (1975:39). Traces of organicism, however, are commonly found in almost all evolutionary or system-theoretical models, including those that place a major emphasis on historical, social, and political determinants of literary periodization. Hermand and Torton Beck's presentation of the formalist concept of evolution completely ignores the historical and systemic elements of the later phases of Russian formalism and Czech structuralism. The authors' flight from technical rigor causes their discussion of Wellek and other "specialized critics," as they call them, to be quite uninformative. For a more rigorous critique of the metaphor of the organism in Russian formalist theory, see Peter Steiner (1984:68–98). Ironically, Wellek himself criticizes what he calls the "organological" point of view, as well as the limited evolutionism of the early formalist model, in "The Concept of Evolution in Literary History" ([1963] 1973:37–53).

17. Guillén traces the historical and sociological research that has led many nonliterary scholars of periodization to similar conclusions. See discussion later in this chapter. Compare Georges Gurvitch's notion of "la multiplicité des temps sociaux," in Guillén (1971:440–41). Gurvitch himself applied his theory to literature in an interesting series of studies of the theater. Available in English is his "The Sociology of the Theatre" (1973).

18. Originally written in Russian during Tynjanov's visit to Prague in the winter of 1928 and first published in Novyj Lef, 12 (1928). English translation in Matejka and Pomorska ([1929, 1971] 1978) and reprinted in Jakobson (1987: 47–49).

19. That Wellek has not made the full transition to a pluralistic view of the literary trend is evidenced by his more traditional discussions of romanticism and realism ([1963] 1973:128–255). On the sustained ambivalences of Wellek's view of literary periods and trends and on the reception history of Wellek's position, see Parker (1991). Perkins describes Wellek as the consolidator of the consensus, dominant until the 1970s, that periods are objective and relatively unified, "while also allowing for a degree of heterogeneity and struggle within them" (1992:64–65).

20. I am referring to Norton Juster's ([1962] 1976) fascinating children's book, which describes a child's travels through a metalinguistic universe of discourse whose geography is made up of words and numbers, from Dictionopolis and Digitopolis to the Castle in the Air. Not very different in its preoccupation with terms rather than concepts is J. Hillis Miller's programmatic reduction of "the problematic of periodization" to "a particularly complex form of the problematic of naming" (1979:14–15).

21. Often referred to in German literary criticism with the confusing label positivism. See Hermand and Torton Beck (1975:11–24) and Wellek ([1963] 1973:256–81).

22. On the association of typology, ahistoricism, and static conceptions of periodization with Geistesgeschichte, see note 4 above. It is important to note, with Hermand and Torton Beck, that Geistesgeschichte is a thoroughly untranslatable concept. "Even its closest English equivalent, the phrase 'history of ideas,' entirely fails to capture the nonrational elements inherent in [it]" (1975:46).

23. See, in addition to the works by Wellek, Weisstein, and Hermand and Torton Beck cited above, Weisstein (1973b), Hermand (1978), and, from the perspective of sociopoetics, Escarpit (1972) and Orecchioni (1972).

24. See "National, Volkish, and Racial Aspects" in Hermand and Torton Beck (1975), especially their discussion of the "nationalization of all concepts of epoch" (p. 48ff). And see the contrasts between the prototype model and the notion of ideal types in chapter 1, note 16.

25. Jasinowski (1937:44); cited in Guillén (1971:434).

26. For material in English on Polish philosophy and logic, see the entry "Polish Philosophy" and the section on Polish logicians in the entry "Logic, History of" in the *Encyclopedia of Philosophy* (New York: Macmillan, [1967] 1972) vols. 5–6:363–70 and 3–4:566–68; and the *Journal of Philosophy* 57(7)(1960), which is an entire issue devoted to Polish philosophy and logic.

27. Szili cites Pawlowski (1980).

28. We need only be reminded of Robert Fogelin's concluding remarks in his commentary on Wittgenstein to realize that such rigid views are logically and methodologically far from necessary:

> In the end, I think that the notion of family resemblance has two chief virtues. 1. It helps dispel the commitment to definiteness of sense by exhibiting a set of concepts that violate this standard but are still perfectly serviceable.... 2. Somewhat differently, the attack upon essences can curb the belief that definitions, of the standard kind, are always possible and, if we are doing things right, actually necessary in the systematic development of a subject matter.... And using the notion of family resemblance need not mean we have taken the easy way out. This notion indicates the form this investigation will take; it does not call a halt to investigation. (1976:122–23)

29. See, for example, "On the Uses of Literary Genre" and "Genre and Countergenre: The Discovery of the Picaresque" in Guillén (1971:107–58).

30. "Tradition and the Individual Talent" (1917), in Eliot (1932:5) and Brooks (1953:418); both are discussed in Guillén (1971:452).

3. Behind the Graph and the Map

1. The historiographic distortions laid bare by critical constructions of Yiddish modernist poetry will be taken up in a future study. In its multiplicity of literary centers and its fundamentally aterritorial stance, Yiddish poetry problematizes—perhaps more than any modern literature—the basic assumptions of literary historiography. It also calls into question the theoretical presuppositions of current accounts of marginality and minor literature. For application of the models of marginal prototypes to Yiddish modernist trends and poets see Chapters 7–8.

2. Note the ideologically charged titles: Gideon Katznelson, *Le'an hem holkhim?* [Where are they going?], Tel Aviv: Alef, 1968; Ortzion Bartana, *La-vo cheshbon* [Settling accounts], Tel Aviv: Alef, 1985; and *Zehirut, sifrut eretz yis-re'elit* [Watch out, land-of-Israel-literature], Tel Aviv: Alef, 1989; Menachem Ben, "ki kol ha-adam eydim" [For all man is vapors] (1986). *Yediot Acharonot*, January 3, 1986.

3. For a theory of modernism based on this fundamental concept in Adorno's aesthetics, see Eysteinsson (1990:39–45, 201–205, ff.).

4. My critique of Wieseltier's account has been influenced by Michael Gluzman's (1991a) discussion.

5. This is Gluzman's analysis of Wieseltier's (1980:405) courtly chronicles of the *moderna*.

6. The most important corrective to this exclusionary model is Ammiel Alcalay's groundbreaking study (1993).

7. On Fogel, see Chapters 4 and 7. Lensky's poetry has been recovered by Miron (1991a:203–233). See discussion of Preil in Yael Feldman (1985:46–48).

8. See, for example, the periodological essay by Ezra Spicehandler (1971) "Hebrew Poetry, Modern" in the *Encyclopedia Judaica*.

9. For a cogent stylistic description of the *nusach*, see Alter (1988:31–58); for the origins and development of the anti-*nusach* in Hebrew prose fiction, see Alter (1988:45–51). Gershon Shaked speaks of Ya'akov Rabinovitch, for example, as between "*nusach* and anti-*nusach*," and has also proposed the somewhat analogous notion of a *nusach she-keneged* (a counter-formula or counter-version). See, for example, his historiographical surveys of Hebrew prose fiction, *Ha-Siporet Ha-Ivrit* (1977:I–468ff).

10. Compare my discussion of Orecchioni (1972) and Gumbrecht and Link-Heer (1985) in Chapter 1.

11. After all, this has already been encoded in the love-as-kinship metaphors of the Song of Songs. See detailed discussion in Chapter 4.

12. As Miron has alleged, in a series of polemic exchanges with Zach. See, for example, Miron (1987b).

13. See, for example, the special issue of *Prooftexts* titled *David Fogel and the Emergence of Hebrew Modernism* (January, 1993).

14. Dan Miron was the first to frame the discussion of early modernist women's poetry in terms of a "poetics of poverty" in his groundbreaking study *Imahot Meyasdot, Achayot Chorgot* [Founding mothers, stepsisters] (1991). Miron's analysis, however, is still argued from a perspective that privileges, directly or indirectly, a poetics of plenitude while reifying literary and linguistic "poverty" (*dalut*) as a quintessentially feminine style. For critiques of Miron's account see Seidman (1993); and Gluzman (1991a) and (1993a), who also offers an illuminating counter-reading of Raab. See also Ann Lapidus-Lerner (1992) for a different perspective on Raab's poetics of gender, especially in its relation to Bialik's poetry.

15. Compare the role of the bramble bush as a symbol of destructive, barren, authoritarian rule in the parable of Yotam, Judges 9.

16. Raab saw no contradiction between her nativist Hebraism and her sense of direct participation in—even influence on—French modernism. See Raab (1981:103). Indeed, the revolutionary features of Raab's poetic language are best understood on the background of French symbolist heritage. In a fascinating study of the stylistics of symbolism, Françoise Meltzer (1978:253–73) describes the dislocation of adjective and noun, and the "verbal vertigo" effect created by this inversion in symbolist syntax. Her observations are

equally illuminating for Raab's poetry and have influenced my reading of Raab's radical syntactic dissonances.

17. Amichai's poem appears in Amichai (1962); Wallach's famous line appears in her poem "Ivrit" ("Hebrew") in Wallach (1985). For a compelling reading of Wallach's poetics and politics of grammatical gender, see Gluzman (1991b).

18. I have provided a literal translation of these highly ambiguous poems. Numerous alternative constructions of each poem's syntax are, in typical symbolist fashion, not only optional but quite obligatory.

19. *Ach* ("hearth, fireplace") is homonymous with *ach* ("brother") and has the suffixless morphological structure of masculine nouns in Hebrew, although in its use as "hearth" it is feminine, as in the expression *lifney ha-ach ha-mevo-eret* ("in front of the burning fireplace"). *Esh* ("fire"), while both grammatically and symbolically feminine, appears masculine because it lacks the typical ending of feminine nouns.

20. Feminine of *tsabar* (the sabra, or prickly pear) is the lexicalized metaphor for the native Israeli. Note that unlike the apocryphal *sabra*, the *atad* does not claim any mitigating sweetness underneath its prickly exterior.

21. I am borrowing Eric Zakim's phrase, from the title of his article "The Cut That Binds: Philip Roth and Jewish Marginality" (1988).

22. *Cherev*, another feminine noun referring to a traditionally masculine instrument. The whole scene enacts a radical reversal of the narrative of Jephtah's daughter in Judges 13, where the young woman falls passive victim / sacrifice (both *korban* in Hebrew) to the law of the warrior father.

4. Beyond Language Pangs

1. Alter suggests, somewhat whimsically, that *melitsah* might be translated as "poesy" (1988:23), and indeed it is the Hebrew textual equivalent of rhetorical decorum and poetic diction. That it would become synonymous, in the period prior to the Hebrew revival, with the emulation of lofty, authoritative—i.e., sacred—textual sources indicates just how far *melitsah* is from any of the connotations of poetic diction in English. *Shibbuts* is the Hebrew name of a long tradition of biblical allusion, but it has come to be associated with the conception of the poetic text as a mosaic of biblical citations. For a more detailed discussion, see Chapter 5.

2. This is the approximate time both on the two-tiered and on the three-tiered accounts of modernism, for the simple reason that Fogel and Shlonsky's first volumes of poetry appeared within a few years of each other.

3. This price was, in my opinion, much more marked in Hebrew prose fiction from the turn of the century through the 1960s. For a detailed account of the ways in which Hebrew fiction handled the language crisis, see Alter (1988).

4. See Bradbury and McFarlane's excellent discussion of this point in *Modernism* ([1976] 1981:191–206). On the parallels between modernism and Hebraism as two central transformations that make up the "Jewish Revolution," see Harshav (1993).

5. See discussion in Erlich (1965:194–97), Steiner (1984:51–52, 58–60), and Bakhtin and Medvedev ([1978] 1985:106–18).

6. See especially Harshav [Hrushovski] (1976); similar ideas are developed by Perry (1979).

7. Important discussions appear in Even-Zohar (1990), an issue of *Poetics Today* devoted to Even-Zohar's theory, and in his "Russian and Hebrew: The Case of a Dependent Polysystem" and "Israeli Hebrew Literature: A Historical Model" (1978:63–94). See also Even-Zohar (1979, 1970, and 1971).

8. For an account of paragons within prototype theory, see Lakoff (1987: 87–88; 527–529). Shaked (1988:157) discusses what he calls "progons" in the context of *moderna* fiction.

9. Both Bialik's Hebrew coinage *chevley lashon* and the English translation suggested to me by Robert Alter, "language pangs," echo—quite intentionally—the expression "birth pangs," *Chevley leyda*. The pains of the language crisis are, then, a natural part of the miraculous process of language (re)birth. The Hebrew term, however, invokes another fixed expression, *chevley mashi'ach* ("Messianic pangs")—the suffering en route to redemption. In fact, unlike pangs, *chavalim* are almost always "positive" pains. The term occurs often within a context of new beginnings: birth, the Messiah, and life in a new country (*chevley klita*—"absorption/adaptation pangs"). It is significant, as Ruth Berman has pointed out to me, that Bialik's title echoes these powerful collocations. As we shall see, Bialik's essay is about the power which collocations—formulaic and fixed expressions—have in sustaining the life of a language. Ironically, and almost in modernist fashion, Bialik's title pays homage to fixed expressions by deviating from one: *lashon* ("language" [literally, "tongue"]) is, after all, not one of the lexical environments in which the genitive construct *chevley* normally occurs in Hebrew.

10. Although initial publication is usually attributed to *Ha-Shilo'ach* 18 (1907), the essay appeared two years earlier in a special edition of *Ivriya* (Odessa, 1905). Translation from the 1965 Dvir edition.

11. See Tynjanov ([1929, 1971] 1978) and Jakobson ([1929] 1971). See also Even-Zohar's entries in Sebeok (1986): "Automatization," "Literary Dynamics," "Literary Interference," and "Literary System."

12. Especially as represented by the work of Even-Zohar, collected first in Even-Zohar (1978). See also the revised version in Even-Zohar (1990).

13. Though formulated here in semiotic terms, Even-Zohar's basic tenets are compatible with Russian formalist literary theory and Prague School structuralist linguistics.

14. I have emphasized here the ways in which Bialik's essay prefigures modern views of language within literary theory. Much more needs to be said, however, about the specific respects in which this essay contains the kernels of some major trends in contemporary linguistics, from the ideas of Noam Chomsky to those of Dwight Bollinger and of Charles Fillmore. Suffice it to say that both an antinormativist approach to "grammaticality" and an emphasis on formulaic collocations are central to contemporary views of

grammatical and lexical structure, and—as Ruth Berman has pointed out to me—to theories of language acquisition.

15. For an analysis of the metaphor of a system as a central model for the formalist theory of linguistic and literary function, see Steiner (1984:99–137).

16. On the role of mechanistic metaphor in formalist thinking, see Steiner (1984:44–67). On a critique of Even-Zohar's theory as a hydraulic model, see Lang (1987).

17. See discussion in Matejka and Pomorska ([1971] 1978:194–97).

18. This phrase was suggested to me by Robert Alter.

19. See Alter (1988) for the ingenious solutions prose writers have found for some of these problems. On the use of monologue and lecture as a way around dialogue, see Harshav (1993:129).

20. Shaked's important multi-volume project, *Ha-siporet ha-ivrit* (1977, 1983, 1988), places consistent emphasis on the relevance of internal and external norms to the development of Hebrew prose fiction. No equivalent study exists for Hebrew poetry.

21. Controversies over periodization have always been the rule rather than the exception in Hebrew literary history.

22. Alter describes the tradition of *melitsah* as "the cult of the biblical phrase. . . . Biblical poetry in particular was mined for such phrases: merely to invoke a figure of speech, a rhetorical maneuver, a *recherché* term from Isaiah, Job, Psalms, or Song of Songs was felt to imprint a magic, to confer a special status on an idea or object" (1988: 23). For more on Hebrew modernism as a reaction against *melitsah*, see Chapter 5.

23. From Fogel's lecture-cum-literary manifesto *Lashon ve-signon be-sifrutenu ha-tse'ira* ("Language and style in our young literature"), delivered during a lecture tour of Poland in November, 1931. First published from archival materials by Moshe Ha-Naomi in *Siman Kri'ah* (Fogel, [1931] 1974: 387–391). A full English translation of this lecture by Yael Meroz and Eric Zakim appeared in the Fogel Issue of *Prooftexts* (1993:15–20). Here cited in my own translation from the Hebrew (Fogel, [1931] 1974:391).

24. All future-tense verbs can also be construed as imperfective and all past-tense ones as perfective. See discussion below.

25. The addressee in the poem is identified morphologically as masculine, and the speaker as feminine.

26. On adverbial gerundives and the distinction between inflected infinitive and gerund in Hebrew, see Berman (1978:287–309) and Kutcher (1982: 45–46).

27. As Ruth Berman has observed, this is consistent with the perfective sense of the KATAL pattern in biblical Hebrew.

28. For another treatment of the tense/aspect system, see Rubinshteyn ([1981] 1985).

29. Evoked text, alluding text, and the marker are some of the basic terms in Ziva Ben-Porat's (1976) theory of literary allusion. For a detailed discussion of Ben-Porat's theory of allusion and intertextuality, see Chapter 5.

30. Alter discusses the analogy between these passages in somewhat different terms in *The Art of Biblical Poetry* (1985:187–88).

31. The context of the "maiden poems" suggests that the speaker is a young adolescent. This context becomes important for Komem's argument (see below) about the conflation of woman and child in Fogel's poetry.

32. One must stress the relative sense of "active" in a poetry reflecting a fundamentally passive orientation of the human agent—male or female—toward the world.

33. See George Steiner (1976) on the connection between modernism and changing norms of erotica.

34. My understanding of metaphor in the Song of Songs has been influenced by Ilana Pardes's discussion, in an unpublished Honors thesis (Berkeley, 1980). See also Pardes (1992:118–142).

35. Komem ties his observations to biographical evidence based on Fogel's diary, since then published as a work unto itself, concerning a complicated relationship that the poet maintained simultaneously with a mother and her young daughter. Intriguing as this information may be, it does little to provide a literary, not to mention a stylistic, understanding of the issue.

36. The concept of a metaphorical system is developed in Lakoff and Johnson (1980) and in a study of poetic metaphor by Lakoff and Turner (1989).

37. Upper case indicates recurring phonemes; lower case, uniquely occurring ones. Here and elsewhere I follow Harshav's [Hrushovski's] method of prosodic analysis (1980).

38. But note the vestiges of a romantic stance toward nature in lines 7–8. For an analysis of the image of the moon slice as wedding band, see Margalith (1971:45); the example was originally offered by Harshav [Hrushovski] as an illustration of the importance of the "erased" features of a metaphorical transfer.

39. On the problematics of establishing relations between sound and meaning in poetry and in the structure of focalizing sound patterns, see Harshav [Hrushovski] (1980).

40. Originally attributed to A. D. Gordon's version of Zionism, the "religion of labor" is meant here more broadly, to indicate socialist-Zionist transpositions of religious and mythical fervor from orthodox Jewish practice to an ideology of valorized labor "on the land."

41. On the variety of ways in which Shlonsky's neologisms rework and revive traditional sources, see Arye Aharoni's introduction to Ya'akov Kna'ani's *Dictionary of Shlonsky's Neologisms* (1989:5–8).

42. Eleazar ben Kalir (6th Century (?), Palestine); great liturgical poet and linguistic innovator.

43. Mayakovsky on Khlebnikov's use of neologisms. In Brown (1976:15).

44. But in doing so he is also invoking—and secularizing—a classical artistic representation of this biblical narrative. As Ilana Pardes has pointed out (in conversation), Rembrandt's "Jacob Wrestling with the Angel" (1660–1661) not only depicts the angel as a woman but the painting also looks more like lovemaking than wrestling.

45. In the song a soldier encounters a woman without knowing her name: *Hu lo yada et shma / Aval ota tsama halcha 'imo le-orekh kol ha-derekh* ("He didn't know her name / But that braid was with him all along the way"). I am grateful to Miri Kubovi for dating this song for me.

5. Theories of Allusion and Imagist Intertextuality

1. Black is referring to the knowledge and belief necessary for the identification and interpretation of metaphor, but his concept can also apply to the conditions for identifying and interpreting a literary allusion.

2. For a critical assessment of this school, see Mintz (1984).

3. In the article by that name, in Eliot ([1920] 1960:47–59).

4. Medieval Hebrew poetry in Spain was the last phase of a strong poetic norm in Hebrew before its revival (*tchiya*) in the nationalist romanticism of the end of the nineteenth century.

5. On the distinction between schools and movements in the arts, see Poggioli (1968:17–18), and my discussion in Chapter 2.

6. The distinction between *shibbuts* and *remizah* is summarized in Pagis (1970:75). And see also Yelin ([1940] 1972:102–49). Although Yelin provides a detailed exemplification of the medieval *shibbuts* and *remizah*, he presents little analysis of the similarities and differences in their function as rhetorical strategies.

7. For criticism of the term *Mussivstil* and its static, decorative connotations, see Shachor (1962). And see also Pagis (1970:70). A traditional account of the use of allusion in medieval poetry as *Mussivstil* is found, for example, in Girscht (1958:46–48).

8. For a critical account of *melitsah* and its connection to *shibbuts,* see Shahevitch (1970). For an example of the attack on *melitsah* by *moderna* poets, see Shlonsky's manifesto "The *Melitsah*" in Harshav [Hrushovski] (1973: 154–55).

9. As in the meticulous but either far-fetched or uninterpretive allusion hunts of Enlightenment-inspired literary criticism, whose vestiges survive well into the twentieth century. *Mekorot* ("source") criticism used to be quite common in Bialik scholarship. Thus, for example, Lachower (1974) tracks down the *mekorot* of Bialik's imagery in order to provide allegorized over readings (which he describes as "symbols"). "Drashic" (homiletical) interpretive strategies are also quite common mostly in the mosaic like (*Mussivstil*) unpacking of allusions. See, for example, in the work of Bahat (1980).

The other extreme position, which is an uninterpretive *mekorot* criticism, is exemplified by textological studies such as Shraga Abramson (1965). The work amasses an impressive amount of information about allusions and versions of allusions in medieval poems and discursive texts, but it does not go far beyond listing the data. See a similar methodology in Avrunin (1953). Even linguistically sophisticated analyses of "borrowings" from the *mekorot* are often not more than refined classifications of examples. See, for example, Mansour (1968:239–49).

The habit of talking about allusions to the Bible in terms of a vaguely defined primitivism or archaism is exemplified in Hillel Bavli's work, *Some Aspects of Modern Hebrew Poetry* (1958). In discussing Abraham Regleson's "Cain and Abel," Bavli, after summarizing what each character "symbolizes," provides the following account of the role of allusion in his work: "A somewhat primitive rawness of style lends an archaic touch to a modernized interpretation of ancient lore" (p. 13).

10. The reference is to Genesis 4, where Cain's jealousy over the divine reception of his brother's sacrifice is described as a motive for the first murder.

11. Contemporary postmodernist poetry, at least in one of its competing prototypes, is moving away from biblical and liturgical allusions to imported intertextual models (especially of seminal classical Western texts).

12. The classical locus of debate on this question is Barukh Kurzweil's famous question: "Our new literature: continuity or revolution?" (in a volume by that name, 1959:11–146). For more recent discussions which are especially relevant for our purposes here, see Abramson (1984) and Sokoloff (1984).

13. Ben-Porat's model, as well as the theoretical components of all the other accounts presented below, are general theories of literary allusion, not of biblical or religious reference. As we shall see, this "universalism" is not accidental but rather an Israeli response to the dominance of classical allusion in Anglo-American imagist and vorticist poetry and poetics. The universalist tendency sometimes expresses itself in attempts to marginalize the centrality of biblical and liturgical allusions within modernist Israeli poetry, even while the radical deployment of such allusions continues to be highly prototypical of the actual poetic practice. Naomi Levy has shown in an unpublished paper (1984) that Israeli critics of Amichai rarely describe his religious allusions as a dominant, prototypical device, whereas his American critics tend to overemphasize it. I believe the same tendency is evident in treatments of other poets' allusions to indigenous sacred texts.

It is nevertheless true that a corollary of the universalist tendency of modernist-inspired Israeli criticism and literary theory is the growing use of allusions to European and other Western sources in modernist (and even more so postmodernist) Hebrew poetry. This increase is perhaps evidence of a gradual shift from center to periphery of the once dominant Hebraic intertextual norms, as the number of readers who can easily activate the evoked religious texts decreases. Ben-Porat's empirical studies of allusion bear this out, especially the article entitled "The Appearance of Japhet in the Tents of Shem" (1979). Her other major discussions of literary allusion are in Ben-Porat (1973, 1976, 1978a, 1978b, and 1985).

14. Sadan's oeuvre is too vast to be adequately represented here. I shall mention only two typical discussions: of S. Y. Agnon's meta-allusive use of allusion as a means for criticizing traditional values, in Sadan (1978:23ff); and of the Aggadic basis of Bialik's (and others') metaphor of the poet as nursing infant, in Sadan (1964:63–67ff).

15. Much as Mendele Moykher Sforim, Shalom Ya'akov Abramovitch's public literary persona, was made by Sholom Aleichem into "The Grandfather of

Yiddish Literature" in order to lend the literature a much needed sense of tradition and legitimacy. Compare Miron (1973).

16. A book-length study which extends the framework of Toury and Margalith's work and has a linguistic rather than a literary focus is Landau (1980). For the role of collocation in the identification of literary allusion, see Ben-Porat (1976:110).

17. For similar conclusions about the literary utilization of the involuntary linguistic allusiveness of Hebrew, see Fruchtman (1968/69).

18. Harshav's [Hrushovski's] terms. See, for example, Harshav [Hrushovski] (1982a:156–90). A modified version of this theory appeared in Harshav [Hrushovski] (1982b).

19. Note that Sternberg, like most theorists of allusion, accepts implicitly the claim that direct quotation or direct reference cannot count as allusion. Carmella Perri, however, challenges this accepted dictum in "On Alluding" (1978). As Perri points out (p. 290, note 2), "Ben-Porat is the only student of allusion other than myself who denies the necessity of covertness for allusion."

20. See note 13 above.

21. Especially, as was suggested above, Israeli poetry which alludes to non-Hebraic sources. Compare Ben-Porat (1979), which deals with allusions to Western texts in modernist and postmodernist Hebrew poetry from the *moderna* to the present.

22. See, especially, Eliot's "Hamlet and His Problems" and, of course, "Tradition and the Individual Talent" in *The Sacred Wood* ([1920] 1960) and "The Metaphysical Poets" in *Selected Essays* ([1932] 1960); and Ezra Pound's "A Few Don'ts by an Imagist" (1913) and "Vorticism" ([1916] 1960: 94–106).

23. An important statement of Russian theories of allusion is available in English in Lotman et al. (1975).

24. Compare a similar ambiguity in Robert Alter's *After the Tradition* (1969) between the two senses of "after."

6. Yehuda Amichai

1. It is typical of Amichai's deflation of poetic discourse to take the form of scientific language, as in this recodification of the well-known geometrical theorem (Amichai, 1962, 1977 ed.: 90–91; English translation in Amichai, 1986: 13–14).

2. See Sandbank (1982) and Fishelov (1992) for an analysis of Amichai's reworkings of the metaphysical conceit. Arpali (1986:119–120) shrewdly characterizes this poem as an example of Amichai's poetics of the uncommon denominator, a poetics that valorizes heterogeneity and unreconciled differences.

3. On the special relationships, often bilateral in the Hebrew cultural system, between poetry and popular song, see Ben-Porat (1989). For a recovery of common Middle Eastern poetic traditions in Arabic and Hebrew cultures, see Alcalay (1993).

4. Compare, for example, the importance of self-reference as a poetic principle within romanticism (especially, romantic irony) and—famously now—within postmodernism.

5. This is also a title of one of his poems, in Amichai ([1968] 1975:160). And see interview with Ya'akov Beser (1971:52–53).

6. Literally, the "square" stanza (*ha-bayit ha-meruba*); Zach cannot resist the pun.

7. I discuss this point in greater detail in Kronfeld (1990).

8. The Hebrew grammatical term for verb pattern, *binyan*, literally means "building" and is derived from the triconsonantal verbal root b-n-h, "build." Thus, the regular name for verb pattern in itself illustrates the point Amichai wishes to make in this poem: ordinary language as a building in which the life of the language users is evolving; a *bildungs* poem contained within the grammatical building.

9. In Sha-ar Ha-Gai (Gate of the Valley), where burnt vehicles from the bitter battles fought there in the 1948 war are still "lying dead" (in the words of the famous song "Bab el Wad") as a roadside monument. It is significant that the speaker wanted to take a trip to that place, of all places, right after the birth of his daughter; it is there that he points to the dying pine trees' great productiveness.

10. On the sustained reversals of "prosaic" and "poetic" norms in this poem, see Scharf Gold (1984:145–47). Her reading of these reversals, however, reiterates the modernist cliché about "language as an unsatisfactory instrument of communication" (1984: 147), precisely the position Amichai is rejecting.

11. See Kronfeld (1990) for a more detailed discussion of the poem's complex uses of the genre of autobiography.

12. A twelfth-century Jewish explorer whose search for lost Jewish communities started a trend in Jewish letters, leading to the satirical *Travels of Benjamin the Third* by Mendele Moykher Sforim, where the genre of the travelogue and the conventional theme of the quest for lost tribes are brilliantly parodied. And see Alcalay (1993: 119ff) for a new perspective on Benjamin of Tudela as a traveler through the glass walls separating/joining the Arab and Jewish Levant.

13. This quantification of hope as a yardstick echoes, in the desert setting of this poem, Israeli perceptions of how Bedouins estimate distance: "two cigarettes away," for example.

14. For a detailed discussion of the philosophy of interims or in-betweenness, see Kronfeld (1990).

7. David Fogel and Moyshe Leyb Halpern

1. Dan Pagis insists in the opening section of his introduction to the critical edition of Fogel's poetry that the poet's name should be spelled "Vogel" following the German. I have nevertheless chosen "Fogel," in line with the common romanization of the Hebrew spelling. See "Kavim le-biyografia,"

in Fogel ([1966] 1975:13). Similarly with Halpern's name, I have chosen to follow the transliteration of the Yiddish, "Moyshe Leyb," rather than the more Germanic "Moishe Leib."

2. For a brilliant analysis of this relationship, see Seidman (1993a). See also Even-Zohar, (1990:121–30).

Research into the bilingual aspects of Hebrew-Yiddish modernism seems particularly necessary in the case of Fogel. It now appears that Fogel was quite familiar with modernist Yiddish poetry (perhaps mainly in its Central and Eastern European manifestations, such as the expressionists of the *khalyastre* and the *albatros* groups). See Pagis's introduction in Fogel ([1966] 1975: 21–22, 42–43) and Feldman (1985:30). With Menakhem Perry's publication of his heavily edited Hebrew translation of Fogel's unfinished Yiddish novel, under the title *Kulam yats'u la-krav (All Have Gone Out to Battle)* in Fogel (1990:65–198), it has become public knowledge that Fogel was also a Yiddish writer himself. The gallows humor characteristic of this novel, which Perry associates with the grotesque in the tradition of Mendele and Gogol (Fogel, 1990:30), in fact bears the mark of the macabre wit salient in modernist Yiddish poetry and most clearly exemplified by Halpern's work. Several translations of Fogel's poetry into Yiddish (some apparently his own) appeared in literary magazines in Vienna, Warsaw, and New York. See Fogel ([1966] 1975: 275, 1983:65).

The situation is less certain with respect to Halpern's association with Hebrew literature. Although his lifelong involvement with the Yiddish press would have exposed him to modernist Hebrew writers in Yiddish translation, he also explicitly declared his separateness from the Zionist revival of Hebrew: compare his mocking criticism of "the Zionist Marxists who expressed their ideals of liberty, equality, and fraternity by practicing birth control and promising that when they went together to Eretz-Yisroel to smell tobacco they would sneeze in Hebrew." (Translation of Halpern's "Introduction" to Zishe Weinper's *Geklibene verk*, 1932; cited in Wisse, 1988:199).

3. Although Hebrew modernism is prototypically exemplified by poetry, prose fiction is perceived to have predated Fogel's early poetic modernism by almost twenty years with the groundbreaking works of Uri Nissan Gnessin and Yosef Chaim Brenner. See, for example, Steinhardt (1989), Alter (1988:49–63), Shaked (1973:57–120, 155–92), Brinker (1990), and Miron (1964: 40). Although Fogel explicitly acknowledges Gnessin as an influential "precursor," stylistically they are construed as members of one and the same literary "generation" of antiformulaic writers. This relationship lends further empirical support to the repudiation of linear conceptions of literary periodization. Fogel's relationships to the older poets who are sometimes associated with the antiformulaic generation—Ya'akov Shteynberg, Avraham Ben-Yitzhak—as well as to women poets who are more rarely associated with it, needs to be studied further.

In Yiddish prose fiction, Dovid Bergelson is usually credited with a position similar to Gnessin's in Hebrew, an interesting fact given Bergelson's familiarity with Gnessin since 1904–5 (see Harshav [Hrushovski], Sutzkever, and Shmeruk, 1964:734). Like Gnessin, Bergelson is considered the creator of an early modernist prose style for his literature and is associated both with impressionism and with explorations of consciousness. The prototypical text of this early modernist style is his "Arum Vokzal" ("At the Depot") ([1909] 1961), fragments of which were originally written in Hebrew.

A critical account of the bilateral bilingualism of Hebrew and Yiddish modernism in the context of the first anti-*nusach* wave of Hebrew literature and the impressionist phase of Yiddish literature still waits to be written, but Seidman (1993: 188–263) makes an important contribution in her discussion of Dvora Baron as a bilingual writer. And see also, Feldman (1985) and Bakon (1986). Feldman's discussion in particular is illuminating on the New York Yiddish-impressionists/aestheticists' links to modernist Hebrew poetry on the one hand and American imagism on the other.

4. Halpern's *In New York* was published in 1919 and Fogel's *Lifney ha-sha'ar ha-afel* appeared in 1923.

5. On the concept of self-modernization in a decentered literature (here, early twentieth-century American, as distinct from European literature), see Robert Alter's perceptive critique of Eliot's relationship to modernism in "What Was T. S. Eliot?" (1989:32ff). In his discussion of Eliot's self-modernization, Alter emphasizes the precociousness of the author of "Prufrock" and quotes Ezra Pound's observation "in a letter after meeting Eliot for the first time in London in 1914 that his young compatriot had 'actually trained himself *and* modernized himself *on his own'* " (italics in the original).

Halpern's choice of Yiddish was also far from automatic but ultimately entailed less isolation from a community of writers and, most dramatically, from a community of contemporary readers than did Fogel's choice of Hebrew. Interestingly, his first poems, written in German, were composed, like Fogel's early Hebrew work, in Vienna, where Halpern was apprenticed to a commercial artist even though he spent a good deal of his time sitting in on German literature classes at the university. See Wisse (1988:76) and the biographical appraisal of Halpern's European period by his *landsman*, the poet Dovid Kenigsberg (1938; reprinted in Eliezer Greenberg's excellent monograph, *Moyshe Leyb Halpern in Ram fun zayn Dor (Moyshe Leyb Halpern in the Framework of His Generation)*, 1942:116–21). Upon returning to his hometown of Zlochev, which had already become a small center of Yiddish letters, he began to write poetry in Yiddish. But only with the addition of two intermediary stops during his travels does the choice of Yiddish become identified with a cultural commitment to the language and with an increasingly modernist sensibility: the Czernowitz Conference he attended as a delegate in 1908 (in which Yiddish was declared for the first time(!) a Jewish language) and his emigration to the United States, which followed almost immediately afterward.

6. A detailed discussion of Fogel's innovative prose style immediately follows this quotation (Alter, 1988:75–94).

7. The diary was given the apocalyptic title *Ktzot ha-yamim (The End of Days)* by its editor, Menakhem Perry (see Fogel, 1990:268–326). However, the poem from which this title is borrowed, "Ayefim anachnu,/ nelkha-na lishon" (referred to at the beginning of this chapter) deflates the apocalyptic

pathos of the "end of days" through a metaphorical concretization of "ends" as physical "edges" or "tails." Rather than conjure up a universal judgment day, the poem—like the diary that predates it by two decades—deals with a mundane ennui: days' ends inexorably lead into nights, which redundantly stand for death. Life is ungracefully stuck or tucked into (*tchuvim*) death, perhaps like the tail ends of a blanket or a pajama top invoked within the poem's dramatic situation: "*Ayefim anachnu,/ nelkha-na li-shon.//Ktsot ha-yamim tchuvim ba-layla,/ tchuvim ba-mavet*" ("Weary are we,/ let us go to sleep.//The edges of days are tucked into the night,/tucked into death"). Translations are my own, unless specified otherwise. For a nuanced reading of Fogel's diary as a laboratory for the forging of a modernist Hebrew self, see Alter (1993).

8. Which Fogel most likely read in the German translation (Hamsun, 1891).

9. Fogel (1990:285). For other renditions of Vilna as the only locus of happiness and its simultaneous association with Hebrew and with love, see Fogel (1990: 276, 279, 283, 291, 303).

10. Wisse comes close to doing just that in her otherwise sensitive and erudite literary biography of Halpern and Mani Leyb, *A Little Love in Big Manhattan* (1988:81). She argues that what was "special about Halpern, that set him apart from even the other individualists and eccentrics of the nascent literary community" in New York was that "for one thing, he resisted employment. . . . Halpern took . . . pleasure in his inability to succeed at a regular job."

11. I am grateful to Nanette Stahl for help with translating Halpern's richly figurative colloquial Yiddish into idiomatic English.

12. The terms in which this theme is expressed in the poetry—as in this early letter—are decidedly Marxist, although Halpern remained ferociously critical of state-controlled Bolshevism even before his break with the Soviet-leaning paper *Frayhayt* in 1929. Just as during his early literary affiliation with *di yunge*, he was one of only a few who consistently maintained a critical distance from the aestheticist dictates of the group, so in his political conviction "it was Halpern alone who remained the local 'Trotsky,' irritant to those who upheld collective discipline" (Wisse, 1988:184). An interesting example of Halpern's resistance to institutional corruptions of the Marxism he was committed to is found in the circumstances under which he left *Frayhayt*. The final break with the paper—for which he paid dearly with the unemployment and total destitution that may have led to his premature death three years later—came, despite his outspoken anti-Zionism, when *Frayhayt* obeyed the Soviet dictate and refrained from condemning the massacre of Jews in Palestine by Arabs during the uprising of 1929.

Halpern was among the first to leave the paper and, with a few temporary exceptions, remained unemployed, literally hungry, and critically ill until his death on August 31, 1932. "The word went out that he had died of neglect. . . . One critic was certain that 'Yiddish literary history would consider his death a murder' " (Wisse, 1988:204; the critic cited is Borukh Rivkin, 1934:110). Rivkin also quotes the poet H. Leyvik's (1932) graveside eulogy of Halpern:

"One of our greatest poets has been murdered." This eulogy is typical of the sense of communal responsibility for the poet's death, in particular for his fellow writers' and readers' failure to assess the severity of his malnutrition and illness, expressed in many contemporary appraisals. This sense of responsibility was enhanced, I believe, by the fiercely ironic dramatization which Halpern's work offered of the ambivalence of self- and social criticism concerning the personal and social dislocations of the poet-as-pauper.

13. A brilliant discussion of this technique, its roots in premodernist Yiddish discourse and fiction, and its political uses in Halpern's poetry is offered in Harshav (1990:100–111); see in particular the section "Halpern's Political Talk-Verse."

14. Compare the unadorned prosaic crudeness of Halpern's 1917 *altz is gornit* with Yehoash's poetic-philosophical translation: *nishtikayt fun nishtikaytn, altz iz nishtikayt* (Yehoash, [1936] 1939). Halpern may also be alluding to the famous Jewish joke about being a nothing as an achievement not everybody is entitled to (see my analysis of this story as a parable on marginality in the Conclusion).

15. On the aesthetics of quietude as practiced and preached by those members of *di yunge* who clustered around Mani Leyb, see Wisse (1988:38ff).

16. Abraham Novershtern discovered, in an innovative study (1986:138), that Glatshteyn's first book of poetry was modeled—in its thematic structure—on Halpern's *In New York*. Thus, Glatshteyn adopted Halpern's radically modernist poetic architecture in the same book that launched his group's "rebellion" against *di yunge*.

17. This effect, so essential to the shock value of the poem, is unfortunately lost in translation.

18. The poem's rhythmic complexity notwithstanding, I offer below a literal translation that follows the poem's semantic and syntactic structure as accurately as I could. But for poetic renditions, see Hellerstein's translation in Halpern (1982) and Roskies (1989).

19. This declaration, as Harshav shrewdly points out, is almost a direct parallel to Kazimir Edschmidt's expressionist manifesto, published not much before the introspectivists', in his *Über den Expressionismus in der Literatur und die neue Dichtung* (1919:56). Edschmidt's influential declaration was first made in a speech in Berlin in 1917. The introspectivists' relation to expressionism—like Halpern's—is, however, rather ambivalent. See Harshav (1990:178) and my discussion below.

20. The distinction between explicit and implicit poetics, by now quite accepted in literary theory, was first introduced by Benjamin Harshav [Hrushovski] in lectures during the 1960s.

21. In discussing their relation to the first group of Yiddish poets in the United States, the so-called proletarian or sweatshop poets, the introspectivists select a "grandfather" who should have been their literary father: "Only one representative of the older Yiddish poets has crossed the boundary of his time and is, for us, not merely a precursor but a fellow poet. This is Yehoash. . . . Perhaps he should have been the initiator of a new trend in Yiddish poetry and perhaps also, at least in part, of our trend. He did not do

this for understandable reasons, and we would like to note that we regard him as one who is close to us" (in Harshav and Harshav, 1986:782).

22. An English translation first appeared in the journal *Yiddish*, 1(1)(1973): 34. Sections of this essay are reproduced in a different translation in Harshav and Harshav (1986:785–88).

23. Recognizing Halpern's liminality may help us become more aware of the importance of women poets to the dynamics of both modernist trends. Novershtern has shrewdly observed Anna Margolin's transitional role between *di yunge* and the introspectivists (1990:460–63). But her recovery project has only just begun.

24. See also numerous retrospective appraisals of their "Americanism" and "imagism" in the December 1939 issue of *In Zikh* devoted to A. Leyeles.

25. For early reviews, see Wisse (1988:248, note 34) and Boaz (1971:169–72).

26. My summary relies on the last two chapters of his posthumously edited book (1976), as well as on my own studies with Professor Ha-Ephrati up to his death in the 1973 war.

27. See note 19 above.

28. Cited from the Hebrew translation, in Harshav [Hrushovski] (1973:81).

29. In his monograph on Halpern (Greenberg, 1942:23); within Yiddish poetry it is the quietude faction of *di yunge*, not Halpern, that developed this genre.

30. Edschmidt (1919), Hebrew translation in Harshav [Hrushovski] (1973: 81).

31. In a study on the relationship between fragmentation and totality in modernist poetry and music (Ph.D. Diss., Berkeley; 1996).

32. My reading of this poem has benefited from the teaching of Boaz Arpali.

33. Idiomatically, the verb to walk (*h.l.kh.*) is used to indicate process (the horses are in the process of melting away). Yet, the surrealism of the imagery allows for a literalization of this idiom. Note that it is not the sound that is "fading away"—as a realist or impressionist would have it. The Hebrew for "melting (and walking) away," *ha-nemasim ve-holkhim,* is masculine, in agreement with "horses," *susim,* but not with "gallops," *daharot.*

8. The Yiddish Poem Itself

1. Poetic translations of both versions are included in Harshav and Harshav (1986:466–471, 488–89).

2. As, for example, in the poetry of Chaim Nachman Bialik. Note that this is one of the few Jewish inflected symbols in this poem.

3. On Halpern's failed attempt to relocate to Los Angeles, see Wisse (1988:188–90).

4. Since the poem is written almost entirely in slang and uses many abbreviated colloquial forms, the transliteration follows the spoken rather than the standard pronunciation.

5. See also Revelation 1:1, 21:6. I am grateful to David Roskies for suggesting this connection.

6. That Hofshteyn may in fact have been affiliated with Hebrew—not just Yiddish—modernism directly is evidenced by the sampling of his Hebrew poems included in Hofshteyn 1977:194–96.

7. Paul Cezanne's *Large Bathers*, Paul Gaugin's *Fatata Te Miti*, Otto Mueller's *Bathers*, for example.

8. In his "Who Am I and What Am I" ("*Mi ani u-ma ani*"), 1911, in Bialik ([1953] 1964/65:57).

9. For traditional expressions of this motif in literature and folklore see, for example, the custom of the "black wedding," a wedding conducted in the graveyard to ward off the plague or to appease the spirits of the dead. Famous fictional examples are found in Mendele Moykher Sforim's *Fishke der Krumer* (Fishke the Lame) and in I. J. Singer's *Yoshe Kalb*; for ethnographic evidence, see Rekhtman (1958:132ff).

There are also numerous depictions of newlyweds dancing on the graves of dead brides and grooms who have been killed in a pogrom in order to share the joy with those who never lived to experience it. This custom forms a central motif in Sh. An-Ski's *Der Dibek (The Dibbuk)* and is documented in An-Ski's famous study, *Folklor un Etnografye: Gezamelte Shriftn (Folklore and Ethnography: Collected Works)* (1925:257–67ff). And see also David Roskies and Diane Roskies (1975:70–72, 79, 199, 232, 247).

10. See, for example, lines 2, 7, 9, 10.

11. Uriel Weinrich has discussed this tendency as it is revealed in Sutzkever's use of rhyme, in "On the Cultural History of Yiddish Rhyme" in Weinrich (1959).

12. Cited in R. Wisse's introduction to Sutzkever's *Green Aquarium* (1975: xi–xii).

Conclusion

1. The story is Bluma Goldstein's. The appropriation is my own. My reading of the joke as a parable on marginality has benefited from discussions with her as well as with David Biale.

2. I owe this coinage to Eric Zakim.

3. For a cogent critique of French and American theories of marginality, see Yudice (1988).

4. An awareness of the ambivalent valorization of nothing and nothingness in Jewish culture is built into Halpern's sarcastic self-reading of the poet/pauper as a *gornisht*. See discussion of his letter to Royzele Baron in Chapter 7.

5. In Trinh T. Minh-ha's words (1990:329).

6. "Introduction: Invisible Center," in Ferguson et al. (1990:9).

7. Although I refuse to describe these works' greatness in immanent or essentialist terms, I take the intersubjective experiential evidence of their re-

ception seriously. Within a prototype model of literary categorization, aesthetic salience of this type does not need more positivist corroboration.

8. For a brilliant historical analysis of the interrelations of canonicity and questions of value, see Jusdanis (1991:199). Of special interest is ch. 3, "The Making of a Canon: A Literature of Their Own," pp. 49–87.

9. The distinction between "intraliterary" and "extraliterary" materials or patterns, customary in formalist and neoformalist poetics, is a methodological idealization. The impossibility of "any absolute separation" of internal and external frames of reference is acknowledged by Benjamin Harshav [Hrushovski], the leading theorist of this school of poetics. See, for example, his "An Outline of Integrational Semantics: An Understander's Theory of Meaning in Context" (1982b:75).

10. In a pioneering study included in his "Suppressed Modernisms: Marginality, Politics, Canon Formation" (1993a).

11. For a discussion of her poetry, see Chapter 3.

12. See Lyotard, Heidegger and "the jews" (1990); lowercase in the original. A brilliant critique of Lyotard's universalizing appropriation of "the jews" was delivered by Jonathan Boyarin and Greg Sarris in "Jews and Native Americans as Living Voice and Absent Other" (1991).

13. Lensky's collected poetry has been reissued in an expanded edition (1986). It includes a long narrative poem entitled "Be-yom ha-sheleg" ("On the Snowy Day"). Miron rightly hails the publication of this poem forty-five years after it was written as "a great literary event, at least for those increasingly numerous readers who see Lensky as one of the greatest Hebrew poets of the twentieth century." See Miron (1991:203). Typically, however, this important recovery project, in which Miron is a major participant, views Lensky as an individual "forgotten talent." It disregards the trend affinities between Lensky and other anti-nusach "minor-key" poets, especially David Fogel, Avraham Ben-Yitzhak, Rachel, and Esther Raab. Lensky's contribution to this latent, though most persistent, strand of Hebrew modernism still remains to be studied.

14. Deleuze and Guattari (1986); see especially the chapter "What Is a Minor Literature?" (reprinted in Ferguson et al., 1990:59–69).

15. For important work in this conceptual framework, see Hever (1990a) and Alcalay (1993).

16. Korman (1928) includes works by seventy(!) poets.

17. Important exceptions are Kathryn Hellerstein's studies of female literary traditions, especially her article "A Question of Tradition: Women Poets in Yiddish" (1988); and Abraham Novershtern's work on Anna Margolin as a transitional figure between di yunge and the Inzikhistn, especially Novershtern's "The Poetry of Anna Margolin" (1990).

Works Cited

Abramson, Glenda. 1984. "Amichai's God." *Prooftexts* 4(2): 111–26.

Abramson, Glenda, and Tudor Parfitt, eds. 1985. *The Great Transition: The Recovery of the Lost Centers of Modern Hebrew Literature.* Totowa, N.J.: Rowman & Allanheld.

Abramson, Shraga. 1965. *Bi-lshon kdumim: mechkar be-shirat yisra'el bi-sfarad* [Quotations: A study in medieval Hebrew poetry]. Jerusalem: Makhon Schocken le-Mechkar ha-Yahadut.

Adorno, Theodor. 1984. *Aesthetic Theory.* Translated by C. Lenhardt. London: Routledge & Kegan Paul.

Aharoni, Arye. 1989. Introduction to *Milon Chidushey Shlonsky* [Dictionary of Shlonsky's Neologisms], by Ya'akov Kna'ani, 5–8. Tel Aviv: Sifriat Po'alim.

Akhmatova, Anna. 1985. *You Will Hear Thunder.* Poems translated by D. M. Thomas. Athens: Ohio University Press.

Alcalay, Ammiel. 1993. *After Jews and Arabs: Remaking Levantine Culture.* Minneapolis: University of Minnesota Press.

Alt, Arthur Tilo. 1987. "A Survey of Literary Contributions to the Post-World War I Yiddish Journals of Berlin." *Yiddish* 7(1): 42–52.

Alter, Robert. 1969. *After the Tradition.* New York: E. P. Dutton & Co.

———. 1985. *The Art of Biblical Poetry.* New York: Basic Books.

———. 1988. *The Invention of Hebrew Prose: Modern Fiction and the Language of Realism.* Seattle: University of Washington Press.

———. 1989. "What Was T. S. Eliot?" *Commentary,* 87(3): 31–37.

———. 1991. *Necessary Angels: Tradition and Modernity in Kafka, Benjamin, and Scholem.* Cambridge: Harvard University Press.

———. 1993. "Fogel and the Forging of a Hebrew Self." *Prooftexts* 13(1): 3–13.

Amichai, Yehuda. 1958. *Be-merchak shtey tikvot* [Two hopes away]. Tel Aviv: Ha-Kibbutz ha-Me'uchad.

————. [1962] 1977. *Shirim: 1948–1962* [Poems]. Jerusalem: Schocken.

————. [1968] 1975. *Akhshav ba-ra'ash: Shirim 1963–1968* [Now in the storm]. Jerusalem: Schocken.

————. 1980. *Shalva gdola: she'elot u-tshuvot* [Great tranquility: Questions and answers]. Jerusalem: Schocken.

————. 1986. *Selected Poetry of Yehuda Amichai*. Translated by Chana Bloch and Stephen Mitchell. New York: Harper & Row.

————. 1989. *Gam ha-egrof haya pa'am yad ptucha ve-etsba'ot* [Even the fist was once an open hand with fingers]. Jerusalem: Schocken.

Andersen, Elaine S. 1978. "Lexical Universals of Body-Part Terminology." In *Universals of Human Language,* vol 3, Joseph H. Greenberg et al., eds., 335–68. Stanford: Stanford University Press.

Andreeva-Popova, Nadezhda. 1985. "Tradition and Changes in Literary History." In *Proceedings of the Tenth Congress of the International Comparative Literature Association* (1982), edited by Douwe W. Fokkema, vol. 1: 65–69. New York: Garland Publications.

An-ski, Sh. 1927. *Folklor un Etnografye* [Folklore and ethnography], Vol. 15 of *Gezamelte Shriftn* [Collected works]. Vilnius, Warsaw, New York: Farlag "An-ski."

Arpali, Boaz. 1987. *Ha-prachim ve-ha-agartal: shirat Amichai 1948–1968 (mivne, mashma'ut, poe'tika)* [The flowers and the urn: Amichai's poetry 1948–1968 (structure, meaning, poetics). Tel Aviv: Siman Kri'ah/Ha-Kibbutz ha-Me'uchad.

Avrunin, Avraham. 1953. *Mechkarim bi-leshon Bialik ve-Yalag* [Studies in the language of Bialik and Y. L. Gordon]. Tel Aviv: Va'ad ha-Lashon ha-Ivrit.

Bahat, Ya'akov. 1980. "Naftuley elohim be-shirato u-va-haguto shel Avraham Shlonsky" [The Struggle with God in Abraham Shlonsky's poetry and thought]. *Moznayim* 51(3–4): 218–29.

Baker, G. P., and P. M. S. Hacker. [1980] 1985. *An Analytical Commentary on Wittgenstein's Philosophical Investigations.* Chicago: University of Chicago Press.

Bakhtin, Mikhail M., and Pavel N. Medvedev. [1978] 1985. *The Formal Method of Literary Scholarship: A Critical Introduction to Sociological Poetics.* Translated by Albert J. Wehrle. Cambridge: Harvard University Press.

Bakon, Yitzhak. 1986. *Brenner u-Gnessin ke-sofrim du-leshoniyim* [Brenner and Gnessin as bilingual writers]. Be'er Sheba, Israel: Yiddish Chair, Ben Gurion University.

Barsalaou, Lawrence. 1983. "Ad Hoc Categories." *Memory and Cognition* 11(3): 211–27.

Bartana, Ortzion. 1985. *La-vo cheshbon* [Settling accounts]. Tel Aviv: Alef.

————. 1989. *Zehirut, sifrut eretz yisre'elit: Megamot ba-shira, ba-siporet, u-va-bikoret be-yisra'el* [Watch out, Land of Israel literature: Tendencies in Israeli fiction]. Tel Aviv: Papyrus.

Barthes, Roland. 1975. *The Pleasure of the Text.* Translated by Richard Miller. New York: Hill and Wang.

Baruch, Miri. 1979. *Ha-romantikan ha-mar: i'yun be-shirav shel Nathan Zach* [The bitter romantic: Studies in the poems of Nathan Zach]. Tel Aviv: Alef.

Bat-Miriam, Yocheved. [1932] 1985. *Me-rachok* [From afar]. Tel Aviv: Ha-Kibbutz ha-Me'uchad.

Bavli, Hillel. 1958. *Some Aspects of Modern Hebrew Poetry.* Pamphlet 2. New York: Herzl Institute.

Beck, Evelyn Torton. 1971. *Kafka and the Yiddish Theater.* Madison: University of Wisconsin Press.

Ben, Menachem. 1986. "Ki kol ha-adam edim." [For all man is vapors]. *Yedi'ot Acharonot* 3 Jan.: 20.

Ben-Porat, Ziva. 1973. "The Poetics of Allusion." Ph.D. Diss., University of California, Berkeley.

————. 1976. "The Poetics of Literary Allusion." *PTL: A Journal for Descriptive Poetics and Theory of Literature* 1(1): 105–28.

————. 1978a. " 'Dantes, lo': li-dmut ha-shir shel Nathan Zach" ["Dantes, No": Analyzing Nathan Zach's poem]. *Siman Kri'ah* 8: 379–90.

————. 1978b. "Ha-kore, ha-tekst ve-ha-remiza ha-sifrutit: Aspektim achadim be-mimush remizot sifruti'yot" [Reader, text and literary allusion: Aspects in the actualization of literary allusions]. *Ha-Sifrut* 26: 1–25.

————. 1979. "Hofa'at Yefet be-ohel Shem: Remizot ve-hityachsuyot le-tekstim mi-sifrut eyropa ba-shira ha-ivrit mi-Shlonsky ve-ad yameynu" [The appearance of Japhet in the tents of Shem: Literary allusions and other references to European texts in modern Hebrew poetry]. *Ha-Sifrut* 29: 34–43.

————. 1985. "Beyn-textu'ali'yut retorit" [Intertextuality, rhetorical intertextuality, allusion and parody]. *Ha-Sifrut* 34: 170–78.

————, ed. 1989. *Lirika ve-lahit* [Lyric poetry and the poetry of pop]. Tel Aviv: Ha-Kibbutz ha-Me'uchad and the Porter Institute for Poetics and Semiotics, Tel Aviv University.

Ben-Porat, Ziva, and Benjamin Harshav [Hrushovski]. 1974. *Structuralist Poetics in Israel.* Papers on Poetics and Semiotics 1. Tel Aviv: Porter Institute for Poetics and Semiotics.

Ben-Yitzhak, Avraham. 1992. *Kol ha-shirim* [Collected poems]. Edited by Hanan Hever. Tel Aviv: Ha-Kibbutz ha-Me'uchad.

Bergelson, Dovid. [1909] 1961. "Arum Vokzal" [At the depot]. In *Ale Verk* [collected works], vol. 1, 15–91. Buenos Aires: ICUF.

Berman, Ruth Aronson. 1978. *Modern Hebrew Structure.* Tel Aviv: University Publishing Projects.

Beser, Yaakov, ed. 1971. *Si'ach meshorerim al atsmam ve-al ktivatam* [Poets talk about themselves and their works]. Tel Aviv: Eked.

Bialik, Chaim Nachman. [1953] 1964/65. *Kol kitvey Ch. N. Bialik* [Collected works]. Tel Aviv: Dvir.

Black, Max. 1962. *Models and Metaphors: Studies in Language and Philosophy.* Ithaca, N.Y.: Cornell University Press.

Blatt, Avraham. 1967. *Bi-netiv sofrim* [In the writers' lane]. Tel Aviv: Menorah.

Bloom, Harold. 1973. *The Anxiety of Influence: A Theory of Poetry.* Oxford: Oxford University Press.

Blumenberg, Hans. 1983. *The Legitimacy of the Modern Age.* Translated by Robert M. Wallace. Cambridge: M.I.T. Press.

Boaz, Chaim. 1971. *Shrayber un verk* [Writers and their work]. Tel Aviv: Menorah.

Boyarin, Jonathan, and Greg Sarris. 1991. "Jews and Native Americans as Living Voice and Absent Other." Paper presented at the Modern Language Association Convention, San Francisco.

Bradbury, Malcolm, and James McFarlane. eds. [1976] 1981. *Modernism 1890–1930.* Harmondsworth, U.K.: Penguin.

Brandes, Georg. 1906. *Main Currents in Nineteenth Century Literature.* 6 vols. New York: Macmillan; London: Heinemann.

Brenner, Yosef Chaim. [1902] 1972. *Shkhol ve-khishalon* [Breakdown and bereavement]. Tel Aviv: Am Oved.

———. 1971. *Breakdown and Bereavement.* Translated by Hillel Halkin. Ithaca, N.Y.: Cornell University Press.

Brinker, Menachem. 1990. *Ad ha-simta ha-Tveryanit: al sipur u-machshava bi-yetsirat Brenner* [On narrative and thought in Brenner's work]. Tel Aviv: Am Oved.

Brooks, Cleanth. 1953. "Tradition." In *Dictionary of World Literature: Criticism, Forms, Techniques,* edited by J. Shipley, 418–19. New York: Philosophical Library.

Brown, Edward J. 1976. "Introduction." In *Snake Train: Poetry and Prose* by Velimir Khlebnikov, translated by G. Kern et al. Ann Arbor, Mich.: Ardis.

Burnshaw, Stanley, T. Carmi, and Ezra Spicehandler, eds. [1965] 1989. *The Modern Hebrew Poem Itself.* Cambridge: Harvard University Press.

Canetti, Elias. 1985. *Das Augenspiel: Lebensgeschichte, 1931–1937.* Munich: Carl Hanser Verlag.

———. 1986. *The Play of the Eyes.* Translated from the German by Ralph Manheim. N.Y.: Farrar, Straus, Giroux.

Carmi, T., ed. 1981. *The Penguin Book of Hebrew Verse.* Harmondsworth, UK: Penguin.

Chapman, Graham, et al. [1979] 1992. *Monty Python's The Life of Brian (of Nazareth).* London: Mandarin Paperbacks.

Cohen, Ralph. 1991. "Genre Theory, Literary History, and Historical Change." In *Theoretical Issues in Literary History,* edited by David Perkins, 85–113. Cambridge: Harvard University Press.

Culler, Jonathan. 1981. *The Pursuit of Signs: Semiotics, Literature, Deconstruction.* Ithaca, N.Y.: Cornell University Press.

———. 1982. *On Deconstruction: Theory and Criticism after Structuralism.* Ithaca, N.Y.: Cornell University Press.

———. 1988. *Framing the Sign: Criticism and Its Institutions.* Oxford and New York: Blackwell.

Cysarz, Herbert. 1926. *Literaturgeschichte als Geistesgeschichte: Kritik und System.* Halle an der Saale, Germany: Niemayer.

―――. 1930. "Das Periodenprinzip in der Literaturwissenschaft." In *Philosophie der Literaturwissenschaft,* edited by Emil Ermatinger, 92–129. Berlin: Junker und Dünnhaupt.

de Man, Paul. 1971. *Blindness and Insight: Essays in the Rhetoric of Contemporary Criticism.* New York: Oxford University Press.

Deleuze, Gilles, and Félix Guattari. 1975. *Kafka: pour une littérature mineure.* Paris: Éditions de Minuit.

―――. 1986. *Kafka: Toward a Minor Literature.* Translated by Dana Polan. Minneapolis: University of Minnesota Press.

Dilthey, Wilhelm. 1906. *Das Erlebnis und die Dichtung: Lessing, Göethe, Novalis, Hölderlin.* Leipzig: B. G. Teubner.

―――. 1985. *Poetry and Experience.* Princeton, N.J.: Princeton University Press.

―――. 1989. *Introduction to the Human Sciences.* Princeton, N.J.: Princeton University Press.

Dubois, J. et al., eds. 1972. *Analyse de la périodisation littéraire.* Paris: Éditions Universitaires.

Ducrot, Oswald, and Tzvetan Todorov. 1979. *Encyclopedic Dictionary of the Sciences of Language.* Translated by Catherine Porter. Baltimore: Johns Hopkins University Press.

Edschmidt, Kazimir. 1919. *Über den Expressionismus in der Literatur und die neue Dichtung.* Berlin: Erich Reiss.

Eichenbaum, Boris. 1965. "The Theory of the 'Formal Method.' " In *Russian Formalist Criticism: Four Essays,* translated and introduced by Lee T. Lemon and Marion J. Reis. Lincoln: University of Nebraska Press.

Eliot, T. S. [1932] 1960. *Selected Essays.* New York: Harcourt, Brace & World.

―――. [1920] 1960. *The Sacred Wood.* London and New York: Methuen and Barnes & Noble.

Encyclopedia of Philosophy. [1967] 1972. Paul Edwards, editor in chief. 8 Vols. New York: Macmillan.

Eric, Max. [1922] 1973. "Leshon ha-ekspresyonizm ha-yehudi [The language of Jewish expressionism]." In *Yorshey ha-simbolizm ba-shira ha-eyropit ve-ha-yehudit* [Heirs of symbolism in European and Jewish literature], edited and translated by Benjamin Harshav [Hrushovski], 138–39. Tel Aviv: Tel Aviv Student Union.

Erlich, Victor. 1965. *Russian Formalism: History-Doctrine.* 2d rev. ed. The Hague: Mouton.

Ermatinger, Emil, ed. 1930. *Philosophie der Literaturwissenschaft.* Berlin: Junker und Dünnhaupt.

Escarpit, Robert. 1972. "Avant-Propos." In *Analyse de la périodisation littéraire,* edited by J. Dubois et al., 7–9. Paris: Éditions Universitaires.

Even-Zohar, Itamar. 1969/70. "Le-berur mahuta ve-tafkida shel leshon ha-sifrut ha-yafa be-diglossia" [The nature and functionalization of the language of literature under diglossia]. *Ha-Sifrut* 2(2): 286–302, 444.

————. 1971. "Ha-sifrut be-lashon ba'alat rav-ma'arekhet chasera: likrat tipologya shel sfot ktav" [Literature written in a language with a defective polysystem: Notes to Paul Wexler's rebuttal]. *Ha-Sifrut* 3(2): 339–41.

————. 1972. "Rashey prakim le-te'orya shel ha-tekst ha-sifruti" [An outline of a theory of the literary text]. *Ha-Sifrut* 3(3–4): 427–46.

————. 1978. *Papers in Historical Poetics.* Papers on Poetics and Semiotics 8. Tel Aviv: Porter Institute for Poetics and Semiotics.

————. 1979. "Polysystem Theory." *Poetics Today* 1(1–2): 287–310.

————. 1986. "Literary System." In *Encyclopedic Dictionary of Semiotics,* edited by Thomas A. Sebeok, 1: 463–66. Berlin and New York: Mouton de Gruyter.

————. 1990. *Poetics Today* 11(1). (Special issue on Even-Zohar's polysystem theory.)

Eysteinsson, Astradur. 1990. *The Concept of Modernism.* Ithaca, N.Y.: Cornell University Press.

Fanger, Donald. [1976] 1981. "The City of Russian Modernist Fiction." In *Modernism 1890–1930,* edited by Malcolm Bradbury and James McFarlane, 467–80. Harmondsworth, U.K.: Penguin.

Feldman, Yael. 1985. *Modernism and Cultural Transfer: Gabriel Preil and the Tradition of Jewish Literary Bilingualism.* Cincinnati, Ohio: Hebrew Union College Press.

Ferguson, Russell et al., eds. 1990. *Out There: Marginalization and Contemporary Cultures.* New York and Cambridge: New Museum of Contemporary Art and MIT Press.

Fichman, Ya'akov. 1948. *Dmuyot kdumim: shira u-proza* [Figures of antiquity: Poetry and prose]. Jerusalem: Mosad Bialik.

Fillmore, Charles J. 1975. "An Alternative to Checklist Theories of Meaning." In *Proceedings of the First Annual Meeting of the Berkeley Linguistics Society,* 123–31. Berkeley: Berkeley Linguistics Society.

————. 1982. "Frame Semantics." In *Linguistics in the Morning Calm,* edited by Linguistic Society of Korea, 111–38. Seoul: Hanshin.

————. 1985. "Frames and the Semantics of Understanding." *Quanderi di Semantica* 6(2):222–53.

Fishelov, David. 1992. "Yehuda Amichai: A Modern Metaphysical Poet." *Orbis Litterarum* 47: 178–91.

Fogel, David. 1923. *Lifney ha-sha'ar ha-afel* [Before the dark gate]. Vienna: Machar.

————. [1931] 1974. "Lashon ve-signon be-sifrutenu ha-tse'ira" ["Language and style in our young literature"]. *Siman Kri'ah* 3–4: 387–91.

————. [1966] 1975. *Kol ha-shirim* [Collected poems, 1915–1941]. 3d. rev. ed. Edited by Dan Pagis. Tel Aviv: Ha-Kibbutz ha-Me'uchad.

————. 1983. *Le'ever ha-dmama* [Toward stillness]. Edited by Aharon Komem. Tel Aviv: Ha-Kibbutz ha-Me'uchad.

————. 1990. *Tachanot kavot* [Stories; Diary]. Edited by Menakhem Perry. Tel Aviv: Ha-Kibbutz ha-Me'uchad.

——. 1993. "Language and Style in our Young Literature." Translated by Yael Meroz and Eric Zakim. *Prooftexts* 13(1): 15–20.

Fogelin, Robert J. 1976. *Wittgenstein.* London: Routledge and Kegan Paul.

Fohrmann, Jürgen. 1988. "Remarks toward a Theory of Literary Genres." *Poetics* 17: 273–85.

Fokkema, Douwe W. 1984. *Literary History, Modernism and Postmodernism.* Amsterdam: John Benjamins.

Fokkema, Douwe W., and Elrud Ibsch. 1987. *Modernist Conjectures: A Mainstream in European Literature 1910–1940.* London: C. Hurst.

Foucault, Michel. [1970] 1973. *The Order of Things.* New York: Random House, Vintage Books.

Frow, John. 1986. *Marxism and Literary History.* Cambridge: Harvard University Press.

Fruchtman, Maya. 1968/69. "Hashpa'atam shel ha-mekorot ha-kdumim ve-ha-sifrut ha-chadasha al leshono shel Aharon Megged be-'Ha-chay al ha-met' " [The influences of ancient Hebrew sources and modern Hebrew literature on A. Megged's *The Living and the Dead*]. *Ha-Sifrut* 1(3–4): 723–25.

Furness, R. S. 1973. *Expressionism.* London: Methuen.

Genette, Gerard. 1982. *Palimpsestes: la littérature au second degré.* Paris: Seuil.

Gilbert, Sandra M., and Susan Gubar. 1991. " 'But Oh! That Deep Romantic Chasm:' The Engendering of Periodization." *The Kenyon Review* (2nd. Series) 13(3): 75–81.

Girsht, Yehuda Loeb. 1958/59. *Tachanot be-sifrut yisrael: Toldot sifrut am yisrael mi-zman chatimat ha-talmud im antologya mevo'eret* [The history of Jewish literature since the completion of the Talmud with an annotated anthology]. Vol. 2. Jerusalem: Yeshurun.

Givón, Talmy. 1977. "The Drift from VSO to SVO in Biblical Hebrew: The Pragmatics of Tense-Aspect." In *Mechanics of Syntactic Change,* edited by Charles N. Li, 181–254. Austin: University of Texas Press.

——. 1986, "Prototypes: Between Plato and Wittgenstein." In *Noun Classes and Categorization,* edited by Colette Craig, Typological Studies in Language, 7:77–102. Amsterdam/Philadelphia: John Benjamins.

Glatshteyn, Yankev [Jacob Glatstein]. 1973. "A Short View of Yiddish Poetry." *Yiddish* 1(1): 30–39.

Głowiński, Michał. 1969. "Ha-genre ha-sifruti u-be'ayot ha-po'etika ha-historit" [The literary genre and the problems of historical poetics, translated from the Polish]. *Ha-Sifrut* 2(1): 14–25.

——. 1975. "Polish Structuralism." *Books Abroad* 49(2): 239–43.

——. 1976. "Theoretical Foundations of Historical Poetics." *New Literary History,* 7(2): 237–45.

——. 1994. "From a Different Perspective." *New Literary History* 25(4): 895–97.

Gluzman, Michael. 1991a. "The Exclusion of Women from Hebrew Literary History." *Prooftexts* 11(3): 259–78.

————. 1991b. "Female Subjectivity in/and Minor Literature: Two Examples of Hebrew Postmodernism." Paper presented at the Association of Jewish Studies Conference, Boston.

————. 1993a. "Suppressed Modernisms: Marginality, Politics, Canon Formation." Ph.D. Diss., University of California, Berkeley.

————. 1993b. "Unmasking the Politics of Plain Style in Hebrew Modernist Poetry: Rereading David Fogel." *Prooftexts* 13(1): 21–43.

Gold, Nili Scharf. 1984. "Images in Transformation in the Recent Poetry of Yehuda Amichai." *Prooftexts* 4(2): 141–52.

Goldberg, Leah. [1952] 1988. *Pgisha im meshorer: al Avraham Ben-Yitzhak Sonne* [Encounter with a poet]. Merchavya: Sifriat Po'alim.

————. 1972/89 *Ktavim* [Collected works, 5 vols.]. Edited by T. Ribner. Merchavya: Sifriat Po'alim.

Goldstein, Bluma. 1968. "Franz Kafka's 'Ein Landarzt': A Study in Failure." *Deutsche Viertel-jahrsschrift für Literaturwissenschaft und Geistesgeschichte* 42: 745–59.

————. 1992. *Reinscribing Moses: Heine, Kafka, Freud, and Schoenberg in a European Wilderness.* Cambridge: Harvard University Press.

Gorsky, D. P. [1974] 1981. *Definition: Logico-Methodological Problems.* Translated from the revised Russian by Sergei Syrovatkin. Moscow: Progress Publishers.

Greenberg, Eliezer. 1942. *Moyshe Leyb Halpern in ram fun zayn dor* [Moshe Leyb Halpern in the framework of his generation]. New York: M. L. Halpern Arbeter Ring.

Grodzensky, Shlomo. 1975. *Otobiografia shel kore: masot u-reshimot al ha-sifrut* [Autobiography of a reader]. Tel Aviv: Ha-Kibbutz ha-Me'uchad.

Guillén, Claudio. 1971. *Literature as System: Essay toward the Theory of Literary History.* Princeton, N.J.: Princeton University Press.

————. 1993. *The Challenge of Comparative Literature.* Cambridge: Harvard University Press.

Gumbrecht, Hans-Ulrich, and Ursula Link-Heer, eds. 1985a. *Epochenschwellen und Epochenstrukturen im Diskurs der Literatur und Sprachhistorie.* Frankfurt am Main: Suhrkamp.

————. 1985b. "History of Literature—Fragment of a Vanished Totality." *New Literary History* 16: 467–79.

Gurvitch, Georges. [1956] 1973. "The Sociology of the Theater." *Les lettres nouvelles* 35: 196–210. Reprinted in *Sociology of Literature and Drama,* edited by Elizabeth Burns and Tom Burns, 71–81. Harmondsworth, U.K.: Penguin.

Ha-Ephrati, Yosef. 1976. *Ha-mar'ot ve-ha-lashon: le-toldot ha-te'ur ba-shira ha-ivrit ha-chadasha* [The presented world: Evolution of the poetic language of nature description in Hebrew poetry]. Tel Aviv: Porter Institute for Poetics and Semiotics.

Ha-Gorni-Green, Avraham. 1985. *Shlonsky ba-avotot Bialik* [Shlonsky in the bonds of Bialik]. Tel Aviv: Or Am.

Halkin, Shimon. [1950] 1974. *Modern Hebrew Literature from the Enlightenment to the Birth of the State of Israel: Trends and Values.* New York: Schocken Books.

Halpern, Moyshe Leyb. [1919] 1954. *In New York.* (in Yiddish). New York: Farlag Matones.

———. 1934. *Moyshe Leyb Halpern.* 2 vols. New York: Moyshe Leyb Halpern Komitet.

———. 1982. *In New York: A Selection.* Translated, edited, and introduced by Kathryn Hellerstein. Philadelphia: Jewish Publication Society.

Halpern, Moyshe Leyb, and Menachem Boreysho, eds. 1916. *East Broadway* (in Yiddish). New York: Literatur Farlag.

Hamsun, Knut. 1891. *Hunger* (in German). Berlin: M. Von Broch.

Harshav, Benjamin [Hrushovski], ed. and trans. 1973. *Yorshey ha-simbolizm ba-shira ha-eyropit ve-ha-yehudit: mivchar manifestim, ma'amarim, hakhrazot* [Heirs of symbolism in European and Jewish literature: A selection of manifestoes, articles and declarations]. Tel Aviv: Tel Aviv Student Union Press.

———. [Hrushovski]. 1976. *Segmentation and Motivation in the Text Continuum of Literary Prose: The First Episode of War and Peace.* Papers on Poetics and Semiotics 5. Tel Aviv: Porter Institute for Poetics and Semiotics.

———. [Hrushovski]. 1979. "The Structure of Semiotic Objects: A Three-Dimensional Model." *Poetics Today* 1(1–2): 363–76.

———. [Hrushovski]. 1980. "The Meaning of Sound Patterns in Poetry: An Interaction Theory." *Poetics Today* 2(1a): 39–56.

———. [Hrushovski]. 1982a. "Integrational Semantics: An Understander's Theory of Meaning in Context." In *Contemporary Perceptions of Language: Interdisciplinary Dimensions,* edited by Heidi Brynes, 156–90. Washington, D.C.: Georgetown University Press.

———. [Hrushovski]. 1982b. "An Outline of Integrational Semantics: An Understander's Theory of Meaning in Context." *Poetics Today* 3(4): 59–88.

———. 1984. "Poetic Metaphor and Frames of Reference." *Poetics Today* 5(1):5–43.

———. 1990. *The Meaning of Yiddish.* Berkeley: University of California Press.

———. 1993. *Language in Time of Revolution.* Berkeley: University of California Press.

Harshav, Benjamin [Hrushovski], Sutzkever Avrom, and Chone Shmeruk, eds. 1964. *A Shpigl oyf a Shteyn* [A mirror on a stone]. Tel Aviv: Goldene Keyt/Peretz Farlag.

Harshav, Benjamin, and Barbara Harshav, eds. 1986. *American Yiddish Poetry: A Bilingual Anthology.* Berkeley: University of California Press.

Hartman, Geoffrey. 1986. "The Struggle for the Text." In *Midrash and Literature,* edited by Geoffrey H. Hartman and Sanford Budick, 3–18. New Haven: Yale University Press.

Hausenstein, Wilhelm. 1921. *Vom Geist des Barock*. Munchen: R. Piper.

Heilke, Thomas N. 1990. *Voegelin on the Idea of Race: An Analysis of Modern European Racism*. Baton Rouge, LA: Louisiana State University Press.

Hellerstein, Kathryn. 1988. "A Question of Tradition: Women Poets in Yiddish." In *Handbook of American-Jewish Literature: An Analytical Guide to Topics, Themes and Sources*, edited by Lewis Fried et al., 195–237. New York: Greenwood Press.

Hermand, Jost. 1978. *Stile, Ismen, Etiketten: Zur Periodisierung der modernen Kunst*. Wiesbaden, Germany: Akademische Verlagsgesellschaft Athenaion.

Hermand, Jost, and Evelyn Torton Beck. 1975. *Interpretive Synthesis: The Task of Literary Scholarship*. New York: Frederick Ungar.

Hever, Hanan. 1983. "Ha-ma'agal ha-shlishi: Dov Sadan al tsmichata shel ha-shira ha-ivrit ha-modernit" [The third circle: Dov Sadan on the growth of modern Hebrew poetry]. *Siman Kri'ah* 16–17: 574–77.

———. 1990a. "Hebrew in an Israeli Arab Hand: Six Miniatures on Anton Shammas's *Arabesques*." In *The Nature and Context of Minority Discourse*, edited by Abdul R. JanMohamed and David Lloyd, 264–93. Oxford: Oxford University Press.

———. 1990b. "Tanchunim nistarim: al reshit ha-modernizm ba-shira ha-ivrit" [Hidden solace: on the beginnings of modernism in Hebrew poetry]. *Chadarim* 9: 93–106.

———. 1992. "Acharit-davar: al chayav vi-yetsirato shel Avraham Ben-Yitzhak" ["Postscript: On the life and work of Avraham Ben-Yitzhak."] In *Kol ha-shirim* [Collected poems], by Avraham Ben-Yitzhak, edited by Hanan Hever. Tel Aviv: Ha-Kibbutz ha-Me'uchad.

———. 1993. *Prichat ha-dumiya: Shirat Avraham Ben-Yitzhak* [The Flowering of silence: The poetry of Avraham Ben-Yitzhak]. Tel Aviv: Ha-Kibbutz ha-Me'uchad.

Hofshteyn, Dovid. 1919. *Bay Vegn* [On the road]. Kiev: Kiever Farlag.

———. 1977. *Lider un Po'emes* [Poems]. Tel Aviv: Yisro'el-Bukh.

Holland, Dorothy, and Naomi Quinn, eds. 1987. *Cultural Models in Language and Thought*. Cambridge: Cambridge University Press.

Howe, Irving, and Eliezer Greenberg, eds. [1969] 1976. *A Treasury of Yiddish Poetry*. New York: Schocken Books.

In Zikh: A Zamlung Introspektive Lider [In oneself: A collection of introspective poems]. [1919] 1920. New York: Maisel.

Jakobson, Roman. [1929, 1971] 1978. "The Dominant." In *Readings in Russian Poetics: Formalist and Structuralist Views*, edited by Ladislav Matejka and Krystyna Pomorska, 82–87. Ann Arbor, Mich.: University of Michigan.

———. 1987. *Language in Literature*. Edited by Krystyna Pomoroska and Stephen Rudy. Cambridge: Harvard University Press.

JanMohamed, Abdul R., and David Lloyd, eds. 1990. *The Nature and Context of Minority Discourse*. Oxford: Oxford University Press.

Janson, H. W. 1970. "Criteria for Periodization in the History of European Art, II." *New Literary History* 1(2): 115–22.

Jasinowski, B. 1937. "Sur les fondements logiques de l'histoire." In *Travaux du IXe Congres International de Philosophie*, Vol. 5, 39–48. Paris: Hermann et Cie.

Jofen, Jean. 1984. "The Jewish Element in the Work of Franz Kafka." *Modern Jewish Studies Annual V, Yiddish* 5(4): 87–106.

Journal of Philosophy 57(7). 1960. "Polish Number," special issue devoted to philosophy in Poland, edited by Max Rieser.

Jusdanis, Gregory. 1991. *Belated Modernity and Aesthetic Culture: Inventing National Literature*. Minneapolis: University of Minnesota Press.

Juster, Norton. [1962] 1976. *The Phantom Tollbooth*. London: Collins/Lions.

Kafka, Franz. 1948/49. *The Diaries: 1910–1923*. 2 vols. Edited by Max Brod and translated by Joseph Kresh and Martin Greenberg. New York: Schocken Books.

——. 1954. "An Introductory Talk on the Yiddish Language." In *Dearest Father*, translated by Ernst Kaiser and Eithne Wilkins, 381–86. New York: Schocken Books.

——. 1977. *Letters to Friends, Family and Editors*. New York: Schocken.

——. 1989. *The Sons*. New York: Schocken.

Kallir, Eleazar. 1930. *Mivchar piyutim* [Selected liturgy]. Annotated by Y. L. Baruch. Tel Aviv: Omanut.

Katznelson, Gideon. 1968. *Le'an hem holkhim?* [Where are they going?]. Tel Aviv: Alef.

Kelly, Joan. 1984. "Did Women Have a Renaissance?" In *Women, History, and Theory: The Essays of Joan Kelly*, 19–50. Chicago: Chicago University Press.

Kenner, Hugh. 1984. "The Making of the Modernist Canon." In *Canons*, edited by Robert Von Hallberg, 363–75. Chicago: University of Chicago Press.

Kermode, Frank. 1988. *History and Value*. Oxford: Clarendon Press.

Khlebnikov, Velimir. 1976. *Snake Train: Poetry and Prose*. Translated by G. Kern et al. Ann Arbor, Mich.: Ardis.

Kna'ani, Ya'akov. 1989. *Milon Chidushey Shlonsky* [Dictionary of Shlonsky's Neologisms]. Tel Aviv: Sifriat Po'alim.

Komem, Aharon. 1982. "Le-fesher shirat ha-ahava shel David Fogel" [On the meaning of David Fogel's love poems]. *Iton* 77(32–33): 24–29.

Korman, Ezra, ed. 1928. *Yiddishe Dikhterins* [Yiddish women poets]. Chicago: Farlag L. M. Stein.

Kristeva, Julia. 1969. *Semiotiké: recherches pour une semanlyse*. Paris: Éditions du Seuil.

Kronegger, Maria Elizabeth. 1973. *Literary Impressionism*. New Haven, Conn.: College and University Press.

Kronfeld, Chana. 1983. "Aspects of Poetic Metaphor." Ph. D. diss., University of California, Berkeley.

——. 1985. "Allusion: An Israeli Perspective." *Prooftexts* 5(2): 137–63.

——. 1990. "'The Wisdom of Camouflage': Between Rhetoric and Philosophy in Amichai's Poetic System." *Prooftexts* 10(3): 469–91.

————. 1993. "Fogel and Modernism: A Liminal Moment in Hebrew Literary History." *Prooftexts* 13(1): 45–63.

Kurzweil, Barukh. 1959. *Sifrutenu ha-chadasha: hemshekh o mahapekha?* [Our new literature: Continuity or revolution?]. Jerusalem: Schocken Books.

Kutcher, Edward Yechezkel. 1982. *A History of the Hebrew Language.* Jerusalem: Magnes Press, Hebrew University.

Lachower, Pinchas. 1974. "Ha-semel be-shirat Bialik" [The Symbol in Bialik's Poetry]. In *Bialik: yetsirato le-suge'ha bi-re'i ha-bikoret* [Bialik: Critical essays on his works], edited by Gershon Shaked, 24–51. Jerusalem: Mosad Bialik.

Lakoff, George. 1972. "Hedges: A Study in Meaning Criteria and the Logic of Fuzzy Concepts." In *Papers from the Eighth Regional Meeting, Chicago Linguistic Society,* 183–228. Chicago: Chicago Linguistic Society. Reprinted in *Journal of Philosophical Logic* (1973):458–508.

————. 1987. *Women, Fire, and Dangerous Things: What Categories Reveal about the Mind.* Chicago: University of Chicago Press.

Lakoff, George, and Mark Johnson. 1980. *Metaphors We Live By.* Chicago: University of Chicago Press.

Lakoff, George, and Zoltán Kövecses. 1987. "The Cognitive Model of Anger Inherent in American English." In *Cultural Models in Language and Thought,* edited by Dorothy Holland and Naomi Quinn, 195–221. Cambridge: Cambridge University Press.

Lakoff, George, and Mark Turner. 1989. *More Than Cool Reason: A Field Guide to Poetic Metaphor.* Chicago: University of Chicago Press.

Landau, Rachel. 1980. *Milim ve-tserufeyhen: i'yunim semanti'yim ba-kolokatsya ha-itona'it* [Collocation in journalistic Hebrew]. Ramat Gan, Israel: Bar-Ilan University.

Lang, George. 1987. "Periphery as Paradigm: Creole Literature and the Polysystem." *Poetics Today* 8(3–4): 529–37.

Lapidus-Lerner, Ann. 1992. " 'A Woman's Song': The Poetry of Esther Raab." In *Gender and Text in Modern Hebrew and Yiddish Literature,* edited by Naomi Sokoloff et al., 17–38. New York: Jewish Theological Seminary of America Press.

Lasker-Schüler, Else. 1920. *Hebraische Balladen.* Berlin: P. Cassier.

————. 1968/69. *Shirim* [Poems]. Translated into Hebrew by Yehuda Amichai. Tel Aviv: Eked.

————. 1980. *Hebrew Ballads and Other Poems.* Translated, edited and introduced by Audri Durchslag and Jeanette Litman-Demeestère, prefaced by Yehuda Amichai. Philadelphia: Jewish Publication Society.

Leenhardt, Jacques. 1972. "Périodisation et typologie." In *Analyse de la périodisation littéraire,* edited by J. Dubois et al., 23–32. Paris: Éditions Universitaires.

Lemon, Lee T., and Marion J. Reis, eds. 1965. *Russian Formalist Criticism: Four Essays.* Lincoln: University of Nebraska Press.

Lensky, Chaim. 1986. *Me-ever nahar ha-leti* [Beyond the Leti River: Collected poems]. Tel Aviv: Am Oved.

Leonard, Henry Siggins. 1957. *An Introduction to the Principles of Right Reason.* New York: Holt.

Levi-Strauss, Claude. 1962. *La pensée sauvage.* Paris: Plon.

Levin, Harry. 1966. *Refractions.* New York: Oxford University Press.

Levin, Yisrael. 1960. *Beyn gdi ve-sa'ar: I'yunim be-shirat Shlonsky* [Between kid and storm: Studies in Shlonsky's poetry]. Tel Aviv: Sifriat Po'alim.

Levy, Naomi. 1984. "The Nature and Function of Religious References in the Poetry of Yehuda Amichai." Unpublished thesis, Cornell University, Ithaca, N.Y.

Leyvik, H. 1919. "Di Yunge" [The young ones]. *Shriften* 4: 29–40.

———. 1932. "Nokhn toyt fun Moyshe Leyb Halpern" [After the death of Moyshe Leyb Halpern]. *Literarishe Bleter* 50(39): 615–16 (Sept 23).

Liptzin, Sol. 1972. *A History of Yiddish Literature.* Middle Village, N.Y.: Jonathan David.

Lloyd, David. 1987. *Nationalism and Minor Literature: James Clarence Mangan and the Emergence of Irish Cultural Nationalism.* Berkeley: University of California Press.

———. 1990. "Genet's Geneology: European Minorities and the Ends of the Canon." In *The Nature and Context of Minority Discourse,* edited by Abdul R. JanMohamed and David Lloyd, 369–93. Oxford: Oxford University Press.

Lodge, David. 1981. *Working with Structuralism: Essays and Reviews on Nineteenth and Twentieth Century Literature.* London: Routledge & Kegan Paul.

Lotman, Jurij M. 1977. *The Structure of the Artistic Text.* Translated by Ronald Vroon. Ann Arbor: University of Michigan Press.

Lotman, Jurij M. et al. 1975. *Theses on the Semiotic Study of Culture as Applied to Slavic Languages.* Press Publications in Semiotics of Culture 2. Lisse, Netherlands: P. de Ridder Press.

Lux, Joseph August. 1925. *Ein Jahrtausend deutscher Romantik zur Revision der Deutschen Literaturauffassung.* Innsbruck: Verlagsanstalt Tryolia.

Luz, Tzvi. 1964. "Lifney ha-sha'ar ha-afel: i'yun be-shirav shel David Fogel" [*Before the Dark Gate:* A study of David Fogel's poetry]. *Molad* 22(189/90): 218–24.

Lyotard, Jean François. 1990. *Heidegger and "the jews."* Translated by Andreas Michel and Mark S. Roberts. Minneapolis: University of Minnesota Press.

McCawley, James D. 1981. *Everything That Linguists Have Always Wanted to Know about Logic—But Were Ashamed to Ask.* Chicago: University of Chicago Press.

McHale, Brian. 1987. *Postmodernist Fiction.* New York: Methuen.

Mains, John W. 1978. "Literary Impressionism: A Study in Definition." Ph. D. diss., University of Washington.

Mansour, Ya'akov. 1968. *I'yunim bi-lshono shel Shay Agnon* [Studies in the language of S. Y. Agnon]. Tel Aviv: Dvir.

Marc, Franz, and Else Lasker-Schüler. 1987. *Der blaue Reiter präsentiert Eurer Hoheit sein blaues Pferd, Karten und Briefe.* Munich: Prestel.

Margalith, Avishai. 1971. "Ha-metafora be-misgeret shel meta-safa semantit shel lashon tiv'it" [Metaphor within a frame for a semantic metalanguage of natural languages]. *Ha-Sifrut* 3(1): 35–52.

Markish, Perets. 1918–19. *Shveln* [Thresholds]. Kiev: Yidisher Folks Farlag.

———. 1921. *Farbaygeyendik: Esseyen* [Passing over: Essays]. Vilnius: Tsentraler Yidisher Shule-organizatsye.

Matejka, Ladislav, and Pomorska, Krystyna, eds. [1929, 1971] 1978. *Readings in Russian Poetics: Formalist and Structuralist Views.* Ann Arbor: University of Michigan.

Mayakovsky, Vladimir. [1918] 1973. "Open Letter to the Workers." In Benjamin Harshav [Hrushovski], editor and translator, *Yorshey ha-simbolizm ba-shira ha-eyropit ve-ha-yehudit: mivchar manifestim, ma'amarim, hakhrazot* [Heirs of symbolism in European and Jewish literature: A selection of manifestoes, articles and declarations], 56–58. Tel Aviv: Tel Aviv Student Union Press.

———. [1922] 1973. "V. V. Khlebnikov." In *Major Soviet Writers: Essays in Criticism,* edited by Edward J. Brown, 83–88. London: Oxford University Press. Translated from "V. V. Khlebnikov," in *Krasneya nov,* Moscow, July-August 1922.

Meltzer, Françoise. 1978. "Color as Cognition in Symbolist Verse." *Critical Inquiry* 5(2):253–73.

Milch, Werner. 1950. "Über Aufgaben und Grenzen der Literatrugeschicte." *Abhandlungen der Klasse der Literatur* (Akademie der Wissenschaft und Literatur in Mainz) 2: 53–77.

Miller, J. Hillis. 1979. "The Function of Rhetorical Study at the Present Time." *ADE Bulletin* 62 (Sept.-Nov.): 10–18.

Min-ha, Trinh T. 1990. "Cotton and Iron." In *Out There: Marginalization and Contemporary Cultures,* edited by Russell Ferguson et al., 327–36. New York and Cambridge: New Museum of Contemporary Art and MIT Press.

Mintz, Alan. 1984. "On the Tel Aviv School of Poetics." *Prooftexts* 4:215–34.

Miron, Dan. 1964. "Gnessin acharey chamishim shana: 'beynatayim' " [Gnessin after fifty years: "In the meantime"]. *Akhshav* 10:33–51.

———. 1973. *A Traveler Disguised: A Study in the Rise of Modern Yiddish Fiction in the Nineteenth Century.* New York: Schocken.

———. 1987a. *Bodedim be-mo'adam: li-dyokana shel ha-republika ha-sifrutit ha-ivrit bi-tchilat ha-me'a ha-esrim* [When loners come together: A portrait of Hebrew literature at the turn of the twentieth century]. Tel Aviv: Am Oved.

———. 1987b. "Matay nechdal 'le-galot' et Fogel?" [When will we stop "discovering" Fogel?] *Yedi'ot Acharonot* (Shavu'ot Holiday Literary Supplement) June 2:2–4.

———. 1991a. "Idilyat ha-borot ve-hakvarim: tsava'ato ha-piyutit ve-ha-tsiyonit shel Chaim Lensky" [The idyll of the holes and the graves: The poetic and Zionist legacy of Chaim Lensky]. In *Noge'a ba-davar: masot al sifrut, tarbut ve-chevra* [Essays on literature and society], 203–33. Tel Aviv: Zmora-Bitan.

———. 1991b. *Imahot meyasdot, achayot chorgot: al shtey hatchalot ba-shira ha-eretzyisre'elit ha-modernit* [Founding mothers, stepsisters: The emergence of the first Hebrew poetesses and other essays]. Tel Aviv: Ha-Kibbutz ha-Me'uchad.

Mundle, C. W. K. 1970. *A Critique of Linguistic Philosophy.* Oxford: Clarendon Press.

Musil, Robert. [1953] 1979. *The Man without Qualities,* Vol. 1. London: Secker and Warburg.

Nash, Stanley. 1985. "The Hebraists of Berne and Berlin Circa 1905." In *The Great Transition: The Recovery of the Lost Centers of Modern Hebrew Literature,* edited by Glenda Abramson and Tudor Parfitt, 44–58. Totowa, N.J.: Rowman & Allanheld.

Neohelicon 1988. 15(1). (Special issue on literary periodization.)

Novershtern, Abraham. 1986. "The Young Glatstein and the Structure of His First Book of Poems." *Prooftexts* 6:31–100.

———. 1990. " 'Who Would Have Believed That a Bronze Statue Can Weep:' The Poetry of Anna Margolin." *Prooftexts* 10(3):435–67.

Orecchioni, Pierre. 1972. "Dates-clés et glissements chronologiques." In *Analyse de la périodisation littéraire,* edited by J. Dubois et al., 29–38. Paris: Éditions Universitaire.

Pagis, Dan. [1965] 1989. "Avraham Ben-Yitshak." In *The Modern Hebrew Poem Itself,* edited by Stanley Burnshaw et al., 50–53. Cambridge: Harvard University Press.

———. 1970. *Shirat ha-chol ve-torat ha-shir le-Moshe Ibn Ezra u-vney doro* [Secular poetry and poetic theory: Moses Ibn Ezra and his contemporaries]. Jerusalem: Mosad Bialik.

———. 1976. *Chidush u-masoret be-shirat ha-chol ha-ivrit: sfarad ve-italya* [Change and tradition in the secular poetry: Spain and Italy]. Jerusalem: Keter.

———. 1991. *Hebrew Poetry of the Middle Ages and the Renaissance,* foreword by Robert Alter. Berkeley: University of California Press.

Pardes, Ilana. 1980. "Metaphor in the Song of Songs." Berkeley, Honors thesis.

———. 1992. *Countertraditions in the Bible: A Feminist Approach.* Cambridge: Harvard University Press.

Parker, Mark. 1991. "Measure and Countermeasure: The Lovejoy—Wellek Debate and Romantic Periodization." In *Theoretical Issues in Literary History,* edited by David Perkins, 227–47. Cambridge: Harvard University Press.

Paulk, Sarah Frances. 1979. "The Aesthetics of Impressionism: Studies in Art and Literature." Ph. D. diss., Florida State University.

Pawlowski, Tadeusz. 1980. *Begriffsbildung und Definition.* Berlin: Walter de Gruyter.

Perkins, David, ed. 1991. *Theoretical Issues in Literary History.* Cambridge: Harvard University Press.

————. 1992. *Is Literary History Possible?* Baltimore: Johns Hopkins University Press.

Perri, Carmella. 1978. "On Alluding." *Poetics* 7: 289–307.

Perry, Menakhem. 1972. "Ma'agalim nechtakhim: al tofa'a ba-kompozitsya shel shiro shel Avidan 'Nechitat-lo-ones' " [Intersecting circles: On a phenomenon in the composition of Avidan's poem 'Non-Emergency-Landing']. *Siman Kri'ah* 1: 269–81.

————. 1979. "Literary Dynamics: How the Order of a Text Creates Its Meanings." *Poetics Today* 1(1–2): 35–64.

Poggioli, Renato. 1968. *The Theory of the Avant-Garde*. Translated by Gerald Fitzgerald. Cambridge: Harvard University Press.

Polan, Dana. 1986. "Translator's Introduction." In *Kafka: Toward a Minor Literature* by Gilles Deleuze and Félix Guattari, xxii–xxix. Minneapolis: University of Minnesota Press.

Pound, Ezra. 1913. "A Few Don'ts by an Imagiste." *Poetry* 1: 200–206.

————. [1916] 1960. *Gaudier-Brzeska*. New York: New Directions.

Preil, Gabriel. 1960. *Mapat Erev* [Map of evening]. Tel Aviv: Dvir.

Prooftexts 13(1). 1993. Special Issue: *David Fogel (1891–1944) and the Emergence of Hebrew Modernism*, edited by Michael Gluzman, Chana Kronfeld, and Eric Zakim.

Raab, Esther. 1981. "Ne'urey ha-shira be-eretz lo zru'a" ["The youth of poetry in an uncultivated land"]. Hillit Yeshurun, interviewer. *Chadarim* 1(Spring): 101–13.

————. 1988. *Kol ha-shirim* [Collected poems]. Tel Aviv: Zmora, Bitan.

Rachel [Bluvstein, Rachel]. 1978/79. *Shirat Rachel* [Rachel's poetry], 27th ed. Tel Aviv: Davar.

Rekhtman, Avrom. 1958. *Yiddishe etnografye un folklor* [Jewish ethnography and folklore]. Buenos Aires: YIVO.

Renza, Louis. 1984. *"A White Heron" and the Question of Minor Literature*. Milwaukee: University of Wisconsin Press.

Richards. I. A. 1936. *The Philosophy of Rhetoric*. London: Oxford University Press.

Rivkin, Borukh. 1934. "Halb Veg tzu Geoynes" [Halfway to genius]. *Brikn* [Bridges] 2: 108–29.

Ronen, Omry. 1977. "A Beam upon the Axe: Some Antecedents of Osip Mandelstam's 'Umyval'sia noc'iu na dvore. . . .' " *Slavica Hierosolymitana* 1: 158–76.

Rosch, Eleanor [Heider]. 1973. "Natural Categories." *Cognitive Psychology* 4: 328–50.

————. 1975. "Cognitive Representations of Semantic Categories." *Journal of Experimental Psychology: General* 104: 192–233.

————. 1977. "Human Categorization." In *Advances in Cross-Cultural Psychology*, edited by N. Warren, 1:1–49. London: Academic Press.

Rosch, Eleanor, and Barbara B. Lloyd, eds. 1978. *Cognition and Categorization*. Hillsdale, N.J.: Lawrence Erlbaum Associates.

Rosch, Eleanor, and Carolyn Mervis. 1975. "Family Resemblances: Studies in the Internal Structure of Categories." *Cognitive Psychology* 7: 573–605.

Rosch, Eleanor, C. Simpson, and R. S. Miller. 1976. "Structural Bases of Typicality Effects." *Journal of Experimental Psychology: Human Perception and Performance* 2: 491–502.

Roskies, David G. 1984. *Against the Apocalypse: Responses to Catastrophe in Modern Jewish Culture.* Cambridge: Harvard University Press.

———, ed. 1989. *The Literature of Destruction: Jewish Responses to Catastrophe.* Philadelphia: Jewish Publication Society.

Roskies, David G., and Diane Roskies, comps. 1975. *The Shtetl Book.* New York: Ktav.

Rubinshteyn, Eliezer. [1981] 1985. *Ha-ivrit shelanu ve-ha-ivrit ha-kduma* [Our Hebrew and ancient Hebrew]. Tel Aviv: Misrad ha-Bitachon/Sifriat Universita Meshuderet.

Rusinko, Elaine. 1979. "Intertextuality: The Soviet Approach to Subtext." *Dispositio* 4: 213–35.

Sadan, Dov. 1964. *Galgal mo'adim* [A wheel of feasts]. Tel Aviv: Massada.

———. [1959] 1967. *Al Shay Agnon: masa, i'yun va-cheker* [On S. Y. Agnon: Research volume]. Tel Aviv: Ha-Kibbutz ha-Me'uchad.

———. 1978. *Al Shay Agnon: kerekh masot u'ma'amarim* [On S. Y. Agnon: Essay volume]. Tel Aviv: Ha-Kibbutz ha-Me'uchad.

Sandbank, Shimon. 1976. *Shtey brekhot ba-ya'ar* [Two pools in the forest]. Tel Aviv: Ha-Kibbutz ha-Me'uchad.

———. 1982. *Ha-shir ha-nachon* [The true poem]. Tel Aviv: Sifriat Po'alim.

Schapiro, Meyer. 1970. "Criteria for Periodization in the History of European Art, I." *New Literary History* 1(2): 113–14.

Scott, Bonnie Kime, ed. 1990. *The Gender of Modernism: A Critical Anthology.* Bloomington: Indiana University Press.

Scott, Clive. 1976. "Symbolism, Decadence and Impressionism." In *Modernism,* edited by Malcolm Bradbury and James McFarlane, 206–27. Harmondsworth, U.K.: Penguin.

Searle, John. 1969. *Speech Acts: An Essay in the Philosophy of Language.* Cambridge: Cambridge University Press.

Sebeok, Thomas A., ed. 1986. *Encyclopedic Dictionary of Semiotics.* Berlin and New York: Mouton de Gruyter.

Seidman, Naomi. 1993a. "'A Marriage Made in Heaven'?: The Sexual Politics of Hebrew-Yiddish Diglossia." Ph. D. diss., University of California, Berkeley.

———. 1993b. " 'It is You I Speak from within Me': David Fogel's Poetics of the Feminine Voice." *Prooftexts* 13(1): 87–102.

Sephiha, H. Vidal. 1970. "Introduction à l'étude de l'intensif." *Langages,* 18 (June 1970): 104–20.

Shachor, M. 1962. "Classical Coinage in Rabbi Yehuda Halevi's Poetry." In *Sefer ha-yovel shel ha-gimnasya ha-ivrit bi-rushalayim* [Fiftieth anniversary of the Jerusalem Hebrew Gymnasium commemorative book], edited by H. Merchavya, 37–48. Jerusalem: Agudat Shocharey ha-Gimnasya ha-Ivrit bi-Rushalayim.

Shaked, Gershon. 1973. *Le-lo motza* [Dead end]. Tel Aviv: Ha-Kibbutz ha-Me'uchad.

————. 1974. *Bialik: yetsirato le-sugeha bi-re'i ha-bikoret: antologia* [Bialik: Critical essays on his works—an anthology]. Jerusalem: Mosad Bialik.

————. 1977, 1983, 1988. *Ha-siporet ha-ivrit* [Hebrew narrative fiction]. Vols. 1–3. Jerusalem: Ha-Kibbutz ha-Me'uchad and Keter.

Shahevitch, Boaz. 1970. "Beyn amur la-amira: le-mahuta shel ha-Melitsah" [On the Nature of the Melitsah]. *Ha-Sifrut* 2(3): 664–68.

Shavit, Uzi. 1981, 1982. *Sefer Shlonsky* [Studies on Avraham Shlonsky and his work]. Vols. 1–2. Tel Aviv: Sifriat Po'alim.

Shen, Yeshayahu. 1988. "Symmetric and Asymmetric Comparisons." *Poetics* 18(6): 517–36.

Shklovsky, Victor B. 1923. *Literatura i kinematograf.* Berlin: Russkoe Universal'noe Zd-vo.

————. [1925] 1990. *Theory of Prose.* Translated by Benjamin Sher from the 2d. ed. (1929). Elmwood Park, Ill.: Dalkey Archive Press.

Shlonsky, Avraham. 1924. *Dvay* [Distress]. Tel Aviv: Hedim.

————. 1947. *Al milet* [Plenitude]. Merchavya: Sifriat Po'alim.

————. 1954. *Shirim* [Poems], 2 vols. Merchavya: Sifriat Po'alim.

————. [1923] 1973. "Ha-Melitsah." In *Yorshey ha-simbolizm ba-shira ha-eyropit ve-ha-yehudit* [Heirs of symbolism in European and Jewish literature], edited and translated by Benjamin Harshav [Hrushovski], 154–55. Tel Aviv: Tel Aviv Student Union Press. Originally published in *Hedim* 1(1923): 189–90.

Silberschlag, Eisig. 1985. "Hebrew Literature in Vienna: 1782–1939." In *The Great Transition: The Recovery of the Lost Centers of Modern Hebrew Literature,* edited by Glenda Abramson and Tudor Parfitt, 29–43. Totowa, N.J.: Rowman & Allanheld.

Sokoloff, Naomi B. 1984. "On Amichai's 'El male rahamim.'" *Prooftexts* 4(2): 127–40.

Spicehandler, Ezra. 1971. "Hebrew Poetry, Modern." In *The Encyclopedia Judaica,* vol. 8: 175–214. Jerusalem: Keter.

Steiner, George. 1972. *On Difficulty and Other Essays.* Oxford: Oxford University Press.

————. 1976. "Eros and Idiom." In *The Modern World,* edited by David Daiches and Anthony Thorlby, vol. 3, 51–82. London: Aldus Books.

Steiner, Peter. 1984. *Russian Formalism: A Metapoetics.* Ithaca, N.Y.: Cornell University Press.

Steinhardt, Deborah. 1989. "The Modernist Enterprise of Uri Nissan Gnessin: Gnessin's Narrative Technique in the Context of Hebrew Fiction of the Late-Nineteenth and Early-Twentieth Centuries." Ph.D. diss., University of California, Berkeley.

Stern, J. P. 1975. "From Family Album to Literary History." *New Literary History* 7(1): 113–33.

Sternberg, Meir. 1976. "Ofaney kvilut ve-yatsrani'yut ba-lashon u-vi-leshon ha-sifrut" [Bound and productive forms in language and literary language]. *Ha-Sifrut* 22: 78–141.

————. 1977. "Mivne ha-chazara ba-sipur ha-mikra'i" [The structure of repetition in biblical narrative: Strategies of informational redundancy]. *Ha-Sifrut* 25: 109–50.

————. 1982. "Proteus in Quotation-Land: Mimesis and the Forms of Reported Discourse." *Poetics Today* 3(2): 107–56.

Sutzkever, Avrom. 1963. *Poetishe Verk.* 2 vols. Tel Aviv: Yovel.

————. 1975. *Griner Akvaryum* [Green aquarium]. Introduced by Ruth R. Wisse. Jerusalem: Hebrew University Yiddish-opteylung.

————. 1991. *Selected Prose and Poetry,* translated by Barbara and Benjamin Harshav. Berkeley: University of California Press.

Sweetser, Eve E. 1987. "The Definition of Lie: An Examination of the Folk Models Underlying a Semantic Prototype." In *Cultural Models in Language and Thought,* edited by Dorothy Holland and Naomi Quinn, 43–66. Cambridge: Cambridge University Press.

Szili, Joszef. 1988. "Les notions de la littérature et la périodisation littéraire." *Neohelicon* 15(1): 25–37.

Tchernichovski, Shaul. 1950. *Shirim* [Poems]. Jerusalem: Schocken.

Teesing, H. P. H. 1949. *Das Problem der Perioden in der Literaturgeschichte.* Groningen, Netherlands: J. B. Wolters.

Todorov, Tzvetan. 1981. *Introduction to Poetics.* Minneapolis: University of Minnesota Press.

Tomashevsky, Boris. [1925] 1965. "Thematics." In *Russian Formalist Criticism.* translated and edited by Lee T. Lemon and Marion J. Reis, 61–95. Lincoln: University of Nebraska Press.

Toury, Gideon, and Avishai Margalith. 1973. "Darkhey ha-shimush ha-sote ba-tseruf ha-kavul" [On deviant uses of collocation]. *Ha-Sifrut* 4(1): 99–129.

Tsvetayeva, Marina. 1971. *Selected Poems.* Translated by Elaine Feinstein. London: Oxford University Press.

Tynjanov, Jurij N. [1929, 1971] 1978. "On Literary Evolution." In *Readings in Russian Poetics: Formalist and Structuralist Views,* edited by Ladislav Matejka and Krystyna Pomorska, 66–78. Ann Arbor, Mich.: University of Michigan.

Tynjanov, Jurij N. and Roman Jakobson. [1928, 1971] 1978. "Problems in the Study of Language and Literature." In *Readings in Russian Poetics: Formalist and Structuralist Views,* edited by Ladislav Matejka and Krystyna Pomorska, 79–81. Ann Arbor: University of Michigan.

Tzara, Tristan. [1977] 1992. *Seven Dada Manifestoes and Lampisteries.* Collected and translated by Barbara Wright. London: Calder Press.

Tzur, Reuven. 1985. *Yesodot romantiyim ve-anti-romantiyim be-shirey Bialik, Tchernichovski va-Amichai* [Romantic and anti-romantic elements in poems by Bialik, Tchernichovski, and Amichai]. Tel Aviv: Papirus.

Tzvik, Yehudit, ed. 1988. *Yehuda Amichai: Mivchar ma'amarey bikoret al yetsirato* [Yehuda Amichai: A selection of critical essays on his writing]. Tel Aviv: Ha-Kibbutz ha-Me'uchad.

Uhlig, Claus. 1982. *Theorie der Literarhistorie: Prinzipen und Paradigmen.* Heidelberg: Carl Winter.

―――. 1985. "Forms of Time and Varieties of Change in Literary Texts." *Proceedings of the Xth Congress of the International Comparative Literature Association,* vol. 2, 247–56. New York: Garland Publishing.

Von Halberg, Robert, ed. 1984. *Canons.* Chicago: University of Chicago Press.

Wallach, Yona. 1985. *Tsurot* [Forms]. Tel Aviv: Ha-Kibbutz ha-Me'uchad.

Weinrich, Uriel. 1959. "On the Cultural History of Yiddish Rhyme." In *Essays on Jewish Life and Thought,* edited by Joseph L. Blau et al., 423–42. New York: Columbia University Press.

―――. 1965. "Yiddish Poetry." In *Princeton Encyclopedia of Poetry and Poetics,* edited by Alex Preminger, 899–901. Princeton, N.J.: Princeton University Press.

Weisstein, Ulrich. 1973a. *Comparative Literature and Literary Theory.* Translated by William Riggan. Bloomington: Indiana University Press.

―――. 1973b. *Expressionism as an International Literary Phenomenon.* Paris: Didier.

Wellek, René. 1941. "Periods and Movements in Literary History." In *English Institute Annual* (1940), 73–93. New York: Columbia University Press.

―――. 1970. *Discriminations: Further Concepts of Criticism.* New Haven, Conn.: Yale University Press.

―――. [1963] 1973. *Concepts of Criticism.* New Haven, Conn.: Yale University Press.

―――. [1965] 1986. *A History of Modern Criticism: 1750–1950.* Vol. 4, *The Late Nineteenth Century.* New Haven, Conn., and London: Yale University Press.

―――. 1986. *A History of Modern Criticism: 1750–1950.* Vol. 5, *English Criticism, 1900–1950.* New Haven, Conn., and London: Yale University Press.

―――. 1991. *A History of Modern Criticism: 1750–1950.* Vol. 7, *German, Russian and East European Criticism 1900–1950.* New Haven, Conn., and London: Yale University Press.

Wellek, René, and Austin Warren. [1949] 1963. *Theory of Literature.* 3d rev. ed. Harmondsworth, U.K.: Penguin.

Wieseltier, Meir. 1980. "Chatakh-orekh be-shirato shel Nathan Zach" [Longitudinal study in the poetry of Nathan Zach]. *Siman Kri'ah* 10: 405–29.

Williams, Raymond. 1989. *The Politics of Modernism: Against the New Conformists,* edited and introduced by Tony Pinkney. London: Verso.

Wisse, Ruth R. 1980. "A Yiddish Poet in America." *Commentary,* 70(1): 35–40.

―――. 1988. *A Little Love in Big Manhattan: Two Yiddish Poets.* Cambridge: Harvard University Press.

Wittgenstein, Ludwig. 1958. *The Blue and Brown Books.* Oxford: Basil Blackwell.

————. 1972. *Philosophical Investigations*. Translated by G. E. M. Anscombe. Oxford: Basil Blackwell.

Wölfflin, Heinrich. 1888. *Renaissance und Barock: eine Untersuchung über Wesen und Entstehung des Barockstils in Italien*. Munich: T. Ackerman Verlag.

————. 1966. *Renaissance and Baroque*. Translated by Kathrin Simon. Ithaca, NY: Cornell University Press.

Wolitz, Seth. 1977. "Structuring the World View in Halpern's *In New York*." *Yiddish* 3(1)/*Studies in American Jewish Literature* 3(2): 56–57.

Yaffe, A. B. 1966. *Shlonsky: ha-meshorer u-zmano* [Shlonsky: the poet and his times]. Merchavya: Sifriat Po'alim.

Yehoash. [1936] 1939. *Tanach* [Bible: translation from the Hebrew]. New York: Forverts.

Yelin, David. [1940] 1972. *Torat ha-shira ha-sfaradit* [The theory of Spanish poetry]. Jerusalem: Magnes Press, Hebrew University.

Yudice, George. 1988. "Marginality and the Ethics of Survival." In *Universal Abandon?: the Politics of Postmodernism*, edited by Andrew Ross, 214–36. Minneapolis: University of Minnesota Press.

Zach, Nathan. 1960. *Shirim rishonim* [First poems]. Tel Aviv: private edition.

————. 1965. *Shirim shonim* [Miscellaneous poems]. Tel Aviv: Alef.

————. 1966a. "Le-akliman ha-signoni shel shnot ha-chamishim ve-ha-shishim be-shiratenu" [On the stylistic climate of the fifties and sixties in our poetry]. *Ha'aretz* July 29: 10, 13.

————. 1966b. *Zman ve-ritumus etsel Bergson u-va-shira ha-modernit* [Time and rhythm in Bergson and in modern poetry]. Tel Aviv: Alef.

————. [1976] 1981. "Imagism and Vorticism." In *Modernism 1890–1930*, edited by Malcolm Bradbury and James McFarlane, 228–42. Harmondsworth, U.K.: Penguin.

————. 1982. *The Static Element: Selected Poems of Nathan Zach*. Translated by Peter Everwine and Shulamit Yasni-Starkman. New York: Atheneum.

Zadeh, Lotfi A. 1965. "Fuzzy Sets." *Information and Control* 8(3): 338–53.

Zakim, Eric. 1988. "The Cut that Binds: Philip Roth and Jewish Marginality." *Qui Parle* 2(2): 19–40.

————. 1983. "Between Fragment and Authority in David Fogel's (Re)Presentation of Subjectivity." *Prooftexts* 13(1): 103–24.

————. 1996. "Fragmentation and Totality in Modernist Poetry and Music." Ph.D. Diss. University of California, Berkeley.

Zemach, Edi. 1962. "Al sfat ha-krakh" [On the banks of the city]. *Gazit* 17: 115–17.

Index

Abbreviations used with page reference numbers are:
n for note, nn for notes, f for figure, and t for table.

Designer: Nola Burger
Compositor: Braun-Brumfield, Inc.
Hebrew Compositor: El Ot Ltd.
Typeface: Galliard, text 10/14
Hebrew/Yiddish Typeface: David, text 10.5/12
Printer: Braun-Brumfield
Binder: Braun-Brumfield